{RISE}

16 REASONS WHY 10% OF START-UPS SUCCEED

MICHAEL W. HARRISON

Powered by

24by7publishing.com

This book RISE: 16 Reasons Why 10% of Start-ups Succeed by Michael W. Harrison

All the printing & distribution process of the book
is powered by

24by7 Publishing
13 New Road, Kolkata - 51, India
https://www.24by7publishing.com
mail@24by7publishing.com
+91 9831 470 133
+91 9433 444 334

First Published in March, 2025

Version 1.00

ISBN: 978-81-984564-8-9

Powered by

24by**7**publishing.com

Dedication

To my daughter, Ashley-Mae,

Your unwavering support and boundless enthusiasm have been the driving force behind this journey. At sixteen, you embody the spirit of resilience, curiosity, and creativity that every entrepreneur aspires to achieve. Your insightful questions, innovative ideas, and genuine belief in my work have inspired me more than words can express.

This book is dedicated to you, Ashley-Mae, for being my muse and my motivation. Your presence reminds me daily of the power of dreams and the importance of perseverance. May you continue to chase your dreams with the same passion and determination that have fueled my own.

With all my love,
Dad

"There is a crack in everything.
That's how the light gets in."

- Leonard Cohen

"Cram as much pleasure as you can into life, and rail against the pain that you have to suffer as a result."

- Shane MacGowan

"We should not say that one man's hour is worth another man's hour, but rather that one man during an hour is worth just as much as another man during an hour. Time is everything, man is nothing: he is at the most time's carcass."

- Karl Marx

Contents

Foreword

"Success consists of going from failure to failure without loss of enthusiasm."

- Sir Winston Leonard Spencer Churchill

Writing the foreword for *RISE: 16 Reasons Why 10% of Start-ups Succeed* is an opportunity to reflect on the journey that began with *FALL: 16 Reasons Why 90% of Start-ups Fail.* This new book continues the exploration of the volatile world of start-ups, but this time, it focuses on the elusive success stories that define the 10% of start-ups that manage to thrive.

In my first book, *FALL: 16 Reasons Why 90% of Start-ups Fail,* I delved into the myriad reasons why the majority of start-ups fail. It was a sobering yet necessary exploration of the pitfalls, mistakes, and unforeseen challenges that can lead to a start-up's downfall. Acknowledging failure is crucial; it allows us to learn from our mistakes, to understand the consequences of bad decisions, and to develop strategies to avoid repeating them. The essence of *FALL: 16 Reasons Why 90% of Start-ups Fail* was to provide a practical guide for understanding and circumventing the common errors that plague start-ups, from funding issues and market misalignment to team dynamics and burnout.

As I wrote *FALL: 16 Reasons Why 90% of Start-ups Fail,* I realized the importance of not only understanding why start-ups fail but also why some succeed against all odds. This realization led to *RISE: 16 Reasons Why 10% of Start-ups Succeed,* a book that examines the other side of the coin. *RISE: 16 Reasons Why 10% of Start-ups Succeed* is about those rare instances where start-ups navigate the treacherous waters of entrepreneurship to find success. This book seeks to uncover the patterns, decisions, and strategies that differentiate successful start-ups from those that falter.

Writing *RISE: 16 Reasons Why 10% of Start-ups Succeed* was an enlightening experience. It required a shift in perspective, from focusing on failure to celebrating success. Success in the start-up world often appears as a confluence of various factors, some within the founder's control and others seemingly influenced by external forces. However, through meticulous research and analysis, I have identified key reasons why start-ups succeed. These reasons are not just about having a great idea or adequate funding but involve a complex interplay of vision, execution, timing, and adaptability.

One of the most significant aspects of start-up success is securing the right funding model. Start-ups must understand the intricacies of different funding avenues, whether it's bootstrapping, venture capital, or crowdfunding. The path to success often involves finding a balance between raising enough capital to fuel growth and maintaining control over the company. In *RISE: 16 Reasons Why 10% of Start-ups Succeed*, I explore case studies of start-ups like Shopify and Shutterstock, which navigated their funding journeys with precision, ensuring they had the resources to scale while keeping their core vision intact.

Another crucial element is developing the right product for the right market. It's not enough to have a groundbreaking idea; the product must address a genuine need or pain point in the market. Start-ups like HubSpot and Udemy exemplify how understanding market dynamics and customer needs can lead to products that resonate deeply with users, driving adoption and growth. These companies didn't just create products; they created solutions that people were willing to pay for, solutions that fit seamlessly into the lives of their customers.

Competition is another area where successful start-ups excel. Beating the competition requires more than just having a better product. It involves strategic positioning, understanding competitor weaknesses, and continuously innovating. Companies like Apple and Google have shown that even in saturated markets, there is room for new players who can offer something unique and valuable. These companies didn't just survive; they thrived by outmaneuvering their competitors with superior strategies and execution.

A successful start-up also requires the right business or monetization model. Whether it's a subscription-based service like Netflix or a freemium model like Spotify, the way a start-up makes money is crucial to its long-term viability. In *RISE: 16 Reasons Why 10% of Start-ups Succeed*, I delve into the various monetization strategies that have worked for different companies, providing insights into how start-ups can choose and implement the model that best suits their product and market.

Marketing and sales strategies are also pivotal. In today's digital age, start-ups need to leverage online platforms, social media, and data analytics to reach their target audience effectively. The stories of companies like Tesla and Red Bull highlight how innovative marketing and sales strategies can create brand loyalty and drive sales. These companies understood that marketing is not just about selling a product; it's about creating an experience and a connection with the customer.

Listening to customers is another fundamental aspect of success. Start-ups that engage with their customers, seek feedback, and adapt their products based on this feedback are more likely to succeed. This customer-centric approach ensures that the product evolves in line with customer needs and expectations, fostering loyalty and advocacy.

The importance of having a focused and passionate team cannot be overstated. Start-ups are often characterized by small, dedicated teams that work tirelessly to bring the founder's vision to life. Finding the right team, with the right mix of skills and a shared passion for the product, is critical. Start-ups like Airbnb and SpaceX have demonstrated that a strong, cohesive team can overcome significant challenges and achieve extraordinary success.

Seeking the right advice and maintaining energy levels are also key factors. Start-up founders often find themselves at the crossroads, needing to make critical decisions with limited information. Having mentors or advisors who can provide guidance and support can make a significant difference. Additionally, maintaining high energy levels and staying motivated through the highs and lows of the start-up journey is essential for long-term success.

Finally, timing and the ability to pivot when necessary are crucial. Many successful start-ups have had to change their direction based on market feedback or changes in the competitive landscape. The ability to recognize when a pivot is needed and to execute it effectively can be the difference between success and failure. Companies like PayPal and

Twitter are prime examples of start-ups that successfully pivoted and found their niche in the market.

As you read *RISE: 16 Reasons Why 10% of Start-ups Succeed*, I hope you find inspiration and practical insights that can help you on your entrepreneurial journey. Whether you are a founder, an investor, or someone interested in the start-up ecosystem, this book offers a comprehensive look at what it takes to succeed in the challenging yet rewarding world of start-ups.

Reflecting on the journey from *FALL: 16 Reasons Why 90% of Start-ups Fail* to *RISE: 16 Reasons Why 10% of Start-ups Succeed*, I am reminded of the resilience and determination that define successful entrepreneurs. While failure is a common and often necessary step in the start-up journey, success is built on learning from those failures, adapting, and persevering. The stories and lessons in *RISE: 16 Reasons Why 10% of Start-ups Succeed* are a testament to the fact that with the right strategies, mindset, and a bit of luck, success is within reach for those willing to pursue it with relentless passion.

Thank you for embarking on this journey with me. I hope *RISE: 16 Reasons Why 10% of Start-ups Succeed* serves as a valuable resource and a beacon of hope for all aspiring entrepreneurs. Let us continue to learn, grow, and rise together.

Michael W. Harrison

Introduction

"Failure is inevitable. Success is elusive."

– Steven Spielberg

Ninety percent of start-ups fail.[1] From the brink of inevitable failure, only a few reaches elusive successes. To be more exact, only one in ten. Will your company ever be the one?

While it may seem as if random luck chooses which start-ups succeed and which do not, we can see patterns in the success stories. Throughout this book, we will keep exploring the choices, the snaking paths, the winding roads, the painful growth, the small yet funny failures, and the sheer joy and confusion that make up all start-up stories.

This book will rediscover those tiny details that made a massive difference in a start-up journey, the natural ease with which some organizations seem to operate, and the small and trivial things these businesses learn and relearn with enthusiasm to succeed.

As a founder, doubts never leave for good. They have several tender spots that keep them awake during the long nights and which they try to keep protected. However, as these founders learn to buck against that instinct, step into their fears, and understand what matters and what doesn't, they start believing in their vision wholly and find that, finally, elusive success is within their grasp.

These success stories open a radiance within the start-up world – the beacon of shining hopes that light up the path for other start-ups. As we overlay each reason for start-up success on top of each other, we will get an outline visible beneath the parchment that is profoundly insightful. We may also find the method to the madness of running a successful start-up.

Come along with me on this beautiful journey of understanding the soul of start-ups. As we navigate the intricacies of running a start-up, try to recognize where your business might be lacking and what you could do right to become the first among equals. Let us look at the cases where the founder or their team did the right thing and aligned the start-up's vision with the world's expectations, and the magic just happened. Let us progress from chapter to chapter, step by step, to see what these start-ups got right and what the other 90 percent didn't.

When you are a kid, you may have simple aspirations. From becoming a traffic policeman, being an artist, or even becoming an astronaut who would go to Mars – your dreams may change as you grow and understand what drives adults to choose the career they eventually choose. It could be job security, money, or the pride of working for an institution. Most people from the previous generation stuck to one job for most of their working lives. However, the times have changed.

From Gen X, who jumped from one job to another to increase their salary or try something new, Gen Y, who started new organizations, and Gen Z, who have grown up with mobile phones as their third arm – the lives of people around us have kept changing. These generations have also realized that choosing a job is not a finite end to a job search. They can switch between organizations or decide to scratch their start-up itch.

Think of what you have been so far in your life. Have you been fulfilled in all your roles? Or have you just landed on something that you wholeheartedly embrace and would love to devote all your time and energy to? It could be a college degree you always wanted, a new job you joined after fierce competition, a marriage with someone you love, a new kid, or a start-up. All of them are ridiculously fulfilling. They require your time, energy, and passion to navigate the initial years before settling into a routine. They will give you reasons to wake up each morning – to stay happy despite the challenges.

A start-up might not seem officially like a job, yet it gives you a platform like nothing you have imagined. My last book tried to understand start-up failure, while this book tries to understand the magic behind the successes. This book processes what takes place when a start-up succeeds and analyses the reasons to know why they did when thousands around them have failed.

Come, let us look at the ingredients for success from each of these stories and then formulate a winning recipe that works again, again, and again.

The Blueprint Of Success

Bootstrapping, grants, incubators, and angel investments have helped several start-ups succeed. However, each start-up has a formula that works for them, and one person's meat could very well be another's poison. *Chapter 1* looks at those organizations that succeeded by *Getting the Funding Model Correct.*

Shopify[2] ran as a bootstrapped organization for several years before raising money from VCs. While bootstrapping was fine, Shopify understood that they would have to get investors on board to succeed.

We will also look at Shutterstock – a company that has made money since its inception and turned into a billion-dollar company very quickly. Yet, it received funding four years after its launch.[3]

For over two decades, Mailchimp[4] ran as a bootstrapped organization – it didn't go in for venture capital funding rounds, didn't spend beyond its means, or ran into debt. More importantly, it ran like a typical start-up without careening out of control.

Since its debut, GitHub has made enough money to run as a bootstrapped organization. It generated enough money to offer a lavish lifestyle to its founders and hire employees to take the business further. However, when they did raise funds, it was from the prestigious Andreesen Horowitz for a whopping $100 million USD.[5]

Collaborative software maker, Atlassian raised one of the biggest IPOs of 2015 by raising $460 million USD and valuing the company at about $4.4 billion USD. However, you would be amazed to see its origins – it started with a $10,000 USD credit card advance[6]—more about such unorthodox journeys in the chapter.

Sometimes, people think they have an excellent idea that could generate good revenue as a side hustle. However, sometimes they create a symphony that showers revenue when they strike the right chord with the audience. We have all heard about how Twitter and Instagram kicked off – and how it was just a side idea that became the focus. Yet, several more start-ups hit the right note by working steadily on their vision.

Udemy began in 2007 when two of its founders built the software for live classrooms in Turkey. Two years later, they moved to Silicon Valley and founded a company. The official launch happened in early 2010, yet investors rejected them thirty times.[7] Nevertheless, they didn't give up and bootstrapped the product development. Within a few months, they had thousands of instructors and courses. Finally, in August, they received their first round of $1 million USD. Today, Udemy has won several awards. Many organizations recognize that it offers an experience that rivals traditional classrooms.

A unique product that solves customer needs will always have a lot of takers. Brian Halligan and Dharmesh Shah started the HubSpot in 2006 at MIT. From a little more than some quarter-million dollars in 2007, HubSpot reported revenues of $1 billion USD in 2021.[8] The magic happened because, for a while, they were the only ones doing what they did.[9] What does it require to find the *right product* that your audience would love? Read about what it takes to find your niche in *Chapter 2.*

As a founder, you may see a problem that needs to be solved. You have identified a pain point, an itch that needs to be scratched, and you know how to build a product/service to solve it. Congratulations! You now have an idea for a start-up.

However, is the problem you are trying to solve applicable to a large populace, or is it only for a select few like you? The truth is, if someone does not purchase your product/service, the only thing you are doing is a side project – not running a start-up. Nevertheless, it is unfortunate that most founders assume that if they build a fantastic product/service, customers will flock to them in droves.

Y Combinator, an early-stage start-up accelerator, understands the importance of being at the right place at the right time. Hence, the company's motto is "*Make Something People Want.*"[10] Marc Andreessen, the co-founder of Netscape and a very prominent investor who is one-half of the firm Andreessen Horowitz, says that the most critical to start-up success is the market.[11] It could make the difference between success and failure. To quote him – "In a great market—a market with lots of real potential customers—the market pulls product out of the start-up."[11]

The product doesn't need to be out of the world; it just needs to work and fulfill the market need. Customers would knock down the doors to get that product. Your job would be merely to answer customer queries and complete the orders. The team and the product would fall in place in such a market. Do you want to know how to find such a market where you can simply glide in and grab all the customers in one fell swoop? Several start-ups have done it before. Delve into *Chapter 3* to see which companies have found the *right market* which brought them astounding success.

The next chapter will discuss the start-ups that have managed to topple the competition – David vs. Goliath, the meeting of the giants, and the scramble between the minions to become the next Kevin.

We all know how Apple took on the giant Nokia to become more successful.[12] Amazon emerged from a small garage to take on Barnes & Noble to become the largest bookseller.[12] Can you believe that Google was not always the undisputed leader in the search world?[12] Though it might be a giant in the search space today, it still faces relentless competition and sometimes loses out to smaller start-ups in some cases. Google Hangouts has still not been able to win against Zoom.[13] GoDaddy remains a leader despite Google Domains slowly creeping into the market.[13] This chapter is all about beating the competition. If you possess the audacity to dream an outrageous dream, you could still win – even against giants.

Start with one product in a market you know is ready for it. Salesforce took on Microsoft and Siebel to become the leader. Even Microsoft was a start-up once which competed with market leader IBM for a share of the pie. The success of several start-ups seems incredible, yet they did – simply because they were more original and profitable. *Beating the competition* may not seem so wild after you have finished *Chapter 4*.

Chapter 5 will look at the companies that succeeded because of the *Right Business or Monetization Model*. PayPal didn't find its niche just like that – it was founded initially as a cryptography company. After several trials and errors, it is where it is now.[14] For a long while, Google did not have a proper business model. It made leaps and turns – some radical ones that changed its course significantly.[14] Some organizations' business models are so unique that they change the world as we know it. Airbnb does not own a single room. Alibaba does not own stocks. These organizations all have business models that deliver, generate, and capture value while others follow. Ikea provides sophisticated products at lower prices with their unique model. Tesla makes electric cars uncomplicated, leading the competition despite being pricey. Wikipedia – the general reference library – is free.

There is no single formula for a suitable business model. Does your company have a good business model that generates revenue? Should you stay on course, or should you pivot? With a pinch of introspection, a dash of a critical eye, and a ladle of raw courage, you could also hit the suitable business model for your company.

This exciting chapter shows that you don't need deep pockets for global marketing. You only need the right amount of creativity and an understanding of markets. You could even opt to market to the local audience – for that could be where your audience lives. Or you could market so well that people all over the globe would think that yours is a local brand and offer you patronage. Red Bull is one company that has nailed it that though based out of Austria, Americans assume that it is a local brand.[15] It hosts extreme sports events worldwide and has a unique packaging that looks European.[15]

McDonald's, another global brand, customizes its menu according to the local cuisine. From offering macaroons in France to spaghetti in the Philippines, their idea was to celebrate local flavors.[15] Elon Musk does not buy traditional advertising, yet they are the most valuable automotive company despite being outsold by Toyota.[16] There is no formula for a proper marketing strategy, yet as you look at all the examples and the various methods used, you will arrive at your secret sauce for the *right marketing strategy* in *Chapter 6.*

Start-ups today also have to think about digital-first sales and technology-driven sales that accelerate the sales cycle of the start-up and bring down the cost of customer acquisition. Focusing on sales is essential because it determines the start-up's sustainability in the long run.

Additionally, traction and sales are some of the significant criteria that investors look for before deciding on funding.

Effective sales strategies get new customers quickly. There are nuances to creating an effective sales strategy – from perfecting cold calls to identifying profitable niche markets, leveraging storytelling, to following up with customers the right way. Also, it must comply with the marketing strategy.

The experience is also central to sales. For instance, if you were to buy a car, you would go to a dealer and discuss the features with the salesperson. Once you decide, you try to reach a consensus on the price. However, Tesla takes a different approach. You go to the company website, select the customizations needed and place the order – no haggling or unwanted chatter that wastes your time. You could pick up your car at a service center or transport it. Would you prefer a traditional selling model or one like Tesla if you sold cars?

There is no right way, but you need to look from the viewpoint of your customers. Read about creating a winning sales strategy and arriving at the *right sales model* in *Chapter 7*.

Successful partnerships have driven so many start-ups to unimaginable success. Evan Williams and Biz Stone (Twitter); Bill Gates and Paul Allen (Microsoft); Steve Jobs and Steve Wozniak (Apple) have built business behemoths. All of them had strong partnerships. Like a collaboration between two people, there could be collaborations between organizations too.

For instance, did you know that Louis Vuitton and BMW have a partnership? What does a French fashion house have in common with a luxury car manufacturer? At first glance – nothing. However, both cater to the luxury segment and offer high-quality craftsmanship. Hence, when BMW manufactured sports cars, Louis Vuitton designed suitcases and bags to fit the parcel shelves.[17]

Also, Nike and Apple have a partnership. How does that work? Apple brings music to Nike customers' workouts, and Nike uses Apple apps to keep track and record workout data.[17] Good partnerships come in all shapes and sizes, between unexpected people and disparate companies. However, successful organizations make them work.

Partnerships can be between siblings – like Warner Bros and McDonald's; between a candle maker and a soap maker who married into the same family – William Procter and James Gamble of P & G; friends at Stanford – Bill Hewlett and Dave Packard of HP, Larry Page and Sergey Brin of Google; or even between co-workers – Gordon Moore and Bob Noyce of Intel. The partners on the list joined forces to make their dream a reality. These wildly successful partners have walked willingly over bushes and thorns to reach unimaginable success. You could do so too – if you examine which is the *right partnering model* for your business. That is what *Chapter 8* is all about.

Customer experience is highly critical for retention. Though many start-ups find it difficult to put their customer first, those who prioritize customers benefit from excellent results. For example, Zoomcar is an Indian start-up offering self-driving cars and rentals. Their team continually sifts through the car renting process to see how best to simplify it.[18]

A lot of your success hangs on identifying and solving the correct problems. As much as solving the right need is essential, listening to the customer is too. Without listening to your customers, there is a higher probability of building unfriendly products, poor marketing, or bad pivots. Listening to customers must be an integral part of your start-up's early days. Quality feedback provides real-time data on your customers' thinking about your company. Once you start engaging your audience in developing the product/service they offer, and when they realize that the organization is implementing their suggestions, there will be increased loyalty.

Honk Mobile Inc. uses cloud-based technology that allows people to search, reserve, pay, and top up parking fees from any device connected to the internet.[19] Since its launch, it has become one of the largest companies in this space despite competition. However, though it can be tempting to lead the race by acquiring new customers, Honk Mobiles focused on listening to customers that it already has. Since most customers may not be very articulate about their needs, they analyzed customer behavior to build new features – like allowing the customers to 'favorite' a location. The organization receives insightful feedback to gauge satisfaction levels and identify pain points with regular analysis. It also monitors comments on social media and uses CRM to track customer calls.

Let us go back to Elon Musk, who is the world's richest man as of 2022 – and see how he listens to customers. In one famous incident, a Tesla owner tweeted with an idea for a steering wheel adjustment while parking the car.[20] As Elon Musk liked it, he implemented the solution. Imagine the customer's satisfaction when the organization's CEO himself addressed their problem directly. On another tangent, directly addressing a customer creates impressive publicity. Wouldn't you think of buying a Tesla even though it is expensive simply because you know that the CEO has your back?

With technology again stepping up to do the "paying attention to the audience" part for the organizations through social listening, several companies have adopted the technology with the best results. For example, when a customer tweeted about an outage, internet provider Spectrum[21] stepped up and solved the problem immediately. A skin safety brand called Black Girl Sunscreen[21] searches for related keywords and quotes tweets to share on its profile. Retweeting or commenting by the brand encourages customers by letting them know that the company listens to what they have to say. In other words, the company shows that the customer's voice is powerful. Social Listening does not mean merely tweeting or replying – it could mean incorporating customer sentiment into your marketing strategy. You could even employ a dash of humor like Netflix did.

We all know that several people use Netflix with the same account. Password sharing costs the companies by limiting the number of individual users who would sign up. However, Netflix made a self-deprecating joke with a funny comment for a fake ad where the offer said that the first thousand callers would get a free Netflix subscription for six months.[22] Netflix stamped out the phony ad saying that it was fake and customers could continue using someone else's account like the rest of them. Though it costs the company money when they share Netflix passwords with others, the organization was not blind to its customers' actions. Yet with a dash of humor, it won its customers' hearts. If you did not guess what the title of *Chapter 9* will be, it's all about *listening to customers.*

There are so many things that a start-up could be doing – however, it is crucial not to lose your vision of the goal and spread yourself thin. Every founder should learn about focus soon. Otherwise, a start-up could quickly become a meandering mess without results. A start-up has fewer resources than established organizations, so you don't have the leeway to spread yourself thin. The possibilities are limitless in a start-up – and so are distractions. Being calm and focused in a chaotic environment will do wonders for your company's growth.

Choose one problem to solve, pick one business model and fire those employees who do not add value to the organization. Sounds harsh? But that is the harsh reality of running a start-up. The more opportunities you say yes to, the less you can accomplish. If you are a small start-up trying to find your footing, remember that your organization is outmanned and outnumbered before saying yes to every new opportunity that comes your way.

Focus, Focus, Focus – we will focus on focus in *Chapter 10*. It is all about learning how successful start-up founders have managed to focus on their tasks, built organizations that stayed in one lane, and outpaced their competition. Instead of frazzled founders who flounder about, we will see calm, efficient, and focused leaders; we will see that what matters is not the number of hours of work you put in – more important is the efficiency with which you work.

When you are an entrepreneur following your dream, you need a team that wants to bring your vision to fruition. From a group of one – you – to hiring your first teammate and building your team, you will transition from doing all the jobs by yourself to delegating tasks to people who are better at it than you are. As Warren Buffet said, associate with people who are better than you. By uniting a team with different skills under a common cause, you will have a diversity of skills and experience required to march towards your dream, and you will have people to take up some of your jobs when you need a break. You hire smart people because they can work independently.

Finding the right team is no mean task, but you will see the difference that it makes to your company when you find it. Start-ups are no walk in the park. You need to hire a resilient team that can hold its own against any force. You will have to look for character traits in your recruits that complement your own and yet believe in your vision. Furthermore, if you have started the company with a friend or a relative as a co-founder, you may have found the right mix of friendship and professionalism that could propel your start-up to success. Read about identifying the *right team* in *Chapter 11.*

Some people are inherently passionate about many things – like photography, baseball, clothes, chocolates, or food. If you manage to convert your passion into work, it will never feel as if you are working each day. Some enterprising entrepreneurs have managed to turn their enthusiasm for a subject into a successful start-up. This chapter is all about *passion* and converting it into something productive to monetize it.

"The only way to do great work is to love what you do."

– Steve Jobs

Humans of New York began as a project in 2010. Not strictly a start-up, but nevertheless a triumphant story of a passion generating revenue, Brandon Stanton had a goal of photographing 10,000 people on the streets of New York. Though ignored for the first year, his photoblog is immensely popular. Today, it has spawned two books and has received great attention.[23]

Jennifer Hyman and Jenny Fleiss were Harvard Business School classmates who used to toss entrepreneurial ideas over lunch. When Hyman's sister wanted a dress for a wedding and yet didn't want to spend a lot of money on a dress she would wear only once, they hit upon their start-up idea.[24] Rent the Runway was a sort of Netflix for clothes where women could rent gowns for a part of the original retail price. Investments from Fidelity, Franklin Templeton, and more poured in. Today it has become a Unicorn with both the founders named Fortunes' lists of "30 under 30" and "40 under 40." Wouldn't you want to know how to convert your passion to earning revenue like this?

Yvon Chouinard loved the outdoors. Founding a Falconry club led him to rock climbing. However, equipment was expensive, so he purchased a forge to build his rock-climbing equipment. To support his climbs, he also started selling the steel pitons out of the back of his car. From steel pitons, he moved to aluminum chockstones to rugged outdoor clothing. Recognizing the financial success, he founded Patagonia[25]

– a company that sells technical apparel for the outdoors. Read more about fusing your ***passion*** and start-ups in *Chapter 12.*

Even business moguls need advice. They do not magically have the formula for success. Did you know that Warren Buffet mentored Bill Gates?[26] Google's Larry Page, Sergey Brin, Eric Schmidt, Sundar Pichai, Marissa Meyer of Yahoo, and Jeff Bezos all have one thing in common – Bill Campbell coached them.[27] If these legends need advice and coaching, don't you think that getting the right direction at the right time could have helped them become who they are today?

Sometimes, ten focused minutes from someone could help entrepreneurs feel more encouraged and optimistic about their work. You could receive advice from mentors, angel investors, personal relationships, or even a random person you meet on the street who could set you off on a more lucrative and fulfilling tangent.

It is imperative to *seek the right advice from the right places.* Entrepreneurs need to acknowledge that they will never know enough to focus on all aspects of the company. For this, they will need help. Recognizing this fact and accepting help from mentors will guide your start-up growth. However, wrong advice could wreak havoc on your start-up too. Learn all about seeking advice and filtering the good ideas from the lousy ones in *Chapter 13.*

There is something intangible yet tangible in start-ups – its soul, energy, or presence that captures the company's spirit. Founders inject this while employees and customers feel it deep within themselves. It inspires people to contribute in any way to the organization's success. As long as the dynamism is there, engagement is very high, and the start-up remains agile. However, if the start-up lacks energy, it fumbles– that extra something that made it unique is gone.

Start-up effectiveness is a function of collective human energy. In their book "The Positive Leader: How Energy and Happiness Fuel Top-Performing Teams," Jan Mühlfeit and Melina Costi state that to set the right example and marshal those you lead, you must turn into the Chief Energy Officer in the organization.[28] Being the Chief Energy Officer will help manage your energy and your team's energy.[28] If you feel that your team gets exhausted when Friday rolls around or the board faces burnout, it is important to pace the team for the marathon instead of the sprint. Learn all about *the importance of energy in a start-up and maintaining that energy* in *Chapter 14.*

Start-ups that launched their ideas ahead of their time have faced failure. Before launching your product/service out into the market, you need to consider many things. Imagine your favorite thing – like your car. Had it been launched a hundred years ago, would there be takers for it? There might be takers, but would the technology be the same? Would it offer the experience that you get out of it now? Though it is an extreme example, it highlights the point that to succeed, you must launch the product/service at the right time.

For example, twenty years ago, the technology that could have made Uber possible didn't exist. On the other hand, though the technology for Airbnb did exist, the cultural mindset to rent a room in another person's house didn't exist. How did that happen? With Facebook, people started getting comfortable talking to strangers and becoming friends. As online reviews also started becoming more common, they gave way for people to develop interactions.

Though online classes were available for several skills before 2020, the number of people registering for those courses increased only after the pandemic. You shouldn't build your product/ service for the immediate future. However, you must think like your audience and perceive what they would feel at the launch, six months or one year away. Work out what it takes to identify the *right timing for your product* in *Chapter 15.*

"It is not enough to be at the right place at the right time. You have to be the right person at the right place at the right time."

– Harv Eker

Apart from launching your product/service at the right time, you may also need to pivot at the right time. There have been competitors in the same space for a few of them, yet they were the leaders in what they did. Examples are Twitter, Instagram, PayPal, Starbucks, and several more. However, what did they do right that the other companies that pivoted did wrong?

Western Union was a telegram service that started dying with the advent of telephones. However, they pivoted to a money transfer service, which is successful to date.[29] IBM was a personal computing giant before the launch of other less expensive products. So, the organization pivoted towards providing consultancy services for other large organizations.[29]

Did you know that the Play-Doh company manufactured it to clean the soot near coal heaters on the walls? However, there were many more oil and gas heaters in about two decades than coal heaters, which declined the sales of Play-Doh. Nevertheless, when they found that one of their sisters-in-law had been using the product to teach a kindergarten class, they had found their new niche.[29] Learn all about *pivoting at the right time* in *Chapter 16.*

Often in a start-up, time seems to twist and leap. The time for reflection is too limited. The velocity is too incredible, making it hard to process what is happening quickly and react according to changes. Each day you might feel as if you are earning your position as the CEO. However, it would help if you had some downtime to regroup yourself and your team to ensure you are right on track before being thrust into the vortex.

You may feel that you couldn't and shouldn't rest. You carry a history with you – that of being in the same place that Steve Jobs, Bill Gates, and lots more were there at one point in time. You carry their histories and the expectations of your families, friends, and teams that lean on you to succeed and lend wings to their dreams.

You could feel pressurized, yet you may also consider it a driving need not fail. It would be best if you stayed focused on not wasting your opportunities.

Sometimes you will need extra strategizing and hard work to get through a phase. It is unreasonable not to worry about the result. And the responsibility is also huge. You may show sluggish yet consistent growth. Yet the critical part is focusing on the development and making sure that it becomes exponential.

The journey of an entrepreneur is surreal. There are quiet and profound moments coupled with noisy and raucous discussions. New winds will gather and blow while old storms will die down suddenly. Though you may dream a little, it is impossible to picture how it would end. However, the effort is worth it.

As you start reading through this book, you will reflect on your journey. Some of the bumps that these organizations encountered might resonate with you. I hope that the successes will resonate as well. As the book progresses, I hope you will share your story – for I believe when you share, you help the community of entrepreneurs to learn and succeed from your trials and triumphs. I am gratified you found your way to this book, and I hope that you enjoy it as much as I relished it while writing this book.

References

1. Patel, N. (2015). *90% of Start-ups fail: Here's what you need to know about the 10%.* Available at: https://www.forbes.com/sites/neilpatel/2015/01/16/90-of-startups-will-fail-heres-what-you-need-to-know-about-the-10/?sh=2fc1c0526679 [Accessed 6 May 2022].
2. Brainstation.io (2010). *Ottawa's Shopify raises $7 million series a funding from Bessemer, Firstmark, and Felicis.* Available at: https://brainstation.io/magazine/ottawas-shopify-raises-7-million-series-a-funding-from-bessemer-firstmark-and-felicis [Accessed 6 May 2022].
3. Bertoni, S. (2013). *Silicon valley's first billionaire aims to dominate images on web.* Available at: https://www.forbes.com/sites/stevenbertoni/2013/10/09/silicon-alleys-first-billionaire-aims-to-dominate-images-on-web/?sh=54fd189f33b2 [Accessed 6 May 2022].
4. Masters of Scale (n.d.). *The case for bootstrapping w/Ben Chestnut.* Available at: https://mastersofscale.com/ben-chestnut-the-case-for-bootstrapping/ [Accessed 7 May 2022].
5. Techcrunch (2012). *GitHub pours energies into enterprise – Raises $100 Million from Power VC Andreessen Horowitz.* Available at: https://techcrunch.com/2012/07/09/github-pours-energies-into-enterprise-raises-100-million-from-power-vc-andreesen-horowitz/ [Accessed 7 May 2022].
6. Quitner, J. (2015). *The secret to Atlassian's successful $460 Million IPO.* Inc.com. Available at: https://www.inc.com/jeremy-quittner/atlassian-ipo-one-of-biggest-in-2015-profitability-is-key.html [Accessed 7 May 2022].

7. Venture Hacks (2010). *How Udemy got oversubscribed.* Available at: https://venturehacks.com/udemy [Accessed 8 May 2022].
8. Ir.hubspot (2022). *HubSpot reports Q4 and full year 2021 results.* Available at: https://ir.hubspot.com/news/hubspot-reports-q4-and-full-year-2021-results#:~:text=Full%20Year%202021%3A,up%2041%25%20compared%20to%202020. [Accessed 8 May 2022].
9. Alspach, K. (2011). *HubSpot: What we're working on now will change the Internet.* Available at: https://www.bizjournals.com/boston/blog/start-ups/2011/12/hubspot-amazon-personalization-marketing.html [Accessed 8 May 2022].
10. Ralston, G. & Seibel, M. (n.d.). *YC's essential start-up advice: Becoming a founder, early stage, talking to users | Y Combinator.* Available at: https://www.ycombinator.com/library/4D-yc-s-essential-startup-advice [Accessed 8 May 2022].
11. Andreessen, M. (2007). *The only thing that matters.* Available at: https://pmarchive.com/guide_to_startups_part4.html [Accessed 8 May 2022].
12. McIntyre, D. (2011). *Nine companies that destroyed their largest competitors.* Available at: https://247wallst.com/investing/2011/08/23/nine-companies-that-destroyed-their-largest-competitors/2/ [Accessed 8 May 2022].
13. Main, K. (n.d.). *10 million-dollar start-ups that prove you can compete with Google and win.* Available at: https://www.inc.com/kelly-main/10-million-dollar-startups-that-prove-you-can-compete-with-google-win.html [Accessed 8 May 2022].
14. Walley, L. (2010). *6 companies that succeeded by changing their business model.* Available at: https://www.chargify.com/blog/6-companies-that-succeeded-by-changing-their-business-model/ [Accessed 8 May 2022].
15. Fleishman, H. (2021). *13 businesses with brilliant global marketing strategies.* Available at: https://blog.hubspot.com/marketing/global-marketing-and-international-business [Accessed 8 May 2022].
16. Kilpatrick, G. (2022). *Market like Elon Musk: 6 genius marketing strategies – Episode 119.* Available at: https://nextlevelpodcast.com/market-like-elon-musk/ [Accessed 8 May 2022].
17. Connects (2021).*Top 10 Successful business partners examples.* Available at: https://connects.world/top-10-business-partners-examples/#Top_10_examples_of_successful_business_partners [Accessed 10 May 2022].
18. Morgan, B. (2020). *10 start-ups leading the way in customer experience.* Available at: https://www.forbes.com/sites/blakemorgan/2020/02/10/10-

startups-leading-the-way-in-customer-experience/?sh=2bd5661069f5 [Accessed 10 May 2022].

19. Cornell, C. (2019). *For small business success, listening to your critics is just as important as listening to your fans | Financial Post.* Available at: https://financialpost.com/entrepreneur/fp-startups/for-small-business-success-listening-to-your-critics-is-just-as-important-as-listening-to-your-fans [Accessed 12 May 2022].
20. Know Online Advertising (n.d.). *4 examples of brands that listen to customer feedback.* Available at: https://www.knowonlineadvertising.com/beyond-digital/4-examples-of-brands-that-listen-to-customer-feedback/ [Accessed 12 May 2022].
21. Needle, F. (2021). *7 companies with great social listening strategies.* Available at: https://blog.hubspot.com/service/social-listening-examples [Accessed 12 May 2022].
22. McNulty, M. (2020). *Netflix Twitter account jokes about 'subscription mooching,' which costs streaming service dearly.* Available at: https://www.foxbusiness.com/technology/netflix-joke-subscription-mooching [Accessed 12 May 2022].
23. Humans of New York (n.d.). *About.* Available at: https://www.humansofnewyork.com/about [Accessed 14 May 2022].
24. Granzella Larssen, A. (n.d.). *What we've learned: A Q&A with rent the runway's founders.* Available at: https://www.themuse.com/advice/what-weve-learned-a-qa-with-rent-the-runways-founders [Accessed 15 May 2022].
25. Forbes (n.d.). *Yvon Chouinard.* Available at: https://www.forbes.com/profile/yvon-chouinard/?sh=216e7d874fb5 [Accessed 15 May 2022].
26. Lebowitz, S. (2018). *Inside the 27-year friendship of Bill Gates and Warren Buffett, who didn't even wants to meet and now have each other on speed dial.* Available at: https://www.businessinsider.in/slideshows/miscellaneous/inside-the-27-year-friendship-of-bill-gates-and-warren-buffett-who-didnt-even-want-to-meet-and-now-have-each-other-on-speed-dial/slidelist/63336784.cms#slideid=63336786 [Accessed 15 May 2022].
27. Kashyap, S. (2021). *[YS Learn] Leadership lessons from Bill Campbell - the man who mentored Larry Page, Sergey Brin, and Steve Jobs.* Available at: https://yourstory.com/2020/06/ys-learn-leadership-bill-campbell-steve-jobs-larry-page-sergey-brin/amp [Accessed 15 May 2022].
28. Mühlfeit, J. & Costi, M. (2016). *The positive leader: How energy and happiness fuel top-performing teams.* Available at: https://books.google.com/

books/about/The_Positive_Leader.html?id=643tjwEACAAJ [Accessed 15 May 2022].

29. Glaveski, S. (2017). *The Top 10 company pivots of all-time*. Available at: https://medium.com/steveglaveski/an-staaethe-top-10-company-pivots-of-all-time-adfd049c99c0 [Accessed 16 May 2022].

CHAPTER 1
Getting the Funding Model Correct

If you're reading this section and reflecting on your choices while funding your start-up or on the trajectory on which you would embark for your start-up in the future, then you're probably more interested in reading this book than at least five others who haven't reached here. For many, the puddle-jumping about knowing what funding right is all about—is scary, let alone negotiating the ocean-diving when talking to potential funders.

A study published by an online platform points out that many start-ups fail at Series A funding, which many refer to as the "Series A crunch."[1] Hence, getting your funding model[2] correct is a solid entry point to building a start-up that will probably reach the market. But how do you do that? How do you figure out investors who would be interested in your business idea? What does it take to convince reputed investors about your business and get your ship sailing? Why do you believe that your business idea will effectively work? Whom are you looking to compete in the market? How much funding are you looking at to get your business kick-started? Now, you do not have to answer these questions in a manner that is not contestable. While your answers should be short and should make sense, you should also be ready with probable strategies to tackle the anticipated challenges that might come your way.

Another important question remains: are your funders going to look at your data on the funding industry and the approach of how you unpack your proposal? Or are they willing to listen more about how your product or service will solve an ignored problem all this while? By now, you would have put on your thinking caps and jotted down points to work on your business's fundamental innovation and problem-solving angle. And by the way, that is a great way to start.

What To Know Before Selecting A Funding Model?

A start-up gets funding from an investor, who can be an individual or a group of individual investors. There are different funding models[2] available, and many start-ups have leveraged these globally. A funding model used by many start-ups currently is the 'equity capital'[3] model, where investors get equity in the form of shares in the company. It means that investors have a say in the decision-making process within the company and are entitled to a share of its profits once the business starts making money. Its first official stage is Seed[4] funding - often used to validate start-up ideas before entrepreneurs invest their time and money into developing products. The current practice for funding depends on 'equity' money or 'debt' money. Debt[5] money is what you borrow from banks at lower interest rates, and equity money is the invested money that individuals or groups are willing to take risks with to make profits. I have discussed many of these in my previous book[6] and will take you through companies that have rightly utilized the correct funding models in the latter part of this chapter. I will discuss the steps you should take to get the funding model[7] right. We will reduce our understanding down to how you can work a few strategies out to anticipate which funding model is going to work more effectively based on your business model.

A part of your business that needs focus is knowing your competitors and the industry in and out. The best way to do this is to spend time on social media and news sites, reading everything you can about the industry and your competitors. As a start-up, this is particularly important because you do not have much money to spend on research, but you will be competing against companies that can pay a lot more than you can. Experts argue that lack of competition[8] might indicate a lack of market need for your product or service - which means that it may not be a good sign. If you want to gain valuable insight into what other companies are doing well or not so well, the best way would be by checking out their websites, press releases, the publications that write about them, and the people who follow them on social media. What are they doing better than you? Are they making any mistakes? What could you learn from them? You will find out where others think the market is heading, which will help you with your business plan.

Competitors are the focal points to start with when you are thinking about your business - knowing who is doing what will help you define your market and differentiate yourself from others. It will also help you understand how to work with customers to keep them coming back to you. Research indicates that a competitive environment, especially at the early stages of a company's functioning, has a positive impact[9] on its long-term prospects. You may not be the only person who has started a similar business - there are probably other companies that are similar in concept or execution. It won't hurt to research them for a few minutes every day or so - what do they do differently? What resources do they have that you don't? How much are they charging for their product or service? Do they have any partnerships with other companies that can help you or hurt you? Is their website user-friendly? Do their employees talk nicely about them on social media?

No matter how different your product is from what people are familiar with, there is always someone who has a similar idea. Your goal, in that case, should be to find something better than what the industry competition is offering already. In the end, it is all about the customer. You might have a great idea, but it won't go anywhere if customers don't like your product or service. For example: if you're selling women's clothing online and you have a better way of displaying the clothes, they look flattering on every body type, that is great! But if your idea doesn't consider that most people do not want to spend hours looking through the clothing they can't afford and won't fit, then you will never get customers buying from you. Always be ready for an unexpected competitor. The best start-ups anticipate their competitors' moves and react accordingly by improving their products or services. It is not just about getting in and staying afloat; it is about ensuring you offer the change that people are probably expecting.

Thorough knowledge of the industry is another focal point for start-ups. This is where research into the industry comes into play. It helps to understand competition through a different dimension. It is not to know whether the industry validates what you will offer as a company, but it is to know if what you will be offering is the change people keep talking about. You may have noticed, for instance, that lotion companies are all trying to push the message that their product will help you look younger. It is because they know there is a ready market of people looking for anti-aging lotions and want to ensure they capture as much of the market as possible. It is not necessarily bad. However, if you were to enter the industry with your brand of anti-aging lotion and claim that it was different, this could hurt your business in the long run. It is because what your company offers would not be different from what others were already selling. In short - not the change that the industry is probably hoping for.

It is rather pleasing to know that many start-ups quickly adapted[10] to the changing times during the 2020-2022 pandemic era, which indicates their quick adaptability. They knew the industry as well as the competition. But what they also learned with time was the change that was necessary to stand out. A primary goal for every brand is to create something people need and want, but it also helps them take a step back and see how much their product improves the industry. It is more important than focusing on just the people to whom they're selling it. If you don't know the ins and outs of your industry, you may think you've hit on a great idea when it's something that others have already tried. Or your idea might be something that will make things worse. Start-ups must know that what they're offering is a reasonable solution to any industry's problems. Trying to force a new product into an industry where it does not belong can not only be unsuccessful, but it can also hurt the people whose problems your start-up was trying to solve in the first place. It is the wrong product conversation I discussed in my previous book, a counter to which I will discuss in the next chapter of this book. For example, if there is an industry meant for people who are looking for a specific type of loan, you cannot be asking the same people to invest in real estate. It means that your business is offering something completely different. In such a case, you are not only going after customers who are not interested in what you are selling; you could be directing them away from what could have truly helped them. But if you research and study the problems, your product will probably be able to solve them.

Selecting The Suitable Funding Model

For a great business idea to take shape, you need funds. It is a well-acclaimed fact that funding is difficult, especially for start-ups. But how does one turn this complex task into an opportunity? While every start-up wishes to move ahead with its desired growth trajectory, knowing which type of funding is suitable is crucial for your business. While numerous sources of capital[5] are available to a budding business, choosing the right one helps secure your company's future and steer it toward a successful operation. Let us look at some things you should consider to identify the correct type of funding model for your business.

Know What Your Company Stands For

When starting a new company, the most important thing for you is to define what your company stands for and to do this with clarity. It is more important than anything else as it will determine the success of your business venture. So, how do you communicate your company's values and principles with clarity? To do so, you must tell the entire world, "What is in it for them?" What benefits can they derive by funding your business or acquiring your products/services? The answers to such questions will enable you to create better strategies for financing your business. You will be able to offer a new meaning to your business venture and help you popularize it faster. Communicating your company's principles with coherence will increase its brand value and create customer trust.

Starting a new company is like sailing in an ocean of unpredictability. Hence, standing true to your company values is rewarding. It helps in sustaining the growth[6] of your company in the years to come. First things first – write down your core values and make them visible. It will help people keep them in mind while working with the company and help define everything that comes next for your company. For example, if "being innovative" or "being professional" is one of the values, everything else you do should support this value. When you make your values[11] actionable, people will endorse them. It helps them to accept your company values quicker and feasibly internalize them.

Make Your Expectations Clear

One of the most crucial aspects you will need to focus on while raising funds for your start-up is the clarity of your company's vision, mission, and objectives. What is it that you want to achieve? What are the goals that you wish to attain? How will you measure your success? Answering these questions and thoroughly understanding the dynamics of various funding models[12] helps you to make a choice that resonates with your expectations. It gives an excellent head-start to your business.

After you have a clear picture of what your start-up stands for and what it's trying to accomplish, it might be time to start writing your vision statement. This statement will serve as a marker for everything that will happen in the future. It should be short but powerful enough that everyone who reads it will get a good idea of where your company is heading. You should also include key points such as the purpose of your business, why you started it, and how it's different from other competitors in the same industry. If this is still too broad for you, try creating separate statements for each primary goal or objective your business has, of course, about what we've discussed in the section above. Your start-up's vision, mission, and objectives will determine the smoothness of the funding process and what it has in store for you. Simply put – if you want to know which models suit your company the best (whether crowdfunding or bootstrapping), have no stone unturned in ensuring as much clarity as possible in its vision, mission, and objectives. Having clear objectives[13] will ensure long-term success for your business.

Knocking At The Right Doors

Funding your start-up should not always be about the cash or resources. I say - *should not* because it is a choice. And the better the option, the merrier the outcome. There is no doubt that money is essential; after all, it is one of the most driving resources in business. But is that the only resource you need? What about leadership and other resources? When looking for funding, how do you decide what to ask and what not to ask? How do you choose whom to ask? Reaching out to the "right people" with our proposal rather than just anybody who can give us money is crucial. It is because the right people[14] will bring something to the table that cannot be easily quantifiable, like experience and connections. While money is a significant resource for funding start-ups or any other company, the right people with the required money create the magic. If you get guides[15] with the right industry experience, they could also help design your start-up's course- something money cannot easily buy. Many have launched their businesses and know what it takes to make a concept a reality. Therefore, it is vital to choose funders familiar with your industry. If you get funding from someone who knows a lot about the area in which you are working, they can help determine whether an idea has the potential to be successful or not.

Industry experience, particularly with a start-up in the same field as your own, is invaluable when guiding your venture. An experienced funder can tell you what to look out for and even direct the course of your business as it grows. No money is enough to buy this kind of guidance, which is why you'll want to do your best to find an investor who shares your background. A mentor is an industry expert who can help an entrepreneur chart a path toward success. Mentors can quickly provide guidance and feedback on areas of a start-up that require more expertise than you might have. A good mentor will help you gain experience and develop ideas about how to proceed with your start-up. When you need to take a massive leap in your business, mentors are the ones who can guide you. If your start-up ever faces a disastrous situation, then a qualified mentor is the only person to direct you toward the actionable steps. The sooner you start looking for a mentor - the more significant their impact on your company's future will be.

Your Ultimate Checklist

Investors are very particular about what drives[16] your company and how you present it to them. They will also want to know if you are clear with your start-up's objectives. Why? Because they are not only interested to see if you have the right idea and approach, but they are also interested to know if you've done your homework and that you're as passionate as they are. They want to hear a good story. They want to listen to your understanding of what's happening in your industry and how it is evolving. They want to hear more than just a pitch; they want to hear about what sets your company apart from others in the same industry. The chances of someone investing in you or even taking time out to listen to you increase when they are convinced that your company has a solid foundation that will allow it to succeed in the long run. In the section below, I have listed four actionable steps to help you get the right investor for your start-up.

Have A Convincing Company Manifesto

The first step in reaching out to the right investors is carefully drafting your company manifesto. It is something that everyone would be willing to have a look at, especially funders. The best way to prepare a good company manifesto is by being very specific about how your start-up or business idea can serve your customers and make them better off. Knowing your pitch and story inside out is essential whether you're writing a business plan or preparing to meet with investors. You need to be able to discuss your company's manifesto without stumbling over your words or getting off track. A good business manifesto should communicate what your company stands for. It should be clear and compelling enough to get someone interested in learning more. People should be able to comprehend the manifesto without any trouble.

MailChimp's Culture Manifesto[17] is a good (and recent) example. It truly reflects their manifesto. In their own words: "We are passionate about our small business customers…." They also succinctly articulate their open culture that supports gender equality, freedom of speech, a living wage for all employees, and even "…adapt, experiment, embrace failure, and create value." MailChimp prioritized the needs of its customers before everything else, which helped it grow significantly as a business. They focused on making their product easier to use and affordable, which meant they could sell more. They also ensured that their product worked well with the most popular email clients because they wanted to make it easy for customers to use MailChimp. They just wanted to make something that worked well for their purposes, but in doing so, they created a phenomenal tool for email marketing.

Work On Proposals

The next step in getting the funding model correct is to design your start-up funding proposal according to industry trends, requirements, and tone. It is crucial to remember that a professional venture funding proposal will make it more likely to attract investors. Many funding proposals are rejected[18] due to the lack of clarity in the start-up's vision. A clear vision is necessary to attract funding. Clear vision lets an investor see if the proposed idea is strong enough. It also helps define a value proposition for investors to understand if it is worth investing in the business. Not all companies have exact needs regarding financing and human resources. What matters most to a start-up having a single product or service may not matter as much to a company with a more extensive portfolio of products or services. The first step would be to examine your requirements for working capital, fixed assets, and other aspects, such as training cycles for new employees.

Leading investors put forth their requirements before deciding to fund a project, which I will discuss in detail in *Chapter 3*. Although these vary from one investor to another, there are some commonalities that you can use while building your company funding proposal. Always ensure that you seek permission from your investors to share the draft proposal with other interested parties, such as banks or lending institutions. It is crucial to have any legalities sorted out before you proceed further. It helps if you can find someone who has already gone through this process and is willing to help you along the way. In addition to a business plan, there are other documents that you will need to make an effective start-up funding proposal. These include:

1. Proposal Letter: You should address this letter to the investor. It briefly explains why your business deserves funding, how much money you need, how long you need it, and what return they will get on their investment.
2. A pitch deck: It is a presentation that shares your company's story and pitches with investors or prospective clients through an infographic-style slide deck consisting of images, charts, and graphs. A

picture[17] can have a more significant impact than words. And the impact is created faster by pictures as compared to lengthy descriptions.

Utilize Social Media

When trying to get funding for your start-up, you might think that social media is only applicable when you have already been funded and have a business up and running. However, what if an investor wants to see the public's reaction to certain features or aspects of your business model? What if they want to know how many people are willing to support the idea behind your business? To prove these things, you do not need any other place than social media. With the right strategy to use social media, you can be more likely to fund your ideas.

Starting a business without social media is like scaling Mt. Everest without oxygen. It is not impossible, but it is not the smartest thing to do. Here are three reasons why:

1. *Your customers will validate your business idea*: In the old days, you could only get feedback from friends and family members. Nowadays, you have thousands of people endorsing or supporting the idea that drives your business model. Not only this, but you also get valuable feedback on the pricing structure of your product or service, which could help you strategically plan the future pricing of your product or service. So, keeping track[19] of what your customers are saying about your business on social media is an effective way to strategize your start-up's action plan.
2. *You can easily connect with prospective customers*: Social media allows you to communicate with potential customers and share your ideas (and products). It is invaluable because it will enable you to build trust among your customers to generate leads and contribute to the rising sales of your products or services.
3. *You can create a community around your brand*: People are always looking for something new or different from what they have had access to for several years. They are looking for some-

> thing to solve their problems and improve their lives. If you can find a niche market to help them achieve that goal, you are on to something.

People will always be the most valuable players in any business venture. And now more than ever, your social media presence reflects your business and brand. On the other hand, you would not want to get too obsessed with growing your number of followers (or friends in social media terms). All you need is to - "be consistent." "Be" because you need to ensure that your presence is felt by those who matter most. In the case of start-ups, that means potential investors and partners. Just having a Facebook account or a Twitter handle will not suffice. You must regularly update them with meaningful content that shows what you stand for, how you operate, and how you impact your community, industry, or even the world. "Consistent" because it takes time before people start noticing you online. It might take months to get all the traction you need from investors, partners, and customers.

Use Data And Stories

The famous saying goes, "You should never put all your eggs in one basket." While everyone agrees that data is king when it comes to growing your business, there is also a significant role that stories can play in getting the funding model right as far as your start-up is concerned. When getting funding for your start-up, the rule is that people should not forget your narrative. As an aspiring entrepreneur, it is easy to get caught up in the idea of your start-up and lose focus on the hard facts. The one thing that will hold you back is not enough data. You need to know how many people use the product you are trying to sell, where they live, if they like it, how they use it, and so on. You need to know what features they want and how much they would be willing to pay. The reason is simple: A business model built on assumptions is doomed before you even try. You can go through hundreds of articles about the importance of customer feedback, but nothing beats getting out there and talking to them about what matters most.

Data is not just a status report but can help you learn things that may not be obvious by looking at your current user base. It would help you in making better decisions. The data you collect depends on the activity you trace and measure. If your goal is to measure customer satisfaction, you will look at indicators,[20] like the quantity of the product used in a given month. If your goal is to identify what makes customers choose an effective product, then the data you collect would include the number of people of a particular age group using the product and their usage pattern. Funders like the idea of data-driven studies[21] when it comes to investments. They are also cautious about the validity of the sources from which you extract the data. Remember, people regard data as good or bad depending on its source. The accuracy of a set of numbers depends on how someone gathers data and who gathers it. Did someone simply guess at the number of new clients hired this year? Did they ask each person involved? Did they write down the answers immediately after getting them or wait until their next weekly staff meeting when it was easier to forget? All of these are essential questions when it comes to convincing investors.

As far as stories are concerned, remember that when data is presented visually appealing, it creates a better ground[22] of understanding for those listening to your strategy. Stories are as powerful as data regarding getting the funding model correct for your start-up. It is easy to get into the fallacy of thinking that you need a business plan. The phrase "business plan" evokes images of spreadsheets and PowerPoint presentations. Most people do not get funding that way. A business plan is essential, but it is unnecessary to make it all about facts and figures. Your business plan needs a narrative[23] that shows why your start-up will create value and how you will capture some of it. Investors want to know if they have enough information about your start-up to make an investment decision, but they do not want to see every detail about how you would run your company. They want a story that helps them understand what your company does, why people would use it, who will pay for it, how much money it could make, and which investors would benefit from the investment. Experienced marketers[24] are masters in storytelling. They know the power of a story and the impact it can have on your brand. Stories are so powerful that they can persuade even the most skeptical investors to buy into your message and fund your start-up. Specific stories will make your business seem more promising, while others will make it seem far-fetched. For example, anecdotes about competitors who have been successful in the market and are now thriving with a similar business model are beneficial in convincing investors that they can make money. Still, they only work if you can show the investors a way to get in early enough to get a piece of the action before the company becomes too big. Stories about companies that launched and failed may help instill confidence that you know what it takes to break through, but only if you can demonstrate why this time will be different.

In other words, there are no coincidences regarding stories about what has been working for other companies. The persuasive power of stories has been well-documented over time. The most successful businesses can connect with their customers on an emotional level. They tell stories about their opportunities and problems that people can relate to and feel invested in, which gives them a reason to become investors and customers. A good story[25] can change a hopeless situation into something that works in your favor as an entrepreneur. A good story can create empathy; it is no secret that investors like to hear stories about start-ups they are funding. But what makes a "good" story? What are the pitfalls of an ineffective one? A good story answers three questions: who is your customer, what problem are you solving for them, and why do they need to have it solved now? You can tell stories in many different forms, but in the case of a start-up looking for funding, the accepted narrative is when entrepreneurs talk about the journey from a problem to a solution. The most compelling stories are those that use both data and emotional context. Think of it this way: how do you feel when someone tells you about their life experiences? Sure, you care about the facts and figures, but there is something more important about how they make you feel. Your heart aches for people who had to struggle with an issue that you never realized was so serious until now. You get angry at people who have done wrong by others because you understand how much damage the others have done. You empathize with people when they share their vulnerabilities, which helps you to establish a proper connection.

The Unsung Stories Of Titans

The question of funding for start-ups has been on the minds of current and aspiring entrepreneurs for years. There are numerous ways for a company to move forward and grow. Some companies use the traditional method of getting investors on board by pitching their business plans and explaining how they plan to use the funds raised. Others take a more unconventional approach, like seeking out wealthy individuals willing to fund their ventures. Whatever the case, the company's goal must be in line with its business model and the people with whom it chooses to work. It is also vital that you do not rush toward funding as a business entrepreneur. The right strike at the right time is what you should target. It will help you to understand your strengths & weaknesses and use them wisely. Also, when you are getting ready to start your business, ensure there is a market.

As an entrepreneur, you know your business won't succeed without the proper funding model. It can be one of the most challenging aspects of business planning. There is no single suitable funding model for all businesses, but there are many great examples of how to work with investors and other resources to start a business. Here are some of the most successful companies in history and what their funding models look like:

Shopify has grown significantly as a company since its inception. It has become a sought-after marketplace for people globally. In the past, it has opened its doors to many different industries, such as manufacturing, technology, and retail. Not only does it help them gain more traffic for their business, but it also helps them grow their business. Shopify's platform makes creating an online store accessible to those who want to expand their business online. They can easily set up payment gateways and shipping methods on this platform. Shopify also makes the customer service process very personal through live chat, email, and phone. The platform also offers many different apps that can be helpful for small businesses looking to grow their customer base or expand their current business. Due to its strong point of being an easy-to-use piece of software, Shopify has had many different companies utilize the platform as a way to get started in e-Commerce selling.

Shopify was started in 2004 by Tobias Lütke, Daniel Weinand, and Scott Lake. The company first bootstrapped and grew without any external funding. In its initial years, it focused on enhancing the customer experience and outreach to ensure that it would successfully bring in even more customers. Switching from sales-driven fees to subscriptions was one strategy that helped them attract more customers and grow their user base. The subscription model also ensured they had steady income over time instead of relying heavily on project-based work. Shopify's Series A funding[26] took place in 2010 when they raised $7 million USD, followed by a Series B in 2011 for $15 million USD. By 2012, the company had over 41,000 merchants[27] using their platform to sell online, and their Series C in 2014 helped them raise $100 million USD. In 2017, the company was worth over a billion dollars.

Company Name: Shopify

Founded: 2004

Net worth:[28] $47.02B

Significant reason(s) for success: The company relied heavily on bootstrapping initially and focused on enhancing customer satisfaction.

Shutterstock is one of the most preferred companies offering images online. It is a multinational provider of licensed photographs, vector graphics, illustrations, and video footage. Shutterstock relies on a subscription-based business model for its operations. It offers subscriptions to businesses, agencies, and individuals to access its vast database. Shutterstock also has a platform allowing users to upload their media assets to the database under custom terms and conditions. Not only do they offer high-quality and affordable images, but they also provide marketing tools for businesses. These tools can help you create more exposure on social media, which will surely increase your popularity and lead to more sales.

From its founding in 2003 to its IPO in 2011, Shutterstock grew at a very rapid pace. The company did not disclose the amount it received from Insight Venture Partners in 2013. Shutterstock focused on offering what its customers wanted - an online reservoir of images they could buy and have the copyright to - and using these images in their blog posts, presentations, websites, etc. The business model[29] was simple: supply a site where customers could browse and search for specific types of images or images that fit a theme. After the purchase, Shutterstock would take the picture and make it available to other customers, saving them from having to find an image that matched their needs.

Company Name: Shutterstock

Founded: 2003

Net worth:[30] $2.18B

Significant reason(s) for success: The company opened to the right venture investors much later after they were sure of their offerings and their impact on the industry.

GitHub has made quite an impression globally since its inception. A software repository and collaboration platform - the site has helped developers worldwide collaborate on open-source projects. It has made a name for itself as one of the leading platforms for sharing repositories. Many developers prefer using GitHub as it allows you to make your code public so that other people can see it and even make changes if it's an open-source project. The site will track any changes made to shared code, so you can see who modified what and when. This type of collaboration is unparalleled compared to other sites that don't have this level of transparency. It helps to keep things organized and allows multiple developers to login from any location with an Internet connection.

GitHub is another example of a successful bootstrapped organization. The company was started in 2008 by Chris Wanstrath, PJ Hyett, and Tom Preston-Werner with the original intention of helping developers share their code. In the beginning, GitHub was self-funded through consulting work and small contracts. In 2012, GitHub received its initial round of funding from Andreesen Horowitz for $100 million USD. In its Series B funding[31] in 2015, GitHub raised $250 million USD. Presently, it claims to have over 83 million developers, 4 million organizations, and over 200 million repositories[32] as a part of its ecosystem. This tool has made it easier for coders to collaborate on projects and opened up new pathways for people who have never coded before to contribute to open-source projects. By making the process of contributing to open source[33] easier and more interactive, GitHub will continue to grow in popularity and enhance its reach in the future.

Company Name: GitHub

Founded: 2008

Net worth:[34] $7.5M (when acquired by Microsoft in 2018)

Significant reason(s) for success: The company worked as a bootstrapped company and raised a considerable amount in its first external funding round by working tirelessly on its products.

Atlassian is a leading name in the software development industry. They're most famous for their highly user-friendly project management and collaboration software, JIRA. JIRA is an issue-tracking system that allows companies to track what's going on with their software projects - bugs, code issues, and other problems that need to be resolved. It also helps teams get their work done by allowing them to communicate quickly and easily. Atlassian offers three tiers of JIRA: Free, Standard, and Advanced. The free version is limited in what it can do (only ten users, no attachments), but the Standard version is surprisingly affordable at $10 USD per user per month. The Advanced tier has no limits on users or storage space and offers priority support from Atlassian themselves.

This Australian company, providing software development tools, has raised $210 million USD in funds. [35] The most recent round was a secondary market[36] funding in 2014, which raised $125 million USD. Participants in the funding round included Accel Partners, T. Rowe Price, and Dragoneer Investment Group. Mike Cannon-Brookes and Scott Farquhar founded the company in 2002 with the idea of software that would let developers share information about projects and collaborate online. The company now has more than 6,000 employees in 13 countries and provides software for managing software projects, sharing files, and communicating. Its products are used by 83% of Fortune 500 companies, with more than 10 million users[37] actively using its cloud products.

Company Name: Atlassian

Founded: 2002

Net worth:[38] $27.77B

Significant reason(s) for success: The company started with a minimal amount as a company and went on to open big with its IPO.

Anyone aware of online course structures has heard of Udemy. The company is synonymous with a revolution in the education industry. The founder Eren Bali wanted to create a platform where ordinary people could learn from experts without spending any money on expensive classes at a college. The number of courses available on Udemy is growing every day, catering to learners from all over the world. One can learn about anything on Udemy, starting from basic skills like programming languages or advanced topics like artificial intelligence. Courses for entrepreneurs teach how to create your start-up or raise funds for your business idea through crowdfunding platforms.

Udemy is one of the largest marketplaces[39] in the world for online courses and has raised considerable funds after operating as a bootstrapped company for many years. It has raised $3 million USD and $12 million USD in Series A funding (2011)[40] and Series B funding (2012). The Series F funding in November 2020 increased the company's valuation to more than $3 billion USD. It was established in 2010 in San Francisco. Udemy caters to students from more than 190 countries,[41] with over 32,000. In 2020, with an additional fund of $50 million USD raised by Udemy, it announced that its valuation[42] crossed over $3 billion USD. The pandemic played a crucial role in enhancing its popularity, especially in the last two years.

Company Name: Udemy

Founded: 2002

Net worth:[42] $3.25B

Significant reason(s) for success: The company continuously bootstrapped their company after moving to Silicon Valley. They got external funding much later and went on to win global awards.

Conclusion

Many factors are involved in getting a business off the ground. You must support a successful business plan with a business strategy that is in sync with the company's goal, and you must back it up with a concrete action plan of what needs to be done to meet those goals. I have discussed these throughout the chapter, focusing on finding a suitable funding model. You must have realized by now that everything we discussed until this point is more accurate for start-ups than anything else.

For a company to succeed and get funded, it must have what it takes to convince potential investors that this company has what it takes to succeed. It's not enough that you have a solid business plan or even a solid strategy. You will have to show that your company has what it takes to outlast the competition, or at least make them work hard enough for you to get funding while they're still trying to catch up.

In the decades, many companies were founded, and many vanished. Many stayed on. We must focus our work and energy on the companies that stood the test of time. If these companies can make it big, so can your start-up. Many companies worked in different ways to get their initial funds right. Some of them went on to receive investment from investors and grow big. Some companies just started small and proved that they could be profitable. It seems like they created the products that people wanted.

I walked you through the nuances of getting the funding model right in this chapter. Of course, some key takeaways will help you focus better on this aspect as you move ahead with your start-up. I will now take a moment to summarize everything we discussed until this point to make it easier for you. I feel that the humongous documented work you now hold in your hand would generate better results if you have concrete, actionable steps to follow. While the research is something that is the essence of this book, laying down the specifics about getting the suitable funding model for your start-up is what I think is essential.

The best thing that journaling taught me is to be clear to myself and more apparent to people who read what I write. It is easy to get caught up in your head when writing and forget that other people might read what you write. It is always good to consider how someone else will interpret what you have written. What will they take from it? Will it get across what you intended? Thanks to my journaling habit - I present, to you, the conclusion below as a ready-reference section. And I shall continue to do so in the chapters that follow, hereafter.

1. Spend time and appoint team members to know the industry and competitors.
2. Know what your company stands for and let the world know.
3. Make your funding proposal clear, creative, and convincing.
4. Network with customers, investors, and fellow companies on social media.
5. Look for the right people along with the right amount of money.
6. Learn how to mix data with stories.

References

1. Prive, T. (2013). *Series a crunch: Why start-ups will use crowdfunding instead.* Available at: https://www.forbes.com/sites/tanyaprive/2013/01/22/series-a-crunch-why-startups-will-use-crowdfunding-instead/?sh=4c43679e4474 [Accessed 10 Jul. 2022].
2. Start-ups (2022). *The 5 types of start-up funding.* Available at: https://www.startups.com/library/expert-advice/5-types-startup-funding [Accessed 10 Jul. 2022].
3. Black, M. (2022). *Equity crowdfunding: What is it & how does it work?* Available at: https://www.forbes.com/advisor/business-loans/equity-crowdfunding/ [Accessed 10 Jul. 2022].
4. Coker, K. (2022). *Council post: Three pieces of advice for entrepreneurs navigating seed funding.* Available at: https://www.forbes.com/sites/forbesbusinesscouncil/2022/04/04/three-pieces-of-advice-for-entrepreneurs-navigating-seed-funding/?sh=8bc3d201e33a [Accessed 10 Jul. 2022].
5. Freedman, J. (2022). *Council post: Securing venture debt you can actually spend.* Available at: https://www.forbes.com/sites/forbesbusinesscouncil/2022/02/03/securing-venture-debt-you-can-actually-spend/?sh=994c18c63b38 [Accessed 10 Jul. 2022].
6. Harrison, M. W. (2022). *FALL: 16 reasons why 90% of start-ups fail.* [Accessed 10 Jul. 2022].

7. Bobbink, W. (2022). *The ultimate guide to financial modeling for start-ups.* Available at: https://www.ey.com/en_nl/finance-navigator/the-ultimate-guide-to-financial-modeling-for-startups [Accessed 10 Jul. 2022].
8. Riani, A. (2021). *Why it's ok to find competitors with your start-up idea.* Available at: https://www.forbes.com/sites/abdoriani/2021/03/18/why-its-ok-to-find-competitors-with-your-startup-idea/?sh=66a7cf301ed1 [Accessed 10 Jul. 2022].
9. Harvard Business Review (2013). *How competition strengthens start-ups.* Available at: https://hbr.org/2013/03/how-competition-strengthens-start-ups [Accessed 10 Jul. 2022].
10. Khosravi, B. (2020). *How start-ups are changing and adapting to the pandemic era.* Available at: https://www.forbes.com/sites/bijankhosravi/2020/09/24/how-startups-are-changing-and-adapting-to-the-pandemic-era/?sh=7a6d17364202 [Accessed 10 Jul. 2022].
11. Martinuzzi, B. (2022). *14 ways to make your company values stick.* Available at: https://www.americanexpress.com/en-us/business/trends-and-insights/articles/why-values-are-good-for-business/ [Accessed 10 Jul. 2022].
12. Peek, S. (2022). *Small business financing to bypass traditional banks.* Available at: https://www.businessnewsdaily.com/1733-small-business-financing-options-.html [Accessed 10 Jul. 2022].
13. Lytvyn, M. (2022). *Council post: Leveraging corporate values to drive business growth and scalability.* Available at: https://www.forbes.com/sites/forbestechcouncil/2021/05/19/leveraging-corporate-values-to-drive-business-growth-and-scalability/?sh=6e27ce134220 [Accessed 10 Jul. 2022].
14. Robinson, J. (2022). *How to find the right investors to fund your start-up.* Available at: https://about.crunchbase.com/blog/investors-for-startup/ [Accessed 10 Jul. 2022].
15. BrandLabs, I. (2022). *How the right mentoring can boost start-up success.* Available at: https://inc42.com/features/how-the-right-mentoring-can-boost-startup-success/ [Accessed 10 Jul. 2022].
16. Ledbetter, J. (2022). *How founders can use data to fund start-ups.* Available at: https://www.worth.com/how-founders-can-use-data-to-fund-startups/ [Accessed 10 Jul. 2022].
17. Mailchimp (2022). *About MailChimp - MailChimp's story.* Available at: https://mailchimp.com/about/ [Accessed 10 Jul. 2022].
18. Ingram, D. (2022). *Financial business objectives.* Available at: https://smallbusiness.chron.com/financial-business-objectives-4072.html [Accessed 10 Jul. 2022].

19. Jain, P. (2021). *How start-ups can use social media to understand customer needs.* Available at: https://returnonnow.com/2021/01/startups-social-media-customer-needs/ [Accessed 10 Jul. 2022].
20. Cleave, P. (2022). *6 ways to measure customer satisfaction.* Available at: https://www.smartsurvey.co.uk/blog/6-ways-to-measure-customer-satisfaction [Accessed 24 Jul. 2022].
21. Payne, K. (2020). *How data visualization can help your start-up get funding.* Available at: https://visme.co/blog/data-visualization-startup-funding/ [Accessed 10 Jul. 2022].
22. Koenigs, M. (2022). *Council post: A key aspect of storytelling to improve your business pitches.* Available at: https://www.forbes.com/sites/forbescoachescouncil/2022/05/06/a-key-aspect-of-storytelling-to-improve-your-business-pitches/?sh=476b9ac65258 [Accessed 10 Jul. 2022].
23. Guber, P. (2014). *The four truths of the storyteller.* Available at: https://hbr.org/2007/12/the-four-truths-of-the-storyteller [Accessed 10 Jul. 2022].
24. Council, F. A. (2019). *Council post: How marketers can tell compelling stories: 13 valuable lessons.* Available at: https://www.forbes.com/sites/forbesagencycouncil/2019/10/10/how-marketers-can-tell-compelling-stories-13-valuable-lessons/?sh=4fac81991241 [Accessed 10 Jul. 2022].
25. All Business (2020). *What angel investors want to know before investing in your Start-up.* Available at: https://www.forbes.com/sites/allbusiness/2020/12/13/what-angel-investors-want-to-know-before-investing-in-your-startup/?sh=6c0414a11a11 [Accessed 24 Jul. 2022].
26. Crunchbase (n.d.). *Shopify - funding, financials, valuation & investors.* Available at: https://www.crunchbase.com/organization/shopify/company_financials [Accessed 24 Jul. 2022].
27. Dean, B. (2022). *Shopify revenue and merchant statistics in 2022.* Available at: https://backlinko.com/shopify-stores [Accessed 24 Jul. 2022].
28. Macrotrends. (2022). *Shopify net worth 2013-2022.* Available at: https://www.macrotrends.net/stocks/charts/SHOP/shopify/net-worth [Accessed 24 Jul. 2022].
29. Chafkin, C. (2022). *How Shutterstock went from zero to IPO.* Available at: https://www.inc.com/christine-lagorio/bootstrappers-bible-shutterstock-founder-success-story.html [Accessed 24 Jul. 2022].
30. Macrotrends. (2022). *Shutterstock net worth 2011-2022 | SSTK.* Available at: <https://www.macrotrends.net/stocks/charts/SSTK/shutterstock/net-worth> [Accessed 24 Jul. 2022].

31. Crunchbase (2022). Available at: https://www.crunchbase.com/organization/github/company_financials [Accessed 24 Jul. 2022].
32. GitHub (2022). Available at: https://github.com/about [Accessed 24 Jul. 2022].
33. Krill, P. (2022). *GitHub expects 100 million software developers by 2025.* Available at: https://www.infoworld.com/article/3599874/github-expects-100-million-software-developers-by-2025.html [Accessed 24 Jul. 2022].
34. Weinstein, P. (2022). *Why Microsoft is willing to pay so much for GitHub.* Available at: https://hbr.org/2018/06/why-microsoft-is-willing-to-pay-so-much-for-github [Accessed 24 Jul. 2022].
35. Crunchbase (2022). Available at: https://www.crunchbase.com/organization/atlassian/company_financials [Accessed 24 Jul. 2022].
36. Kenton, W. (2022). *Learn about secondary market.* Available at: https://www.investopedia.com/terms/s/secondarymarket.asp [Accessed 24 Jul. 2022].
37. Atlassian (n.d.). Available at: https://www.atlassian.com/customers [Accessed 24 Jul. 2022].
38. Macrotrends (n.d.). *Atlassian net worth 2014-2022 | TEAM.* Available at: https://www.macrotrends.net/stocks/charts/TEAM/atlassian/net-worth [Accessed 24 Jul. 2022].
39. Raouna, K. (2020). *The 11 best online learning platforms.* Available at: https://www.learnworlds.com/online-learning-platforms/ [Accessed 24 Jul. 2022].
40. Craft (n.d.). *Udemy funding rounds, valuation, and investors.* Available at: https://craft.co/udemy/funding-rounds [Accessed 24 Jul. 2022].
41. Udemy (n.d.). *140% year-over-year growth in a number of online courses taken in the UK.* Available at: https://about.udemy.com/press-releases/140-year-over-year-growth-in-number-of-online-courses-taken-in-the-uk/ [Accessed 24 Jul. 2022].
42. Adams, S. (n.d.). *Udemy adds more than $1 billion to its valuation in new funding round.* Available at: https://www.forbes.com/sites/susanadams/2020/11/18/udemy-adds-more-than-1-billion-to-its-valuation-in-new-funding-round/?sh=3e24f3ef2993 [Accessed 24 Jul. 2022].

CHAPTER 2
Right Product

The world is changing, and so are people's perceptions of their everyday products. Some trends in the past century have been constant, and many have changed. Some people still want that wash of color that only lipstick can give, and others want to feel like they are wearing something different and unique[1] when they buy new clothes. They want to use technology[2] that enables and tools that empower. The idea of a new product or service is exciting - the possibilities seem endless, and the potential for success seems high. However, when it comes to identifying and launching a successful product, many start-ups struggle because they do not have any real-life context from which to draw.

Sometimes, the problem is the lack of clear understanding of a particular industry.[3] If you are going after an existing industry, you need to understand its needs and wants before creating a new product that fits it. Great ways of doing this include reading reviews, researching products similar to yours, and even interacting with the target audience through user testing. It can give you insights into how customers will receive your product and whether there is a market. Other times, the issue is more about identifying what people want from your product. You already know what your product will do - but do people want what you offer? You might get carried away with your creative vision, but even if it is something that seems like it would be popular or revolutionary, you still have to ask yourself if people want or need it. You may be surprised by the answer!

What Do I Mean By A Unique Product?

A unique product[4] is not always one that is different from the other existing products. But it is a product that would attract customers nonetheless. The most important reason for choosing this type of product is because it will be better than the others and provide more benefits to your customers. Creating a new product can lead to trends and opportunities for success, but before you go in that direction, I have some tips for you to consider. First, you must research[5] whether or not that idea is feasible in the market. If people are already familiar with similar kinds of products, then they might not accept your invention as quickly as you think. That's why you have to do some testing first and see if people are open to trying out something new or not. Another thing you need to consider is how much profit is associated with your invention. If there's no profit, then there's no point in doing it since inventing something that doesn't bring in money won't help your business.

When you are a budding entrepreneur, it's tempting to look at your competitors[6] and think that you have to have a product similar to theirs. But you must be mindful that different industries have different outcomes. Any specific industry will have a product range in the market that sets different consumer expectations[7] and has other purposes. As you plan your product, ensure you understand your customers' needs before determining what's best for them. For a product to be successful, it ideally fulfills a necessity in a way that's not currently being fulfilled. If you're trying to create a product where the only thing it does is satisfy the need or want, then you're not innovating—only competing. To innovate, you have to provide something different from what already exists. When developing a product, it's easy to forget that the person using it probably doesn't have the same set of worries that you do. As a designer (or engineer, or marketeer, etc.), you must remember that the end user will probably not care about specifications, weight, or even how many hours it takes to charge - they'll just want something that works.

How does one achieve uniqueness in a product? The first thing is to ensure that the product differs from the others from a certain angle. For example, let's look at the smartphone-case market. A case can be considered an isolated product with its features and functions. It must not only match your device, but it must also fit your style and personality. A person who wants to buy a smartphone case would like something that protects their phone and looks good at the same time. There are so many companies that compete, which makes it harder for the customer to choose one specific item from all of them. When selecting a cell phone case online, people tend to compare their prices and reviews rather than look at how cool or stylish these cases are. When creating or designing an item, the most important thing to remember is to put yourself in the customer's shoes and try to understand what they want and need from your product. Following are three factors to consider before you choose what could be the right product for you:

Utility

In today's business environment, start-ups must carefully analyze the utility aspect of new products. Its utility is the foremost factor that decides how a product will perform[8] in the market. Factors like need, pricing, and sustainability will only come into the picture if the utility meets the customer's expectations. This is why start-ups should always be prepared to create innovative products with broader applications. For example, people may use electronic devices in homes, offices, and even vehicles. A product like this can add immense value to the firm by making it more popular amongst people already using it. However, if the product is used only in the home, it will not generate the same revenue because of its limited usage. Thus, a start-up that wants to create a new product must consider utility[9] just like any sizeable established company. You can often determine the utility by developing prototypes and testing them with potential customers. Prototypes allow companies to test the usability of their concepts by letting consumers try out the product themselves in a controlled environment. By watching real people interact with different models and materials, product developers can understand which features should be incorporated into future iterations and which should be removed altogether.

A successful business is built upon a good product.[10] The quality of a product is determined by its utility. A product that does not solve a problem or satisfy a need will surely not be successful. A start-up must ensure that its product offers added value to the customer. As I mentioned, it should either solve an existing problem or create a new market for the customer. It is necessary to analyze[11] a product thoroughly and ensure that it has all the features needed to succeed in the market. It is important to note that utility drives the modern world - a good product enables your customers to fulfill their needs and keeps them returning for more. If a customer feels that your product offers valuable features and benefits, they will be more inclined to use it repeatedly and recommend it to others. For example, when Johnathan and the other old MySpace[12] users switched to Facebook, they could transfer all of their photos, friends list, and status updates from MySpace. It was a very appealing feature for many users who had spent years creating an extensive social network on MySpace. Another feature that made Facebook more attractive was the ability for users to send private messages to friends without going through an email server. It enabled instant communication between Facebook users. These two features helped Facebook surpass MySpace in less than five years.

Need

The need for the product is another crucial aspect you must know. If you're launching a new product, then this fact is vital for a successful[13] start-up. You must see the need factor in and out. Understanding your customer or client's challenges is one of the most critical components of product development. You can only create a product that satisfies their needs if you understand them. The most effective way to gather this information is by speaking directly with your customers and clients. It does not just apply to the products and services you provide but also to the problems you help solve. It means that not only do you need to know your market but also the problems your market faces. As a start-up, it is necessary to have intimate knowledge of their problems and challenges to create products that solve the issues. If your product idea addresses a current problem or fulfills a new need, then you have done the research. But it's good to test it on actual customers during the launch phase by performing surveys[14] and interviews. Building a compelling product requires a deep understanding of the customer's needs.

The success of a product will depend highly on how well it will meet the needs of the customer or buyer. You must be clear with what your customers want and build a product around them. If you know the condition of the product you are trying to launch, it becomes easy for you to tap your customers. The only thing that you need to do is take a stand and build trust[15] among your target audience. Subsequently, you must review the website, research, and target people according to their requirements. If you can do this, then it's always great for any business. As they say, once a customer is converted into a regular buyer, they will have greater loyalty to your company and recommend your products to others. Think about it: a client who has been coming back to you for years without fail and you have always taken care of their needs is a solid foundation for building a relationship. You know what they like, don't like, and how to keep them happy. The same is true when it comes to your customers or even potential customers. If you can convince them that you are reliable and trustworthy in handling their first purchase, there is a better chance of them choosing you again and referring others to do so, too.

Sustainability

Sustainability is another aspect that decides whether your product is suitable. Many start-ups tend to ignore the dimension of sustainability while launching new products, but it goes beyond saving money and making the product more environmentally sound. The success of a product depends not only on its features but also on how well it fits and addresses the needs of people in all demographics, geographies, and user groups. Sustainability[16] is a crucial element of the product development process. You can do it by identifying a new product that meets consumer requirements and has a sustainable impact on society and the environment. The company will benefit in many ways if this is what it achieves and maintains. If your product impacts the environment more positively than similar existing products, you would have already made a forward step in the league. The impact factor is one of the most important things to consider before launching a new product. For instance, when it comes to water bottles, there are many alternatives to plastic bottles. Though not all these bottles are made of biodegradable materials, they can still be considered more environment-friendly. These alternatives include metal, glass, and paper. An excellent example of an environmental-friendly water bottle is a stainless-steel bottle. Compared with other options, this bottle requires less energy and fewer resources to produce. Even though stainless steel is non-biodegradable like many different types of material, it still has a lesser environmental impact than plastic since people can recycle it easily.

Improved product quality, increased sales, and repeat business will be just some advantages gained by focusing on sustainability. It is a crucial element for any company regarding the core of the business, the environment, and responsible practices. Where green initiatives have always been important, many businesses have started striving hard to go beyond reducing their carbon footprint and setting goals around sustainability. Several sustainable businesses have come a long way since their inception, creating new opportunities and raising awareness of the importance of sustainability as an element of business. Some of these start-ups are now big names in their respective fields, and a few are still growing. Dow Chemical Company[17] was one of the first businesses recognized for its environmental efforts. In 1991, Dow teamed up with other major companies to create the Green Lights Program, which focused on phasing out the use of chlorofluorocarbons (CFCs) from aerosol cans. Dow estimated that it stopped 35 million pounds of CFCs from entering Earth's atmosphere by voluntarily blocking their use in aerosols. Dow also started the Powering Our Future program to educate consumers about energy conservation and reuse. The company has also worked towards reducing greenhouse gas emissions at each stage in its production process by making every aspect more efficient in its energy and water use. Dow's headquarters are located in Midland, Michigan, which is fitting because Midland was ranked number 16 on Forbes' list of America's Cleanest Cities in 2009. Over two decades after its launch, Seventh Generation continues to be an environmentally conscious company by providing safe products for people and the planet.

How To Create A Unique Product?

Idealism is a hard thing to fight. The idea of the perfect product, the best design,[18] the "big idea" that will revolutionize how people do something and make a ton of money is intoxicating. It's what drives many start-ups, and it's also what keeps them from being successful. Start-ups need to launch, but when they don't have a clear vision of what their product should do, they waste time trying to get it right. Not only does this delay getting their product out into the world and making revenue, but it can also lead to a product that doesn't have any customers because it doesn't solve any problems or fulfill any needs. Talking about feedback,[19] a company's founder is no different from anyone else. The founders of a company may have no previous experience in comparing their organization or its products. They can be very hard on themselves, and it's easy for them to lose touch with the reality of how others view their work. That's why it's so valuable for founders to solicit feedback from those who regularly interact with their products, whether internal employees or external customers. Founders must also understand that even the most direct feedback can help them learn about the functionality of their product. Even if a founder doesn't respond to every single bit of feedback they receive, they can at least take note of its existence and consider how it could affect their product. Founders need to understand that people will always have different opinions about the product, and that's a good thing - there's room for improvement. The only way for a founder to make an informed decision about how to move forward is to hear as many opinions as possible first. It's an opportunity to find out whether people love or hate your product, and it also lets people get their hands on what you've created as soon as possible so they can start using it and provide feedback.

The reality TV show Shark Tank[20] has inspired many worldwide to take a chance on their business ventures. The show's premise is simple: entrepreneurs pitch their products or services to a panel of "sharks." If the sharks like the idea, they can make an offer, which could be an investment in exchange for equity or a percentage of the business. But this isn't just any reality TV show; millions of people have watched it worldwide, and the show has inspired many who have never considered starting a business. It made pitching a business product glamorous, easy, and worthy of the risk. The question here is - what do we know about products that did well at their launch? How many of these products are still dominating the markets? And what could we possibly be deriving as lessons by studying some of these revolutionary products? Below are certain factors to keep in mind while creating a unique product:

Think About Resources

Businesses constantly face one challenge: how can they minimize the use of resources while ensuring that the product is sound?[21] It is something that all new companies should consider because they want their product to go the distance. A perfect example of this would be an app with the absolute minimum features, but those features are necessary for making the app work well. In doing so, you consider what features your users need and what is just extra fluff – this helps ensure you don't waste any time or money on unnecessary parts of your app or platform. Availability of resources is significant in deciding on a product launch. You must be mindful of the industries offering these resources as a start-up. For example, if a firm plans to launch its product catering to the automobile industry, it should know where these resources are available. The resources can be money, human capital, market access, and technology. For your business, you must know where these resources are available at economical[22] prices. It will help you decide where to target your strategic investments to succeed in the market. You can also ensure you do not overinvest in any particular resource without knowing how much the product strategy and marketing plan are required. It will also help them manage their overall costs of operation and profit margins throughout their existence.

Knowing what materials are used is essential before deciding to use them. The materials used in a product, whether a phone or a pair of jeans, are critical. These materials determine the quality of the product and its price. When choosing materials for your product, you must consider cost and marketability factors. When coming up with a start-up idea, it's easy to think only about the function of your product and not how you will make it. It's easy to overlook material costs when focusing on creating the perfect clothes or the most effective phone software. But you should also consider the materials needed to make your product. For example, if you want to create a new phone that people can use in any weather condition, how much would the waterproofing feature cost?

Will it affect your profit margin if you decide to use certain materials? What is the cost you would pay to sell a new water-repelling fabric? Are there enough people who would like this type of fabric to be worth spending money on manufacturing? Many factors decide what materials to use in your products and business. You should find out how common they are, what they cost, and what alternatives you have. A producer is also responsible for considering all environmental factors[23] from start to end of a products usage. It means being aware of the availability of resources and those that could harm the environment the least. If you start a small business, you might be surprised at how much consideration you should exercise regarding the natural environment. As with many large companies, start-ups are usually in the business of creating something new, which may include materials that can hurt the environment. So, being mindful is the key.

Think About Other Similar Existing Products

While the goal of a new business is to have customers who like their products and services so much that they'll continue to buy from them year after year, companies have to look to the future. How will the business stay relevant when it grows? One way to ensure long-term success is to look at other products and evaluate what you can do better. New businesses need to find their niche within a market by performing thorough market research. Conducting solid market research is essential for building a successful business and brand. The key to finding a way to stand out from your competition and make yourself preferable. It helps new companies gain insight into the current industry landscape and identify areas where they can stand out. While establishing a business, a business owner should conduct market research regularly. Researching your industry lets you identify trends that show what consumers are looking for and allows you to stay ahead of the curve. Regular reviews of your competition will enable you to notice changes in the marketplace and develop a strategy for adapting your brand accordingly. The rules surrounding market research aren't set in stone. They can be applied differently depending on your business model. But there's one thing most agree on: entrepreneurs need to go out there, study the trajectory of other similar products, talk with potential customers, and learn as much as they can about what customers have to say about products that resemble what you wish to offer. Thus, all start-ups must indulge in solid market research, especially to study similar products in the industry.

Working on case studies is an effective way to conduct market research[24] for your competitors' products. Case studies help marketers to understand what their target audience wants and how to provide it better. Working on a case study that involves a competitive product can give you an idea of why your competitor's products are more successful than yours. Case studies[25] are helpful because they give you a bird's eye view of the competitive landscape. When you have a detailed description of their strategy, marketing, and challenges, it is easier to understand where your competitors fit in and how your product stacks up. When working on a case study, you should be careful not to copy your competitors. Instead, take notes on the components of their strategy that show the most promise and then come up with ideas for how you would tweak those strategies to suit your business model better. Avoiding in-depth comparisons between yourself and your competition when indulging in a case study is essential. It would help if you did not argue about why one company is better or explain why someone should choose you over another company; this could turn off potential clients. Remember to follow these steps during case studies: before contacting anyone, figure out which questions you want to be answered by reading through their website or doing some of your research; make sure that you have an idea of what kind of customer you're trying to attract with your product or service; make your goals[26] clear from the beginning - for instance, if you want feedback on pricing, make that known from the very beginning; and as soon as you get someone on board, get them started as quickly as possible after they agree - don't wait!

Think About People

You can't build a better mousetrap if you don't know where the mice are. In the same way, it is impossible to launch your product successfully unless you understand who will be using it. While there are many ways to know your potential customers, conducting market research is one of the most valuable factors for understanding what people[27] want and need in today's market. Launching the right product is not possible without considering the people who would be potentially using it. Decision-makers should seek customer feedback to improve, strengthen, and validate the product they are creating. This way, they can make a practical solution that will satisfy all their customers' needs. Any person developing a product can benefit from seeking their customers' input. These people are the ones who will be using your product depending on how the product performs;[28] they have the most to gain or lose. That is why it is important to seek feedback from your customers. Feedback is information that will provide you with a detailed analysis of what they like, what they don't like, and what they would change about your product. Not only will this give you invaluable information regarding your product, but it will also allow you to develop a solution that fits the needs of all of your customers. The best part about seeking customer feedback is that it can be done in various ways: surveys, interviews, focus groups, etc. The key is determining which method will work best for you based on your goals and resources. For example, a survey can be sent out electronically through email or posted online to reach a wide variety[29] of people. This way, you will receive responses from anyone who feels compelled to fill one out. An online survey makes it easier for customers to visit and respond when they have time and under no pressure. People are the flagbearers[30] of your products, especially when you are starting up. Aspects like age, region, gender, and education play an essential role in shaping who your target audience is.

As a start-up, you must address these relevant aspects alongside other business goals. For example, if you want to produce a cold drink with no sugar content, the audience you would need to promote it to would be people who are trying to reduce their sugar intake. You must develop a clear image of your target audience to tell them what you have in store for them. The nature of your products or services will change depending on the category of people you are catering to. As a start-up, you must have a clear idea of your target market before you can begin marketing to them effectively. A company's biggest mistake is casting its net too wide, so vast that it ends up not reaching anyone. Before thinking about marketing, you need to determine your target market. If you're just starting, it's best to narrow your focus as much as possible. While it's great to be open to the possibility that your business idea may eventually appeal to a variety of people with different interests and needs, it's important not to spread yourself too thin from the get-go. The more specific your target market is at first, the better off you'll be in the long run. If you're a small start-up, chances are you haven't been able to test out the interest level for your product or service just yet. Selling something specifically for niche[31] markets is one way of safely starting without making mistakes before getting into more significant markets.

How To Know Your Product's Potential?

Start-ups must know the potential of the products they plan to launch. Before you build and launch a product, you should validate it. The validation process helps you understand how well your envisioned product will perform in the marketplace. For example, if your product requires building artificial intelligence capabilities, it is essential to check how people react to a minimum viable product (MVP). You can validate MVPs[32] by sending out prototypes and conducting customer interviews. Knowing your product's potential will help you get many things right in the first place. You will also be able to identify any additional product needs or if you have enough inventory for the launch. Every product's potential is different. Its journey will be unique. Much hard work, prototyping, and user testing go into every effect, but there's nothing like seeing a customer using your product to make you feel like it was worth the effort. There are different opinions about the best way to develop your future product's demand: by solving a problem, knowing your competition, or reaching out directly to people.[33] Some business owners feel that studying their competition and what their customers want is good enough. In contrast, others think better products are achieved by talking with potential customers and finding the necessary solutions.

Whatever your strategy, identifying your product's potential before moving ahead with its launch is a sound idea. Taking the time to perform marketing research can help you avoid mistakes, save time and money, and ensure that your marketing investments produce the results you expect. Knowing your intended buyers[34] and their needs will help define your product's success.[35] It matters the most because it's the reason for doing all of this in the first place. It might sound obvious, but it's not easy to do. It requires you to be mindful of what most of your intended customers want and need. You need to study the market, read articles, notes, and books, and conduct surveys to find out what they want/need/like. The latest trends in the market can show you where your product/service fits in. For example, if your intended product is an iPad case, you should know that people are changing their iPad cases more often than ever before because they're getting more stylish and colorful these days. So, it's more likely that potential customers will buy an iPad case with a unique design instead of just one that is practical (an iPad case with a built-in stand). To know your product's potential, you must do three things: understand the products that are successfully selling in the market and how they are being marketed to customers; understand what type of people would want to buy your product based on their needs; determine a market[36] environment that is conducive for launching your particular product. The following pointers would help you to move ahead to know your product's potential strategically:

Learn From Others' Mistakes

While most people learn from their own mistakes, more intelligent people learn from others' mistakes. It is also true for start-ups trying to launch a new product. Rather than throwing a new development in the hope that it will succeed, those who originate good ideas will look at past successes and failures. Study what made them successful and what failed; use this information to create products that may not be exactly like those but will be similar enough to compete with them in the marketplace. If you want to utilize your time judiciously as an entrepreneur, then simply see what others have done wrong in the industry and avoid such mistakes. For example, one of the biggest mistakes you can make is spending time on tasks that won't bring much value to your business. Creating a professional Facebook page may be more productive than a personal one if you are a social media expert. If all you care about is making connections with people in your industry and getting traffic on your website, then creating an individual page, which will likely be unused after some time, might be a waste of time.

Thus, brilliant entrepreneurs[37] study similar products that have done well in the market. They will try to find out what others are doing right as much as what they are doing wrong. The most common mistake start-ups make is not doing enough research on their competitors, which can be detrimental to success. Learn from the successes and setbacks of others. When you are starting your own business and planning to launch a new product, you should always look at examples of things that have been made or missed in the market. Gain insight from ideas that hit big in the past and see if they could work the same with your audience. There may be some features of specific products that you might want to change for your product. For example, you could have a superior quality product and a lower price point than similar products that do well in the market. Or maybe you want to make a niche product for a particular segment of customers who might otherwise not have access[38] to these products. If you are hoping to impact your new product, it is essential to understand how other companies made or missed the mark when they launched their products.

Production Cost And Profit Margin

To introduce a product still in development, you must be mindful of the production[39] costs. You want to show that your product has great potential, but it must also be affordable to the consumer. It would help to consider how much your competitors charge for their products. Creating a market plan and ensuring it fits your business goals is crucial. To launch your product, you need to use various production methods and materials. The most common way is to outsource some work to different factories based on your needs. Due to this reason, you should build a strong relationship with other companies/factories/businesses to accept orders and execute them quickly. In case you find out that there are some problems with the production process or if you need additional money, you must be prepared to cover the extra production costs.[40] After all, it is worth what your product will bring back to your company. As a start-up, your company will go a long way if your calculations about the product costs are accurate. When planning and executing your product's production, you must be conscious of how much each part of the process will cost. If you are a person with much capital, you can use that money for prototyping. But what if you don't have access to lots of money? How do you get the initial capital to start your own business? It would help if you thought out of the box and used your network well in this regard. When you're the CEO of an up-and-coming company, it's your job to know how much everything will cost. You have to get it right the first time - not only because you don't want to lose money, but you also want to avoid disappointing your customers and associates. They're counting on you, so you have to be sure that your projections are accurate.

When you are in the business of selling things, the profit margin is one of the most critical metrics to focus on. Profit margin tells you how much money you make after deducting the cost from your sales figures. Having a favorable profit margin helps increase your business's adequate cash flow. Therefore, start-ups need to understand its significance and find ways to improve it. As a start-up, your focus should be a balance of quality offerings and substantial profit. While pricing the product, you must be thorough with all the implications of profit margin. The critical point is that when you think about pricing,[41] you need to separate your thinking into two different steps: establishing a price and calculating a profit margin. As a new market entrant, offering a superior product at a very high value may backfire on you as there is no market history to prove this will work. Also, if the price is higher than that of your competitor, you are likely to lose a part of your consumer base and might not be able to recover from it. Your pricing strategy depends on several factors, including the type of product or service and the industry in which your company competes. Pricing[42] is a calculated decision you will have to make as an entrepreneur.

Know What People Using Such Products Have To Say

If you are unsure that your product will perform[43] well in the market, reach out to people using similar products and ask them for feedback.

You can even ask them to test the product so that you can make adjustments before it goes on the market. You should know the needs of your potential customers and be open to reaching out to them. You should also try to give them a chance to test your product to get their feedback. If you know what people say[44] about products similar to what you want to launch as a start-up, the journey ahead will be easier. It can help you avoid mistakes that could lead to the failure of your start-up. For example, if you wish to launch a new makeup brand, you should research other brands available in the market. You may want to check out their prices and compare them with your products. Also, find out if people like the packaging of these brands and study how they market their products. It will help you understand the aspects of your product that need improvement and what changes need to be incorporated before it hits the market.

If people test your product before its launch in the market, you could improve it as per the feedback received. It is one of the effective ways to make sure that your product is successful. Many companies are using this strategy. They are getting better results after getting feedback from their customer. It will help to increase customer satisfaction.[45] You can use customer feedback in various ways to improve product quality. You can use this feedback to know customers' expectations and fulfill their requirements by giving them the best products at affordable prices. It also helps build a strong rapport with your customers and may lead to winning over new customers in your company in the future. For example, Apple Inc.[46] has used this technique to understand its users' needs and develop new products. Their main goal is to deliver innovative products to differentiate themselves from their competitors. When Apple launched its first iPad in 2010, it received around 100 million pre-orders worldwide in just 60 days. The pre-order list was 25 times longer than the number of iPads Apple had produced then. In this case, Apple used user surveys to understand the consumers' needs and wants and developed the iPad accordingly.

In the same way, Google[47] has introduced its new operating system by conducting surveys. The feedback the users gave helped them create a product that could fulfill all the requirements of new users and older users who were previously using Windows or Mac OS X systems. Google also used surveys to determine what type of products and services it should provide its users. Surveys are practical tools for understanding users' needs and expectations.

Companies That Made It Big With The Right Products

HubSpot

Good products are for users as well as companies. Companies create good products that serve the needs of their users and make them successful. HubSpot[48] offers one such good product; its software provides small businesses with inbound marketing and sales solutions. It consists of content designed to attract traffic that would otherwise go to the website through organic search, social media, and email marketing. HubSpot has successfully built its brand awareness, becoming one of the most talked-about software providers globally. The company has been featured in Bloomberg BusinessWeek and The Wall Street Journal. The company started as a start-up in 2006 in a space shared with other start-ups in Cambridge, MA. During the first two years after its inception, it focused on developing its product and engaging customers. In 2008, people still perceived it as just another start-up trying to sell software services. The company changed this perception by making itself a household name among small business owners. HubSpot started blogging on topics such as how to build an effective website, what tools small businesses should use for social media engagement, how email marketing could make a customer base, etc. It also created a series of videos featuring tips on how to run a campaign or get more out of the accessible version of HubSpot's software.

In just six years, it has grown to become one of the leading marketing automation platforms in the world. The software allows companies to do much more than they could before with other platforms, communicating proactively with customers and prospects instead of simply reacting. HubSpot's success lies in its ability to find a niche in the market and fill it with a high-quality product. Its founder, Brian Halligan, realized a need for a more modern way to manage sales and marketing. The existing platforms were good at tasks like sending out mass emails or managing social media campaigns, but they didn't do much else. Using HubSpot's software, however, meant that small businesses could have their dedicated marketing team - one that would be able to handle everything from blog posts to Twitter interactions and beyond. Not only that, but it would do it all without requiring them to hire a new employee! The software is intuitive enough for people without prior knowledge of web development or coding to use it. It runs on an intuitive drag-and-drop interface so that you can make changes on the fly.

Company Name: HubSpot

Product: CRM Platform

Significant reason(s) for success: Created a flexible product. The company has been focused on its offering since year one and has only done better with time by cementing its product focus.

Y Combinator

Y Combinator[49] is another example of a company with an outstanding product. It offers funds for start-ups and has made a mark in the funding industry. Y Combinator is a well-known company that provides seed funding for start-up companies. Paul Graham and Jessica Livingston cofounded the company in 2005. It has funded over 500 start-ups, including Dropbox, Airbnb, Scribd, Loopt, Disqus, and Posterous. Many of these companies have raised Series A rounds from top VCs like Sequoia Capital, Andreessen Horowitz, and Union Square Ventures. Many have praised the company for its unorthodox approach to funding young companies. The program is designed for three months, during which the start-ups receive $20,000, as well as three weekly meetings with Y Combinator partners. The program culminates on Demo Day when the founders present their companies to a carefully selected audience of investors.

When start-ups are looking to fund, many of them look at Y Combinator. Founded in 2005 by Paul Graham and Jessica Livingston, the organization's motive was to support others. The business model is simple: Y Combinator will take a small percentage of equity in the start-up in exchange for money. The program lasts three months and ends with a Demo Day where the start-ups display their work to investors. Since its inception, Y Combinator has funded over 860 companies and helped them raise $5 billion USD. One reason why Y Combinator is so successful is that it has this product down to a science. The first step of the application process requires the start-up to submit a two-minute video about their business. It allows Graham and Livingston to get a feel for what the company does and whether or not they fit into the program. If accepted into the program, they meet with each member of Y Combinator's staff individually and discuss the details of their business. Each staff member has a different and specific role within Y Combinator; some are only there for moral support, while others offer advice on strategic decisions. It allows them to target each company's needs individually instead of treating every company as an identical entity. Some people credit its success to the connections made through the program or the resources they receive while they're there; others mention that their mentors and advisers have been critical to their success. Still, others attribute their success to the experience of working with other start-ups in the same boat or the extreme amount of support they get during their time in the program. One cannot ignore its product angle.

Company Name: Y Combinator

Product: Funding for Start-ups

Significant reason(s) for success: Created an outstanding product that would essentially drive other start-ups. The success of others always ensures success for them.

Netscape

To know what a great product looks like, you must consider Netscape's success over the years. Netscape[50] has been an innovator in Internet browsing and set the standards for a good browser. Microsoft's Internet Explorer was developed as a quick response to Netscape's Navigator. Netscape's basic premise was that a browser should be easy to use, fast, and have many features; in other words, it should be convenient. It should also allow for customization. The modern web user is all about customization; people want things that reflect their personalities, tastes, and interests. Netscape's popularity proved that it was possible to create software with all these qualities in one package. It is why people preferred it over competitors such as Mosaic and ViolaWWW. People love options—and Netscape gave them opportunities. In 1995, Netscape released a software development kit that allowed developers to create applications that used Netscape's navigation tools. In 1996, Netscape announced its integration with all new computers sold by Sun Microsystems, which made Netscape's user base grow even more. As the popularity of the browser grew, so did the company's revenue and profits. This success caused Netscape to be acquired by AOL in 1999 for $4.2 billion USD, later rebranded as AOL Time Warner when AOL merged with Time Warner in 2000.

It was one of the early-known browsers that made the Internet much more accessible to regular users and technology enthusiasts. Netscape had many features that were very helpful to amateur learners in the web space. For example, it allowed you to add your bookmarks easily (you could drag the icon of any page to your bookmark list). It also had features that let you see how a website looked on different browsers and platforms. The Netscape Navigator could use plugins to render content, another cool feature. It meant you could add functionality to your browser by downloading a plugin. Plugins for Netscape included Flash, QuickTime, RealPlayer, and Java. It meant that Netscape could function as an extensible platform that allowed other developers to build plugins for it without making changes to Netscape itself. This plugin support also allowed users to use Netscape as a platform for running applications. The most famous application developed using Netscape as a platform was Mozilla Application Suite (also known as Sea Monkey), which many people use today.

Company Name: Netscape

Product: Computer Services

Significant reason(s) for success: Created a breakthrough product as per the timeline and adapted to the changing needs of users.

Conclusion

"What one thinks is right is not always the same as what others think is right; no one can always be right."

- Roy T. Bennett

Selecting the perfect product for your start-up is like playing a game of guesses, where you collect all clues and build upon them to find the answer. While selecting a product with umpteen choices in the market, it is normal for entrepreneurs to doubt their choice of the right product. But the parameters I discussed in the chapter will surely be a torchlight in the maze. The tips I have put forth and the examples laid down will enlighten you to guess the most appropriate product for your business.

The old saying that "risk-taking is the only path to success" speaks volumes in this regard. As the internet has become increasingly popular, it has opened up many opportunities for new entrepreneurs to succeed. It has also enabled people to start businesses without leaving the comfort of their homes. Every company can utilize technology to launch and spread awareness around your product. It will help you reach people across the globe, and you can use it to gain valuable feedback on your product.

When you're planning to launch your product, the first thing is to create a plan of action. Start small, stay focused, and always remember that there is always room for improvement. In addition, it's essential to keep track of your progress to see what works and what doesn't. To make it easier, consider using a template or software to create an organizational chart with all your plans and provide reminders of things you may have forgotten about and information you could use later.

The following pointers will help you summarize what I have spoken about in this chapter:

1. A unique product is what stands out from others. The uniqueness can also be a difference in the features and offerings.
2. The utility precedes all other expectations.
3. The product need is another dimension to consider while trying to get the right product.

4. You should not ignore sustainability as an entrepreneur leading a start-up.
5. Knowing the industry in and out will help you focus on the right product.
6. Tracking people's feedback on similar products and performing a litmus test of your product before launch will give you perspectives.
7. Learning from others' mistakes will save you time and effort.
8. Learning from others' success stories will add value to your vision.

Now that you know what a good product looks like and how to launch the right product, you can follow my tips and trust your efforts to build a successful start-up.

References

1. NerdWallet (2022). *40 best start-up ideas to make you money in 2022.* Available at: https://www.nerdwallet.com/article/small-business/small-business-startup-ideas [Accessed 25 Aug. 2022].
2. The Official Cloudways Blog (2022). *70 best start-ups you need to watch out for in 2021.* Available at: https://www.cloudways.com/blog/best-startups-watch-out/ [Accessed 25 Aug. 2022].
3. Bplans (2022). Available at: https://articles.bplans.com/know-your-industry-before-you-start-your-business/ [Accessed 25 Aug. 2022].
4. Strauss, K. (2022). *8 weird and unique products from start-ups and small businesses.* Available at: https://www.forbes.com/sites/karstenstrauss/2014/03/25/8-weird-and-unique-products-from-startups-and-small-businesses/?sh=54fc6f9f49a0 [Accessed 25 Aug. 2022].
5. Savchenko, V. (2022). *Council post: Where and how to find ideas for a new start-up.* Available at: https://www.forbes.com/sites/forbesbusinesscouncil/2021/05/24/where-and-how-to-find-ideas-for-a-new-startup/?sh=-204decbd8c4f [Accessed 25 Aug. 2022].
6. Polson, B. (2022). *Council post: Three steps for start-ups to get ahead of competition.* Available at: https://www.forbes.com/sites/forbescoachescouncil/2019/05/31/three-steps-for-startups-to-get-ahead-of-competition/?sh=2fffcb514234 [Accessed 25 Aug. 2022].
7. Yehiav, G. (2022). *Council post: The evolution of customer expectations and how businesses can meet them.* Available at: https://www.forbes.com/sites/forbestechcouncil/2021/06/17/the-evolution-of-customer-expec-

tations-and-how-businesses-can-meet-them/?sh=6ef1a72a70cf [Accessed 25 Aug. 2022].

8. Kunaparaju, V. (2022). *Council post: Six lessons from start-ups for product development projects.* Available at: https://www.forbes.com/sites/forbestechcouncil/2021/09/29/six-lessons-from-startups-for-product-development-projects/?sh=b08ec6843b07 [Accessed 25 Aug. 2022].
9. Chron (2022). *Why is utility such an important feature of marketing?* Available at: https://smallbusiness.chron.com/utility-such-important-feature-marketing-80482.html [Accessed 25 Aug. 2022].
10. Houston, M. (2022). *How to build a successful product-based business, told by the experts.* Available at: https://www.forbes.com/sites/melissahouston/2021/02/25/how-to-build-a-successful-product-based-business-told-by-the-experts/?sh=c4be24b6850f [Accessed 25 Aug. 2022].
11. Ahuja, B. (2022). *Council post: A 10-step guide to designing the perfect product offering for an early-stage start-up.* Available at: https://www.forbes.com/sites/forbesbusinesscouncil/2022/07/29/a-10-step-guide-to-designing-the-perfect-product-offering-for-an-early-stage-startup/?sh=408ce322dcbd [Accessed 25 Aug. 2022].
12. Hartung, A. (2022). *How Facebook beat MySpace.* Available at: https://www.forbes.com/sites/adamhartung/2011/01/14/why-facebook-beat-myspace/?sh=4be6e716147e [Accessed 25 Aug. 2022].
13. Taylor, T. (2022). *How to determine product market fit in your industry.* Available at: https://blog.hubspot.com/sales/product-market-fit [Accessed 25 Aug. 2022].
14. Keone, M. (2022). *Council post: Get creative with customer feedback efforts.* Available at: https://www.forbes.com/sites/forbescommunicationscouncil/2020/08/14/get-creative-with-customer-feedback-efforts/?sh=30a4c0b74fd5 [Accessed 25 Aug. 2022].
15. Harvard Business Review (2022). *How business can build and maintain trust.* Available at: https://hbr.org/2022/02/how-business-can-build-and-maintain-trust [Accessed 25 Aug. 2022].
16. Scheel, R. (2022). *Council post: How star-tups can become more sustainable in 2021.* Available at: https://www.forbes.com/sites/forbesbusinesscouncil/2021/03/31/how-startups-can-become-more-sustainable-in-2021/?sh=5bcaaa2b343a [Accessed 25 Aug. 2022].
17. Encyclopedia Britannica (2022). *Dow Chemical Company | history, products, lawsuits, & facts.* Available at: https://www.britannica.com/topic/Dow-Chemical-Company [Accessed 25 Aug. 2022].

18. Stirworld (2022). *Remarkable product designs of 2021 that champion innovation and sustainability.* Available at: https://www.stirworld.com/see-features-remarkable-product-designs-of-2021-that-champion-innovation-and-sustainability [Accessed 25 Aug. 2022].
19. HubSpot (2022). *Customer feedback strategy: The only guide you'll ever need.* Available at: https://www.hubspot.com/customer-feedback [Accessed 25 Aug. 2022].
20. Investopedia (2022). *8 most successful products from "Shark Tank".* Available at: https://www.investopedia.com/articles/investing/082415/10-most-successful-products-shark-tank.asp [Accessed 25 Aug. 2022].
21. McKinsey (2022). *Winning formula: How Europe's top tech start-ups get it right.* Available at: https://www.mckinsey.com/industries/technology-media-and-telecommunications/our-insights/winning-formula-how-europes-top-tech-start-ups-get-it-right [Accessed 25 Aug. 2022].
22. Business Insider (2022). *Scarce natural resources are start-up idea goldmines.* Available at: https://www.businessinsider.com/scarce-natural-resources-are-startup-idea-goldmines-2014-5?IR=T [Accessed 25 Aug. 2022].
23. Gordontredgold (2022). *7 Start-up ideas for environment conscious entrepreneurs - Gordontredgold.* Available at: https://gordontredgold.com/7-start-up-ideas-environment-conscious-entrepreneurs/ [Accessed 25 Aug. 2022].
24. Morais, R J., Jedidi, K. (2022) *Why entrepreneurs should use 360-degree market research.* Available at: https://www.forbes.com/sites/columbiabusinessschool/2019/08/10/why-entrepreneurs-should-use-360-degree-market-research/?sh=63cac0b370a0 [Accessed 18 Sep. 2022].
25. Grinnell, C. (2022). *Council post: Traditional market research is fine, but there's a better solution.* Available at: https://www.forbes.com/sites/forbesagencycouncil/2021/03/23/traditional-market-research-is-fine-but-theres-a-better-solution/?sh=2dd061ea58fb [Accessed 18 Sep. 2022].
26. Podolsky, M. (2022). *Council post: Understanding market research for your business plan.* Available at: https://www.forbes.com/sites/theyec/2020/02/28/understanding-market-research-for-your-business-plan/?sh=58421cb96458 [Accessed 18 Sep. 2022].
27. Harvard Business Review (2022). *Know what your customers want before they do.* Available at: https://hbr.org/2011/12/know-what-your-customers-want-before-they-do [Accessed 25 Aug. 2022].
28. Railsware (2022). *Key start-up metrics applicable for your product - start-up growth metrics.* Available at: https://railsware.com/blog/a-full-guide-on-startup-metrics-for-product-success/ [Accessed 25 Aug. 2022].

29. Irigoyen, D. (2022) *10 ways to reach customers who don't know they need you.* Available at: https://blog.hubspot.com/marketing/10-ways-to-speak-to-customers-who-dont-know-they-need-you [Accessed 25 Aug. 2022].
30. O'Connor, S. (2022). *Step 6 for a successful start-up: Know your audience.* Available at: https://www.forbes.com/sites/shawnoconnor/2013/07/09/step-6-for-a-successful-startup-know-your-audience/?sh=12b355767ec4 [Accessed 25 Aug. 2022].
31. Ahuja, J. (2022). *Why should entrepreneurs serve a niche market?* Available at: https://inc42.com/resources/why-should-entrepreneurs-serve-a-niche-market/ [Accessed 25 Aug. 2022].
32. Forbes. (2022). *Council post: A review of the minimum viable product approach.* Available at: https://www.forbes.com/sites/theyec/2021/12/08/a-review-of-the-minimum-viable-product-approach/?sh=19d4c0822e20 [Accessed 25 Aug. 2022].
33. YC Startup Library (2022). *How to talk to users: YC start-up library.* Available at: https://www.ycombinator.com/library/6g-how-to-talk-to-users [Accessed 25 Aug. 2022].
34. Techcrunch (2022). *TechCrunch is part of the Yahoo family of brands.* Available at: https://techcrunch.com/2020/08/03/when-building-a-startup-think-like-a-buyer/ [Accessed 25 Aug. 2022].
35. UserGuiding (2022). *Product success metrics: How to measure the success of a new product.* Available at: https://userguiding.com/blog/product-success-metrics/ [Accessed 25 Aug. 2022].
36. Harvard Business Review (2022). *Strategy for start-ups.* Available at: https://hbr.org/2018/05/strategy-for-start-ups [Accessed 25 Aug. 2022].
37. Masterclass (2022). *Business 101: How to develop an entrepreneurial mindset.* Available at: https://www.masterclass.com/articles/how-to-develop-an-entrepreneurial-mindset [Accessed 25 Aug. 2022].
38. CommBox (2022). *Why you should create a niche category for your product in 2021? 10 Tips You Can Use.* Available at: https://www.commbox.io/why-you-should-create-a-niche-category-for-your-product-in-2021-10-tips-you-can-use/ [Accessed 25 Aug. 2022].
39. Black, M. (2022). *Business start-up costs: How to calculate and budget.* Available at: https://www.forbes.com/advisor/business-loans/business-startup-costs/ [Accessed 15 Sep. 2022].
40. Business Insights Blog (2022). *Cost-benefit analysis: What it is & how to do it.* Available at: https://online.hbs.edu/blog/post/cost-benefit-analysis [Accessed 15 Sep. 2022].

41. Forbes Business Council (2022). *Council post: 12 techniques for selecting the right pricing strategy*. Available at: https://www.forbes.com/sites/forbes-businesscouncil/2021/02/16/12-techniques-for-selecting-the-right-pricing-strategy/?sh=3ae8839f3fae [Accessed 15 Sep. 2022].
42. Riani, A. (2022). *How to price your early-stage start-up product*. Available at: https://www.forbes.com/sites/abdoriani/2020/07/29/how-to-price-your-early-stage-startup-product/?sh=1fdff1d3203e [Accessed 15 Sep. 2022].
43. Medium (2022). *9 key metrics to track your product performance*. Available at: https://eliecasa.medium.com/9-types-of-metrics-you-need-to-track-for-your-product-s-success-314e530a218f [Accessed 25 Aug. 2022].
44. HubSpot (2022). *How to figure out what (products) people want & need*. Available at: https://blog.hubspot.com/service/what-people-need-want [Accessed 25 Aug. 2022].
45. HubSpot (2022). *How to increase customer satisfaction, according to HubSpot experts*. Available at: https://blog.hubspot.com/service/how-to-increase-customer-satisfaction [Accessed 25 Aug. 2022].
46. Kocienda, K. (2019). *Creative selection*. [Accessed 16 Sep. 2022].
47. Schmidt, E., & Rosenber, J. (2017). *How Google works*. [Accessed 16 Sep. 2022].
48. Bootstrapcreative (2022). *What is HubSpot used for? What are the benefits? 2022*. Available at: https://bootstrapcreative.com/glossary/hubspot/ [Accessed 25 Aug. 2022].
49. Kofi Group (2022). *7 things you need to know about Y Combinator*. Available at: https://www.kofi-group.com/7-things-you-need-to-know-about-y-combinator-and-seed-stage-startup-funding/ [Accessed 25 Aug. 2022].
50. Fortune (2022). *The rise of Netscape*. Available at: https://fortune.com/2012/02/05/the-rise-of-netscape/ [Accessed 25 Aug. 2022].

CHAPTER 3
Right Market

The right market[1] is another significant dimension for start-ups to succeed. Just as start-ups seek to create something people need; they should also look for a market where they can get the same feedback loop that a product needs. It is essential to identify the right market to ensure that a start-up can sustain robust and long-term growth. In the case of Google,[2] it initially faced several challenges when it launched its search engine in 1998. However, the company could overcome these challenges by focusing on its core competencies and carefully choosing which markets it wanted to compete in. Instead of being distracted by entering every possible market and thus spreading itself too thin, Google focused on a few markets with high potential. It first targeted the United States and countries that spoke English, as well as Germany; this was a big market for Google to gain traction among users without overburdening itself with trying to attract users from other countries at once. As Google grew, it eventually expanded into other markets, such as France and Japan. However, Google did not try to rush into those markets simultaneously. It gradually grew into each market while perfecting its comprehensive search.

Choosing where to focus your energy is essential to growing a successful business as a start-up. As you wouldn't buy a house in a neighborhood where no one lives or rent office space in an area with enough traffic to keep your door open, you can't expect to successfully market your company if you're trying to appeal to everyone.[3] There are many ways to identify the right market for your business. One way is by thinking about the question, "Who do I want my customers to be?" and then looking at who they are now. For example, if you sell T-shirts, maybe you have mostly college students buying them. In that case, consider how you can turn your current customers into referees who will tell their friends about your shirts. You may get some help from social media to make it easy for people to share what they bought with others. If all of your customers are older employees of the same company, however, these strategies won't work - you'd want to look for other opportunities to sell T-shirts or find a new audience.

This chapter will delve deeper into ways of identifying the right market and tips to stick to it. It will also talk about successful companies that have capitalized on the right market and emerged as successful players.

How To Know If The Market Is Right?

As a start-up, you must know the market[4] well when you are set to move ahead with your business. It will ensure that you do not waste time and money on a market that does not have the potential to grow or even survive. Marketing for small businesses is different from marketing for large corporations. Most people think that marketing is a one-size-fits-all process. In reality, this is not the case. It takes much research and planning to determine your target audience and what they want to see in your product or service. If you have a start-up, you must learn how to target the right audience so your marketing efforts are well-spent. Marketing is an art form, not just a science. It requires creative thinking, intuition, and good old-fashioned trial and error. But some tried, and proper strategies will help any business owner develop a winning marketing plan. The key to marketing success is to find your niche and fill it. Look at what your competitors are doing, but don't try to copy them directly. Instead, find out what makes you unique and then use that to set yourself apart from others in your industry. Marketing is all about getting people's attention[5] so they'll want to buy from you. It doesn't matter if you're selling dog treats or luxury cars - you have to grab the attention of potential customers before they can even think about making a purchase decision.

Knowing the right market as a start-up will benefit you in more than one way. It will allow you to focus on the right things and avoid problems[6] that might arise if you need to know your target audience. The first thing that most people think about when starting a business is who will buy their products or services. Knowing it can make or break your business before it gets off the ground. It is essential to consider what kind of market you want to go after and why. There are many different types of markets out there, but some are better suited for certain businesses than others.[7] For example, if you sell to consumers, targeting young adults would be intelligent because they are more likely to spend money than older people with families and other responsibilities that take up their time and money. On the other hand, a market that targets engineers would be more beneficial if you were selling industrial equipment since they could tell other engineers about your product and make more sales for you in return (the concept behind word-of-mouth marketing). Below are some dimensions to consider when you are identifying the right market[8] for your business: I have talked about how you must align your start-up's goals via-a-vis the market; how the validity of the product you wish to sell will help you know if the market is right for it; and how to use product flow and market size to your advantage.

Alignment Of Goals

The first mantra of getting the right market for start-ups is to align the business goals[9] per the market's demands. For this, it's essential to have a clear understanding of what your customers want and deliver it to them in an effective manner. In today's world, where technology[10] is rapidly evolving and global competition is rising, it is easier for entrepreneurs to focus on marketing strategies. The alignment of your start-up goals will do wonders in this regard. To achieve market success, you need to identify your target customers and understand their needs and wants before creating a product or service that meets them. The more you know about your target customers, the easier it will be for you to develop a marketing plan that will reach them effectively with products and services they want at the prices they're willing to pay.

When you are starting a business, it is crucial to have an idea of where the company is headed. You should know your overall vision and how you plan to achieve it. Your vision will help you determine the best marketing strategies[11] for your business. Once you have decided on your vision, it's time to align that goal with the rest of your business goals. It will ensure that all aspects of your business move toward the same objective. If your business goals don't align, they will compete against each other instead of working together in harmony. For example, if one goal is to increase sales while another is to lower costs, then both objectives will compete against each other instead of working together towards a common goal. If you figure out such objectives well, you can get to the right market quicker as an entrepreneur.[12] Having aligned market goals enables you to make better decisions that can help improve the efficiency of your business.

Validity Of The Product

As a start-up, the right market is something you have to prioritize. You can efficiently deliver it to them when you know that customers validate[13] your product. If you are sure of the validity of your product, then determining the proper market becomes easy. You have to look at your competitors and see what they are doing wrong and what they're not doing. For example, if you're building an app that allows people to book flights, you need to find out what other apps are already in this space. What features do they offer? What kind of customers do they cater to? How much money do they make? And how many people use their apps? Once you know these things, you can build your app accordingly and target an audience looking for just what your app has to offer. You can sell your product to anyone who needs it. So, before you start making any assumptions about who will buy your product and how much they are willing to pay for it, make sure that you clearly understand the problem that your customers face and how much they are eager to pay to solve it.[14] It is where user research comes in handy. Researching your target audience in the right market helps you understand their needs and requirements[15] better than anyone else. It also allows you to identify different segments within a larger group and cater to each piece accordingly.

One of the first decisions you will have to make is about the market for your product. Should it be a local market, or should it be for an international audience?[16] The answer to this question will depend on several factors, including your budget and your capabilities as a business owner. You also need to know what you want from your business and where it stands in the global economy. The world has become increasingly integrated thanks to globalization. It means that markets are no longer confined to local or national boundaries. Consumers now have access to goods produced anywhere in the world at affordable prices and vice versa. There are no limits to where you can sell your products or services as long as there is demand for them. An excellent example is how computers were first introduced into homes around the world during the 1980s and 1990s; they were expensive, but people bought them because they saw how useful they could be for their daily lives. Today, these machines are commonplace in most homes and offices around the world. There are even more sophisticated versions on sale that can play video games or run programs designed by computer programmers worldwide who have created them using one of these machines. So, product validation vis-a-vis market analysis[17] is the key.

Product Flow And Market Size

The right market will ensure that your start-up product flow happens without hassle. The wrong market can be a huge problem and cause many issues for your business and its people. How do you know which market is right for you? How do you know if this market is the right one? It's not easy to answer these questions because the answer depends on many factors. Product flow[18] is transferring a product from the manufacturer to the consumer. It can either be done through stores or online. A start-up must know the market's product flow when identifying the right market for their businesses. Companies that can establish themselves in an industry with a high volume of business have ample opportunity for growth and success. The product flow can be divided into two categories: retail and wholesale.[19] The best way for a start-up to determine which type they should focus on is by looking at the current state of their industry and how it works. If there's already much competition in wholesale sales, then it might not be worth it for them to pursue this route because there's no guarantee that they'll earn enough money back to cover their overhead costs.[20]

Before launching your business, you must know what kind of market you want to enter. You should consider the market size[21] carefully because it will help determine how profitable your business will become over time. The market size will also affect whether there's enough room for competition and potential customers who need what you're offering. It would help if you also looked at the demographics[22] of your potential customer base and their buying habits and behaviors when making this decision. It can help you determine if there's enough demand for your product or service once it's been launched into the marketplace through marketing efforts such as advertisements.[23] If you're entirely aware of the market size and demographics of buyers in the market, you are sure to succeed. It will help you to focus on the right target audience and develop your marketing strategy accordingly. You should also know where they are located, how much they earn, and their needs[24] and wants. Understanding these critical aspects will help you achieve valuable insights into your customers' mindsets, expectations, buying behavior, etc. It can help you to create effective marketing strategies that will yield positive results for your business.

How To Sustain In The Right Market?

The right strategies enable start-ups to sustain and thrive in the right market. The success of your business largely depends on how[25] you choose the market for your product or service. You need to be careful about your marketing strategy to increase your chances of getting more customers and making more profits. Marketing is one of the most important aspects of any business. It helps you reach a wider audience and make your presence felt. You can use various marketing strategies, including social media marketing, Search Engine Optimization (SEO), email marketing, or content marketing. As a start-up company, you must know how to go about choosing the right market and the apt marketing strategy.[26] Before you can choose one, it is essential that you analyze all the options available and then decide which one works best for your business. For example, if your business caters mainly to local clients, traditional marketing forms like advertising may not be a good idea. One effective way is using social media platforms like Facebook and Twitter, which can help you reach out to your clients.

One successful strategy for start-ups that is often underestimated is daring to take risks. Without risks, you cannot make it big as a start-up. Sustaining in the right market is all about catering to the needs of the hour in every way possible. You need to be fearless and ready to take on any challenge that comes your way. You have also got to be flexible, open to new ideas, and willing to change your business model accordingly. One example of this would be Uber,[27] which started as a luxury car service but later shifted its focus towards providing low-cost transportation options for people who could not afford a taxi or even rent a car on their own. Uber managed to do this by changing its business model and coming up with something new that people were looking forward to using. Another example would be Airbnb, which started as an online platform where people could rent their spare rooms or homes for travelers looking for accommodation while traveling around town or abroad. Nowadays, Airbnb[28] has expanded its services and become an accommodation provider like any other hotel company. In the section below, I have talked elaborately on the aspects that will help you to sustain in the market you enter: how you must have a dynamic start-up mindset as an entrepreneur; what good will it do to you when you offer beyond or better than what already exists in the market; and how a product that impacts people's lives in appropriate ways help entrepreneurs sustain in the market.

Have A Dynamic Start-Up Mindset

Start-ups that are dynamic[29] and ready to change with the changing needs of the industry will stick longer in the right market. Businesses that improve existing products or services through innovation, creativity, and imagination make a difference. They don't necessarily need to prove a point but make life easier for customers by making products more accessible, helpful, or cheaper than before. Start-ups must be flexible and ready to adapt. It might be as good as dead if your start-up cannot adapt[30] quickly. Some of the best examples of successful start-up companies are Apple and Google. All these companies have managed to become successful because they were able to adapt their products according to customer needs and demands. They changed their business models when they saw that their existing models were not working well with customers.

When you start a business, it's important to remember that the vision of your start-up is reflected in the products and services you offer and in the people who work for you. If your start-up has a dynamic mindset, it will come across to people in various ways, making your business sustenance more likely. It is not only about having a receptive attitude in your talks but also about being open-minded to new ideas and perspectives. In such a situation, employees and customers feel encouraged to share their thoughts and feedback, regardless of whether they are right or wrong. It also means that there is less resistance to change within your company. A dynamic business mindset focuses on customers and clients before focusing on profits or other aspects of the business. Stakeholder values are regarded highly and will always be ahead of everything else. It also means that customer needs are a priority. For example, people who shop online should get what they want; if their order is delayed due to delivery issues, they should be compensated for their inconvenience.

Offer Beyond Or Better Than Existing Products

Your market sustenance[31] also depends on what you offer as a company compared to other existing products. Always offer better than or beyond what customers are already getting. If you are selling a new product to the market, it may be difficult for your customers to compare it with some other similar product. However, if you have an existing product in your portfolio, it is easy for your customers to compare the new product with the older one. You can use this fact to your advantage by examining all the features of both products and highlighting those different features. It will help you differentiate between them. For example, suppose your company has been selling cosmetics for years now and suddenly comes up with another line of cosmetics that promises better performance or is priced moderately than before. In that case, it might work in your favor. The more niche your product is, the easier it will be to find success in the marketplace. The fewer people who want it, the fewer competitors you'll have, and the more likely you will make money from your creation.

Sometimes, it is not only about the product itself but also about its packaging, design, color, and other aspects influencing customers' buying decisions. The product should be unique, but never at the expense of quality. The main goal of your brand is to create a connection between customers and your product. This connection should be based on honesty and trust - knowing your audience well before launching a new product or service is crucial. Also, make sure that people will be able to understand how they can benefit from using your product or service. If they don't see any value in it, there's no point in trying to sell it to them. People drive your product in the market. And if you offer better than what others have for them, they will return to you. Take Apple Inc. as an example. When the company was founded in 1976, Steve Jobs and Steve Wozniak were not the first to think about computers. There were already many companies that had tried their hands at building personal computers, but none of them succeeded. However, Apple's founders did not give up easily. They continued working on their vision until they had created something that no one else could match at that time - a computer that was intuitively easy to use and was made with high-quality components. In other words, they provided their customers with an experience unlike anything they had ever seen.

Impact People's Lives

A company that can create products that can change people's lives in the right way and impact for a longer time will ensure your start-up's sustenance in the market. The key to building a sustainable business is first to have a product or service that customers are willing to pay for. Once you have the right product and customer base, you must create efficient systems that allow you to grow exponentially. Having a valuable product and a good customer base is not enough. You must also have plans to scale your business as quickly as possible while maintaining high-quality standards across all areas of your operations. For a start-up to be successful, it needs to build a brand that people want to buy into and stand by. A brand is an association between an idea or image and the offered product or service. The same applies to marketing, too. People may not always respond to advertisements and promotions[32] just like that, but they do respond when they feel that what you are offering can help them in their lives.

If you're wondering why your business is suffering, it could be that you've been building a business that looks good on paper. The problem with doing something like this is that it's easy to lose track of whether or not customers are enjoying their experience with your products and services. If customers feel your products make their lives easy but not as meaningful, your business may not survive in the market. While it may seem counterintuitive, focusing on making life more accessible all the time can hurt your company. Sure, it's an easy way to get customers excited about the benefits of your product or service. But what does the consumer want? Let's consider how we feel about our lives to answer this question. We are always looking for ways to simplify things, and we can find ways of accomplishing this in almost every area of our lives - from cooking dinner to working out to cleaning our homes. We're so good at finding ways to make our lives easier that we often go through life without experiencing much joy or fulfillment. When it comes to it, people aren't only interested in making their lives easier; they're equally interested or even more in making them more meaningful and fulfilling.

How To Offer The Right Product In The Right Market?

The key to marketing success is knowing what the market wants. The first thing you have to do is make sure your product is something people want. You must research what your target consumers are looking for, including their demographics and what they expect in a product before you can effectively begin marketing. You have to get inside their heads, understand their needs, and be able to meet them with a product that will bring them back again and again. It's also essential to study the market closely before you begin marketing to know where there is room for improvement. If a competitor has a particular advantage over you, like lower prices or better brand name recognition, don't just give up - you can still find ways to keep your customers happy. You may want to offer incentives to buy your product instead of theirs, like providing free accessories or a bonus gift card. In addition, it's essential that you follow the guidelines of social media marketing so that people will be more likely to share photos of your beautiful products on their social media accounts. For example, when someone wants to post an image of something stylish on Instagram, they will be more likely to post about an item if it's from one that reflects their style.

When you're an entrepreneur, you can easily get caught up in your product or service details and forget that an entire market is at play. You may have the best product in the world, but if no one knows, you're only cutting off potential customers. And if you have a solid system for marketing your business and its products, then you can grow that market base over time, and that's when you'll start seeing some real growth. Marketing strategies[33] is the key to getting your product out there, and they're essential before you even launch your start-up. When you advertise your business or product on social media, what social networks are you targeting? How are you targeting them? What demographics do you want to reach? What are the prices people would be willing to pay to buy your products? What kinds of posts will appeal to those people? Will you pay for ads on social media? Do those ads target specific demographics, or do they also try to reach as broad an audience as possible? The answers to these questions will all impact your marketing strategies success. Read ahead to learn more about the secrets to offering the right product in the right market. I have written about knowing the worth of your product, relying on segmentation to analyze your customers better in the market, and using social media to optimize your prediction about whether customers will continue using your product to help you make relevant changes.

Know What The Product Is Worth

Product pricing is an essential factor for marketing a product right. It can make or break a product. Pricing it too high means the customer will not purchase the product. On the other hand, if it is priced too low, companies tend to lose money. One of the first things customers do when they enter a store is look at the prices of products. When customers see prices that are within their budget, they will buy them. When it comes to pricing a product, there are several ways to do it successfully. The price anchoring method, for instance, has two different strategies.

The first way is for retailers to place higher-priced items next to lower-priced items. The second way is to identify the most expensive item at the end of an aisle and the least expensive item at the beginning so that customers have to walk through all of the products to get to the one they want. This method makes customers think that all other products are a reasonable price because they have to walk past them to get to where they want.

Price skimming[34] is another strategy in this regard. It is when a company sets a high price for its product at the start of production and then gradually lowers the cost as the product becomes more popular. The idea is that those less sensitive to price will purchase the product at a higher price, and those more sensitive to price will wait until it goes on sale. Price skimming is another sales tactic where products are initially priced at a premium, then gradually lowered over time as demand increases and supply decreases. While it's common for new products to be released at a higher price than their initial cost, brands using price skimming in their pricing strategy believe that their products are perceived as more desirable when they're first released. Then the price lowers to reflect the increased demand. It is an effective strategy for companies that want to maximize revenue by appealing to early adopters, who are willing to pay more for a new product since they're confident in its future success. This strategy can also help eliminate competition from lower-priced alternatives, which companies can use as a selling point when lowering their prices. Also, remember that price skimming can alienate customers who aren't early adopters.

Using Segmentation To Analyze Customers In The Market

As a start-up, you must be flexible, agile, and responsive to your customers' needs. However, this is not always easy to do. One way to overcome the problem is by analyzing the market and your customer's behavior. The first thing you need to do is simplify the big picture by adopting segmentation. Segmentation[35] is dividing a large group into smaller groups with similar characteristics. For example, selling a product aimed at teenagers might divide the market into teenage boys and girls. Then, you could make different versions of your product for each group - a different color for the girls and a different game for the gadget for the boys. You can use segmentation to determine how many people in your target market fit into these smaller groups. Psychographic segmentation analyzes customer behavior based on their lifestyles and values. By grouping consumers according to their lifestyles and values, marketers can tailor their marketing strategies to target the groups most likely to purchase a product. It focuses on the reasons for buying rather than statistical information such as age, gender, or income. The lifestyle and values of an individual can change over time, so you must update this segmentation regularly to ensure that companies choose the best target market to focus on.

On the other hand, demographic segmentation analyzes customer behavior based on where they live, their age group, or their income level. It aims to examine the market in terms of its various subgroups. Typically, companies will identify a particular audience and then look at other factors influencing their behavior as customers. Then, they'll divide this larger audience into smaller groups based on these factors. It allows companies to target only the most likely customers and focus on specific aspects of their behavior. You can do this by looking at the potential customers' long-term needs and preferences. The advantage of demographic segmentation is that it's relatively easy to analyze large numbers of people and gives you a good general picture of whom you're targeting.

Use Social Media To Study Consumer Sustainability Trends

Social media helps greatly in knowing which way the consumers are headed[36] and how long they will continue using specific products. Social media is an excellent source for discovering what is trending on the internet and how many people are talking about it. It can also be used as an avenue for advertising purposes. Social media has helped companies reach out to customers and improve customer service. It has become a platform where companies can interact with their clients more personally and get feedback regarding their products or services. It has also become an essential medium for communication between companies and customers, making it easier for them to connect. Social media helps companies get feedback on their products or services from their target audience. The main objective of any company is to increase sales while maintaining high levels of customer satisfaction. It can only be achieved if they know what exactly their customers want from them. You can accomplish this by using social networks such as Facebook, Twitter, and Instagram, where one can post questions or ask for suggestions from users regarding their business activities.

Social media allows entrepreneurs to reach out to their target audience, get feedback, and even get new customers. But for this to work, start-ups must stay updated and relevant. They must keep up with the latest trends and technologies and provide the best customer experience possible. There are many people who want to know more about your company and what you do. Ensure they have access to information they can use whenever they want. It will help them see you as an expert in your industry, increasing their trust and giving them more reasons to buy from you when the time is right. One of the best ways to sustain people's interest in your business is by keeping them up-to-date with everything happening. Suppose someone follows your brand on social media. In that case, they should be able to find out about any new products or promotions within minutes of their release - not days or weeks later when everyone else has already heard about it from someone else.

Companies That Succeeded In The Right Market

Apple

Apple is not just a tech company; it's a lifestyle brand. The company has created a loyal following by creating products that are easy to use, intuitive, and aesthetically pleasing. Apple has also created a brand for itself where its users are loyal customers who follow its every move in the market. Apple has been able to keep up with the times by changing its offerings per the era's demands. It has changed from desktop computers to laptops and then smartphones. One such change was when Apple launched its first iPhone handset in 2007. Many more launches followed this in different versions and features.

Apple[37] has always been a trailblazer in the technology industry. The company started with computer products and then moved on to smartphones. In the past few years, Apple has introduced new products such as smartwatches, earbuds, and even innovative home automation systems. We must look at its business model to understand how Apple makes money from these products. Apple has always been a vertically integrated company that designs, manufactures, and markets its products. It means that Apple makes all its products in-house instead of outsourcing them to other companies. Apple's business model is based on controlling both the supply chain and customer experience across all product categories. The company relies heavily on luxury branding, which allows it to charge higher prices than other manufacturers simply looking to make money from volume sales. Apple offers its customers convenience in many ways: you can buy music through iTunes or listen to it using your phone; pay for goods and services using Apple Pay; connect with friends via iMessage or Facetime; get directions using Google Maps or Waze; play games like Candy Crush Saga; talk about sports scores with Siri and many more.

Company Name: Apple

Founded: 1976

Significant reason(s) for success: Highly functional and appealing products. Focuses on the changing needs of the market and offers products accordingly.

Volkswagen

Volkswagen's success in the market is not a secret. It has done tremendously well for itself since its inception. It is one of the top most selling brands in the automotive industry and has consistently been voted one of the best brands in its category by several surveys. Volkswagen[38] vehicles are known for their reliability, performance, comfort, and style. Some popular Volkswagen cars include Golf GTI, Jetta, Passat, and Polo. One can attribute the company's success to its innovative ideas, which customers have well received around the globe. Many analysts attribute the success of Volkswagen to management decisions made at different stages in its history.

Volkswagen has catered to the market's changing needs with every passing year. It has stood to the test of time by constantly adapting its offerings as an automobile company. Volkswagen is also renowned for being innovative with its marketing strategies and advertising campaigns. The company has been involved in several high-profile advertising campaigns over the years. One of these was the Fun Theory project, launched in 2010. This campaign was aimed at encouraging people to use their bicycles more often. To do this, Volkswagen set up an experiment that would show just how much time it took cyclists to get from point A to point B compared to motorists. The results showed that it took cyclists about two minutes longer than motorists to reach their destination using their bikes versus driving a car or public transport. This experiment encouraged people reluctant to cycle because they thought it would take too long and be too difficult for them. Many people who had never cycled joined the experiment to see whether it was worth doing so.

Company Name: Volkswagen
Founded: 1937
Significant reason(s) for success: Innovation, performance, and comfort drive its offerings. Involves public outreach by adequately using strategies to be a key player in the market.

Nike

Nike's innovative ad campaigns and marketing strategies have generated success for the company year after year. Recent campaigns have focused on everyday athletes, encouraging consumers to push their limits in sporty but fashionable clothing. Nike has created a culture around empowerment, encouraging people to make their dreams a reality. The slogan "Just do it" is well-known worldwide and has become synonymous with the brand. Nike has worked hard to build an image that inspires action and self-confidence through engaging ads, celebrity endorsements, and heartwarming stories of athletes overcoming obstacles to achieve greatness.

Nike[39] has successfully launched many new products by utilizing the popularity of individual athletes and celebrities. This strategy is called "celebrity endorsement." It increases sales for Nike and creates positive publicity for the celebrity. For example, Tiger Woods, an international superstar in golf, was in a Nike commercial viewed by millions of people worldwide. The commercial made golf more popular and helped Nike sell more golf clubs and shoes. Nike also uses "athlete endorsements" for the same purpose. They employ famous athletes to wear their shoes and clothes during sporting events. For example, LeBron James, arguably the best NBA player, was featured in a Nike commercial. In the ad, he performed special moves that were only possible because he was wearing his signature basketball shoes. The result of both strategies is increased revenue for Nike. Michael Jordan is another name that has boosted Nike's market presence remarkably. Michael Jordan is recognized as one of the greatest basketball players globally. He has been covered in Nike advertisements and promotions since he was signed in 1984. He played a vital role in the success of Nike by endorsing their products and using the shoe giant's gear during his games.

Company Name: Nike
Founded: 1964
Significant reason(s) for success: Celebrity endorsement and innovative marketing ad campaigns enhance the popularity of its products; it has become a leading name in the market for its industry.

Porch

Porch[40] is a real estate technology company that connects homeowners, home maintenance, and repair contractors. Porch's mission has been to make it easy for homeowners to find, book, and pay for home service professionals. They believe that homeowners should be able to book services from anyone in their neighborhood and have a great experience with their service provider. Their platform offers a single source for homeowners to find reliable contractors, compare bids, and learn about their contractor history. The company has been changing the way homeowners connect with contractors by making it easy for them to get recommendations from other homeowners and make informed decisions about who they want to work on their homes.

It is interesting to note that the company went through layoffs two years after its launch. However, with a clear vision and dedicated workforce, it was able to reshape its future course and went on to become a successful company. The company was successful because it was mindful of the market's requirements. It did not try to create a new wheel; instead, it looked at how other companies already had solved problems relevant to the customers. It allowed them to innovate on top of existing solutions. It knew that it needed to be innovative and different from its competitors, so it made sure that its products were unique and had a lot of features. It allowed it to stand out from the crowd and get more customers.

Company Name: Porch
Founded: 2012
Significant reason(s) for success: Quickly adapted to the changing needs of the markets vis-a-vis product choices, variety, etc.

Filippo Loreti

Filippo Loreti[41] is booming as a company designing stylish watches. The brand's growth has been driven by its smartly designed timepieces, which include a range of styles for men and women. The company also offers a wide variety of leather straps and bracelets that can be added to its watches for extra customization options. The brand has been around since 2015, but only in recent years has it gained the attention of the luxury watch world.

Filippo Loreti watches are based on the belief that good design can compensate for any shortcomings in materials, construction, or price. They are created to be fashionable and timeless, with clean lines, a sense of style, and an understated elegance that appeals to both men and women alike. Filippo Loreti watches are made of high-quality materials such as stainless steel, gold-plated brass, and titanium. They come in many styles, appealing to various customers, keeping up with the trends of the fashion and lifestyle industry. Each one has its unique style that is sure to appeal to people across all age groups. Their goal was to design something stylish yet still functional and affordable for people who may need help to afford a high-end watch every day. They want to ensure everyone can enjoy wearing a watch, regardless of their budget or social status. The company's watches have made an impact and are gaining more and more popularity with time, especially in a market that was predominated by a variety of luxury watch options.

Company Name: Filippo Loreti
Founded: 2015
Significant reason(s) for success: A solid understanding of the market; created products that had an existing competition yet tapped into the essence of the market.

Conclusion

"Good marketing makes the company look smart.
Great marketing makes the customer feel smart."

– Joe Chernov

Congratulations, you are at the end of this chapter. You've read about how to start your business, get your product right, and achieve the right market for it. The world is yours. Your start-up is going to make a difference. Many entrepreneurs have given up mid-way through the market, but your start-up will succeed. The right market strategies, the efforts to offer better and beyond others, and the tips for sustaining in the right market will create the magic for your start-up. It's essential to be prepared when you're starting by knowing how you're going to tackle critical components of the right market, and I have helped you in this regard with this chapter. Successful start-ups have great ideas, good funding, and an effective market plan. Market strategies set up the basis for the goals of a business. As I discussed, strategies can be based on the target market's wants and needs. One of the critical points in making your start-up successful is ensuring that you have a good marketing plan in place. In other words, your marketing plan should target your ideal buyers instead of just making a general statement about who your ideal buyers are.

Just because yours is a start-up does not mean you cannot succeed. You can and you will. By following the tips and strategies I have shared in this chapter and reflecting on the success stories of the phenomenal companies I mentioned, your company will make it big. If you know the right things to do and you put in the effort, your business can become a success. That is the message I hope to leave you with after reading this chapter. Whether you're an established company or a start-up, surround yourself with people who not only understand your business principles but who also can anticipate the changes and challenges that await you in the future. Also, remember that you'll want both digital and traditional marketing strategies in place for your business to thrive. Trust your market and trust what you offer. Be confident of who you hire and be sure of your company's adaptability to the changing marketing needs - that's the mantra of success.

Before you move ahead with the succeeding chapters, below are the pointers that you must focus on and keep coming back to, ones that summarize this chapter for your ease:

1. Know that the market is crucial for your start-up's success.
2. Align your company's goals to ensure that the market is right.
3. Know your product's validity for it to yield results in the right market.
4. The product flow and market size are significant aspects of identifying and entering the right market.
5. As an entrepreneur, you must have a dynamic mindset to perform well and sustain your business.
6. Even while offering a product similar to existing ones, always strive to provide better and beyond with time.
7. Impact people's lives in the right market, and the market shall be yours.
8. Product pricing is essential when delivering the right product in the right market.
9. Segmentation enables you to analyze customers in the market effectively.

10. Social media can help you predict whether your customers will stick around for a long time and ensure your company's sustenance in the market.

References

1. Gantz, R. (2022). *Council post: Bearish markets are sending a signal to growing start-ups: Meet the public market earlier.* Available at: https://www.forbes.com/sites/forbesbusinesscouncil/2022/08/02/bearish-markets-are-sending-a-signal-to-growing-startups-meet-the-public-market-earlier/?sh=3dff2f7736f9 [Accessed 16 Oct. 2022].
2. Klobuchar, A. (2021). *Antitrust.* [Accessed 16 Oct. 2022].
3. Praxis (2022). *Start-ups that last.* Available at: https://praxis.ac.in/start-ups-that-last-an-article-from-harvard-business-review/ [Accessed 16 Oct. 2022].
4. The Guardian (2022). *Knowing your market and competition is crucial when starting up*. Available at: https://www.theguardian.com/small-business-network/2013/mar/13/james-caan-market-research-startups [Accessed 16 Oct. 2022].
5. Braze (2022). *5 ways to grab your customer's attention in a distracted world.* Available at: https://www.braze.com/resources/articles/5-ways-grab-customers-attention-distracted-world [Accessed 16 Oct. 2022].
6. Business News Daily (2022). *Mistakes to avoid when starting a business.* Available at: https://www.businessnewsdaily.com/7398-startup-mistakes-to-avoid.html [Accessed 16 Oct. 2022].
7. Expert Panel (2022). *Council post: 10 smart ways for new-to-market businesses to establish credibility.* Available at: https://www.forbes.com/sites/forbesagencycouncil/2021/12/07/10-smart-ways-for-new-to-market-businesses-to-establish-credibility/?sh=6199d9c44e54 [Accessed 16 Oct. 2022].
8. Stewart, C. (2022). *How to determine if there is a market for your business.* Available at: https://blog.marketresearch.com/how-to-determine-if-there-is-a-market-for-your-business [Accessed 16 Oct. 2022].
9. Verma, S. (2022). *Align marketing with business goals that work every time.* Available at: https://aritic.com/blog/aritic-pinpoint/align-marketing-with-business-goals/ [Accessed 16 Oct. 2022].
10. Harvard Business Review (2022). *A survival guide for start-ups in the era of tech giants.* Available at: https://hbr.org/2020/02/a-survival-guide-for-startups-in-the-era-of-tech-giants [Accessed 16 Oct. 2022].

11. Dearsley, B. (2022). *Start-up marketing strategy: 18 ideas and tactics that actually work.* Available at: https://blog.hubspot.com/marketing/start-up-marketing [Accessed 16 Oct. 2022].
12. Google (2013). *The new business road test.* Available at: https://books.google.co.in/books?hl=en&lr=&id=svJFDwAAQBAJ&oi=fnd&pg=PT4&dq=understanding%2Bmarket%2Bbefore%2Bstartup&ots=GrWQSf2-bC&sig=Aaju4t-MIVOzyAEK926rTKgO9LQ&redir_esc=y#v=onepage&q=understanding%20market%20before%20startup&f=false [Accessed 16 Oct. 2022].
13. Business Insights Blog (2022). *5 Steps to validate your business idea.* Available at: https://online.hbs.edu/blog/post/market-validation [Accessed 16 Oct. 2022].
14. Business Insider (2022). *Nine steps to effective business problem solving.* Available at: https://www.businessinsider.com/nine-steps-to-effective-business-problem-solving-2011-7?IR=T [Accessed 16 Oct. 2022].
15. Conductor (2022). *How to anticipate, identify and meet your customer's needs.* Available at: https://www.conductor.com/learning-center/customer-needs/ [Accessed 16 Oct. 2022].
16. Naveh, M. (2022). *6 ways to identify the target audience for your business.* Available at: https://elementor.com/blog/how-to-identify-target-audience/ [Accessed 16 Oct. 2022].
17. SingleMind (2022). *A step-by-step guide to product-market validation | SingleMind.* Available at: https://www.singlemindconsulting.com/blog/a-step-by-step-guide-to-product-market-validation/ [Accessed 16 Oct. 2022].
18. Dotactiv (2022). *Here's how to create a great product flow.* Available at: https://www.dotactiv.com/blog/create-a-great-product-flow [Accessed 16 Oct. 2022].
19. Snelling, B. (2022). *Why large retailers and wholesale platforms are critical to small brands.* Available at: https://www.forbes.com/sites/brinsnelling/2022/06/16/why-large-retailers-and-wholesale-platforms-are-critical-to-small-brands/?sh=44e72fa0307d [Accessed 16 Oct. 2022].
20. Investopedia (2022). *Business start-up costs: It's in the details.* Available at: https://www.investopedia.com/articles/pf/09/business-startup-costs.asp [Accessed 16 Oct. 2022].
21. Cremades, A. (2022). *How to effectively determine your market size.* Available at: https://www.forbes.com/sites/alejandrocremades/2018/09/23/

how-to-effectively-determine-your-market-size/?sh=f7f524c13d82 [Accessed 16 Oct. 2022].

22. Start-ups. (2022). *Customer segmentation for start-ups and small businesses.* Available at: https://www.startups.com/library/expert-advice/customer-segmentation [Accessed 16 Oct. 2022].
23. Ruggieri, R., Savastano, M., Scalingi, A., Bala, D., & D'Ascenzo, F. (2018). *The impact of digital platforms on business models: An empirical investigation on innovative start-ups.* Available at: https://sciendo.com/article/10.2478/mmcks-2018-0032 [Accessed 16 Oct. 2022].
24. ConvergeHub (2022). *Know your customers | The importance of knowing your customer.* Available at: https://www.convergehub.com/blog/six-principles-knowing-your-customers-better [Accessed 16 Oct. 2022].
25. Hotjar (2022). *What is product-market fit? How to find it.* Available at: https://www.hotjar.com/grow-your-saas-startup/product-market-fit/ [Accessed 16 Oct. 2022].
26. Mailchimp (2022). *How to develop a start-up marketing strategy.* Available at: https://mailchimp.com/resources/startup-marketing-strategy/ [Accessed 16 Oct. 2022].
27. Gaskell, A. (2022). *Study explores the impact of uber on the taxi industry.* Available at: https://www.forbes.com/sites/adigaskell/2017/01/26/study-explores-the-impact-of-uber-on-the-taxi-industry/?sh=4c5bf98b16b0 [Accessed 16 Oct. 2022].
28. The Guardian (2022). *How Airbnb took over the world.* Available at: https://www.theguardian.com/technology/2019/may/05/airbnb-homelessness-renting-housing-accommodation-social-policy-cities-travel-leisure [Accessed 16 Oct. 2022].
29. Harvard Business Review (2022). *The soul of a start-up.* Available at: https://hbr.org/2019/07/the-soul-of-a-start-up [Accessed 16 Oct. 2022].
30. Bcombinator (2022). *A successful business must always adapt to the changing world.* Available at: https://www.bcombinator.com/a-successful-business-must-always-adapt-to-the-changing-world [Accessed 16 Oct. 2022].
31. Harvard Business Review (2022). *Start-ups, it's time to think like camels — not unicorns.* Available at: https://hbr.org/2020/10/startups-its-time-to-think-like-camels-not-unicorns [Accessed 18 Oct. 2022].
32. Roesler, P. (2022). Available at: https://www.inc.com/peter-roesler/new-study-shows-deals-promotions-affect-every-part-of-shopping-experience.html [Accessed 18 Oct. 2022].

33. Coleman, A. (2022). *The secrets of a successful social media strategy for start-ups.* Available at: https://www.forbes.com/sites/alisoncoleman/2022/05/26/the-secrets-of-a-successful-social-media-strategy-for-startups/?sh=1ea1954217d6 [Accessed 18 Oct. 2022].
34. Investopedia (2022). *Price skimming definition: How it works and its limitations.* Available at: https://www.investopedia.com/terms/p/priceskimming.asp [Accessed 18 Oct. 2022].
35. Investopedia (2022). *Market segmentation: Definition, example, types, benefits.* Available at: https://www.investopedia.com/terms/m/marketsegmentation.asp [Accessed 18 Oct. 2022].
36. Harvard Business Review (2022). *To Keep your customers, keep it simple.* Available at: https://hbr.org/2012/05/to-keep-your-customers-keep-it-simple [Accessed 18 Oct. 2022].
37. Lovejoy, B. (2022). *20 years of Apple company growth in one 40-second video.* Available at: https://9to5mac.com/2022/04/08/20-years-of-apple-in-40-seconds/ [Accessed 18 Oct. 2022].
38. Forbes (2019). *Can Volkswagen's passenger car segment push top line growth for 2019?* Available at: https://www.forbes.com/sites/greatspeculations/2019/11/04/can-volkswagens-passenger-car-segment-push-top-line-growth-for-2019/?sh=67376f136a88 [Accessed 18 Oct. 2022].
39. Investopedia (2022). *Nike Is a growth company.* Available at: https://www.investopedia.com/stock-analysis/081815/nike-inc-growth-company-nke.aspx [Accessed 18 Oct. 2022].
40. Kirsch, N. (2020). *From pullback to Nasdaq: How Proptech start-up Porch used a shortcut to snag a $500 million valuation.* Available at: www.forbes.com/sites/noahkirsch/2020/08/05/from-pullback-to-nasdaq-how-proptech-startup-porch-used-a-shortcut-to-snag-a-500-million-valuation/?sh=3b99efc918e9 [Accessed 18 Oct. 2022].
41. Business Insider (2018). *How a pair of 20-something brothers from Eastern Europe is shaking up the luxury watch scene.* Available at: www.businessinsider.in/home/how-a-pair-of-20-something-brothers-from-eastern-europe-is-shaking-up-the-luxury-watch-scene/articleshow/63276753.cms [Accessed 18 Oct. 2022].

CHAPTER 4
Beating the Competition

It's exciting to be in an industry with constant advancements, and the growth potential is limitless. But, with these exciting advancements comes a great deal of competition. Having the odds against you is certainly not new to our field, but does that make it any easier? With the ability to compete internationally,[1] many business owners have turned to outsourcing or overseas manufacturing to save money and keep costs low. While this seems like a good idea, it's crucial to remain competitive in today's market and, thus, know about your competition inside and out.

David and Goliath give us a fair idea of what competition looks like. David started with a disadvantage from the start: he was small (Goliath was a giant), his weapons were limited (he only had one rock), and he had no armor (his clothing was not of the finest quality). Despite these disadvantages, David won the battle. In case you're wondering how - well, I'd like to refer you back to your childhood: what did David do when he faced Goliath? He had no choice but to fight him head-on. The same rings true for business today. You have to do what you must do when faced with business competition. Business competition happens every day. Some people try to make money by selling their products and services to those who most need them. When facing a competitor or competing with yourself, you've got to think fast, act fast, and respond quickly. As much as possible, keep your emotions from getting in the way of doing what you must to succeed in business. Remember that there is a purpose for everything. What you want to achieve will happen when you put your mind to it and believe it can happen!

How To Spot Competition?

Spotting competition for start-ups is essential. The internet hosts many blogs, articles, and forum posts on new business ideas[2] and how to launch them - and that's just the tip of the iceberg. Anyone can find tons of information about any industry, including yours, by visiting a few dedicated websites. Uncovering competition for your start-up is vital because it helps you know where you fit in the marketplace. You want to be aware of what your competitors are up to so that you can tailor your business plan accordingly. Suppose you're launching a new company in an industry with many similar businesses already in place. In that case, you'll want to be sure that your product is unique enough that people will buy from you instead of the competitor down the street. It's also essential to monitor your competitors' progress so that you remain aware of their strengths and weaknesses. Keeping tabs on competitors ensures that you're keeping pace as well. You can only grow by knowing what's out there. You can only be as good as you can be by understanding everything offered. Start-ups that succeed on the first try are few and far between, so it's essential to learn from your mistakes. Consider re-evaluating your strategy if you constantly compete with a larger company. But suppose your start-up is still growing, and you're funnelled into the same industry as some big players. In that case, you may have more to worry about than just the quality of their product - you might also have to contend with their marketing budget, advertising campaigns, and dollars.

I have said this before - competition should not discourage[3] any start-up. It should drive all start-ups to try better and deliver better. With increased competition, the market keeps growing, and new opportunities keep emerging. And this competition makes all start-ups work harder to surpass their competitors and reach higher heights in the market. By learning about many companies, we see outstanding examples of how competition has helped them to improve. Competition is always good because it encourages you to do better and keep your rivals on their toes. It also forces start-ups to try harder, innovate, and deliver better products. This is especially true in the e-commerce market. If one company finds success selling a particular product, other companies will rush to put out similar products to grab some of that market share. It's more than just the start-ups that get a push from the competition - more prominent companies, like Amazon and Google, can't afford to rest on their laurels for too long, or they'll quickly lose out to smaller, hungrier companies. In other words, competition is suitable for everyone involved.

When you're a start-up, the easiest thing to do is to compare yourself with other, seemingly more successful companies. You might wonder whether you could be doing better[4] or whether you are competing in a suitable space. But if you focus too much on just one aspect of competition, you lose track of other matters like your customers. The only way to find out how your business can succeed is by talking directly to the people who use your product and service. Are they happy? Is there anything else that would help them do their job better? In the long run, that will keep them returning for more. What does this mean for your business? Keep doing your best, and you will beat the competition eventually. If you can delight your customers consistently, no matter how many new players enter your market, you'll still be able to do well and maintain a loyal customer base. I have discussed three ways to spot competition in the market: ways that will help you to be aware of what can bring you down and what needs to be your benchmark as a start-up. Firstly, you must look at leaders and see what they are doing and how they are doing their business. This will give you an idea of what went right in their journeys so that you can take inspiration from their ideas or business strategies. Secondly, you must closely look at potential companies and learn their strategies for shaping a potentially successful business. Companies that show clear signs of success in the initial phase are mostly bound to boom. You must be aware of such companies and the kind of work they are doing. Thirdly, you must also know about the changing demands of investors[5] in the market. Investors are your backbone. They can help your business and take it to immense heights of success. But investors are constantly tracking the market and expect you to adapt to the changing times as an entrepreneur.

Look At The Leaders

As a start-up, you must look at the industry leaders to understand what competition looks like. When you start looking, though, don't get intimidated or discouraged by them. You'll see that there are so many people out there who are successful and doing well. Focus on what your company can offer[6] and how it differs from the rest. Be confident in your product or service. If you believe in it and know it's going to be great, then it will be! When you're in a start-up, the last thing you want to be doing is trying to compete with big brands. If your company's goal is to make an impact, you quickly realize there are only so many opportunities. If your company wants to win customers[7] over from well-respected players, you will have to do more than you had initially planned. How do you do this? It would be best if you first evaluated what your direct competition looks like. Even if you feel that no one else is doing exactly what your start-up does, the truth is that there are always other similar products out there. By studying the industry leaders, you'll get a good idea of what the market is looking for, giving you a sense of your product's direction. It will also help you understand how customers may perceive your brand - is it trendy and young or safe and established? What can other companies teach you about the industry in general? Who are their competitors? What has made them successful? What trends are on their way out? What will be in demand next year or even five years from now? How can you take advantage of these products and services becoming obsolete?

The leaders in the industry tell you best where your start-up competition[8] is headed. A wise businessperson doesn't only rely on their vision when deciding where to shop. These people will also look to their competitors to see what they're up to, which can often be a more accurate indicator of where a market is headed than any other research. So, if you're interested in getting into any industry, make sure you are familiar with the leaders in that field, and how they position themselves.[9] Before getting into the business, a few key things to consider are - What are the market leaders doing? What kinds of products have they launched lately? How have their websites changed? What's new about their social media strategy? What types of demographics are they targeting? Are there things about their sourcing policies that you'd like to emulate? And how is their customer service policy different from what it was five years ago? You need to know who these businesses are. You also need to understand how you'll compete with them or how they're competing with you.

Look At Potential

Another way to look at industry competition as a start-up is to look at potential.[10] Which names have the potential to make it big in the next five years? How are these names similar or different from your brand? When you're in charge of a new company, you want to know what you're up against. You want to know who your competitors are and how they stack up. One way is to look at what other companies are doing right now. Another way is to know if their business names give off certain vibes, which could have specific implications, and so on. Besides being a more exciting way of looking at things, this method can help you figure out what sort of company you're in. If your competitor has a "better" name than yours, that might mean there's already an established clientele[11] interested in the kind of business your company offers. If your competitor is more established and well-known, your company will be a smaller fish in a bigger pond (for now). But if your competitor has been around for ten years but has yet to make much headway, that might mean there's room for two or three strong players within the next five years.

As an entrepreneur, you must always keep track of the competition. When you're a start-up, the alternative is to see what's trending, which is a great way to delve into insights into consumer behavior[12] and ensure your brand stays relevant. However, another way to get this information is to keep an eye on potential. The potential is different from trends. Trends are what is currently happening in a particular industry. The potential is what could happen in the future if certain conditions come together. Looking at possibilities allows you to observe how trends will evolve and understand how they will shape consumer tastes. It also lets you see which brands have the most excellent chance of growing and dominating their market in the next five years. To do this, keep an eye on a brand that doesn't belong to any niche or category you're interested in but could be an excellent fit for your business model. Keep track of them by checking their social media every few months and seeing if they've been able to gain any traction with consumers or if they're partnering with any big-name companies[13] that would help them expand their audience.

Look At Changing Investor Demands

After you build your first product and make it ready enough to be sold to the market, you have no choice but to think about taking your business to the next phase. All business people do this. But most are too concerned with their products, so they ignore the investors[14] who will fund them and their changing demands. But if you want to make a big company in the future, you must do it right - not just focus on your products or even customers. It would be best if you also considered the investors' dynamic priorities. It is a must-do thing if you want to succeed in the business world. The reason is that investors can help you grow your business and make it sustainable. They will fund your initial product and provide you with necessary resources such as money, advice, and experience. In return, they will take a significant portion of your company's ownership or request substantial future profits. They can also advise you on how to run the business better and where you should spend your money wisely, saving you time and resources, as I discussed earlier in this book.

It is clear that entrepreneurs need investors for their businesses, but what about investors? They need entrepreneurs[15] for their companies too! Investors are after great ideas because those can bring more benefits to them. Investors are looking for people they can rely on; who have what it takes to succeed. They have a specific vision of success, and they will be eager to find somebody who has the same idea so that they can help them reach it. It would be best if you also remembered that the demands of investors would keep changing, and studying this trend is significant. It's essential to have a particular influence over your investors. Investors will be looking at you as a leader and want to know that you can help guide their investment in the right direction. It's also important to understand what investors are looking for to ensure that your idea meets their expectations and requirements. How do you get an investor interested in your business idea? Investors are always looking for growth and sustainability,[16] so you should be very careful about presenting your idea to them. You need to give them all the information about your vision for them to be able to determine if it is worth investing in or not. It would be best if you focused on ensuring that your business plan is well written and thought out, and from there, you can sell yourself as an entrepreneur who can put all the pieces together into one coherent picture. Keep revising your offerings as time passes by. An investor might be interested in your business today. However, if you continue offering the same products and services five years from now, this investor will likely pull out from your company. Hence, a critical aspect for you to note is the changing needs of investors in a highly dynamic capitalist market. Change is good. And change, driven by contexts and the requirements of whom it impacts, is better for any business. It is the change I am talking about and the change you should be keeping track of.

How To Beat The Competition?

As so many start-ups have gone ahead of industry competition by adopting[17] the right strategies, your business can make it happen! For any start-up to enter the market and become successful, it needs to be aware of several factors, such as customer requirements, competitors in the market, marketing strategies, etc. While it is easy to say that you need to think about all these things before introducing your product to the market, it takes work to do precisely that. Competition is life for start-ups, and there's no right way to view it. You can see your competitors as people out to get you or as other entrepreneurs on the same journey as you are. You'll be inclined to fight dirty and break the rules in the first case. In the second case, you'll be more likely to rise above their tactics and focus on your strengths.[18] As such, people in your organization must understand the right spirit of competition so they don't fall into the trap of viewing their competitors with enmity. That will only lead them to make impulsive decisions that might hurt your business in the long run. Keeping this in mind will make everyone more conscious of how they present themselves - both internally and externally - and help ensure that you maintain a positive image even when going up against tough competition.

A good competitor will force you to be a better version[19] of yourself, which can help you improve your character, skillset, and company. A competitor can be a great source of inspiration for a start-up or a small business. But if you're not careful, a competitor can become an enemy - and turn from a push into an obstacle you'll never be able to overcome. How do you treat a competitor? Do you treat them as an inspiration? Or do you treat them as an enemy who has the power to crush everything that you have worked so hard for? Do you take them as a friend who wants the best for both of you or do you look at them as the last person on earth who wants to see your company succeed? When it comes to competition - especially in business competition - there are always two sides to the story: yours and theirs. And yet, sometimes, we all forget that there's our competitors' side. We always put ourselves into their shoes and imagine how we would react had we been in their shoes - but we rarely stop and think about how they are responding from their perspective instead. In the section below, I will discuss the three strategies to beat coemption. Firstly, you must know what can beat you. This is vital to know the potential threats to your business and companies that can take you down as a competitor. Having clarity on this will help you go a long way. Secondly, you must know what you, as a company, have the potential to beat in the industry. When you are starting a business, it will have the potential to challenge other existing companies. Knowing this will help you increase your visibility and conquer the right markets as per the products and services you offer. Thirdly, you must know the companies or strategies that can beat the best players in the industry.[20] The best businesses in the industry do not remain the best forever. Other companies challenge them and beat them to become bigger and better. So, knowing the strategies to beat the best is crucial.

Know What Can Beat You

Start-ups must know the companies or products/services that can beat their business. It is called identifying potential business threats.[21] The task is to determine who will compete with you, how they will do it, and what you can do about it. Your competitors can come from any direction - you might already have some, or your research may reveal that a new, unexpected competitor has entered the market. The best way to identify your competitors is through competitive intelligence. It will give you an insight into your competitors' capabilities and allow you to anticipate their next move. Businesses like yours will likely operate in several different markets and sectors. Competitive intelligence involves identifying all of these and gathering information on them, including details of customers and suppliers. You will also need to understand how your competitors operate and what sets them apart from other businesses in their sector.

Competitive intelligence[22] aims to provide information about your competitor's strengths and weaknesses that you can use to improve your business offering – for example, by making your product or service even better than theirs! This valuable information can help you to customize your marketing plan, sales strategy, product innovation, and pricing to better position your company against its competition. You may decide that there is scope for collaboration between two rival companies, or perhaps it will encourage you to focus on different aspects of your business. Competitive intelligence is not necessarily a new concept: it has been around for decades, but the rise of the internet has made it easier for businesses, small and large, to identify potential threats and opportunities. Competitive intelligence is a crucial aspect of managerial decision-making in business, and there are many benefits associated with using it. First, it can improve an organization's performance and competitiveness by gathering information about competitors and using that information to adapt or adjust its strategy. Second, it can help businesses understand their competitors' processes and priorities, which can help them identify weaknesses and better position themselves against those competitors. Competitive intelligence is also essential for helping businesses identify opportunities for market growth and expansion and identifying threats from new market entrants.

Know What You Can Beat

As an entrepreneur, you can handle most of your competition pressure[23] if you know what or whom your start-up can beat in the industry. When starting up your own business, there will be much competition from the other companies that have already started and developed. Therefore, knowing whom you can beat is essential. It will help you to develop strategies for facing the challenges in the upcoming days of your business. When you see someone or something doing better than your start-up, it is time to think and plan on improving yourself and defeating the competition. When starting a new business, you need to be more creative than thinking about how to beat others in the industry. The best way is by knowing and seeing what they are doing critically and then picking up the points where they are doing well. This way, you will get a better idea of where exactly you need to improve and then work on those things effectively so that it can also impact your business.[24]

To compete with large companies and corporations, you must find where your company will beat them. There are several ways to do this. Firstly, consider differentiating yourself from competitors by changing your product or service. For example, if you sell smartphones, you can incorporate new features that no other company has yet. It will make your customers feel valued, increasing their loyalty. Secondly, consider how much your competitors will spend on marketing and advertising, such as TV commercials and newspapers. Then, decide whether you should spend more than them. An intelligent way to do this is by looking at the return on investment of such marketing activities. Lastly, look at your competitors' strengths and try to find weaknesses in that system so that you can exploit these weaknesses to achieve more tremendous success than your competitors. Make a plan to beat the competitors by knowing what or who the competitors are and their strengths. Try to avoid beating everyone at once. If a competitor is beating you in one way, then focus on beating that specific area or product. Gather information about your competitor through research[25] and ask your friends and family members who may be using the same products or services as your competitor. Every start-up has its competitors in the market. You must narrow your competitors' list to succeed and become a leader.

Know What Can Beat The Best

As an entrepreneur, you may have noticed that the big guys in the industry sometimes become complacent. They are too confident in their business model,[26] and sometimes, they are too big to be overtaken. However, a good business idea can consistently beat the best. Knowing what has the power to overtake the best business in the industry is another aspect of staying ahead as a start-up. Many companies have grown on the foundation of providing something better than their competitors. Apple started by designing computers that were easier to use and cheaper than those that came before it. Netflix created a media streaming service faster and more accessible than its predecessors, like Blockbuster Video. In a way, these companies took over from those leading in their respective industries[27] because they understood what made their competitors fail and how they could beat them.

Brands have a habit of clinging too tightly to their image,[28] using the same tactics they used when they were hot on the market and trying to bring in new customers with the same branding methods. This cycle leads to devastating consequences as it will cause a business to fall behind and become irrelevant. When this happens, companies must be willing to make drastic changes, such as revamping their writing and marketing style or changing their product line altogether. The worst mistake you can make as a business owner is not identifying complacency. As a start-up, you must watch out for such signs. It would be best if you took immediate action when you feel there are no more ways to improve yourself or your business. Otherwise, someone else will be able to beat you by doing just that thing. The first step is to understand what complacency[29] means for your business. When you stop pushing yourself and your business forward because it's the easier route and feels right, that's when the disaster begins.

On the other hand, putting effort into keeping your business relevant is the key. Non-complacency will lead to success and consistency. The second step is to identify that complacency is already present in your company. You can do this by conducting an honest self-assessment of how things are going in your company and talking with your staff to identify their feelings or concerns about the current state of affairs at work. The most important thing here is not to make decisions based on feelings but facts. It is also necessary to monitor what's happening around your company so that you're always aware of any changes or new trends. You can only achieve success with a high level of awareness. So, sometimes complacency in your own business is a more significant threat[30] than external players in the industry.

Why Is Competition Essential?

Competition among start-ups is essential because it helps ensure that the market is always in equilibrium. There can always be a few businesses within an industry, which would lead to an imbalance in power between consumers and vendors. Competitive start-ups also promote innovation by creating a strong incentive for each business to improve its product or service offerings, either directly or indirectly. It ensures that customers constantly receive the best possible value for their money and that quality standards are consistently rising. The competition also promotes sustainable growth, which is essential for a successful start-up. Without competition, businesses stagnate.[31] There is no motivation to aspire toward anything more significant than what has already been attained. To avoid your business being challenged by competitors, you should refrain from entering an industry where others successfully do what you're trying to do. Since that sounds like a bad option, you should enter such an industry with more solid strategies instead of avoiding it. A lack of competition might be a warning sign that your idea isn't genuinely viable. It may mean that you're not doing it in a way that anyone else would care about enough to compete with you - you may need to rethink how you operate and what your goal is if you want people to take notice of your start-up.

Indeed, competition has its perks. It forces a company to stay on its toes and improve daily. If a company can keep up with the pace of the competition, then it will eventually retain its market share. But how far are you willing to go? Can your company be pushed too far for betterment? And if so, what does it mean for your future? Nowadays, there is no shortage of companies in almost all industries that compete with each other. However, whether these companies are competing against each other on an equal footing depends on their market value. In many cases, one of the companies in the industry is far ahead of others in resources and experience. These companies have already worked out all the roadblocks in their system. They have established a solid brand[32] name and gained enough experience to identify their target market and perform well in it; they have a supply chain that can produce mass quantities of products anytime. Most importantly, they know how to adapt to changes in their environment and develop new ways to increase sales. In the section below, I have elaborated on why competition is essential. Firstly, it helps to minimize monopoly. Competition helps to create and sustain a thriving market since it gives scope for more businesses to function. In this way, businesses will thrive instead of being stagnant. Secondly, it allows companies to remain new and updated as per the changing trends. Competition means that businesses will watch out for trends and changing expectations of customers and thus keep updating themselves. Thirdly, it ensures that people get what they love: variety![33] Giving a variety of options in terms of products and services to people is essential for business prosperity. And this can only happen in an environment of healthy competition.

Minimize Monopoly

Competition is the essence of a market economy.[34] It brings in rejuvenating forces and helps create an atmosphere of trust. Without competition, industries are monopolized, and there is scope for the manipulation of prices by the producers. When there is competition, the market remains rejuvenated, and companies do not tend to monopolize.[35] In a competitive environment, companies are involved in making better products to retain their share of the market. They refrain from resorting to price manipulation as competing with other products on price alone would be difficult. Producers must also improve their marketing skills and provide better services to gain customer satisfaction. Consequently, customers get value for money from their purchases and gain from emerging economies of scale. It leads to improvement in infrastructure and education systems, which help the overall development of a nation's economy.

A start-up or any business's consistency in products and services is mainly determined by its contemporaries. If a product or service is consistent with the nature of other products or services of that same period, it will have a greater chance of success. It can be attributed to the fact that if one product or service is successful, others will likely follow suit. For example, if a company can create the perfect smartphone, competitors are expected to try and create something similar. They will not copy the product itself; however, they will attempt to make something comparable and just as good, if not better, than the original product. If a company comes out with a revolutionary product, it must follow through with that revolution by consistently producing more revolutionary things. To succeed as a company by creating revolutionary products, you must stay ahead of your competitors by consistently revolutionizing these products and services. Consistency[36] is a hallmark of any successful business. A business that continually changes its menu, layout, or services will find it challenging to build a loyal customer base. Similarly, a company that offers different service levels to its customers will fail to gain the credibility[37] and trust vital for success. Similar changes in quality and quantity can be observed in new businesses. Early on, a company is constantly adjusting to its competitors' policies and products. It may also be changing how it treats its customers. However, once a company has gained market share, it should focus on consistent products and services. While new technology influences business entities to change how they conduct their operations and interact with the public, these changes must be well thought out.

Your Business Remains New

If you want your start-up to remain new and updated as per the industry trends, participate in healthy competition. You can be a part of the competition by finding the best businesses in your niche; likewise, they will have their eyes on you, too. This way, you can get acquainted with your competitors and know their strengths. It is also an excellent chance for you to hone your skills[38] to match up to them. As an entrepreneur, you always look for ways to improve your business. With the help of healthy competition, it would be easier to figure out what works and what doesn't. Plus, it is an excellent way of learning from other people's mistakes so that you don't end up doing it yourself.

Businesses with a solid market strategy and a keen eye on their competitors are better positioned[39] to succeed and grow. When you study your competitors, you will always be able to find new and exciting ways of doing things. It helps you create value for your customers; you can find out what they want and how best it can be delivered. It creates more scope for evolution as a company, so you always have fresh ideas to explore. Competitors can help you strategize your business in such a way that it stands out from the rest of the crowd. You can also learn about their strengths and weaknesses and choose the right strategies to stay ahead. The real trick is not to copy them but to be original and unique with your products or services so that people prefer coming back to you every time because they know that only you can provide them with what they want. Today's businesses have so much to learn from each other about how to make their services more effective, efficient, and responsive to customers. Please take the time to check out what other people are doing to get valuable information for improving your business practices.[40] You can even take inspiration from their successes and failures, so you can avoid making similar mistakes. You can make your company more dynamic and innovative when you're always looking around at what everyone else is doing. It will help you grow into an even more considerable success than you would have been on your own.

People Love Variety

Isn't it all about people in the end? Your start-up can consistently offer various products and services only if you allow it to grow with time. And competition is an essential part of the process. People love variety, and they love labels that stay, but also labels that remain fresh! People love it when they get many options to choose from. They also love labels that last and brands that stay fresh! It's important to offer various products and services, but it's also vital to remain competitive. The best way to do this is to ensure that your business stays up-to-date. It means making sure you stay charged up. If people think you're not offering something they need or want, they'll go elsewhere.

Keeping your brand fresh[41] and up-to-date is critical in today's ever-changing marketing world. Your brand is your reputation; it's the first thing people will see, hear, and learn about you and your business when they visit your website, read your company bio, or Google you. It's everything from the colors and fonts you use to the words you say in an interview to the image you have on your business card. By updating it and always being aware of ways to improve its effectiveness, you'll position yourself as a professional expert that people will trust. You might only think about some of the touchpoints where your brand gets conveyed. It could be an ad on Facebook or a section on your most recent blog posts. Whatever it is, you would want everything to make sense: if something on your site links back to another page on your site, make sure those two pages match. If someone tweets about something from one of your blog posts, make sure it's a tweetable quote (one that has impact and can be said without explanation). Keep joining back together all of the pieces that make up who you are as a professional so that at any point, visitors can easily navigate through all of the information about you and still feel connected!

Companies And Competitions To Learn From

LinkSquares

LinkSquares[42] is considered to be a revolutionary name in the Artificial Intelligence industry. The technology has been used by the company in its work and licensed to numerous other companies for use in their AI systems. In addition, the company has been a leader in AI research and development, contributing to many academic papers on AI and releasing research results online for free to benefit others in the area. The critical thing about the company is that it has been able to combine different technologies previously used separately. It has been made possible by the unique solutions developed for various tasks such as text recognition, image processing, data analysis, etc. It helps the users save time by connecting them with viable businesses that can provide their services. Companies also find this to be a great marketing tool as they can connect with a large number of clients at one time.

Company Name: LinkSquares

Founded: 2015

Significant reason(s) for success: They are involved with one of the most in-demand niches globally. They are offering unique solutions to existing technical issues.

Instawork

Instawork[43] is one of the newer companies in the industry. The company connects workers with jobs that need to be done, allowing users to fill them by simply showing up and doing them. Over 500,000 job seekers are already using the app, and its easy-to-use interface makes it simple for anyone who needs a quick job done to contact someone who can do it. It allows restaurant owners to recruit workers temporarily with an ease of use similar to that of the popular social media site Instagram. It takes a photo-sharing app and turns it into a business platform. For users, Instawork provides convenience - they can fill out one form and send it to restaurants in the area where they live. When the restaurant receives the completed form, they receive an alert on their phone or computer. It alerts them to contact the prospective employee directly, allowing for faster communication than many other job recruiting sites. It also benefits restaurants because of its simplicity.

Company Name: Instawork

Founded: 2015

Significant reason(s) for success: They ensure effective and simplified communication between employers and employees. They greatly believe in being user-friendly.

CloudTrucks

Start-up, CloudTrucks,[44] was named by the prestigious Silicon Valley firm Andreesen Horowitz as one of their following billion-dollar companies. They are the same people who invested in companies like Facebook, Twitter, and Instagram—and now CloudTrucks. This San Francisco-based start-up has transformed how trucks get loaded for many years. They've pioneered a cloud-based system for tracking and organizing all the necessary components for a cargo shipment. It's a complicated process that requires careful monitoring of multiple moving pieces and coordination between various parties to ensure everything is ready to go on time. They continue to set new records with each passing quarter, which may be why they were recently named one of the most promising start-ups in Silicon Valley by various industry leaders.

Company Name: CloudTrucks

Founded: 2019

Significant reason(s) for success: They simplify solutions for an existing problem. They are utilizing technology to the best of their abilities.

Nokia And Apple

Nokia and Apple[45] are exciting case studies that tell us a lot about the dynamics of competition in mobile phones. Nokia started as a paper mill then ventured into rubber before finally settling on wood pulp-based cellophane for its primary product. Apple started as a company that made video games and calculator machines before branching into computers. Both companies are leaders in their respective market segments: Apple dominates the mobile phone industry in terms of profits, while Nokia is the market leader in cell phones. Through this lens, it might seem like a foregone conclusion that Apple will eventually take over the mobile phone industry entirely. Yet many consumers are loyal to Nokia despite their product offerings being inferior to Apple's. Nokia has managed to grow its share of the mobile phone industry during the same period that Apple has been increasing its market share. It's not just about marketing. It's about more than just having a better product, too. It's about gauging the consumer's needs and responding to them with new technology and offerings that meet those needs even better. That can mean offering innovative products or tweaking existing ones (such as by releasing more color options). The competition's history has shown us that we can see two basic patterns. Firstly, a dominant firm eventually gets challenged by another firm, often resulting in a fierce battle until one of the parties wins. Secondly, the dominant firm gets challenged by many firms and is forced to split up into several competing units.

Company Name: Nokia, Apple

Founded: 1865, 1976

Significant reason(s) for success: Knowing that the industry you enter as an entrepreneur will have successful companies. It only means that you have a benchmark to reach.

Amazon And Barnes & Noble

Barnes & Noble, the brick-and-mortar giant, has long stood in the shadow of Amazon's online bookstore. Almost everyone recognizes Amazon, and

Barnes & Noble[46] has struggled to compete with its online counterpart. It hasn't helped that Amazon's stock skyrocketed in 2017 while Barnes & Noble's fell 9 percent. However, we can learn many important lessons from how these two companies have competed against each other. One key difference to note is how they cater to their customers: Amazon continues to focus on low-priced books and various e-readers and tablets for shoppers, while Barnes & Noble offers coffee shops, magazines, and best sellers, as well as many books. Even though Barnes & Noble sells e-readers and tablets, it also provides an experience for shoppers who want more than just a good deal - but don't necessarily want to interact with employees. Borders Group Inc., which merged with Barnes & Noble in 2011, has been trying to catch up with its online counterpart by lowering prices on eBooks and expanding its selection. However, it has yet to match the ease of use and reduce costs customers demand from Amazon. Borders' approach was too similar to that of Barnes & Noble: many customers feel that they are being forced into buying a book when they go into either store. They want to browse the bookshelves at their leisure, but neither Borders nor Barnes & Noble allows this. By contrast, Amazon lets you read reviews and descriptions and look at pictures of covers without ever having to buy anything.

Company Name: Amazon, Barnes & Noble

Founded: 1994, 1886

Significant reason(s) for success: Listening to customers patiently and offering what they were looking for.

Hangouts And Zoom

The next exciting tiff you must know as an entrepreneur is between Hangouts and Zoom.[47] They have made up for one of the spectators' most exciting business analyses. The year 2016 was when the companies were considered to be in a very close business tie-up. However, this did not work out well because the companies competed against each other. Zoom's CEO, Eric S. Yuan, witnessed this and said that he would sue Google for trademark infringement if it did not stop using the name

Hangouts in another product. The two companies have been competing since 2016 when Google bought Jibe Mobile, which specializes in internet calling services. Eric Yuan, Zoom's CEO, said that Google had copied his competitor's business model by creating Hangouts Meet and started to expand into different fields like video conferencing. In October 2018, Zoom released an update with video conferencing features almost identical to those found on Google's products. According to Bloomberg, zoom is now worth more than $1 billion USD after its latest round of financing, which Sequoia Capital led. Meanwhile, Google paid $186 million USD for Jibe Mobile in 2016 and then shut down most of the products related to it.

Significant learning for start-ups:

Company Name: Hangouts, Zoom

Founded: 2013, 2011

Significant reason(s) for success: Focusing on services as a start-up, especially when they are similar to another company. Knowing how to offer better even with something similar.

Salesforce And Siebel

The question of which business solution is best having long been debated, and this debate will likely continue for years to come. It's hard to find two companies in the same industry that have been as successful at competing with each other as Salesforce and Siebel.[48] Siebel was founded in 1993, and Salesforce in 1999. Both companies started their journeys by selling their cloud-based CRM software. Despite being headquartered across the country from each other (Salesforce in San Francisco, Siebel in Chicago), they've been locked in a battle for market share ever since. Salesforce is known for having a user-friendly interface that allows users to easily create reports and dashboards and track email opens and click-throughs on outbound marketing emails. While on the other hand, Siebel - once considered more professional - has faltered in recent years, with some cloud-based solutions requiring costly third-party integrations. Their WebCGM solution also came under fire after an outage caused by an Amazon Web Services failure left customers without access to critical data for up to a week.

Significant learning for start-ups:

Company Name: Salesforce, Siebel

Founded: 1999, 1993

Significant reason(s) for success: Being mindful of contemporaries as a start-up entrepreneur. Knowing that even if a rival company has more resources, new companies can always make it bigger than those.

Microsoft And IBM

In the tech industry, the competition between Microsoft and IBM[49] remains well-known. The industry is fueled by competitiveness, and this fierce rivalry has kept the industry in a fast-paced evolution. Microsoft has been an innovator in the technological and computer industry since its inception by Bill Gates and Paul Allen. IBM was founded in 1911 with no technical background, so it was surprising to investors that they began competing in the computer industry. The first desktop computers were created by IBM and sold to businesses, while Microsoft created MS-DOS to be used with their computers. Later, IBM tried to compete with OS/2 but was unsuccessful as Microsoft Windows became more popular. Eventually, IBM partnered with Apple Computers to create OS/2, which evolved into OS/2 Warp. At this time, Microsoft had already developed Windows 95, which led them to dominate over IBM. Microsoft continued on its success path with MS-DOS and Windows. At the same time, IBM created OS/2 Advanced Server, which could have been more successful because it was different from Windows or other operating systems at the time. Later on, in 1991, IBM launched AIX Advanced Server, which eventually became open-source software for use on different operating systems involving more than one CPU core. We now know that both IBM and Microsoft have other markets and clients to cater to. Microsoft has become a household name for people all over the world, whereas IBM is something that is niche-specific.

Name of Company: Microsoft, IBM

Founded: 1975, 1911

Significant reason(s) for success: Offering what the market demands and being ready as a start-up to take on a company as big as an empire.

Conclusion

Like many companies out there, your start-up has the potential to be successful, and it will surely go ahead in the league. Being consistent in your business offerings is something you must consider as a rule of thumb if you want to be successful as an entrepreneur. The business world is full of surprises, ups, and downs; the same goes for your company. The foremost step while starting a new business is finding the right niche for that particular company. Your company can provide you with both profitable and non-profitable outcomes. Investing money in a new start-up can be challenging. It's more about consistency with your customers' needs for satisfaction and success.

Before venturing into business, remember that many things matter. An important thing to remember is that to build a solid business foundation, you must know the latest trends and technologies in the market today. Constant research will help you learn more about the market and how to take adequate measures to boost your product development and growth. When running your own business, it's easy to get caught up with daily affairs. The hours can be long, and the goals are never-ending. There are always new business dimensions that need attention, and some days it feels like you need to do more than what's happening at the moment. But if you want to run a successful business, you must make time for reflection. To stay on track with your business goals, take some time to step back and analyze what's going well and what needs improvement. It may be tempting to try new things, but if that means dropping something else in the process, it could hurt your long-term stability. If you've been offering the same products or services for a while now and they've worked out well for your customers, then only switch them up with a good reason. Also, keep notes on how things are going - this isn't just helpful for documentation; it can also help you improve as an entrepreneur. It's all about an opportunity that a market creates and an opportunity that you make the most of.

I am offering that opportunity right now. Sit down, relax, and go through the pointers below that summarize the entire chapter for your convenience:

1. Know what beating the competition means to you.
2. Learn what it means to other businesses that inspire you and carefully analyze their contexts.
3. While spotting competition, look at the leaders in the industry and see what they are doing.
4. Look at potential companies in the industry and the changing demands of investors.
5. You must know what companies can beat your business idea.
6. You should also be aware of what your start-up can beat.
7. Be mindful of companies considered the best in the industry. Understand what business offerings and strategies can beat the best.
8. Embrace competition, as it is crucial for the growth of your start-up.
9. It helps to minimize a monopolized market, enabling businesses to remain active and competitive.
10. Business competition also creates a scope for variety, which is how the market continues to offer products and services per the changing times and demands.

References

1. Franzen-Rodriguez, D. (2022). *Council post: How start-ups can expand to global markets*. Available at: https://www.forbes.com/sites/forbescommunicationscouncil/2022/08/17/how-startups-can-expand-to-global-markets/?sh=5a89c65544c1 [Accessed 22 Nov. 2022].
2. Prater, M. (2019). *50 small business ideas for anyone who wants to run their own business*. Available at: https://blog.hubspot.com/sales/small-business-ideas [Accessed 22 Nov. 2022].
3. Taulli, T. (2017). *How start-ups can thrive against fierce competition*. Available at: https://www.forbes.com/sites/tomtaulli/2017/08/17/how-to-

thrive-against-fierce-competition/?sh=2c8d161f3909 [Accessed 22 Nov. 2022].

4. McKinsey (2022). *Lessons from the best start-ups in Europe.* Available at: https://www.mckinsey.com/industries/technology-media-and-telecommunications/our-insights/what-makes-the-difference-for-europes-top-start-ups [Accessed 22 Nov. 2022].
5. Arora, K. (2022). *Council post: The rise of the retail investor.* Available at: https://www.forbes.com/sites/forbesagencycouncil/2022/11/04/the-rise-of-the-retail-investor/?sh=1e9188381755 [Accessed 22 Nov. 2022].
6. Goldstein, G. (2018). *Staying in your lane: Why start-ups must stay focused.* Available at: https://www.entrepreneur.com/starting-a-business/staying-in-your-lane-why-startups-must-stay-focused/309236 [Accessed 22 Nov. 2022].
7. Oracles, T. (2019). *Council post: Nine secrets to winning (and keeping) customers for life.* Available at: https://www.forbes.com/sites/forbesleadershipcollective/2019/01/29/nine-secrets-to-winning-and-keeping-customers-for-life/?sh=7814d07f6411 [Accessed 22 Nov. 2022].
8. Biggart, A. (2018). *How to identify your competitors: Your 6-step guide.* Available at: https://www.conductor.com/blog/2018/02/identify-competitors/ [Accessed 22 Nov. 2022].
9. Patel, N. (2017). *10 marketing lessons big brands can teach start-ups.* Available at: https://neilpatel.com/blog/big-brand-marketing-lessons/ [Accessed 22 Nov. 2022].
10. Resnick, N. (2019). *These 6 signs indicate your start-up is destined for booming success.* Available at: https://medium.com/startup-grind/these-6-signs-indicate-your-startup-is-destined-for-booming-success-7574194735a [Accessed 22 Nov. 2022].
11. Craig, W. (2018). *10 key principles for truly understanding your clients.* Available at: https://www.forbes.com/sites/williamcraig/2018/07/10/10-key-principles-for-truly-understanding-your-clients/?sh=4a2c72a46504 [Accessed 23 Nov. 2022].
12. McKinsey (2020). *Understanding and shaping consumer behavior in the next normal.* Available at: https://www.mckinsey.com/capabilities/growth-marketing-and-sales/our-insights/understanding-and-shaping-consumer-behavior-in-the-next-normal [Accessed 23 Nov. 2022].
13. Prashantham, S. (2019). *The two ways for start-ups and corporations to partner.* Available at: https://hbr.org/2019/01/the-two-ways-for-startups-and-corporations-to-partner [Accessed 23 Nov. 2022].

14. Merixstudio (2021). *What do investors look for in entrepreneurs and their teams?* Available at: https://www.merixstudio.com/blog/what-do-investors-look-for-in-entrepreneurs-and-their-teams/ [Accessed 23 Nov. 2022].
15. Cremades, A. (2019). *Here is what startup investors look for in entrepreneurs before investing.* Available at: https://www.forbes.com/sites/alejandrocremades/2019/01/31/here-is-what-startup-investors-look-for-in-entrepreneurs-before-investing/?sh=3e4b98e7eb85 [Accessed 23 Nov. 2022].
16. Warren, B. (2020). *Why investors are putting sustainability first.* Available at: https://www.ey.com/en_gl/power-utilities/why-investors-are-putting-sustainability-at-the-top-of-the-agenda [Accessed 23 Nov. 2022].
17. Baremetrics (2018). *How to handle competition in business: 10 tips to beat competition.* Available at: https://baremetrics.com/academy/handle-competition-in-business [Accessed 23 Nov. 2022].
18. Juetten, M. (2019). *Best company traits: Focusing on strengths.* Available at: https://www.forbes.com/sites/maryjuetten/2019/11/12/best-company-traits-focusing-on-strengths/?sh=68aa7cb23e1a [Accessed 23 Nov. 2022].
19. Krasny, J. (2013). *Why Competition may be the best thing for your business.* Available at: Https://www.inc.com/magazine/201311/Jill-krasny/more-competition-is-better-for-start-ups.html [Accessed 23 Nov. 2022].
20. Ryan, C. (2018). *Council post: How to take on (and beat) the giant companies in your industry.* Available at: https://www.forbes.com/sites/forbesagencycouncil/2018/08/28/how-to-take-on-and-beat-the-giant-companies-in-your-industry/?sh=7d3e8dd55eb6 [Accessed 23 Nov. 2022].
21. Kenton, W. (2022). *SWOT analysis: how to with table and example.* Available at: https://www.investopedia.com/terms/s/swot.asp [Accessed 23 Nov. 2022].
22. Bloomenthal, A. (2019). *Competitive intelligence: Eyeing your business rivals.* Available at: https://www.investopedia.com/terms/c/competitive-intelligence.asp [Accessed 23 Nov. 2022].
23. Graham, A. (2017). *Great recent examples of competitive strategy successes.* Available at: https://www.toptal.com/finance/business-model-consultants/competitive-strategy-examples [Accessed 23 Nov. 2022].
24. Salesforce (2017). *The most important factors for start-up success.* Available at: https://www.salesforce.com/ca/blog/2017/11/important-factors-start-up-success.html [Accessed 23 Nov. 2022].

25. Maksimava, M. (2019). *How to perform a best-in-class competitor analysis (w/ template)*. Available at: https://buffer.com/library/competitor-analysis/ [Accessed 23 Nov. 2022].
26. Lyons, R. (2017). *Three ways overconfidence can sink your ship*. Available at: https://www.forbes.com/sites/richlyons/2017/08/15/three-ways-overconfidence-can-sink-your-ship/?sh=134f7d1b2f0e [Accessed 23 Nov. 2022].
27. Up-Rev (n.d.). *How start-ups can overtake corporates in the innovation race*. Available at: https://up-rev.com/startups-can-overtake-corporates-innovation-race/ [Accessed 23 Nov. 2022].
28. Flying Saucer (2021). *The abridged branding bible for start-ups - flying saucer studio*. Available at: https://blog.flyingsaucer.nyc/article/the-abridged-branding-bible-for-startups [Accessed 23 Nov. 2022].
29. Rampton, J. (2018). *Don't be complacent: 13 proven ways to improve your business*. Available at: https://www.entrepreneur.com/growing-a-business/dont-be-complacent-13-proven-ways-to-improve-your-business/309816 [Accessed 23 Nov. 2022].
30. Ruisi, C. (2017). *Complacency: The silent business killer*. Available at: https://www.americanexpress.com/en-us/business/trends-and-insights/articles/complacency-silent-business-killer/ [Accessed 23 Nov. 2022].
31. Forbes (2019). *Council post: 12 ways to tell if your business has stagnated and how to fix it*. Available at: https://www.forbes.com/sites/forbescoachescouncil/2019/06/26/12-ways-to-tell-if-your-business-has-stagnated-and-how-to-fix-it/?sh=400e131a1bb2 [Accessed 23 Nov. 2022].
32. Business (2022). *Make it memorable: 8 tips for creating an effective brand name*. Available at: https://www.business.com/articles/5-tips-for-creating-an-effective-brand-name/ [Accessed 23 Nov. 2022].
33. Desai, P. (2022). *Council post: Variety is the spice of... your CX strategy*. Forbes. Available at: https://www.forbes.com/sites/forbestechcouncil/2022/02/10/variety-is-the-spice-of-your-cx-strategy/?sh=5a4369166bc2 [Accessed 23 Nov. 2022].
34. Boushey, H. & Knudsen, H. (2021). *The importance of competition for the American economy*. Available at: https://www.whitehouse.gov/cea/written-materials/2021/07/09/the-importance-of-competition-for-the-american-economy/ [Accessed 23 Nov. 2022].
35. Hayes, A. (2021). *Monopoly*. Available at: https://www.investopedia.com/terms/m/monopoly.asp [Accessed 23 Nov. 2022].

36. Patterson, R. (2020). *Council post: The power of consistency.* Available at: https://www.forbes.com/sites/forbescoachescouncil/2020/11/02/the-power-of-consistency/?sh=4949ef3628c7 [Accessed 23 Nov. 2022].
37. Pulido, A., Stone, D. & Strevel, J. (2014). *The three Cs of customer satisfaction: Consistency, consistency, consistency.* Available at: https://www.mckinsey.com/industries/retail/our-insights/the-three-cs-of-customer-satisfaction-consistency-consistency-consistency [Accessed 23 Nov. 2022].
38. Forbes (2021). *Council post: 10 essential leadership skills every entrepreneur should continually hone.* Available at: https://www.forbes.com/sites/theyec/2021/11/04/10-essential-leadership-skills-every-entrepreneur-should-continually-hone/?sh=48bed5f54fe9 [Accessed 23 Nov. 2022].
39. Forbes (2022). *Council post: What brand positioning is and why it's important for your business.* Available at: https://www.forbes.com/sites/theyec/2022/01/14/what-brand-positioning-is-and-why-its-important-for-your-business/?sh=2890289a5a63 [Accessed 23 Nov. 2022].
40. The Balance (2022). *6 ways to improve your small business.* Available at: https://www.thebalancemoney.com/improve-your-small-business-2951413 [Accessed 23 Nov. 2022].
41. Crew, D. (2018). *Council post: Four key ways to keep your brand fresh and relevant.* Available at: https://www.forbes.com/sites/forbescommunicationscouncil/2018/12/12/four-key-ways-to-keep-your-brand-fresh-and-relevant/?sh=7e5a5df14c62 [Accessed 23 Nov. 2022].
42. Businesswire (2022). *LinkSquares secures $100 million in series c funding led by G Squared.* Available at: https://www.businesswire.com/news/home/20220401005521/en/LinkSquares-Secures-100-Million-in-Series-C-Funding-Led-by-G-Squared [Accessed 23 Nov. 2022].
43. Fluhr, J. (2021). *Why we led the series c for Instawork.* Available at: https://medium.com/craft-ventures/why-we-led-the-series-c-for-instawork-f09b40a6f06a [Accessed 23 Nov. 2022].
44. Bellan, R. (2021). *CloudTrucks raised $115m series B to help truck entrepreneurs manage their business.* Available at: https://techcrunch.com/2021/11/30/cloudtrucks-raised-115m-series-b-to-help-truck-entrepreneurs-manage-their-business/ [Accessed 23 Nov. 2022].
45. UKEssays (2017). *Nokia vs Apple Case study.* Available at: https://www.ukessays.com/essays/marketing/case-study-report-apple-versus-nokia-marketing-essay.php [Accessed 23 Nov. 2022].

46. Cheng, A. (2018). *Barnes & noble's problem is no longer just Amazon.* Available at: https://www.forbes.com/sites/andriacheng/2018/09/06/barnes-nobles-problem-is-no-longer-about-amazon/?sh=4649166d44d0 [Accessed 23 Nov. 2022].
47. Zuckerman, A. (2020). *Zoom vs Google Hangouts comparison 2021.* Available at: https://comparecamp.com/zoom-vs-google-hangouts-comparison/ [Accessed 23 Nov. 2022].
48. Techila (2020). *Siebel Vs Salesforce | Difference between Siebel and Salesforce.* Available at: https://techilaservices.com/blog/salesforce-vs-siebel/ [Accessed 23 Nov. 2022].
49. Stadler, C. (2021). *To understand the future of diversification, compare Microsoft and IBM.* Available at: https://www.forbes.com/sites/christianstadler/2021/11/15/to-understand-the-future-of-diversification-compare-microsoft-and-ibm/?sh=76adebb2446d [Accessed 23 Nov. 2022].

CHAPTER 5
Right Business or Monetization Model

It's easy to get caught up in the myth that there's a right way to do business and that you're at a disadvantage if you're not doing it. We've all heard big-name companies like Google and Amazon talk about changing the game, but even they have changed their business models[1] over time. You, too, might have to. Finding the right business model for your company can be one of the most challenging decisions you'll make as an entrepreneur. The reason is simple: different business models are suited to varying types of companies, and as your company grows, it might need to change its model to thrive. Look at start-ups across Silicon Valley. You'll see that many of them have had multiple iterations before hitting it big - and even after that, they sometimes stick with their original idea or business model. One of the biggest mistakes entrepreneurs make is thinking that their business model is the best one. To grow, they try to force their business model upon all markets, and they fail because they're trying to use a one-size-fits-all approach when it's clear that different markets require different strategies and tactics. The suitable business model for your company depends on several factors, including your investors' objectives and location. A franchise or multi-level marketing model might be perfect if you want to sell and not expand beyond your current market. However, if you're going to grow rapidly through different locations and storefronts, you may need more of a mobile app or e-commerce solution to reach customers[2] across the country.

The best business model may not be the right one, and the right one may not be the best for your business. The traditional approach to business is to start a company with a clear vision of what you want your end goal to look like and then develop a model that best fits that vision.

The alternative is to start using what you have and then make changes[3] as they become necessary and new opportunities present themselves. Before you settle on a business model, it's helpful to ask yourself some questions about your motivation for starting the venture in the first place. Is it to make money? Is it to grow a social movement? Or is it to solve a problem? The best model for your start-up may differ from the one you must have heard about. You might have solid beliefs or values that conflict with the business model you'd like to pursue. Try out multiple models and decide what works best for your business[4] and company values.

The Different Types Of Business Models

When starting a new business, one of the most important decisions you have to make is what kind of business model you want to choose. Is it a franchise? Is it a chain? Are you going to be an independent entrepreneur with your own business, or will you sell your services through someone else's company as an independent contractor? You must know the difference between all these options so that as soon as you know what type of business model would work best for your start-up, you can make sure you're picking the right one. Why would it matter what kind of business model your start-up picks? The answer is simple: businesses use different strategies to succeed, and there is no "best" strategy.[5] The only way to ensure that your business will succeed is by ensuring that its strategy fits with the model it's using. If your strategy fits well with the model, it will work well for your company.

Choosing the right model for your start-up can take time and effort with many business models. However, you'll want to go through the process carefully to ensure you choose the appropriate model for your product. The easiest way to start is to know that the many different business models have unique strengths and weaknesses. It can be helpful to think about your product in terms of what your customers want and how you deliver it. For example, some products will naturally lend themselves more to a subscription-based model (like magazines or music streaming services). Other products will work well as one-off transactions (like restaurant meals or haircuts). When considering the business model you want, take into account the strengths and weaknesses[6] of each type of model. For example, subscription-based models have some advantages in that they have predictable recurring revenues, but they also have some disadvantages in that they have limited data on individual users. On the other hand, one-time transaction models don't have as much data available, giving users full ownership of their products. It can take time to determine which strategies are suitable for which models. Fortunately, I am here to make this task simpler for you. I have written about the Business-to-Business (B2B) model, which will help you understand the model's nuances and see if your business fits into the same. It will help you to learn the specific features of this model. I have then written about the Business-to-Consumer (B2C) model. Many companies focus on this model for various reasons, and you will learn about some of these reasons to have more clarity on the model. I have then written about the subscription-based model and the on-demand model. Some of the top companies in the world follow these models[7] and have been doing significantly well in the industry. I have also written about some of these companies in the last section of this chapter to give you more ideas about them and their business models.

Business To Business

A Business-to-Business (B2B) model[8] focuses on selling a product or service to other businesses. It is a great model for companies with limited resources since it cuts down on the number of salespeople needed. The company can also use its resources to create a product specific to its customers' needs. A B2B model can be used for many types of start-ups for business, but there are several things you should know before jumping in. Your target market is much smaller than your typical consumer market, so you must find ways to stand out from the competition while still being seen positively by your customers. It would help if you also had clear policies regarding what you will and will not develop. This way, if someone asks you to do something outside your normal range, it will be easy to say "no." A B2B company can take many forms, for instance, a firm that sells templates or designs for other companies' marketing efforts. These services sell templates other businesses can use when creating marketing materials, such as newsletters and brochures. The designers who provide these services are always looking for new ideas and strategies that they could include in their products and services.

A business-to-business model has many advantages.[9] In a business-to-business model, the seller will likely spend less time and money on marketing and advertising than selling to consumers. This is because the customer in a business-to-business model usually makes purchasing decisions based on what will benefit the company. For this reason, businesses that sell products or services to other businesses tend to be more innovative and often create new products or services for their clients. Firstly, in a B2B model, you'll be targeting the decision-makers in any given organization, which means you'll be able to reach a broader audience. Instead of worrying about reaching consumers who make decisions on behalf of their families, you'll be pitching your product or service directly to the people with the final say. It's much easier and more efficient this way. Secondly, it also makes it easier for you to spread the word about your product or service.[10] With B2B marketing, there are no worries about convincing people that they should buy something they don't necessarily need; instead, your job is to let them know they can find the product they need at your store. Since these products are bought by businesses and not individuals, you don't have to worry about getting people excited enough about something they may need help understanding to buy it.

Business To Consumer

The following model is a Business-to-Consumer model[11] or B2C. E-commerce companies and online retailers most often use the B2C model. Some direct sales companies and subscription services also use it. Examples of companies that use the B2C model include Amazon, Expedia, and Netflix. Several factors can impact a company's decision to use a B2C model. First, consumers are increasingly comfortable shopping online and making purchases from home. It means that many businesses have an opportunity to reach consumers directly. Secondly, the ease and convenience of shopping online[12] help remove any barriers that could lead a consumer to choose another option over purchasing on the company's website or app. The business-to-consumer model is one of the more common business models in today's society. This model is used by many different companies that sell products and services to the public. The primary purpose of this model is to generate revenue through sales and then increase this revenue by expanding its customer base. By using this model, companies can grow their businesses in a very short time.

The Business-to-Consumer model (B2C) has many advantages[13] that reflect its name. In this model, entrepreneurs can avoid the costs of traditional intermediaries, such as wholesalers and retailers, by producing a product or service and selling it directly to the consumer. It allows businesses in this category to offer lower prices. This model also allows for greater flexibility in the product offering since inventory is directly linked with demand. Businesses can also react quickly to changing market conditions by changing their product offerings and marketing materials. For example, if a company produces hats and the demand for baseball caps declines, the business can switch resources from producing baseball caps to producing something else. Suppose a company was working with a wholesaler or retailer. In that case, it might not have that option, as it needs to maintain relationships with all retailers to maintain its market share. Similarly, businesses in this category can customize their communications and advertising[14] efforts by being direct with their target customers. Sometimes, this is done by gathering data on consumers' shopping habits or buying preferences through surveys or other means. Businesses in this category also have an advantage in providing customer support and customer service because they deal directly with the end user of their products or services.

Everything Beyond

The next two business models that I am going to talk about are the subscription-based model[15] and the on-demand model.[16] The subscription-based model means the consumer purchases a product or service regularly and is automatically billed for it. The advantage of this model is that the consumer does not have to worry about whether he can afford the next installment because he has already decided to buy it. The disadvantage of this model is that it may cause consumers to overindulge in their purchases. If a consumer has a credit card, she can purchase anything she wants, so she may be more likely to spend more money using credit cards than if she had to write checks for her expenses. Many companies have become magnificent by opting for the subscription-based business model. Netflix and Amazon Prime are great examples of this, where people pay a monthly fee to access a great library of content. The benefits[17] of this model are tremendous. It allows companies to provide customers with an extremely valuable service for a rate that may be less than the cost of buying the items separately. It also allows customers to cancel any time, which is incredibly convenient when you're wondering how long you want or need to use the service. Also, it makes it much easier for customers to ask for help if they need support - all they have to do is call or email. They're connected immediately with a representative who can help them fix whatever issue they may have.

On-demand business models are a popular choice for start-ups to use because these types of businesses have the potential to be quite cost-effective.[18] With Software-as-a-Service (SaaS)[19] and Delivery-as-a-Service (DaaS),[20] companies can save money on overhead costs, such as renting large office spaces and purchasing expensive computer hardware. This way, they can retain more of their profits. Many companies that use the on-demand business model are internet-based, but it is also used in other industries. Food delivery is one example of an on-demand business model that is not internet-based. Some fast-food restaurants have partnered with delivery services such as Uber Eats or GrubHub so that customers can order their food and have it delivered to them within minutes. With the rise of on-demand companies like Uber, Lyft, and Postmates, it's becoming clear that the on-demand model[21] is viable. On-demand start-ups are very popular for a couple of reasons. Firstly, for a company to be successful using this business model, it needs to have an easily scalable product. It doesn't necessarily mean it needs to be technology-based; most companies using this model provide services. They're so successful because they're highly scalable and can offer huge margins despite being services often performed in person by independent contractors. On-demand companies are similar because they provide services or products where demand can be scaled quickly by adding more customers or drivers. The on-demand business model also delivers convenience to customers, which is a huge win-win situation, especially for start-ups.

How To Know What Suits Your Start-Up

The mantra that every start-up needs to crack is what business model or monetization strategies[22] suit your start-up. It's not enough to reach out to people with your product; you need to figure out how you will profit from it. Many people only focus on this aspect of business too late when they are already over their heads and running low on cash flow. That's why a thorough analysis of what business model would suit your start-up has to be one of the first things you should do when deciding on an idea for your start-up. Monetizing a start-up is a tricky task. You need to figure out which monetization model suits your start-up sooner than later. In the early days, it's best to keep it simple and focus on one aspect of your business at a time.

The nature of your start-up's products will determine your business or monetization model. A software company will have a different approach from a retailer, a publisher, and so on. Some companies follow a traditional model where the majority of revenue is generated from their existing customer base, with others coming from new customers. Others will launch with a premium model and only sell premium features to customers at higher price points. A successful business plan will provide investors with the necessary information[23] to decide whether they wish to invest in your company or not. It should include details on the nature of your product, marketplace, customers and potential, competition, funding requirements, and projected returns. If you are looking to raise capital, investors will likely want to know how much you've already spent and how much it will cost you to launch the product. They'll also want detailed forecasts showing how you intend to generate income through sales and advertising. I have collated it into three main pointers to make this more accessible and feasible. To do so, you must first understand these models' features and your company's offerings. This analysis will make it easier for you to choose the model you want for your company and how it will work in the market. Syncing both these are crucial for your start-up's success. I have then written about understanding the stakeholders involved in your business. If you know what your investors want, you can achieve remarkable funding, and if you know what your customers/subscribers want, you can quickly improve your products and services. Therefore, an insight into stakeholder interests will help you. Thereafter, I have written about the funding strategy and the specific market[24] your company belongs to so that planning for the most appropriate business or monetization model becomes hassle-free for you.

Understanding The Features And Offerings

Many models have been created to help new businesses succeed, but there is no perfect formula to follow. Some business models that may seem advantageous at first may be harmful in the long run. Therefore, it is necessary to understand and evaluate each business model before implementing them.[25] To understand if a business model suits your start-up idea, know the model's features and what your start-up promises to offer. A business model is more than just the basic elements of an idea and its implementation – it also involves a set of resources, ways of doing things, and a measure of success. These models have specific features and can be used separately or combined with other models. Hence, knowing what your start-up promises to offer and how these can fit into your chosen model is imperative. If you are unsure about how your start-up works, you will likely need more time to develop your ideas and figure out a way for them to succeed. So, instead of jumping into a business that does not seem fitting for you, take the time you need to figure it out thoroughly.

Start-up offerings are the foundation[26] of any business. It gives you an idea about the nature of the products and services that your customers need. The offerings should be such that it gives you a clear picture of the business model it is fit for. Once you know the nature of products and services and the right market for these, it is easier for you to go for a suitable business model. Identifying the right business model for your start-up is essential because it will give clarity to you, your customers, your investors, and the industry. After years of observing trends, the entrepreneur's role has evolved to encompass much more than just a place to make money.[27] Many entrepreneurs view their companies as missions. Most entrepreneurs have a vision that they are working hard to bring to fruition, whether it be as simple as making a better mousetrap or as complex as making a world-changing discovery. And working with the right business or monetization model is crucial in this regard. While there is no single path to success in business models, certain characteristics are common among successful businesses. One of these qualities is the ability of an entrepreneur and their team to adapt quickly in a volatile industry.[28] Even if the business is doing well now, the competition may soon do something new to take away some of its market shares. If this happens, the company may need to change its focus and find ways to increase revenue through other means. For example, if a company finds itself competing with other companies in its field that sell its products online, it may need to find another way to make money through brick-and-mortar stores. The key here is flexibility; entrepreneurs need to be willing and able to alter their business model[29] based on current trends or events.

Understanding The Stakeholders

One of the biggest issues in breaking the ice with your ventures is ensuring you are working from a solid understanding of handling the business and approaching the different stakeholders since you can only progress with them on your side.[30] For example, one of the biggest milestones for many new start-ups is figuring out your stakeholders and their interests.[31] It means that you have to be able to know precisely who is involved and which people or businesses will be affected by your decisions. It's essential not just in terms of working out how best to move forward with these people but also the fact that you need to be aware of how they feel about things to know what sort of PR image your company has and how much support it's getting. Before you even decide on a business model, consider what model would suit your start-up vis-a-vis the stakeholders.[32] So, fixing a particular model must mean that you are considering all kinds of impacts it will have on the stakeholders.

Stakeholders in B2B companies are different from that of a B2C company.[33] Companies working across these two models differ significantly in their approaches to the market. We know that while a B2C company focuses on delivering a product or service to a consumer, a B2B company focuses on delivering value and is, therefore, specialized in its service or product. This specialization creates demand for each business' products and services within the business community. As such, many different stakeholders are involved in the decision-making process of a B2B organization that is not typically involved in the decision-making process of a B2C organization. In addition to being focused on the business community, B2B organizations must also be aware of other stakeholders, such as employees and suppliers. There are also regulations and standards, both governmental and industry, which may affect how a company handles the needs of its stakeholders. In general, however, all customers are considered stakeholders because they provide an external market for goods or services produced by the organization. Stakeholders can also include creditors, who provide capital; government agencies, who provide legal protection; and owners, who provide equity capital through loans or stock ownership. So, the business or monetization model[34] you choose will impact all these stakeholders.

Understanding The Funding Strategy And Market

A clear understanding of funding strategies[35] will also help you to know which business model is the perfect match for your start-up. One of the entrepreneurs' most common mistakes is focusing on the wrong funding strategies. At best, this leads to wasted time; at worst, it could lead to a fatal cash flow crunch. A company's funding will determine the level of expectations that come with that investment. If angel investors or venture capitalists fund a start-up, they will likely have to meet high expectations to receive follow-up funding and continue operating. When it comes to debt financing, the implications are less severe, but there is still some pressure for companies to perform. Start-ups financed by private equity and institutional investors will have the less pressure - they can make mistakes without worrying about going out of business or losing money. When you talk to a venture capitalist about funding your business, they will have very different expectations than when you approach a crowdfunding platform. If you go to an investor or business partner with your idea, they will want to know about your market, your competitors, what differentiates you from them, and how you plan to compete. They will ask you for a comprehensive business plan[36] that outlines how much money you'll need, where it will come from, and how it will be spent. They won't care about whether or not the crowd is involved in the process; they may even see them as potential obstacles to reaching your goal.

The market for a product is always an important consideration when starting a business. The best place to test a concept is where you will sell it, and if you're raising funds to get your idea off the ground, you'll likely need to raise that money from investors who expect a return on their investment. Suppose you're bringing your product to market in another country. In that case, investors may not be as interested in an equity stake in the company as they would be if they were investing in a local business. If you're building a consumer product, it may make sense to seek out venture capital or angel investors who are accustomed to funding technology start-ups; if you're building a service, it might make sense to bring the business to the attention of angel investors or even lending institutions who may be more interested in helping fund a profitable operation than betting on equity with an unproven concept. If you're seeking investments outside your home country, pay attention to your backyard. Some countries[37] are friendly toward foreign investors and have laws that make it easier for non-citizens to start and run businesses there.

How To Make Your Model Work

Your business model is only as good as you can make it work.[38] It would be best if you put in the time and effort to get your start-up up and running and sustain it. Just because it's a popular business model doesn't guarantee it will work for you. If the business model isn't appropriate[39] for the market you're trying to sell into, or if other factors make it unsustainable, then giving it your best effort won't be enough. For example, if you're selling organic, non-GMO food at a price that's too low for your market, or if you're selling an art piece at an opening that ends up flopping with no buyers, then all of the efforts in the world aren't going to save your start-up from failure. You must learn how to make your business sustainable to move forward with it. Many entrepreneurs are familiar with start-up life, but it's not all fun and games.[40] When you're a start-up, and your entire business is based on one person's vision, you must remember that your work is constantly scrutinized. Entrepreneurs need a business model to run their business, but the question is, "Will my model work?"

No matter how much you're doing, customers and investors will always look that extra mile.[41] The extra mile, or the walk beyond the extra mile, or whatever you want to call it, sets start-ups apart from all other kinds of businesses. Every moment counts for a start-up because there is no time to waste. If you want to be successful in the business world, you'll have to work hard and put in extra effort to make things happen. If you're a start-up owner and you're still brainstorming about how to grow your business, then it's about time that you realized that your business model would only work out if you took the extra mile. Business owners must identify their niche and what makes their service or product special. They should also ask themselves why their customers should buy from them instead of from their competition. They should have a clear picture of what they are trying to achieve and how they will achieve it. A good business model should include how much you can earn, how much money you will need, and how long it will take you to reach that point. A business plan is not just about money; it is also about understanding what your start-up stands for and where it fits in the market so that you can continue growing in the right direction even when things get challenging. If there is one thing I learned from various success stories, it is that the right people are more important than all the other resources combined. The right people can take your company a long way, while only some other resources can do so much. So, before you decide on a business model, ensure you have the right people. I have elaborated on three crucial aspects in the section hereafter. The first is to pitch like a king – knowing how to market your brand and position your business model correctly. The second is keeping your investors and subscribers happy. You must know which direction your investors and subscribers are headed and mend the features of your business model accordingly. The third is to evolve as you move ahead regarding products and services. You must modify what you offer and how you offer to stay relevant and stay ahead.

Pitch Like A King

One remarkable way to make your business model work is to pitch like a king.[42] It means you are creative when you work through the specifics of your business idea, see things from multiple perspectives, and get others' buy-in on what you're doing. The process starts early in your planning stages. It involves asking yourself questions like - do I have a suitable model for my start-up? What makes this business unique? How can I sell it so that it becomes self-sustaining? This process is about getting people excited about what you're doing so that they want to be part of it. In other words, it's more about selling them something than your product or service. You must go into this with the mindset that you are not pitching from desperation; instead, you're confident that this business model will work if everyone gets on board.[43] If you start by saying, "I don't know if it will work," people won't get excited about joining your endeavor and helping it succeed. If you do this right, people will feel good about being part of something larger than themselves - and that is how your business model will prosper.

A start-up is all about the team. It will only happen if you have a team that believes in your idea and can make it happen. You may have a great plan, but if your team is not on board or is actively rebelling against it, you will have difficulty bringing your vision to fruition. Your team must be on board[44] with a business model for many reasons. In some cases, the business model may be doomed from the start because you cannot accomplish your company's goal within the parameters of its business model. The most obvious case is when a new technology fails to perform as expected and, therefore, fails to meet the standards required for success. How you present your idea to potential investors and acquire funding for it can influence how well your team feels about the business model. If you are using a high level of hype to attract investment, then this creates subconscious pressure on your team members to live up to that hype and create results that are consistent with their messaging.

Even though you can show the viewer that your product has traction and prove that people are interested in what you are doing, your team may be more excited and confident. Your team needs to feel comfortable with the product or service they are providing and how they interact with one another. As a leader, you must be transparent with why you chose each person on the team and how they contribute to the company's overall goals.[45]

Keep Your Investors And Subscribers Happy

For your business or monetization model to work, keep your investors and subscribers happy.[46] It might seem cliche, but it goes a long way. The reason why successful businesses need to manage their business model so carefully is that they are dependent upon their investors and subscribers. When you keep your investors happy and offer them what they're looking for, they will be willing to fund your business and sustain the funding. Investing in a start-up company is a risk[47] that investors take, and they want to ensure that the company they invest in can develop and run smoothly. The more the investors are satisfied with what the company can offer them, the more inclined they will be to give you money and sustain their support for your business. If you can address what an investor is looking for, you have a better chance of securing funding. Investors would rather see a company grow slowly, steadily, and successfully than one that had a quick rise only to fall into oblivion later on. To keep your investors happy and maintain their support, you need to give them what they want. Start by identifying your target investors, which could be family members or friends with some experience with start-ups or professional investors. Once you know who they are, start exercising due diligence on them by finding their investment preferences, and the ball is in your court - make sure you play it right.

The success of a start-up can also be measured by its subscriber base. If you can convince your subscribers to trust you with your business model, it is likely for the business to succeed. It is an important factor that investors consider before investing in a start-up. You must establish a cordial relationship with your subscribers so that they are willing to use your services and buy your products. Customer satisfaction and trust[47] are among the most important factors for a successful business. Suppose you want to know why the franchise industry is so successful. In that case, franchises have credibility because the customer knows that if he buys a product from a franchise, there will be uniformity with the product and service quality. Many McDonald's franchises don't sell half-cooked or raw food items or provide poor service. So, how do you build customer trust? It would help if you were consistent in your dealings with them. You should be very clear about what problem you are solving for the customer and how exactly you plan to go about it. You must understand that you cannot solve all problems with the same solution[48] or approach. The moment someone realizes your product is not solving their problem, they will move on to something else. People don't care much about what you want to do as long as they know how it will help them personally. So, if they see the value of your product or service, they will stick around long enough to find out if they ultimately get value from it later down the line.

Modify What You Offer And How You Offer

It's no secret that the most successful companies are the ones that have a suitable business model[49] - that is, they offer something that people need or want at a price that will generate profits for them. But even the best business model will only work if your customers know it exists and can find you to buy from you. That's why it is so important to adapt how your company works and what it offers - including pricing, product selection, etc. The effort you put into making these changes depends on how fast you want to grow and how quickly you want to make money from your business. Remember that no matter how much you change your business model and how quickly you do it, there are ways to ensure that things go smoothly. Creating a plan for the changes you want to make and taking the time to execute that plan will help keep your customers happy and ensure your business doesn't lose money. The simplest way to do this is by testing: try out new features or options in a small section of your audience (for instance, a 10% sample of all website visitors), see whether they're interested in them, and then expand or remove them based on customer reactions. When communicating with customers about these changes, provide clear reasons for the difference in products and services.[50]

Your business is not a machine; it's a thriving thing.[51] For it to prosper, it must be nurtured and taken care of. The end-user has more choices than ever before, and they want newness. Earlier, companies could do what they wanted, and customers had to accept it. Now, there's a much more dynamic relationship between the two parties. The customer is no longer just spending money on a product or service - they are actively shaping products and services to meet their needs. Companies have to focus on making sure that the customer is happy, which means that companies have to be able to change with the times and deliver new products/services as needed. So, customers will always be up for companies that work on their business model and bring innovation and modification in their products and services as and when required. If you are starting, remember that the more evolved products and services you offer, the greater will be your customer traction. It is easier to start small, with a narrow focus on what you are delivering. Still, as you grow your business and gain experience in the marketplace, you will want to become increasingly more diversified. It will allow for greater customer satisfaction and broader market reach.[51] And above all, it will help you sustain your business model for many years.

Companies Whose Success Stories Will Motivate You

StackBlitz

StackBlitz[52] is one company whose success story has become a motivation for many start-ups. Starting with a clear vision, the company built a platform allowing users to develop and deploy applications without downloading or installing software. StackBlitz, a development tool created by a team of university friends, has inspired many start-ups. The company was founded in 2018. StackBlitz has emerged as a clear market leader in web development tools in recent years. It's no surprise that several up-and-coming developers are paying extra attention to this company's progress and successes. The idea stemmed from the founders' experience in their educational journeys. In their view, today's students have it easier than their generation. They saw that most restrictions on web developers came from the fact that they could not write code how they wanted to, and they set out to create an advanced code editor to break these limitations. Gone are the days when learning how to code for aspiring programmers would mean figuring it out on their own - the Internet now has many user-friendly today, and StackBlitz is a fine example. It allows users to create an entire application without installing software or dealing with any command line interface. These days, StackBlitz is entering a new phase of its life cycle - it has started working on new products and services but is still relying on its flagship product for most of its revenues.

Company Name: StackBlitz

Founded: 2018

Significant reason(s) for success: The company solves a real problem and makes the product accessible to the masses.

Linktree

Every company needs to have a solid business plan and strategy early on. One company that has achieved this is Linktree,[53] a start-up founded in 2016. Their mission is simple: to organize the world's information and make it universally accessible and helpful. They've created an easy-to-use system for posting links, quotes, articles, and videos - which you can use to share your content or content from the sites you run. This system makes it easier for you to curate content with your voice while significantly reducing the time needed to find and post new material. It's also more effective than simply sharing content through your social media - it allows you to get more traffic to your site through a network of like-minded people. Linktree offers an alternative to some of the more famous social networking sites clogging up our online experience with spammy advertisements and other offensive material. Their model allows for a much higher level of engagement with users, making it a fun way to share different types of information with people who will appreciate what you have to say and who are much less likely to be turned off by spam or offensive materials. While many start-ups are drawn to Uber as a model for creating a valuable company out of thin air, Linktree's success reminds us that there are other ways to make it big as a start-up.

Company Name: Linktree

Founded: 2016

Significant reason(s) for success: The company streamlines information and makes it more convenient for users to access. It gives optimal attention to user requirements.

Preply

Preply[54] is a start-up that grew from the founders' frustration with inefficient online tutoring and learning platforms. As they were trying to improve their language-learning skills, they realized there were some great resources, but finding them challenging, and all the existing platforms needed fixing. It is a classic example of how entrepreneurs solve real problems and improve their customers' lives by offering better products. And yet, Preply's story shows that it can be tricky to start from scratch and create an entirely new business concept. The history of Preply is a story that is not often told, but it's one that every new entrepreneur should take note of. It's a story about getting the best out of your team and finding the most brilliant ideas by letting your employees fully engage in the process. Preply was founded in 2012. At the time, it didn't have any clients, nor did it have funding. But there was a desire to impact the world - to improve education through technology and help teachers do their jobs better. The plan was to create an online platform that would allow teachers and students to connect quickly, improving communication and increasing the productivity of teachers to help improve the quality of education worldwide. The first step was creating a prototype of what this online platform might look like. To keep things streamlined, they decided to use only resources they already had available: no full-time developers or designers on staff, only part-time talent from all over the world, willing to explore a new avenue for freelance work. And today, Preply is rapidly growing.

Company Name: Preply

Founded: 2012

Significant reason(s) for success: The company targets specific communities of customers and conveniently connects them across the globe.

Oura Health Oy

Oura[55] has been creating quite a buzz across the world. It is a company that has made a name for itself in a short time frame. Few products can compare to Oura's quality regarding design, technology, and functionality. Oy, the Finnish word for "health," is not just the name of this new company. It's a cultural and spiritual value for the founders that drives everything about their business. The brand was founded by three Finnish entrepreneurs who wanted to find a way to make all the positive changes they were making in their own lives more tangible and accessible to other people. The Oura ring has been regarded as an exemplary innovation by many across the globe. The ring measures body temperature, heart rate, galvanic skin response (which is an indication of how much someone's sweat glands are active), activity level, sleep metrics, personal stress levels, and daily resting heart rate variability (the changes in your heartbeat that occur naturally throughout the day). The data is then uploaded to the app, where users can track it over time.

Company Name: Oura Health Oy

Founded: 2013

Significant reason(s) for success: The company caters to one of the most critical industries. It designs its products keeping the regular consumer in mind.

PayPal

Most of the companies we've looked at could take advantage of the power of network effects, but PayPal[56] had to come up with a unique value proposition based on something other than the strength of its network. When PayPal started in the late 90s, it had a simple business model. It was a free service that let users transfer money to each other and charged merchants a fee for accepting payments through its platform. It worked very well in its early days when the company mainly attracted people who were already technology literate and comfortable with online payments. Not surprisingly, PayPal established itself as a significant player in online payments. But then, something unexpected happened: eBay acquired PayPal in 2002. Even though eBay had been using PayPal for years before this acquisition on its site, after joining forces with eBay, PayPal began receiving criticism from merchants who said that it became harder to do business on eBay because of the high fees they had to pay to accept payments through PayPal. By separating from eBay, PayPal became a brand in itself. It allowed customers to trust and focus on PayPal's reliability and ease of use rather than be distracted by concerns about eBay. The separation benefited both companies by creating competition and giving consumers more choices. On the business side, PayPal has always focused on what it does best - it provides a secure way for people to transact online. And its ads reinforce this message by showing PayPal users having fun, being social, and engaging in rewarding activities without worrying about their financial security. On the marketing side, PayPal's ads are memorable because they feature celebrities such as LeBron James using their service to do something extraordinary. In this way, they've built an image around themselves as cool and fun - a brand identity that people have come to trust.

Company Name: PayPal

Founded: 1998

Significant reason(s) for success: The company has been customer-centric since its inception. It has utilized its business model quite well, irrespective of its acquisition and spin-off phases.

Airbnb

Airbnb[57] is a success story worth learning from. This company was founded on a simple idea: renting out your home to travelers. It seemed an exciting way to make some extra cash and see the world, but most people thought it was too good to be true. But the founders believed in the idea so much that they decided to travel around their country to prove that it would work: they wanted people to see how easy it was for them to rent out your extra space for extra cash. They started small, but every time someone tried their idea, more people started signing up to be hosts on Airbnb. They let everyone know about Airbnb through social media and word-of-mouth marketing. Airbnb has become one of the most visited websites in the world and has raised billions of dollars in funds. It took advantage of a global trend - increased awareness and interest in local experiences. It can be attributed to the growth of social media networks and the increase in transient lifestyles (especially among millennials). Secondly, Airbnb was able to tap into a massive market in the hospitality industry. By creating an online marketplace for accommodations, Airbnb was able to minimize costs while also maximizing exposure for hosts and renters. The company has also taken a unique approach to the market. Instead of spending millions on advertising campaigns as other major sharing economy companies do (i.e., Uber), Airbnb decided to invest significant sums in user-generated content; this helped them gain traction early on and build their brand. They also ensure their listings are incredibly accurate, providing a pleasant experience for both renters and hosts alike.

Company Name: Airbnb

Founded: 2008

Significant reason(s) for success: The company has quickly adapted to the changing times and has been offering services as per the requirements of customers since its foundation.

Alibaba

It is no doubt that Alibaba[58] is one of the most successful Chinese companies in the world today. But how did it all start? What made the company one of the world's most significant, most valuable, and most successful internet companies today? It's all because of its founders, Jack Ma, and his partners. In 1999, Jack Ma, a former English teacher in China, co-founded Alibaba as an online marketplace where small businesses, manufacturers, and exporters can trade their products with other companies and consumers. At first, Alibaba functioned as an online platform enabling suppliers to sell their goods to retailers through a website. The following year, Alibaba's vision became apparent; the company established itself as a professional business-to-business trading platform, allowing people and businesses to sell their products quickly. By 2008, Alibaba had grown into an e-commerce giant with more than 70 million users worldwide. In 2012, Alibaba was worth $231 billion USD – making it more valuable than Amazon and eBay combined. Hence, the story of Alibaba is both exciting and inspiring. If you want your start-up to succeed, then you must learn from Alibaba's growth over the years. To achieve massive success and eventually become the world's largest online retailer, Alibaba experienced a lot of ups and downs, especially during the early years when it was just starting. But it stayed undeterred and moved ahead with conviction and the right intent. Also, it focused on suitable business models and strategies.

Company Name: Alibaba

Founded: 1999

Significant reason(s) for success: The company has had a fantastic team since its inception. Everyone in the team believed in their business model, values, and vision.

Tesla

Tesla[59] is said to be the world's most innovative car manufacturing company. The company has made much progress quickly and has become the leader in its industry today. What are the reasons behind Tesla's success? For one, Tesla is not just any other electric car company. Besides vehicles, Tesla also manufactures lithium-ion battery packs for various clients. In addition, it has designed battery charging stations for commercial and home use. The company's founder, Elon Musk, was able to transform his vision into reality with a bit of help from the financial backing of several investors like the Founders Fund, Daimler Ventures, and Elon Musk himself. With this funding, Tesla has made a giant leap in the automotive world. Tesla's success comes not only from its team members but also from its investors, who were very patient with it during its early stages of operation. The most extensive learning from Tesla should be its vision and focus when it comes to business. One thing that impresses me is how much effort and resources Tesla spends on getting the word out. Everything it launches is done in grand fashion and with well-planned events. Such kind of visibility generates a tremendous amount of excitement, which can be seen from the customers' responses.

Company Name: Tesla

Founded: 2003

Significant reason(s) for success: The company has taken innovation to a new level. The leaders' connection to customers, especially on social media platforms, is noteworthy.

Ikea

Ikea, the Swedish multinational furniture retailer, has revolutionized materials for people worldwide. Ikea[60] is also one of the most successful business models in the world. Can you learn lessons from Ikea to turn your start-up into a success? You can. Ikea was founded in 1943 by 17-year-old Ingvar Kamprad, who started out selling pencils and seeds. In 1950, Kamprad began selling furniture made at local manufacturing plants. It allowed him to build a massive network of suppliers and create national retail chains. He opened the first store in 1958 in Almhult, Sweden. Ikea's core product range comprises furniture, kitchen appliances, and home accessories. The company has been consistently growing since it was founded, opening new stores across the globe every year. The Ikea concept has since expanded globally with a tremendous increase in popularity through franchising opportunities worldwide. Today, over 500 million customers shop at Ikea annually, and there are more than 360 stores in more than 40 countries worldwide. The secret behind Ikea's success is not only in its flat packs but also in its business strategy. To build up an Ikea store, they don't rent or buy land; they create a building shell and fill it with their products. It means that when they move on, they leave nothing behind, making them one of the most environmentally friendly companies. They are also known for their typeface, which is used in every communication material they produce – from catalogs to billboards. Ikea's simple design philosophy is based on honesty, modesty, equality, and durability.

Company Name: Ikea

Founded: 1943

Significant reason(s) for success: The company remained committed to simplistic designs. It has made life easier for people since its inception and has always prioritized customer needs.

Conclusion

A business model is a tool that helps you define your business in a way that enables you to achieve your goals. It also allows you to consider the market trends and other aspects vital for a successful business. A suitable business model will surely mean that your start-up is ready to tread the path of success. To take your start-up to the next level and make it successful, you need to understand your strengths and weaknesses and then make strategic decisions accordingly. The business model you choose will directly impact your start-up's success because it will decide how the product is designed, produced, and delivered to the end customer. Depending upon your business strategy, the revenue model adopted could be anything from selling advertisement space to an online retailer who handles shipping and delivery, or you could sell products directly at a trade show. Choosing the suitable business model should be made keeping in mind all aspects, including legal issues, tax implications, technological feasibility, and most importantly, profitability. Much depends on how well you assess your target audience and their needs before strategizing to come up with a solution. The focus should always be on building a sustainable business model with maximum returns.

As discussed in this chapter, the right business or monetization model would be vital to your company's progress. Many start-ups get their product out there first, then consider how to make money later. While this is good, knowing your business model is essential before developing. Your business model is how you plan to make money from your creation - if you know this upfront, it will be much easier to figure out which features are worth implementing and which aren't. Following are the summary pointers of this chapter so that you can carry the understanding of this chapter in a ready-reference format and keep coming back as and when required:

1. Thoroughly study the different business models and see which suits your start-up flavor.
2. Understand the features of each model well and tally them with the products and services of your start-up to know the compatibility levels.
3. A comprehensive understanding of stakeholders is fundamental if you want your business model to succeed.
4. The funding processes discussed in this chapter and one before play a crucial role in identifying the suitable monetization model.
5. For your model to work, you must keep your strategies in place.
6. Pitch like a king and let people know what your company stands for.
7. Treat your investors and subscribers with equal respect and regard. Their loyalty will take your start-up a long way.
8. Be dynamic in your offerings. Your business model, products, and services will need to evolve.

References

1. Sweeney, D. (2019). *How today's business model is changing.* Available at: https://www.forbes.com/sites/forbeschicagocouncil/2019/05/13/how-todays-business-model-is-changing/?sh=7366297e2fe4 [Accessed 18 Dec. 2022].
2. Moore, K. (2019). *Five E-commerce customer service strategies to supercharge your brand's growth.* Available at: https://www.helpscout.com/blog/ecommerce-customer-service/ [Accessed 18 Dec. 2022].
3. Burns, S. (2020). *4 things to consider when changing your business model.* Available at: https://www.forbes.com/sites/stephanieburns/2020/01/11/4-things-to-consider-when-changing-your-business-model/ [Accessed 18 Dec. 2022].

4. Krajewski, R. (2022). *10 proven business models for start-ups to try in 2022.* Available at: https://www.ideamotive.co/blog/proven-business-models-for-startups [Accessed 18 Dec. 2022].
5. Gans, J., Scott, E.L. & Stern, S. (2018). *Strategy for start-ups.* Available at: https://hbr.org/2018/05/strategy-for-start-ups [Accessed 18 Dec. 2022].
6. Pennington, A. (2022). *SWOT analysis: The most overlooked business tool, and how to use it.* Available at: https://www.forbes.com/sites/forbesbusinesscouncil/2022/02/24/swot-analysis-the-most-overlooked-business-tool-and-how-to-use-it/ [Accessed 18 Dec. 2022].
7. Thales Group (2020). *Six creative companies using subscription models in brilliant ways.* Available at: https://cpl.thalesgroup.com/blog/software-monetization/six-creative-companies-using-subscription-models-brilliant-ways [Accessed 18 Dec. 2022].
8. Chen, J. (2020). *Business to business (B2B).* Available at: https://www.investopedia.com/terms/b/btob.asp [Accessed 18 Dec. 2022].
9. Gibbons, C. (2020). *Top 10 B2B ecommerce benefits.* Available at: https://www.truecommerce.com/uk-en/blog/top-10-b2b-ecommerce-benefits [Accessed 18 Dec. 2022].
10. Israr, S. (2021). *How to promote a product: 15 highly effective ways (2022).* Available at: https://www.cloudways.com/blog/how-to-promote-a-product/ [Accessed 18 Dec. 2022].
11. Kenton, W. (2020). *Business to consumer (B2C).* Available at: https://www.investopedia.com/terms/b/btoc.asp [Accessed 18 Dec. 2022].
12. Morgan, B. (2020). *More customers are shopping online now than at height of pandemic, fueling need for digital transformation.* Available at: https://www.forbes.com/sites/blakemorgan/2020/07/27/more-customers-are-shopping-online-now-than-at-height-of-pandemic-fueling-need-for-digital-transformation/ [Accessed 18 Dec. 2022].
13. Tycoon Story (2022). *07 advantages and disadvantages Of B2C Ecommerce.* Available at: https://www.tycoonstory.com/resource/07-advantages-and-disadvantages-of-b2c-ecommerce/ [Accessed 18 Dec. 2022].
14. Zantal-Wiener, A. (2020). *These 9 brands take personalized marketing to a new level.* Available at: https://blog.hubspot.com/marketing/marketing-personalization-examples [Accessed 18 Dec. 2022].
15. Tarver, E. (2019). *How do subscription business models work?* Available at: https://www.investopedia.com/ask/answers/042715/how-do-subscription-business-models-work.asp [Accessed 18 Dec. 2022].

16. Jungle Works (2020). *On demand business models.* Available at: https://jungleworks.com/on-demand-business-models/ [Accessed 18 Dec. 2022].
17. Baral, A. (2022). *The evolution of the subscription model and what's on the horizon.* Available at: https://www.forbes.com/sites/forbesbusinessdevelopmentcouncil/2022/09/12/the-evolution-of-the-subscription-model-and-whats-on-the-horizon/ [Accessed 18 Dec. 2022].
18. Peerbits (2022). *Why the on demand business is a successful model for start-ups.* Available at: https://www.peerbits.com/blog/on-demand-business-a-successful-model-for-startups.html [Accessed 18 Dec. 2022].
19. Altaf, Y. (2022). *Tips and insights on building a successful Saas platform.* Available at: https://www.forbes.com/sites/forbestechcouncil/2022/10/03/tips-and-insights-on-building-a-successful-saas-platform/?sh=79323f05eeb8 [Accessed 18 Dec. 2022].
20. Newman, D. (2017). *Data as a service: The big opportunity for business.* Available at: https://www.forbes.com/sites/danielnewman/2017/02/07/data-as-a-service-the-big-opportunity-for-business/?sh=3f83471224d9 [Accessed 18 Dec. 2022].
21. Magneto (2020). *6 reasons why on-demand business is a successful model for start-ups.* Available at: https://magnetoitsolutions.com/blog/on-demand-business-successful-model-for-startups [Accessed 18 Dec. 2022].
22. Startup Jedi (2021). *The top 7 start-up monetization models.* Available at: https://startupjedi.vc/content/top-7-startup-monetization-models [Accessed 18 Dec. 2022].
23. Forbes (2020). *What angel investors want to know before investing in your start-up.* Available at: https://www.forbes.com/sites/allbusiness/2020/12/13/what-angel-investors-want-to-know-before-investing-in-your-startup/?sh=632c98af1a11 [Accessed 18 Dec. 2022].
24. Bizjournals (2019). *How to find the right financial strategy for your business.* Available at: https://www.bizjournals.com/bizjournals/how-to/growth-strategies/2018/02/how-to-find-the-right-financial-strategy-for-your.html [Accessed 18 Dec. 2022].
25. Tirakyan, V. (2021). *A checklist for selecting the right business model for your start-up.* Available at: https://www.forbes.com/sites/forbesbusinesscouncil/2021/08/25/a-checklist-for-selecting-the-right-business-model-for-your-startup/?sh=5e4ff2e039a4 [Accessed 18 Dec. 2022].
26. Taulli, T. (2018). *Building the right tech foundation for your start-up.* Available at: https://www.forbes.com/sites/tomtaulli/2018/10/14/build-

ing-the-right-tech-foundation-for-your-startup/?sh=4da1317f3c7b [Accessed 18 Dec. 2022].

27. Hyken, S. (2020). *Your company's purpose (and it's not profit).* Available at: https://www.forbes.com/sites/shephyken/2020/12/13/your-companys-purpose-and-its-not-profit/?sh=37f2dce143a1 [Accessed 18 Dec. 2022].
28. Holaspirit (2021). *5 tactics to adapt your business to a vuca world.* Available at: https://www.holaspirit.com/blog/how-vuca-affects-business [Accessed 18 Dec. 2022].
29. Lawal, R. J. (2020). *Business model innovation: is it a good move?* Available at: https://www.forbes.com/sites/forbesbusinesscouncil/2020/09/24/business-model-innovation-is-it-a-good-move/?sh=1425a96a1b82 [Accessed 18 Dec. 2022].
30. Schoenmaekers, R. (2021). *6 tips for start-ups to negotiate with investors.* Available at: https://thefactory.works/6-tips-a-startup-founder-should-know-before-negotiating-with-an-investor/ [Accessed 18 Dec. 2022].
31. YEC (2019). *Seven strategies for ensuring stakeholders are pleased with your company's performance.* Available at: https://www.forbes.com/sites/theyec/2019/03/14/seven-strategies-for-ensuring-stakeholders-are-pleased-with-your-companys-performance/?sh=4ae94d703ca4 [Accessed 18 Dec. 2022].
32. Mckinsey (2021). *Five steps to stakeholder capitalism.* Available at: https://www.mckinsey.com/capabilities/strategy-and-corporate-finance/our-insights/from-principle-to-practice-making-stakeholder-capitalism-work [Accessed 18 Dec. 2022].
33. Wolff, N. (2019). *B2B and B2C product management: Reality and myth.* Available at: https://medium.com/theventurecity/b2b-and-b2c-product-management-reality-and-myth-f3d386b591b0 [Accessed 18 Dec. 2022].
34. Contributor, D. (2021). *How stakeholders can make or break companies' sustainability efforts.* Available at: https://www.forbes.com/sites/deloitte/2021/05/13/how-stakeholders-can-make-or-break-companies-sustainability-efforts/?sh=141efccc476d [Accessed 18 Dec. 2022].
35. Iyer, R. (2022). *Fundraising tips for early and midstage start-ups in 2022.* Available at: techcrunch.com/2022/07/20/fundraising-tips-for-early-and-mid-stage-startups-in-2022 [Accessed 18 Dec. 2022].
36. Chi, C. (2017). *7 sample business plans to help you write your own.* Available at: https://blog.hubspot.com/marketing/sample-business-plans [Accessed 18 Dec. 2022].

37. Glasner, J. (2021). *These countries have the most start-up investment for their size.* Available at: https://news.crunchbase.com/startups/countries-most-startup-investment/ [Accessed 18 Dec. 2022].
38. Jespersen, S. (2020). *Council post: Building a business model that is unique for you.* Available at: https://www.forbes.com/sites/forbesagencycouncil/2020/01/08/building-a-business-model-that-is-unique-for-you/?sh=66543be77683 [Accessed 18 Dec. 2022].
39. Sahu, A. (2022). *Council post: Finding product-market fit in open-source business models.* Available at: https://www.forbes.com/sites/forbesfinancecouncil/2022/07/29/finding-product-market-fit-in-open-source-business-models/?sh=38865c457ae6 [Accessed 18 Dec. 2022].
40. Worsley, B. (2021). *No joke: Now is a great time to start a company.* Available at: https://medium.com/masterplans/no-joke-now-is-a-great-time-to-start-a-company-c95c7049df28 [Accessed 18 Dec. 2022].
41. Cook, J. (2021). *Six ways to go the extra mile for your customers.* Available at: https://www.forbes.com/sites/jodiecook/2021/03/08/six-ways-to-go-the-extra-mile-for-your-customers/?sh=63786d855fbc [Accessed 18 Dec. 2022].
42. Heim, A. (2021). *How pitch training can help start-ups get their story right.* Available at: https://techcrunch.com/2021/07/16/how-pitch-training-can-help-startups-get-their-story-right/ [Accessed 18 Dec. 2022].
43. Gleeson, B. (2021). *Why core values matter (and how to get your team excited about them).* Available at: https://www.forbes.com/sites/brentgleeson/2021/03/30/why-core-values-matter-and-how-to-get-your-team-excited-about-them/?sh=1aea00f74afd [Accessed 18 Dec. 2022].
44. Frost, A. (2019). *6 elevator pitch examples to inspire your own.* Available at: https://blog.hubspot.com/sales/elevator-pitch-examples [Accessed 18 Dec. 2022].
45. YEC (2022). *Leadership keys to help your team produce great results.* Available at: https://www.forbes.com/sites/theyec/2022/08/01/leadership-keys-to-help-your-team-produce-great-results/?sh=b6c6f1c642f3 [Accessed 18 Dec. 2022].
46. Cashdrop (2021). *Forbes EQ brandvoice: Keeping customers happy to grow your business.* Available at: https://www.forbes.com/sites/forbeseq/2021/03/10/keeping-customers-happy-to-grow-your-business/?sh=60ae575d9fdf [Accessed 18 Dec. 2022].
47. Carosa, C. (2020). *Why successful entrepreneurs need to be calculated risk takers.* Available at: https://www.forbes.com/sites/chriscaro-

sa/2020/08/07/why-successful-entrepreneurs-need-to-be-calculated-risk-takers/?sh=1ddff0102f5b [Accessed 18 Dec. 2022].

48. McKinsey (2020). *Business problem solving.* Available at: www.mckinsey.com/capabilities/strategy-and-corporate-finance/our-insights/six-problem-solving-mindsets-for-very-uncertain-times Accessed 18 Dec. 2022].
49. Indeed Career Guide (2021). *The 10 key components of a business model.* Available at: https://www.indeed.com/career-advice/career-development/components-of-a-business-model [Accessed 18 Dec. 2022].
50. Needle, F. (2022). *How to increase customer satisfaction, according to Hubspot experts.* Available at: https://blog.hubspot.com/service/how-to-increase-customer-satisfaction [Accessed 18 Dec. 2022].
51. Gibbons, S. (2021). *5 principles to keep your business thriving in 2021.* Available at: https://www.forbes.com/sites/serenitygibbons/2021/02/16/5-principles-to-keep-your-business-thriving-in-2021/?sh=4d66e0139765 [Accessed 18 Dec. 2022].
52. Crunchbase (n.d.). *StackBlitz - crunchbase company profile & funding.* Available at: https://www.crunchbase.com/organization/stackblitz [Accessed 18 Dec. 2022].
53. Swant, M. (2021). *The URL renaissance: Linktree raises $45 million to fuel 'link in bio' social commerce.* Available at: https://www.forbes.com/sites/martyswant/2021/03/25/the-url-renaissance-linktree-raises-45-million-to-fuel-link-in-bio-social-commerce/?sh=2fb8b34e649c [Accessed 18 Dec. 2022].
54. Wallen, J. (2018). *Ed-Tech firm preply announces european expansion after successful summer funding.* Available at: https://www.forbes.com/sites/joewalleneurope/2018/10/31/edtech-firm-preply-announces-european-expansion-after-successful-summer-funding/?sh=3899c44c7d47 [Accessed 18 Dec. 2022].
55. Konrad, A. (2021). *Oura's sleep-tracking ring raises $100 million to move further into personalized health.* Available at: https://www.forbes.com/sites/alexkonrad/2021/05/04/ouras-sleep-tracking-ring-raises-100-million-to-move-further-into-personalized-health/?sh=486b53d32be6 [Accessed 18 Dec. 2022].
56. Kagan, J. (2019). *PayPal.* Available at: https://www.investopedia.com/terms/p/paypal.asp [Accessed 18 Dec. 2022].
57. Folger, J. (2021). *Airbnb: Advantages and disadvantages.* Available at: https://www.investopedia.com/articles/personal-finance/032814/pros-and-cons-using-airbnb.asp [Accessed 18 Dec. 2022].

58. Johnston, M. (2019). *How does Alibaba make money?* Available at: https://www.investopedia.com/articles/investing/121714/how-does-alibaba-make-money-simple-guide.asp [Accessed 18 Dec. 2022].
59. Wu, A. (2019). *Tesla's got the keys: A history of its success.* Available at: https://www.investopedia.com/articles/personal-finance/061915/story-behind-teslas-success.asp [Accessed 18 Dec. 2022].
60. Oliveira, N. (2021). *Behind Ikea's success: The creation of approachable design.* Available at: https://medium.com/melted-design/behind-ikeas-success-the-creation-of-approachable-design-aa643e9c17df [Accessed 18 Dec. 2022].

CHAPTER 6
Right Marketing Strategy

Working with a solid marketing strategy[1] is something that many successful start-ups have done aptly. It can be tricky to identify the right strategies and implement them in the best way possible, but getting them right is essential. There are many types of marketing strategies that entrepreneurs can use for businesses, ranging from start-ups to large corporations. Some of the most common are direct marketing, viral marketing, guerrilla marketing, and word of mouth. Even when you've decided which strategy is ideal for your business, several factors can make or break the success of your campaign. And trust me, I am here to help you make it!

Marketing strategies are essential to your success: [2] you will go a long way with them. It can sometimes mean spending a lot of money on flashy ads or hiring expensive marketing firms. Sometimes, it can also suggest focusing on building a solid foundation through marketing strategies that will last, such as creating relevant content for your target audience and reaching out directly to people who might be interested in your product or service. The earlier you start investing[3] in your marketing strategy, the easier it'll be to get results. And once you have successfully built a customer base, there is no looking back. So, instead of dreaming up ideas and immediately starting work on development, sit down with a clear head and plan the marketing strategy you want to pursue. If you do so, it will put you ahead of dozens of other businesses that are only thinking about getting started without having any idea where they're going. It would help if you always appreciate the value of good marketing strategies - they can give you the edge in the marketplace to build a successful brand and your customer base. And this chapter will make that easy for you.

How To Know The Right Marketing Strategies?

As the saying goes, there are lies, damn lies, and statistics.[4] We've all experienced those times when we look at data to get a clear answer. That's not reality. Marketing is about finding the signal in a noisy world full of lies, damn lies, and statistics. There's so much data out there that we need more clarity on how to proceed. The right marketing strategies will give you the clarity you need! Knowing what marketing strategies to use is critical for success for small businesses[5] that need more resources, like giant corporations. It can be incredibly challenging if the company is new - there must be established best practices to follow. Start-ups may want to take advantage of many different marketing strategies at once. Still, they must develop a baseline knowledge of which will be most effective for their product or service before they invest too much time or money into any tactic. Being able to measure your success in a boisterous environment can be daunting. But by looking at your marketing and competitors' actions, you will find a clear picture that gives you an edge[6] over others in your field.

It would be best to determine how much of your marketing budget to spend on marketing strategies. It is pointless for anyone to give you a number because it depends on your business's nature, your budget's size, and what works for your audience. To get the most out of your marketing budget, you must first decide where and when to spend it. A good rule of thumb is to compare the amount of traffic you are getting from different platforms against each other and see which gets the most significant response rate. It can be easy to fall into the trap of using one marketing strategy for all your businesses. But in reality, companies have different needs and should, therefore, have different strategies.[7] For example, a clothing retailer will benefit from advertising in fashion magazines such as Vogue or Glamor. However, if you are a car manufacturer, the best place to advertise would be in a magazine like Popular Mechanics. Fashion magazines serve a different audience than Popular Mechanics. If you can sell your product after a while, you want an advertising strategy that keeps customers returning over time. It is a great way to build loyalty with customers and also helps you achieve repeat sales. On the other hand, if your product needs to be sold right away or the window of opportunity will pass, you want an advertisement[8] that shows people how to get what they want right now. This advertisement will immediately give people something to do, involving them in buying your product. Using both strategies as part of your overall marketing strategy would be best. Try to focus more on strategies that involve repeat sales[9] and building loyalty than on strategies that only work with pitching. I have written about how you can know the right marketing strategies by highlighting three dimensions. Firstly, I have discussed understanding enduring strategies. You will implement tested and reliable pathways if you know which strategies have worked for decades and will stay for good. Secondly, I have written about why you should look for strategies you can apply across markets. Some strategies work in various markets, and you must be aware of such strategies to make them big. Thirdly, I have written about the people or elements that drive market strategies. Knowing about the key players[10] will also help you a great deal in moving ahead with your start-up.

Understand Strategies That Transcend Time

One of the most exciting things about established brands is that they've been able to stay strong through constant evolution. Take Nike[11] as an example: it started by making shoes for runners and has since branched out into sportswear and a wide range of accessories. Other companies have done similar things and expanded their offerings, but Nike's story is an excellent example of why this growth strategy works. That's because it demonstrates that brands can continue to be relevant even when changing up what they offer, as long as they do it organically and with the same commitment[12] to quality as their original products. It is something new businesses can use as a model for their development. A good brand should make consumers want to buy your product because they know it will meet their needs, and it should also stand for something recognizable and valued by society. It's important to remember that this identity needs to evolve with time if you want to continue being successful. You need to keep up with the times, and you need to stay relevant. To keep your brand strong through the years, focus on consistently delivering good products and services, and be bold and expand into new areas. Just make sure you keep your brand's integrity intact by maintaining standards[13] in all you do.

Some marketing strategies transcend time. These have remained valid for years now. One such method is referred to as Pre-selling.[14] It involves creating an interest in the product or service before it hits the market. It happens when you see your product and how the market will receive it. When you pre-sell, you can determine if your product idea has a future and whether you can sell it before going into production. This method is best used with a group of people you already know, like friends, family, and colleagues. Gather them together in one place and start describing your idea[15] to them. If the people show enough interest, then you can use this to indicate that you are on the right track and move on to pre-selling to other groups of people. It involves gathering feedback from potential customers about the benefits they think your product or service will offer them and what price they would be willing to pay. This method uses focus groups to gauge customer reaction[16] before entering mass production. Another important aspect is branding. Branding is creating, communicating, and delivering value to your target audience. It defines your business identity through the words, images, sounds, and touchpoints you convey to your customers. The correct brand positioning[17] will help you determine your business goals and objectives. It will set your company apart from its competitors, create a specific place in the minds of consumers, and provide clear direction for all aspects of your marketing communication.[18]

Look For Strategies That Are Transferable Across Markets

As I have discussed earlier - to change your business's markets and approaches, you must be aware of marketing strategies that apply to various markets.[19] Three essential marketing strategies are product differentiation, market segmentation, and niche. Product differentiation[20] involves the development of products or services that are unique in some way from competitors. It can be as simple as a new product flavor or color that has been around for a while. It can also be as complex as an entirely different product category. Take, for example, the iPod shuffle. We all know that the iPod is a music player that stores songs on an external device. By removing the screen, Apple created a new product category (music players without screens) and integrated new technology (voice control) into its design. This differentiation led to its success over other brands and products. Product differentiation strategy has many advantages. The most significant advantage of this approach is that it enables the company to stand out from its competitors and differentiate itself from other companies. This way, the company can build brand equity, which makes the customer more loyal to that brand and entitles the company to charge higher prices and enjoy better profit margins. Focusing on existing customers also helps minimize marketing costs because it doesn't require heavy advertising. The more attractive benefits of one product will make consumers feel they made a good choice in buying it over another. When companies use differentiation, they can appeal to a much wider audience than if they were trying to match their competitors' offerings. They can also attract customers on the fence about buying. You must be careful about implementing this approach because it requires resources and time to implement correctly.

Market segmentation[21] is another strategy that can help start-ups to succeed. The market segmentation strategy is a technique companies use to identify their target markets and differentiate the products and services they offer to those markets. The main objective of this technique is to increase the market share of a company by making the company's products more appealing to the customers. This technique will help companies to understand their competitors, find profitable opportunities in the market, and develop strategies for their product or service offerings. It will also enable them to maintain a competitive advantage in the market, attract new customers, and retain old ones. One of the most significant benefits of market segmentation is that it will enable small companies to compete against large companies. These small companies can use this strategy to gain access to larger markets that are not accessible to small businesses with limited resources. Another benefit of this technique is that it helps companies focus on profitability rather than volume. Niche[22] is another dimension that allows start-ups to prosper. You don't need to be the biggest fish in the pond; you need to be the biggest fish in your pond. To succeed in business, you must understand and focus on what makes your business unique and different from all the others. Niche enables you to focus on a specific sector of the market, which helps you to do a better job for your clients and generate greater satisfaction. It is also known as targeting. There are many benefits of building a niche as a start-up. It allows you to grow on a smaller scale and focus on your product or service. By creating a niche, you can set yourself apart from your competitors and create an innovative product or service that will attract new customers. Your strategy for creating a niche should change over time as your company's needs change, but having the ability to move rapidly when necessary is an integral part of having business success.

Know Who Drives These Strategies

Marketing strategies are not the sole responsibility of entrepreneurs. Many people play vital roles in a company's marketing strategies. Entrepreneurs, especially those with little experience in marketing, often assume they are solely responsible for every marketing function in their business.[23] While they may be the most important players, they're certainly not the only ones involved. Many others help make marketing strategies a reality: the media and advertising[24] departments, customers, social media users, and competition. Your advertising teams and customers truly drive your marketing strategies. As a critical player in the communication process, a strong marketing department becomes an essential part of a successful business. For example, your marketing team[25] determines the kind of advertising that reaches the target audience. They decide where to place advertisements and how to implement them effectively. Your marketing team also tracks the effectiveness of each campaign and makes changes accordingly. In many cases, your customers are the driving force behind your marketing strategies. Through surveys and focus groups, your marketing department can determine the best way to appeal to potential customers based on their wants and needs (this I have discussed earlier). This process ensures that your company appeals to everyone interested in its products or services. It also allows you to keep your efforts distinct since many campaigns have overlapping target audiences.[26] As you plan for upcoming campaigns, remember that every element should be geared toward your audience's needs and interests, as well as the goals of your business. By understanding who your audience is and what they want from you, you can create a more successful strategy that increases profitability and brand awareness for years to come.

The other two crucial groups are social media users[27] and the competition[28] that affects your marketing strategies. Many consumers[29] will consult their friends and family before purchasing, and many rely on word-of-mouth communication when making a purchase decision. That's not just "any" word-of-mouth communication, either. It has to come from people who are active online. We've all seen it: someone who posts about every little thing that happens in their life on social media sites, whether going to lunch with friends or getting up at 4 a.m. for work. These people are the ones who tend to share the most information about themselves without even realizing it, and they're often the first people that come to mind when we need someone to ask for advice. People who post frequently have an audience, as well as an influence on that audience, so they're worth paying attention to when you're trying to build your base - and if you can get them posting about you, too, then you've got your foot in the door! As I mentioned, competition is the next force driving your marketing strategies. Hence, marketers must know their competitors' strengths, weaknesses, and overall plans. It will help them to create long-term business plans. For a business to develop an effective marketing strategy, it must first understand its competitors' approaches to the market and how they differ from its own. If two companies are selling similar products or services, they must each determine how they will differentiate themselves. Marketers need to be aware of any new competitors[29] entering the market and what they do to increase their products or service sales. They need to know how each competitor uses advertising, public relations, and brand management to develop strategies based on their unique strengths and weaknesses compared with other brands.

How Can The Right Strategies Help You?

If you're starting a business, chances are you've already decided to move forward in the face of uncertainty. You're going to start with a plan[30] and the hope that your business will succeed. However, if you're like most entrepreneurs, you're also aware that you can't control everything that happens. There will be setbacks and unexpected twists, but how you handle them, adapt, and move forward matters. You may already have a plan for when things go wrong—and even a few ideas about what could go right. But whether or not you've got those things covered yet, there's one thing that can help your business stay on track: marketing strategies. Just as the proper steps toward your destination help you to move ahead, the right marketing strategies are crucial for your start-up's progress. These keep your company moving forward, even when something unexpected happens. Marketing strategies will help guide your business through the rough patches, whether it's a technological glitch or a legal issue. Without them, you might have trouble staying on course as changes arise. Marketing strategies[31] are essential no matter what stage your business is in - from starting up to getting out of a slump - but they become increasingly important as your company grows and begins to depend on the revenue it brings in each month. As you embark on your journey to become a successful entrepreneur, it is essential to understand the importance of marketing strategies. It is how you position and distinguish your business from the competition.

There are various aspects of this process, such as identifying and evaluating[32] target markets, creating advertising messages that appeal to those markets, and establishing relationships with customers, clients, and other parties who will help spread the word about your business. The key to developing a sound marketing strategy is knowing your target market. It would be best if you had a detailed understanding of their wants and needs, as well as their limitations and possibilities. Focusing on the right people can save time and money on efforts that yield no results. Partnerships[33] are vital to spreading awareness about your business. However, you have to be careful about selecting partners who will do some good for your company rather than take advantage of you. Marketing strategies are essential in such cases. You need to pay attention to this aspect of the business to ensure progress. It means that clarity will be your companion. You may already have some ideas about these things. Still, it is better to be as clear and specific as possible when making this decision. Once you've figured out what you're looking for from a marketing strategy, you will quickly get one built. A good start for marketing is getting the word out about your new business or product. You can take advantage of free media like blogs and social media sites. If you are willing to spend some money on advertising, it can be effective if done correctly. By using creative ads, you can reach new customers while simultaneously giving them a reason to buy from you instead of a competitor. I have touched upon three aspects of how your marketing strategies can help you. Firstly, I have written about how it can enable you to identify whether your start-up is going in the desired direction. This certainty will empower you as an entrepreneur, and many decisions will fall into place. Secondly, I have written about how it will be beneficial for your company's transition if the need arises in the future. Changes in a company can be done for various reasons, and only with the most functional marketing strategies can you transition seamlessly. Thirdly, I have written how it will allow you to remain relevant despite growing demands. As every start-up or established company wishes to be noticeable till eternity, your company too can dream of achieving this with the appropriate marketing strategies.

To Know If Your Start-Up Is On The Right Track

Marketing strategies help you know whether your start-up is on the right track[34] or, quite the contrary, whether it needs some tweaking. By doing thorough research, you can easily understand what will work best for your product and service. The first step towards marketing is to research the market thoroughly and make an informed decision about your target audience. The main reason behind this is that research helps you identify your ideal customer profile, which will help you decide which mediums will be most effective for reaching out to them. Market research[35] also helps you know about the competitors already in the market and how much money they have spent on their marketing campaigns. It is easy to assume that you have a successful start-up on your hands when you are beginning a new company. However, most businesses fail within the first year (as discussed in my previous book), and of course, the last thing you want is to put your money and time into something that will not work. One of the reasons why start-ups succeed is that they understand the need to analyze their marketing strategy[36] and whether it is effective for them. To ensure that your start-up grows, you need to ensure that it uses effective marketing strategies. You need to understand the product or service you are selling clearly. You should also know why people buy your product instead of a competitor's. This information can help you position yourself in the market to gain a competitive advantage. If your start-up is an online business, it must be correctly optimized for search engines.[37]

Not only do you need to be able to trust your start-up's internal processes, but you also need to trust that the market will want your product.[38] You also have to believe that people will be interested in it and buy it. You can look ahead more confidently if you've saved some money and a decent amount of time before your seed money runs out. You can plan for the future as well as execute short-term goals. When you need clarification about any of these things, you can feel uncertain about everything, from how much marketing to do (if any) on a particular day to whether or not your customers will stick around once the initial hype settles down. You won't know what your company's future holds or if you're doing the right thing by staying with this strategy. It can cause second-guessing.[39] When you implement the right marketing strategies and know that your start-up is doing fine, you can plan securely. Strategic planning[40] is crucial to success in any sector, and the start-up world is no exception. As an entrepreneur, you're constantly bombarded with information you need to process and keep track of to make intelligent business decisions. And this is where the most relevant marketing strategies can help your start-up prosper.

To Transition Better, If Ever You Need To

Your start-up can transition[41] better if you have the best marketing strategies. One of the best ways to prevent a company from completely crashing and burning is to provide consistency. Consistency[42] in your marketing strategy ensures growth. When you are starting up, it is easy to get caught up in the excitement of a business and make decisions without thinking them through. You want people to notice you, and you want results right away. It can cause you to make mistakes, making your business crash and burn if they need to be corrected quickly enough. Hence, marketing strategies should be simple and effective, especially in the beginning. The more complicated they are, the less likely you will be able to maintain consistency in them. While you may have found a genius way to promote your business, if no one else knows about it or how to do it, then it is useless because no one else has been taught how to do it either. Having consistency across the board would be best when something requires change. Changes[43] can happen quickly, and consistency in strategies is integral here. It can also benefit a company if there is an underlying plan if things go awry. It will allow the company to transition gracefully even if things go differently than planned or if an idea does not work out as well as expected.

When you want to take a different path for your start-up than initially planned, your marketing strategies will come in handy. You will likely change your business model along the way, which can be a good thing. It would be helpful if you have an idea and, as you move forward, you see another opportunity that would fit your current plan or be better than what you first thought. Growing[44] a company is hard work—you need to be able to adapt and change your strategy as you go along. When starting, you might have a specific plan, whether creating a new product that fits perfectly into a niche market or expanding your business's services. But as you get deeper into the process, plans can change. New opportunities may arise that could be more lucrative than what you had initially set out to do. Having marketing strategies in place will help you make these decisions quickly and easily. It is essential to keep in mind that no matter the decision, a successful business relies on marketing. You cannot market if you do not know who listens to your message[45] and how to reach them. Hence, marketing strategies are essential to implement and maintain even if your start-up needs changes. You should evaluate your marketing goals, develop a proper plan for your company, and set up a timetable for each purpose.

To Remain Relevant Even With Growing Demands

Your company will remain relevant with the right marketing strategies, especially with the growing industry and market demands.[46] It is imperative to your success that you stay on top of all the latest trends and developments. If a new product hits the market or a celebrity endorses a competitor, you must be aware and ready to act. Marketing is an expense, but it's an investment in your company that will reap dividends for years. Your customers are constantly changing and evolving, so it's your job to change along with them. Marketing involves much more than just advertising or selling. The key to increased sales is being aware of everything around you and adjusting[47] accordingly. No matter what industry your company is in, it is vital to keep up with the current trends. Businesses are constantly growing and expanding to meet their customers' needs better. Pay attention to the growing industry[48] and market demands, as these can impact your company. To stay relevant, you will need a marketing strategy. Before making changes, you must know what's happening to avoid damaging your brand.

Marketing is the lifeblood[49] of any business, and a start-up is no exception. Even though the idea was born out of a vision, it needs to be marketed effectively to make it a living, breathing entity that can attract customers and serve them sustainably. It's not enough that you offer an excellent product - you need to market it so that your target audience recognizes its value and takes notice. Selling your brand well will help you start right and ensure visibility, regardless of changing times or other circumstances. For instance, if you are running a successful business of making paper balloons, you should be able to differentiate your product from others and make it more attractive to your customers. You can do this by using the latest design patterns on your balloons or adding new features that appeal to your target customers. Your sales can increase manifold when all these factors work in your favor. Good marketing is about more than just finding the right keywords for your website and posting to the appropriate social media sites. As I mentioned, you could do better marketing for a small business; your customers and others do it. Many successful small businesses still need a physical location. Thus, marketing helps an unknown company make itself known and keeps an established business relevant in the minds of its customer base. Once the marketing strategy has been established, stay relevant and up-to-date with the ever-changing business environment.[50] A review should occur annually (preferably more often) to ensure that changes have been identified and adjustments can be made when necessary. Changes may occur within the marketing environment due to new competitors, technologies, regulations, or economic factors. Whatever the reasons for change, you can review the business environment. It will help you if you need to adjust the marketing strategy.

Why Is Maximizing The Effects Significant?

The success of a company and its product can often be attributed to the successful marketing strategies of the company. When a new business launches, the founders focus on making the product and figuring out how you will use it. Much time goes into perfecting the product and getting it out there. When this is done, marketing can take over, but how do you successfully market your product? Often, a company's success can be attributed to its marketing campaign. A great example of this is Apple Inc.'s iPhone 5s/5c. The 5c was marketed as the cheaper alternative to the 5s, but in reality, they were both very similar products with little difference. People were still willing to buy the 5s because Apple's marketing team told everyone it was better than the 5c. The power of sustaining marketing effects[51] cannot be understated. It's vital to get your product out there and get people to know about it so that you can make as much money as possible. Even if your product is an improvement on an already existing one, you need to market yourself for people to have any interest in your product. How successful a business is in its infancy depends largely upon how well its products are sold and how well they sustain favorable marketing outcomes.

One aspect many businesses overlook[52] in marketing is how easily their success could be increased with little effort. In most cases, a business owner will have yet to learn if their marketing strategy or technique could have been even more successful if they had just tried harder or put more time into it. Various methods can achieve marketing success, but all require high involvement and attention to detail. The work that goes into your marketing strategies is essential because it will make all of the difference in the success of your business. But how do you know that you are doing enough work to guarantee the maximum effect from your efforts? It is where ultimate impact evaluation comes in handy. When evaluating a marketing strategy's effectiveness, you're trying to gauge whether or not it's worth keeping around. And if it is, then sustaining it is even a wiser decision. It can also help you anticipate what might work in the future so you can plan accordingly and have a better shot at success. It can be imperative when the strategy is an annual campaign. For example, if you know that some of your ads are drawing more attention than others, you can arrange for more of those ads to appear to get the most out of them while they're still relevant. More so, you can keep them in autopilot launch mode. I have elaborated on three reasons why maximizing the effects of marketing strategies is significant. First, it enables your start-up to evolve into a stable company. When you sustain[53] and maximize the impact of your solid marketing strategies, you are more likely to make it big in the industry by expanding your company in the following years. Second, it helps your company to diversify its products and services as it grows. Sustaining customer relationships takes work when you change the features of your products and services. The effects of marketing strategies help you in this regard. Third, it helps your start-up team to take care of other company objectives. When your marketing strategies are in place and in autopilot mode, you can take care of other significant aspects of your business.

To Let Your Start-Up Evolve Into A Stable Company

If you want your start-up to become stable in just a few years, sustain the best marketing strategies and implement them repeatedly.[54] Relying on some of the best marketing strategies over the years will help you achieve your purpose and stabilize your business. Marketing a business is like maintaining a car. It's essential to keep your vehicle in good condition to serve you for a long time. The same goes for your business. It would be best if you marketed it well to keep it strong for as long as possible. If you do not sell your business well and do not maintain it, you will see your profits fall while your expenses rise at an alarming rate. Not only that, but you will also find yourself scrambling to try and improve things when there is still time. Hence, it pays to look at what marketing is all about, how you can apply the right strategies to make your brand known, respected, and reputable, and how you can sustain your brand for many years to come instead of letting it lose steam in just no time.

Some of the best start-ups have quickly become established companies because of their solid marketing strategies. For example, in the early days, Airbnb[55] positioned itself as an alternative to the hotel industry by providing a more local and friendly experience, even though Airbnb hosts mostly rented out spare rooms in their own homes. But the company realized this was getting them nowhere, so they decided to change course and market themselves as offering a unique travel experience to people who wanted to use something other than a hotel. And we know where Airbnb is right now. When it comes to marketing, the power of compounding is significant for businesses of all sizes. It allows you to build a foundation for future success and move toward your goals steadily. The power of compounding applies to solid strategies in the same way it applies to investment strategies. It would be best to start with a solid foundation and then build upon it. Otherwise, you're just throwing money away. Small businesses must focus on creating similar foundations with their marketing strategies. Instead of jumping from one thing to the next to find something that works, companies need to look at their current situation and develop a strategy to help them progress over time. Even if they have to take baby steps along the way, those steps are better than not. Creating an effective marketing strategy is all about planning and knowing what you'll do down the road. That's why new businesses must figure out where they want to be in five years and what they need to do daily. The more concrete your objectives are, the better your chances for success will be down the road!

To Enhance Or Diversify Offerings With Growth

The importance of marketing strategies is something business owners are well aware of. The initial step in any business plan is developing a marketing strategy to help generate revenue, establish brand identity, and create a customer base. Having a marketing strategy in place gives you the confidence to carry out your objectives without worrying about losing customers.[56] When you've established your marketing strategies, you can be sure that your customers will identify with your brand. It allows you to diversify products and services, which in turn will help your business survive the market's ups and downs. Business owners know the importance of diversifying their products and services to avoid unnecessary risks. However, it is sometimes hard to find a new product or service that would benefit the company and its customers without causing harm. Some businesses need to make better decisions so they retain market share. Fortunately, when your marketing strategies are in place, you can be sure that your customers will identify with your brand. It allows you to diversify products and services, which in turn will help your business survive the market's ups and downs.

Many companies have just changed their products and maintained their marketing best practices. And this has helped them a great deal. For instance, Colgate started making just toothpaste, but then they moved to a variety of other oral care products like toothbrushes, mouthwash, and dental floss. Apple used to make computers and mobile phones, but now they also make watches, music players, and tablets. Dell started as a computer manufacturing company but produced all kinds of electronics, such as monitors and printers. Gillette started selling razors but has since diversified into shaving gels, aftershaves, and even hair removal products for women. Google started as an internet search engine but later started offering web-based email services, office software, and even operating systems for mobile devices (Android). Trying to get your product noticed amongst the other products in the same category is easy if you have the best marketing practices. It means finding new ways or sustaining the proven ones to promote your product or service. Maintaining your marketing best practices[57] will attract more customers. Another year of business means another year of customer service and marketing. Even if you don't have to consider how many customers you're attracting, you still have to consider their experience with you and your company. If people are happy, they will repurchase your products or services and tell their friends and family what a fantastic experience they had with your products and services.

Hence, if you're investing in your business long-term, stay up-to-date on the best practices for attracting customers.

To Help You Focus On Other Goals

The best way to grow a business is by focusing on everyday operations and marketing efforts to grow your business quickly. However, looking at other ways to market your business is essential. The marketing strategy is an ideal way to allow you to shift your attention to other aspects of your business, such as customer support, product development, etc. Marketing is a cyclical process, and planning is one of its critical components. With this, it becomes easier to succeed in the business world. Marketing planning involves creating a strategy that supports your business vision and helps you achieve your organizational goals. If you have marketing strategies, you can easily focus on other things. Not only will you be able to focus on the different aspects of your business, but your customers will also benefit from finding your products and services quickly. By having your marketing strategies planned out and ready, you will be able to make more money and gain more customers.

Automating your marketing plans[58] is something you should consider if you want to focus on other dimensions of your start-up. If you're like most entrepreneurs, you only have a little free time to pour into your business. Like all entrepreneurs, you want to do the things that will give you the most significant return on your investment, so when it comes to marketing, you want to focus on activities that connect with the right customers and work for your business. The problem is, there's an overwhelming amount of different things you can do to market your business - and it can take a lot of work to know which ones are worth the time and effort. Many new entrepreneurs need help to keep up with the marketing aspects of their business because they're so focused on research and development. If you have a tight budget for staffing, it makes sense to automate your marketing efforts[59] so that you can free up your time and energy for other aspects of the business. With the right tools, you can set things in motion and take care of these tasks at a later date or even regularly without worrying about them needing your attention immediately. If you have little money to hire an outside firm or pay for outside help, investing in high-quality automation tools can be just as beneficial as spending money on hiring an agency or consultant. You'll still be able to invest in marketing without having to keep track of everything yourself.

Companies That Mastered Marketing Strategies

Red Bull

Red Bull[60] has established an image of a company that excels in marketing strategies. They have successfully changed the common perception of energy drinks from a soft drink to a necessity for a person wishing to stay energized throughout the day or during different activities. Red Bull is known to be one of the most commercial companies in the world. Red Bull from Thailand inspires the Red Bull drink, whose slogan is "Red Bull gives you wings." There are many strategies that Red Bull uses to maintain its popularity. Red Bull uses extreme sports and social networking sites to better its public image and promote its products. The company also uses celebrity athletes to promote its company and its products. They advertise themselves through commercials and different events with other companies as well. For example, Red Bull and Monster Energy teamed up for a summer tour. These two companies could reach out to thousands of people interested in either one or both of those drinks by having them travel across the country and hold competitions such as BMX bike riding. It is an example of how they can get people to try their product because they are trying it out while doing something they enjoy. Red Bull has succeeded in making their product seem necessary for an active lifestyle and promoted their development to everyday people as well.

Company Name: Red Bull

Founded: 1987

Significant reason(s) for success: The company collaborates with the most fitting industries to make its product attractive. It has been able to maintain an outstanding market presence by doing so.

Toyota

Toyota[61] has ruled the market with its strategic planning since its inception. Toyota quickly surpassed Ford and General Motors as the leading car manufacturer in Japan. Even today, Toyota's management philosophy heavily influences what they cater to. They focus on meeting customer demands instead of setting up a marketing strategy alone. Although they have been criticized for being too conservative and lacking innovation, their focus on customer demands has been one of the key strengths that have allowed them to be successful in the automobile industry. Toyota was founded in 1937 by Kiichiro Toyoda, who manufactured automatic looms for Japan's clothing industry. Sakichi was always able to implement many innovative ideas that would become crucial parts of Toyota's strategic planning process. Toyota's early success was mainly due to its focus on producing small cars instead of larger, more expensive ones like other auto manufacturers did at the time. This decision has allowed them to pull ahead of the pack and remain there for decades. It also helped establish its reputation as a company that makes quality automobiles for people with modest budgets but still looking for reliable transportation options.

Company Name: Toyota

Founded: 1937

Significant reason(s) for success: The company has remained one of the most sought-after in its industry by offering the best to customers every decade. Its presence in the market syncs with what it offers.

Udacity

Udacity[62] is another company that has made it big. Sebastian Thrun, David Stavens, and Mike Sokolsky founded it. Sebastian has won awards for his science and technology work and was the Stanford Artificial Intelligence Laboratory director. He's also an expert in robotics and Google X's director of self-driving cars. As the founder of Udacity, he and his co-founders created an online Artificial Intelligence class in 2011 to help make education more accessible. This course brought in

200,000 registered students from 190 different countries. The company started with a single class but now offers more than 300 courses, including analytics, web development, and Android development. The classes have received praise from people from all different backgrounds. Even though Udacity courses are free, around 15% of students continue onto the second term, which is priced - this is where Udacity makes its profits. Udacity also has a high completion rate. It has been able to offer some of the most sought-after courses. More than anything else, it has marketed itself extremely well and has been able to attract users from all over the world. It currently has more than 1.6 million users and has carved a name for itself in the online world of educational courses.

Company Name: Udacity

Founded: 2011

Significant reason(s) for success: The company focuses on differentiation as far as its courses are concerned. It knows how to stay relevant in an ever-growing industry.

DraftKings

DraftKings[63] is one of the most innovative companies, according to many in the sector. DraftKings is a company that has truly revolutionized the fantasy sports industry. Since its inception in 2012, DraftKings has dominated the industry and improved every aspect of its business to provide a more robust and user-friendly product than any other fantasy sports provider. DraftKings was founded in 2012 by Jason Robins, Matt Kalish, and Paul Liberman. The three entrepreneurs created a company based on their love of fantasy sports. The idea was to create a platform where users could play daily fantasy sports games for money. Few entrepreneurs had explored the concept before, so the founders knew they would need to take significant risks to ensure success. DraftKings grew into one of the world's fastest-growing tech start-ups. It was because of hard work and perseverance. The three founders began by launching a beta version of their website in February 2012. They also spent that year raising funds to hire employees, open office space, and start marketing their new business. DraftKings is a company that has gone from nothing to funding rounds of more than $600 million. The company has grown since its founding and now hosts millions of users. It has had an impressive take on marketing strategies and has established itself as a significant company in the industry.

Company Name: DraftKings

Founded: 2012

Significant reason(s) for success: The company has made it big by being focused on its offerings. It has consistently appealed to users by repeatedly using strategies that have worked well.

Zenefits

In just a short time, Zenefits[64] has become a leading industry name. They've developed a competitive edge in the market that other insurance brokers can't compete with. Zenefits is a company that offers free benefits and HR software to its users. The software allows companies to streamline their benefits by using technology. In addition to facilitating its benefits, Zenefits offers payroll services and health insurance quotes. They have annual revenue of $400 million USD and 500 employees. Zenefits was founded in 2013 by Parker Conrad and Laks Srini. Since then, it has become one of Silicon Valley's hottest start-ups because of its innovative approach to HR software and unique value proposition. The company has seen tremendous growth over the past few years, which can be attributed to its strong branding and marketing strategies. As a company, they excel in marketing strategies that have solidified their lead over others. For instance, they have succeeded with "growth hacking," which involves implementing extra marketing techniques to accelerate business growth. One way they've achieved this is by using social media as an advertising platform. It has been incredibly effective for them because of its low cost and high volume. It's low cost because there is no money involved, and its high volume because people use social media all the time! To implement this strategy, they made their blog posts catchy and exciting enough to share, exposing them to thousands of potential customers. The company also offers attractive referral bonuses to those who get friends and family to sign up for Zenefits. It incentivizes users to share the platform with others to make some extra cash! Zenefits has also been effective in its use of content marketing. They can produce quality content consistently via their blog, which drives traffic back to the website and increases leads for the sales team. In 2022, TriNet acquired Zenefits.

Company Name: Zenefits

Founded: 2013

Significant reason(s) for success: The company makes a vital job easy for people. It focuses on authenticity and knows the right marketing strategies to appeal to customers.

TripCandy

TripCandy[65] is a crypto-based travel start-up that's seen success in a notoriously tricky industry. It's easy to think of TripCandy as a travel company, but it's much more. Founded by Jeremy Foo, TripCandy has been hailed as a great example of a start-up that started small and made it big with the right marketing strategies apart of many other things. The team's focus helped it raise funding for expansion and make its name known across the country. TripCandy is a company revolutionizing travel planning through social media and technology. TripCandy is a fantastic service that helps you and your business travel better with your crypto. They collect the best travel deals and share them with you, but they also provide tips to help you travel more effectively and save you time. They allow you to plan trips by suggesting activities and points of interest relevant to your niche based on your personal preferences. The most valuable part is that they streamline finding flights, hotels, and vacation packages. Since they're all in one place, you can spend fewer hours going from site to site like you would with traditional search engines. TripCandy is an invaluable tool for those who travel often. As someone with a busy schedule, there are few opportunities to get away from work

- but with TripCandy, you can easily plan a trip for any occasion: family vacations, business trips, or even a staycation in your city. It's up to you!

Company Name: TripCandy

Founded: 2021

Significant reason(s) for success: The company knows how to appeal to customers and ensures convenience for its users.

EcoCart

EcoCart[66] is another company you can learn business and marketing strategies from. EcoCart is a local organic food delivery service that started in 2019 and has since expanded to many places. The goal of EcoCart when it was founded was to help people fight climate change, and it has been accomplished significantly since its inception. They've set an example for other companies using technology to increase efficiency, reduce waste, and be socially responsible. They have some innovative strategies in EcoCart's success isn't surprising, given its innovative approach to business. The company has helped many customers to calculate ecological footprints and make sustainable decisions while buying products. It has revolutionized the mindset of many consumers across the globe. It is due to its unique approach to the issue of climate change. EcoCart is a company that knows how to market itself. They have created an image that fits precisely with the idea of their target audience in all their marketing material. They make their visions clear with every online presence. Customers know what they're signing up for when they use EcoCart's services. What they want to share with the world resonates with many global conversations, contributing to their rapid growth. They also have a prominent presence through advertising, making it easy to find them online.

Company Name: EcoCart

Founded: 2019

Significant reason(s) for success: The company resonates with a significant crisis of the present time. It has marketed its vision well and has grown significantly.

Conclusion

If the mountain doesn't come to Peter, then Peter must go to the mountain. It means you will need help to achieve your goals and dreams. It is why knowing how to market your own company is so important. You've probably heard of big companies like Nike, Pepsi, and Apple. They've all achieved great success because they had a carefully planned marketing strategy that worked. And now they're huge! But how? It wasn't a miracle; they worked hard and created an effective marketing plan. They learned how to make their brands stand out in a crowd of competitors. They knew how to appeal to their target audiences effectively and created winning strategies that led them to success.

Knowing how your company will present itself to the world and how you will get the word out about what your company does is essential. You must do whatever it takes to identify strategies that will work for your company. Many start-ups have gone under because they needed to market themselves correctly. If your product is what people can use, promoting your product as widely and cheaply as possible makes sense. If your product is something people buy once (like clothing), it may be more effective to put ads in stores where those clothes are sold. You could try many different strategies depending on what your business does! As an entrepreneur, you should consider marketing strategies as signposts to success. A successful marketing strategy focuses on the audience and how to reach them in the most effective way possible. It also focuses on your business objectives; you must align the strategies to achieve your goals. A solid marketing strategy will guarantee a successful start-up and help provide a solid foundation from which to grow big. As I have done for other chapters, I will summarize what I have discussed in this chapter so that you can refer to it whenever you need. Remember to highlight these pointers and come back to them often to master marketing strategies for your start-up.

1. Remember that marketing strategies fuel your start-up; the better the quality, the more distance it will cover.
2. Identifying the right marketing strategies is crucial for any business, start-ups included.

3. Focus on strategies that stay relevant across time.
4. Embrace marketing strategies that apply to various markets while expanding a start-up.
5. Identify the people who drive market strategies. They are the ones you need to most to master and sustain these.
6. The right marketing strategies can help you as an entrepreneur by guaranteeing success for your start-up.
7. These enable you to know which track your start-up is on and whether it is the right way ahead.
8. The appropriate strategies will help your start-up transition better if the need arises.
9. Marketing strategies are your best tools if you want your company to remain relevant despite growing demands.
10. Maximizing the effects of these strategies ensures performance and sustainability for your company.
11. It means that your start-up will soon evolve into a stable company.
12. It will boost your confidence to diversify offerings with growth, helping you to sustain your existing customer base and market presence.
13. The best marketing strategies and their sustenance will help you focus on other goals of your start-up, allowing room for better prospects.

References

1. UserGuiding (2021). *15 fundamental start-up marketing strategies + examples and ideas.* Available at: https://userguiding.com/blog/marketing-startup/ [Accessed 22 Dec. 2022].
2. Dearsley, B. (2021). *8 start-up marketing ideas that actually work [+ examples].* Available at: https://blog.hubspot.com/marketing/startup-marketing [Accessed 22 Dec. 2022].
3. Bina, A. (2018). *Five essential marketing strategies for any start-up.* Available at: https://www.forbes.com/sites/forbesagencycouncil/2018/05/30/five-essential-marketing-strategies-for-any-startup/?sh=393906505795 [Accessed 22 Dec. 2022].
4. Anderson, H. (2022). *The numbers can lie: When data stifles strategy.* Available at: https://www.forbes.com/sites/forbesagencycouncil/2022/01/03/

the-numbers-can-lie-when-data-stifles-strategy/?sh=5fa50e345b2e [Accessed 22 Dec. 2022].

5. Boyarsky, K. (2022). *26 ideas for your 2020 small business marketing strategy*. Available at: https://blog.hubspot.com/marketing/small-business-marketing-guide [Accessed 22 Dec. 2022].
6. Wijayasinha, R. (2020). *How to start marketing your start-up or small business*. Available at: https://www.forbes.com/sites/forbescommunicationscouncil/2020/05/28/how-to-start-marketing-your-startup-or-small-business/?sh=5bdbfb486db3 [Accessed 22 Dec. 2022].
7. Houraghan, S. (2020). *5 brands with the best marketing strategies*. Available at: https://brandmasteracademy.com/brands-with-best-marketing-strategies/ [Accessed 22 Dec. 2022].
8. Wijayasinha, R. (2022). *Five tips for picking your start-up's marketing channels*. Available at: https://www.forbes.com/sites/forbescommunicationscouncil/2022/09/16/five-tips-for-picking-your-startups-marketing-channels/?sh=50da6972fc96 [Accessed 22 Dec. 2022].
9. Leighton, N. (2022). *7 ways leading companies boost repeat sales*. Available at: https://www.entrepreneur.com/growing-a-business/7-ways-leading-companies-boost-repeat-sales/430917 [Accessed 22 Dec. 2022].
10. Kastenholz, C. (2021). *The importance of influencer marketing in the 'new normal' digital sphere*. Available at: https://www.forbes.com/sites/forbesagencycouncil/2021/03/02/the-importance-of-influencer-marketing-in-the-new-normal-digital-sphere/?sh=61bf61341448 [Accessed 22 Dec. 2022].
11. Garrett Moon (2016). *Nike marketing strategy: A guide to selling benefits and not products*. Available at: https://coschedule.com/blog/nike-marketing-strategy [Accessed 22 Dec. 2022].
12. Ellevate (2020). *Culture matters: How great start-ups will thrive in 2020*. Available at: https://www.forbes.com/sites/ellevate/2020/02/11/culture-matters-how-great-startups-will-thrive-in-2020/?sh=f21435c7c76d [Accessed 22 Dec. 2022].
13. Bothe, B. (2020). *Building brand integrity through ESG reporting*. Available at: https://www.forbes.com/sites/forbesagencycouncil/2020/08/28/building-brand-integrity-through-esg-reporting/?sh=1942a09c5369 [Accessed 22 Dec. 2022].
14. Riani, A. (2021). *Why running presales is becoming industry-standard for start-ups*. Available at: https://www.forbes.com/sites/abdoriani/2021/10/30/why-running-presales-is-becoming-industry-stander-for-startups/?sh=4fc3a957e751 [Accessed 22 Dec. 2022].

15. Darley, L. (2017). *The 'lightbulb' moment for entrepreneurs: Finding clarity and curiosity.* Available at: https://www.forbes.com/sites/forbescoachescouncil/2017/02/03/the-lightbulb-moment-for-entrepreneurs-finding-clarity-and-curiosity/?sh=56050b6752fa [Accessed 22 Dec. 2022].
16. Anjoran, R. (2019). *Why a pilot run before mass production is helpful.* Available at: https://www.agiliantech.com/blog/pilot-run-before-mass-production-helpful/ [Accessed 22 Dec. 2022].
17. Kraus, N. (2022). *The how and why of developing a brand positioning strategy.* Available at: https://www.forbes.com/sites/forbesagencycouncil/2022/10/06/the-how-and-why-of-developing-a-brand-positioning-strategy/?sh=6fb6b7bf1af3 [Accessed 22 Dec. 2022].
18. Wijayasinha, R. (2022). *What corporate marketing can learn from start-up marketing.* Available at: https://www.forbes.com/sites/forbesbusinesscouncil/2022/01/10/what-corporate-marketing-can-learn-from-start-up-marketing/?sh=75a7d64a6cf6 [Accessed 22 Dec. 2022].
19. Woschnick, V. (2022). *Top 10 most effective marketing strategies for B2B and B2C.* Available at: https://www.weidert.com/blog/most-effective-marketing-strategies [Accessed 22 Dec. 2022].
20. Kopp, C. M. (2021). *Product differentiation.* Available at: https://www.investopedia.com/terms/p/product_differentiation.asp [Accessed 22 Dec. 2022].
21. Tarver, E. (2022). *Market segmentation.* Available at: https://www.investopedia.com/terms/m/marketsegmentation.asp [Accessed 22 Dec. 2022].
22. Kontozopoulos, H. (2022). *How to find your start-up's niche.* at: https://www.entrepreneur.com/starting-a-business/how-to-find-your-startups-niche/424748 [Accessed 22 Dec. 2022].
23. Musayev, S. (2022). *Researching and marketing in the early stages of entrepreneurship.* Available at: https://www.forbes.com/sites/forbesbusinesscouncil/2022/10/05/researching-and-marketing-in-the-early-stages-of-entrepreneurship/?sh=242d94781a74 [Accessed 22 Dec. 2022].
24. Moorman, C., Ryan, M. & Tavassoli, N. (2022). *Why marketers are returning to traditional advertising.* Available at: https://hbr.org/2022/04/why-marketers-are-returning-to-traditional-advertising [Accessed 22 Dec. 2022].
25. Wijayasinha, R. (2022). *Five tips for building a start-up marketing team.* [online] Forbes. Available at: https://www.forbes.com/sites/forbescommunicationscouncil/2022/06/01/five-tips-for-building-a-startup-marketing-team/?sh=556fbe377f44 [Accessed 22 Dec. 2022].

26. Carmicheal, K. (2020). *How to find your target audience.* Available at: https://blog.hubspot.com/marketing/target-audience [Accessed 22 Dec. 2022].
27. Barysevich, A. (2020). *How social media influence 71% consumer buying decisions.* Available at: https://www.searchenginewatch.com/2020/11/20/how-social-media-influence-71-consumer-buying-decisions/ [Accessed 22 Dec. 2022].
28. Grinnell, C. (2022). *Marketers: Here's why it's important to pay attention to the competition.* Available at: https://www.forbes.com/sites/forbesagencycouncil/2022/04/01/marketers-heres-why-its-important-to-pay-attention-to-the-competition/?sh=5ab1dec075ef [Accessed 22 Dec. 2022].
29. Marketing Charts (2020). *Friends and family still the most trusted sources of brand information.* Available at: https://www.marketingcharts.com/cross-media-and-traditional/word-of-mouth-113276 [Accessed 22 Dec. 2022].
30. Ferriolo, J. (2021). *Seven sections your business plan should have.* Available at: https://www.forbes.com/sites/forbesbusinessdevelopmentcouncil/2021/08/27/seven-sections-your-business-plan-should-have/?sh=2e3442101310 [Accessed 22 Dec. 2022].
31. YEC (2022). *Marketing through the various stages of your business.* Available at: https://www.forbes.com/sites/theyec/2022/05/18/marketing-through-the-various-stages-of-your-business/?sh=43464b0d36a9 [Accessed 22 Dec. 2022].
32. Indeed (2022). *Target market analysis: What it is and how to make one.* Available at: https://www.indeed.com/career-advice/career-development/target-market-analysis [Accessed 22 Dec. 2022].
33. Forbes (2021). *14 tips for launching a successful partnership marketing campaign.* Available at: https://www.forbes.com/sites/forbesagencycouncil/2021/03/18/14-tips-for-launching-a-successful-partnership-marketing-campaign/?sh=3677ce8d2ee9 [Accessed 22 Dec. 2022].
34. Krommenhoek, B. (2020). *Put your start-up on the right track in 30 days.* Available at: https://medium.com/swlh/put-your-startup-on-the-right-track-in-30-days-913a91353eeb [Accessed 22 Dec. 2022].
35. Cint (2022). *Why market research is important | Benefits of market research.* Available at: https://www.cint.com/blog/why-market-research-is-important [Accessed 22 Dec. 2022].
36. Ahern, P. (2017). *How to run a marketing strategy analysis [+ rebuild your marketing efforts].* Available at: https://inter-growth.co/marketing-strategy-analysis/ [Accessed 22 Dec. 2022].

37. Forbes (2020). *12 actionable tips for search engine optimization novices.* Available at: https://www.forbes.com/sites/forbesagencycouncil/2020/02/18/12-actionable-tips-for-search-engine-optimization-novices/?sh=221c2b56360f [Accessed 22 Dec. 2022].
38. Fit Small Business (2018). *How to market a product in 5 steps.* Available at: https://fitsmallbusiness.com/how-to-market-a-product/ [Accessed 22 Dec. 2022].
39. Forbes (2021). *How to stop second-guessing yourself and trust your decisions as a leader.* Available at: https://www.forbes.com/sites/melodywilding/2021/02/22/how-to-stop-second-guessing-yourself-and-trust-your-decisions-as-a-leader/?sh=5a2f93c11d15 [Accessed 22 Dec. 2022].
40. Livemint (2022). *Marketing strategies for start-ups: 5 tactics that actually work.* Available at: https://www.livemint.com/brand-stories/marketing-strategies-for-startups-5-tactics-that-actually-work-11666015836095.html [Accessed 22 Dec. 2022].
41. Abdullah, E. (2021). *How to transition your business from a start-up to a mid-sized company.* Available at: https://www.forbes.com/sites/forbesbusinesscouncil/2021/10/22/how-to-transition-your-business-from-a-startup-to-a-mid-sized-company/?sh=d11948417315 [Accessed 22 Dec. 2022].
42. Wong, J. (2022). *Why consistency is vital to your branding efforts.* Available at: https://www.entrepreneur.com/starting-a-business/why-consistency-is-vital-to-your-branding-efforts/425791 [Accessed 22 Dec. 2022].
43. Start-up Buzz (2022). *5 tips to keep your business running smoothly – start-up buzz.* Available at: https://startup-buzz.com/5-tips-to-keep-your-business-running-smoothly/ [Accessed 22 Dec. 2022].
44. Shaikh, K. (2021). *Growing a company is hard: Turning around a grown-up company is harder.* Available at: https://www.forbes.com/sites/forbesbusinesscouncil/2021/05/25/growing-a-company-is-hard-turning-around-a-grown-up-company-is-harder/?sh=118527ec4c18 [Accessed 22 Dec. 2022].
45. Pandey, R. (2022). *How actively listening to your customers can help your start-up grow.* Available at: https://inc42.com/resources/how-actively-listening-to-your-customers-can-help-your-startup-grow/ [Accessed 22 Dec. 2022].
46. Startuplab, T. T. (2022). *Start-up trends: Top 7 trending sectors that are expected to boom in 2022.* Available at: https://thestartuplab.in/startup-trends-top-7-trending-sectors-that-are-expected-to-boom-in-2022/ [Accessed 22 Dec. 2022].

47. Welsh, T. J. (2020). *Three tips for quickly adjusting your online marketing strategy.* Available at: https://www.forbes.com/sites/forbescommunicationscouncil/2020/04/28/three-tips-for-quickly-adjusting-your-online-marketing-strategy/?sh=7617e9fc68ec [Accessed 22 Dec. 2022].
48. Forbes (2022). *13 industry experts predict rising business tech trends of 2023.* Available at: https://www.forbes.com/sites/forbestechcouncil/2022/12/16/13-industry-experts-predict-rising-business-tech-trends-of-2023/?sh=1209b3f7f310 [Accessed 22 Dec. 2022].
49. Yohn, D. L. (2019). *Marketing matters now more than ever.* Available at: https://www.forbes.com/sites/deniselyohn/2019/01/08/marketing-matters-now-more-than-ever/?sh=57db559d117a [Accessed 22 Dec. 2022].
50. Singh, D. (2020). *Strategies to be followed by start-ups in the #newnormal.* Available at: https://www.entrepreneur.com/en-in/growth-strategies/strategies-to-be-followed-by-startups-in-the-newnormal/355064 [Accessed 22 Dec. 2022].
51. Techfunnel (2018). *Marketing impact on business.* Available at: https://www.techfunnel.com/martech/marketing-impact-on-business/ [Accessed 22 Dec. 2022].
52. Currall, D. (2021). *The compound effect: A secret weapon for e-commerce marketing.* Available at: https://www.forbes.com/sites/forbesbusinesscouncil/2021/12/14/the-compound-effect-a-secret-weapon-for-e-commerce-marketing/?sh=39869ba0228d [Accessed 22 Dec. 2022].
53. Forsey, C. (2020). *How to maximize your marketing efforts with these high-impact techniques.* Available at: https://blog.hubspot.com/marketing/high-impact-marketing-channels-list [Accessed 22 Dec. 2022].
54. Eisner, J. (2020). *The secret to successful marketing: repeat, repeat, repeat.* Available at: https://www.kochiesbusinessbuilders.com.au/the-secret-to-successful-marketing-repeat-repeat-repeat/ [Accessed 22 Dec. 2022].
55. iGMS. (2019). *Airbnb marketing strategy: 6 techniques to crush your competitors.* Available at: https://www.igms.com/airbnb-marketing-strategy/ [Accessed 22 Dec. 2022].
56. Peleg, V. (2021). *Losing clients – How to avoid it & handle it well.* Available at: https://atarim.io/blog/losing-clients/ [Accessed 22 Dec. 2022].
57. OptinMonster. (2020). *8 digital marketing best practices for 2021 and beyond.* [online] Available at: https://optinmonster.com/digital-marketing-best-practices/ [Accessed 22 Dec. 2022].
58. CMSWire (2022). *What is marketing automation and how does it help marketers?* Available at: https://www.cmswire.com/marketing-automa-

tion/what-is-marketing-automation-and-how-does-it-help-marketers/ [Accessed 22 Dec. 2022].

59. Zapier (2022). *4 ways to automate your marketing operations.* Available at: https://zapier.com/blog/automate-marketing-operations-and-processes/ [Accessed 22 Dec. 2022].
60. CoSchedule (2022). *Red bull marketing strategy.* Available at: https://coschedule.com/marketing-strategy/marketing-strategy-examples/red-bull-marketing-strategy [Accessed 22 Dec. 2022].
61. Mainwaring, S. (2018). *Purpose at work: How Toyota is driving growth, innovation and impact.* Available at: https://www.forbes.com/sites/simonmainwaring/2018/11/13/purpose-in-action-how-toyota-is-driving-growth-innovation-and-impact/?sh=60cd3b0847fb [Accessed 22 Dec. 2022].
62. Lunden, I. (2020). *Udacity raises $75M in debt, says its tech education business is profitable after enterprise pivot.* Available at: https://techcrunch.com/2020/11/03/udacity-raises-75m-in-debt-says-its-tech-education-business-is-profitable-after-enterprise-pivot/ [Accessed 22 Dec. 2022].
63. Globenewswire (2022). *DraftKings reports YoY third quarter revenue increase of 136% to $502 million; Raises 2022 revenue guidance and improves 2022 adjusted EBITDA guidance; Introduces 2023 revenue and adjusted EBITDA guidance.* Available at: https://www.globenewswire.com/news-release/2022/11/04/2548627/0/en/DraftKings-Reports-YoY-Third-Quarter-Revenue-Increase-of-136-to-502-million-Raises-2022-Revenue-Guidance-and-Improves-2022-Adjusted-EBITDA-Guidance-Introduces-2023-Revenue-and-Adju.html [Accessed 22 Dec. 2022].
64. Feldman, A. (2021). *Zenefits, once worth $4.5 billion, does deal with private-equity firm that gives it control.* Available at: https://www.forbes.com/sites/amyfeldman/2021/03/18/zenefits-once-worth-45-billion-does-deal-with-private-equity-firm-that-gives-it-control/?sh=145e51d63873 [Accessed 22 Dec. 2022].
65. The Week (2022). *Will TripCandy replace Fiats in tourism?* Available at: https://www.theweek.in/leisure/lifestyle/2022/06/17/Will-TripCandy-Replace-Fiats-in-Tourism.html [Accessed 22 Dec. 2022].
66. Daso, F. (2021). *EcoCart helps digital consumers offset their carbon footprint at checkout.* Available at: https://www.forbes.com/sites/frederickdaso/2021/01/20/ecocart-helps-digital-consumers-offset-their-carbon-footprint-at-checkout/?sh=459682cb25a1 [Accessed 22 Dec. 2022].

CHAPTER 7
Right Sales Model

The right sales model is essential for start-ups to expand like a niche.[1] It allows the company to be adaptable and responsive to the market. It doesn't mean that every business has to be different from another, but it does mean that they have to be able to adapt their offering as demand changes. One of the most significant advantages of having a good sales model is that it allows you to have multiple channels for selling your product or service. You don't just have one channel; you have various channels, each with its purpose and function. For example, if you are an online retailer, you may want one channel for sales directly through your website and another through affiliates or other partners. The truth is that some businesses are built on a sound and sustainable sales model, while others are not. There are many different types of sales models, and they all have different pros and cons. I have discussed some of these in the sections below. So, if you want a good sales model, this is the chapter you choose to focus on.

The best sales models will help you make more money, attract new customers, and grow your business. Implementing effective sales models is essential for any business looking to increase revenue and grow its customer base. Such a model helps companies understand their target audience, identify their needs, and develop strategies to meet them. You can make it big if you get the right sales model for your business.[2] The best sales models help you sell more products, increase customer loyalty, and maximize profits. Even if you aren't a great salesman or marketer, a solid sales model can improve your results dramatically. Sales for start-ups can be challenging and complex, requiring careful planning and execution. From developing your sales strategy to building a sales team and measuring your success, there are many aspects to consider. In this chapter, I have discussed the key elements of sales for start-ups, including defining your target audience, creating a sales process, selecting the right sales channels, building a successful sales team, and everything beyond that. Whether you're a first-time entrepreneur or a business owner with experience, this guide will provide the tools and insights you need to drive revenue and grow your business. I am sure the following sections will benefit your business strategies concerning sales. Clear your goals and follow your passion for creating a business that will thrive for many years. I have crafted this chapter with confidence and precision for all your concerns about sales.

Types Of Sales Models

Choosing the right sales model is a critical decision for any start-up.[3] Your sales model will define how you approach customers, generate revenue, and grow your business. The wrong sales model can lead to inefficiencies, wasted resources, and missed opportunities. The right sales model can be a critical factor in the success of a start-up. When a start-up is in its early stages, choosing a sales model aligned with the company's goals, resources, and target audience is essential. The right sales model can help a start-up generate revenue, acquire customers, and build a foundation for future growth. For example, suppose a start-up is targeting enterprise customers. In that case, a direct sales model may be the best option as it allows for personalized interactions and a higher level of trust-building. On the other hand, if the start-up targets a larger and more diverse customer base, an online sales model may be more appropriate as it allows for scalability and efficiency. Selecting the right sales model for a start-up is not a one-size-fits-all approach. It requires careful consideration of the start-up's product or service, target audience, competitive landscape, and resources. By choosing the right sales model, a start-up can maximize its revenue potential, accelerate its growth, and establish itself as a leader in its industry.

The right sales model for your start-up will determine how long the business will go. As they say, "morning shows the day." The sales model sets the foundation for how a start-up will generate revenue, acquire customers, and ultimately sustain its growth.[4] A poorly chosen sales model can lead to wasted resources, missed opportunities, and failure. It's essential to consider not only the current needs of the start-up but also its future goals and scalability. For example, if a start-up's sales model relies heavily on in-person interactions, it may face challenges scaling the business beyond a certain point. On the other hand, if the sales model is too reliant on online channels, it may struggle to build the necessary customer relationships and trust. By selecting the right sales model, a start-up can establish a strong foundation for growth and create a sustainable business model that can adapt to changing market conditions. For example, if a start-up chooses an inbound sales model, it can generate leads and build relationships with potential customers, even as the market evolves and new competitors emerge. The right sales model can also help a start-up to establish a competitive advantage in its industry. By focusing on a unique approach to sales and marketing, a start-up can differentiate itself from competitors and attract customers looking for something different. Investing time and resources into evaluating different sales models and selecting the one that best aligns with the start-up's goals and target audience is essential. I have written about four types of sales models you could opt for your start-up - inbound sales, outbound sales, account-based sales, and self-service sales. I have defined each model with examples wherever possible. These will give you a clear idea of what each of them looks like.

Inbound Sales

Inbound sales have become increasingly popular in recent years as a more effective and customer-centric approach to sales.[5] Unlike traditional outbound sales, where sales representatives cold-call or email prospects, inbound sales involve attracting potential customers to your business through content marketing, social media, and other online channels. For start-ups, inbound sales can effectively drive revenue, acquire customers, and build a foundation for long-term growth. Inbound sales have proven to be a profitable strategy for many businesses. Inbound sales focus on attracting and engaging potential customers through content marketing, social media marketing, search engine optimization, and other digital marketing tactics. Companies can generate leads and build relationships with potential customers by providing valuable information and solutions to their target audience, increasing sales and revenue. Before effectively attracting potential customers to your business, you need to understand your target audience. It involves creating a buyer persona and a detailed description of your ideal customer. By creating a buyer persona, you can tailor your inbound sales efforts to the needs and preferences of your target audience. It will help you attract the right prospects to your business and increase your chances of converting them into customers. I have written more about buyer persona in the later part of this chapter.

Once you clearly understand your target audience, you must also focus on developing a content strategy to attract and engage potential customers.[6] It is an essential dimension of inbound sales. It involves creating high-quality content, such as blog posts, videos, infographics, and social media posts, that addresses your target audience's pain points and interests. Your content should be optimized for search engines, making it easy for potential customers to find your business when searching for relevant keywords. It should also be shareable on social media and other online channels, helping to increase your brand's visibility and reach. Many companies work on attracting potential customers by nurturing them through the sales process. It involves implementing a lead nurturing process that provides value to potential customers and helps move them closer to purchasing. Lead nurturing can include email marketing, social media engagement, and personalized content recommendations. The goal is to build a relationship with potential customers and provide them with the information and resources they need to make an informed purchase decision. Inbound sales can be an effective way for start-ups to drive revenue, acquire customers, and build a foundation for long-term growth.

Outbound Sales

Outbound sales is a crucial aspect of business development, particularly for start-ups.[7] Outbound sales reach potential customers through various channels, such as cold calling, email outreach, and social media messaging, to generate leads and sales. Start-ups must engage in outbound sales to acquire new customers and grow their business, but doing so can be challenging. The first step in outbound sales for start-ups is identifying the target market. Start-ups must conduct market research to understand their potential customers, their pain points, and how their product or service can solve those pain points. Once they have identified their target market, start-ups can create a list of potential customers and reach them through outbound sales channels. Working on a sales pitch tailored to the target market is the next step you must focus on as an entrepreneur. The sales pitch should clearly explain the product or service's benefits and how it can solve the customer's pain points. The sales pitch should also address any objections or concerns the customer may have, such as cost or implementation. Start-ups should test their sales pitch on a small group of potential customers before scaling up their outbound sales efforts.

Many companies go for multiple outbound sales channels. Many experts feel start-ups should not rely solely on one outbound sales channel, such as cold calling. Instead, they should use a combination of channels, such as email outreach, social media messaging, and direct mail. Using multiple channels helps start-ups reach potential customers differently and increases the chances of generating leads. You must also categorically measure outbound sales performance. Start-ups must use data and analytics to understand which outbound sales channels are working and which are not. Track metrics such as open rates, response rates, and conversion rates to determine the effectiveness of outbound sales efforts. This data can be used to refine the sales pitch and adjust outbound sales strategies. Technological evolution has made things easier for businesses of today. You must use technology to support outbound sales efforts. Many tools are available to help start-ups manage their outbound sales efforts, such as customer relationship management (CRM) and marketing automation software. These tools can help start-ups streamline their outbound sales processes, track customer interactions, and automate tasks such as follow-up emails. By structuring an outbound sales strategy, start-ups can successfully engage in outbound sales and generate new leads and sales.

Account-Based Sales

Account-based sales is a highly effective sales strategy that can help start-ups acquire new customers and grow their businesses.[8] It involves targeting high-value accounts and developing personalized sales strategies to win their business. The first dimension of account-based sales is to identify high-value target accounts. Start-ups must conduct market research to determine companies that fit their ideal customer profile and have the potential to generate significant revenue. Once they have identified these target accounts, start-ups can begin developing personalized sales strategies for each account. Entrepreneurs then have to build a deep understanding of the target account. As a start-up owner, you must research the target account's industry, business objectives, pain points, and decision-making processes. This information can be used to tailor the sales pitch and develop a customized solution that addresses the target account's specific needs. A good idea would be to engage multiple stakeholders within the target account. Account-based sales involve selling to a team of decision-makers rather than a single individual. Start-ups must identify the key stakeholders within the target account, such as the CEO, CIO, and CFO, and develop customized messages and strategies for each stakeholder. This approach ensures that the sales message resonates with each stakeholder and increases the likelihood of winning the business. Creating personalized content also helps in this regard.

It is recommended that you use multiple communication channels. Account-based sales require a multi-channel approach to sales and marketing. Start-ups should use a variety of channels such as email, social media, direct mail, and phone calls to engage the target account. A multi-channel approach ensures the sales message reaches the target account through their preferred channels. Another vital aspect to consider in mastering account-based sales is to measure and optimize performance. It requires continuous measurement and optimization to ensure an effective sales strategy. Start-ups should track metrics such as engagement, response, and conversion rates to determine the effectiveness of the account-based sales strategy. This data can be used to refine the sales pitch, messaging, and strategy for each target account.

Account-based sales are considered an effective sales model and can significantly benefit start-ups wishing to acquire new customers and grow their businesses.

Self-Service Sales

Self-service sales have become increasingly popular among start-ups due to their cost-effectiveness and ability to scale quickly.[9] Self-service sales refer to selling products or services through an automated system, allowing customers to purchase without human interaction. This type of sales model benefits start-ups, enabling them to reach many customers without investing in a large sales team. There are several benefits of using a self-service sales model for start-ups. It allows companies to reduce their costs significantly by eliminating the need for a large sales team. Instead, the focus can be on creating a user-friendly and efficient sales platform that can handle a high volume of transactions. It means start-ups can allocate resources toward other essential business areas, such as product development or marketing. Self-service sales also provide start-ups with the ability to scale their business quickly. With a traditional sales model, the number of sales a company can make is limited by the size of its sales team. However, with self-service sales, the number of customers a company can reach is unlimited. The business can multiply as long as the sales platform can handle the volume of transactions.

Start-ups that opt for self-service sales can provide customers with a convenient and streamlined purchasing experience. Customers can browse products or services, make purchases, and track their orders from the comfort of their homes. This convenience factor can lead to increased customer satisfaction and repeat business. Having said that, some potential challenges are associated with self-service sales for start-ups.[10] You must be aware of these challenges before you take a call regarding the sales model for your company. In self-service sales, it can be challenging to establish trust with customers when no human interaction is involved in the sales process. It can be mitigated by providing high-quality product descriptions, reviews, and a customer support team to address any issues. Furthermore, start-ups must ensure that their sales platform is user-friendly and easy to navigate. A poorly designed platform can lead to frustrated customers and lost sales. Investing in an intuitive platform that provides a positive user experience is essential. It would help if you also had a solid marketing strategy to drive traffic to the sales platform, which could add to the existing operational costs.

Critical Points For Maximizing Sales

Starting a business can be an exciting and challenging venture, but maximizing sales is one of the most critical factors for success.[11] As a start-up, you need to generate revenue to stay afloat and grow; making sales is the only way to do that. Maximizing sales is crucial for the success of any start-up, and it offers several benefits. The primary advantage of maximizing sales is generating revenue, which is essential for the survival and growth of any start-up. Increased sales lead to increased revenue, which can be used to invest in product development, marketing, hiring new staff, and expanding the business. Maximizing sales also helps to build a loyal customer base. Customers are more likely to return and refer others to your business when satisfied with your product or service. Building a customer base is vital for start-ups as it can help to establish a brand identity and increase market share. Maximizing sales is a good indicator that there is a demand for the product or service you are offering as a company. By generating sales, you can validate your business idea and ensure that there is a market for what you are offering. It can also help to increase brand awareness. When your business generates a lot of sales, more people are likely to hear about your brand, which can lead to more exposure and opportunities.

Another one of the most significant benefits of maximizing sales is that it creates room for innovation. When your business generates revenue, you can invest in research and development to improve your product or service or develop new products to meet customer needs. As I mentioned, maximizing sales is essential for the growth and success of start-ups. With sales, generating revenue and keeping the business afloat is easier. In the early stages of a start-up, it is critical to focus on maximizing sales. Start-ups need to create a sense of urgency and convince potential customers that their product or service is the best solution to their needs. Maximizing sales also helps start-ups to understand their customers better. Sales data can provide insights into the effectiveness of a start-up's marketing and sales strategies, including which channels generate the most leads and which campaigns drive the most sales. This information can help start-ups make data-driven decisions about where to invest their resources and which strategies to prioritize. Customer feedback is also a valuable source of information for start-ups. By collecting customer feedback, start-ups can gain insights into how their product or service is being used, what customers like and dislike about it, and what features or improvements they want to see. This feedback can be used to make necessary changes and improvements to the product or service to meet customers' needs better. Thus, by analyzing sales data and customer feedback, start-ups can identify areas for improvement and make necessary changes to their product or service. It leads to increased customer satisfaction, loyalty, and repeat business.[12] By maximizing sales, start-ups can demonstrate to investors that they have a solid business model and are well-positioned for long-term success. I have elaborated on three dimensions you need to focus on while attempting to maximize sales – customer-centric sales, buyer's journey and persona, and aligning the sales with the buyers' needs. The section below will give you a clear idea of all these and help you maximize sales for your start-up.

Customer-Centric Sales

In today's highly competitive market, start-ups must focus on customer-centric sales to stand out.[13] Customer-centric sales is a sales approach that places the customer's needs and preferences at the center of the sales process. This approach involves understanding the customer's pain points, preferences, and buying behavior and tailoring the sales process accordingly. There are innumerable benefits of customer-centric sales for start-ups. Customer-centric sales help start-ups to build customer loyalty by providing a personalized and satisfying buying experience. When customers feel valued and heard, they are more likely to return and refer others to the business. By understanding the customer's needs and preferences, start-ups can offer targeted solutions that meet their specific requirements, increasing the chances of a successful sale. A customer-centric sales approach builds trust between the business and the customer. Customers who feel their needs are prioritized are more likely to trust the company and develop long-term relationships. By offering tailored solutions, start-ups can improve customer satisfaction, which leads to positive reviews and referrals, ultimately contributing to the growth of the business.

Start-ups should invest time and effort in understanding their customers' needs, preferences, and pain points. It involves conducting market research, gathering customer feedback, and analyzing data to gain insights into the customer's buying behavior.[14] Once the customer's needs and preferences are understood, start-ups should tailor their sales process to meet those requirements. It can involve offering personalized recommendations, addressing specific concerns, and providing exceptional customer service. As I have often stated, technology can significantly implement various business strategies, including customer-centric sales. Start-ups can use Customer Relationship Management (CRM) software to store customer data and track their interactions with the business, which can be used to offer personalized solutions. Sales are driven by staff. Start-ups should ensure that their sales staff is trained in customer-centric sales techniques. It teaches them to listen actively, ask the right questions, and offer tailored solutions. Start-ups should continually evaluate and improve their customer-centric sales approach. It involves analyzing customer feedback, monitoring sales data, and making necessary changes to the sales process to meet customer needs. Hence, customer-centric sales is an integral approach for start-ups to stand out in today's competitive market. By focusing on customer-centric sales, start-ups can establish a solid customer base and set themselves up for long-term success.[15]

Buyer's Journey And Persona

For start-ups, understanding the buyer's journey and buyer persona is crucial for building effective sales and marketing strategies.[16] It is where I will talk about the buyer's persona and journey in detail. The buyer's journey refers to a potential customer's research and purchasing steps. The buyer persona is a fictional representation of the ideal customer based on demographic and psychographic data. By understanding the buyer's journey, start-ups can identify the customer's pain points, needs, and preferences at each stage of the buying process. It enables them to offer targeted solutions that meet those specific requirements, improving the chances of a successful sale. By mapping out the buyer's journey, start-ups can identify the most effective sales strategies for each process stage. It involves tailoring the sales message and approach to meet the customer's needs and preferences. By understanding the buyer's journey, start-ups can improve the customer experience by providing the correct information at the right time and format. It ensures the customer is informed and engaged throughout the buying process, increasing satisfaction and loyalty. By developing a buyer persona, start-ups can identify the ideal customer and create targeted marketing messages that resonate with them. It helps to build brand awareness and attract the right customers to the business.

Implementing this strategy needs planning. Start-ups should conduct market research to gain insights into their target audience. It involves analyzing customer data, conducting surveys, and researching industry trends to understand customer needs and preferences. Once the target audience is understood, start-ups should map the buyer's journey. It involves identifying the stages of the buying process and the customer's needs and preferences at each stage. Using the insights gained from market research, start-ups can develop a buyer persona. It involves creating a fictional representation of the ideal customer based on demographic and psychographic data.[17] Start-ups should tailor their sales and marketing strategies to meet the needs and preferences of the ideal customer. It involves developing targeted messaging, using the right channels, and offering the right solutions at each stage of the buying process. Start-ups should continuously monitor and improve their sales and marketing strategies based on customer feedback and changing market trends. It involves analyzing sales data, monitoring customer feedback, and making necessary changes to the sales and marketing approach. Hence, understanding the buyer's journey and persona is critical for start-ups to develop effective sales and marketing strategies. By investing in the buyer's journey and persona, start-ups can set themselves up for long-term success.

Align The Sales With The Buyer's Needs

Aligning sales with the buyer's needs is essential to building long-term relationships and increasing revenue.[18] The focus should be on creating a customer-centric approach that caters to the buyer's needs at every stage of the sales process. The first step in aligning sales with the buyer's needs is understanding what the buyer wants. Start-ups should conduct market research and analyze customer data to identify their target audience's needs and pain points. This information will help them tailor their sales approach to meet the buyer's needs. Start-ups should focus on providing solutions to the buyer's needs rather than just selling a product or service. The sales message should revolve around how the product or service can solve the buyer's problem or meet their needs. By focusing on solutions, start-ups can build trust with the buyer and establish long-term relationships. Start-ups should customize the sales process to meet the needs of the buyer. It involves identifying the buyer's preferred communication channel, providing the necessary information, and addressing concerns. By customizing the sales process, start-ups can create a personalized experience for the buyer and improve the chances of a successful sale.

Start-ups must also focus on building relationships with the buyer. The sales approach should be more than transactional and focus on building trust and establishing long-term relationships. By building relationships, start-ups can create loyal customers who will likely return and refer others. Excellent customer service is crucial to aligning sales with the buyer's needs. Start-ups should be responsive to the buyer's inquiries, provide timely and accurate information, and resolve any issues promptly. By providing excellent customer service, start-ups can establish themselves a trusted partner in the eyes of the buyer.[19] Hence, aligning sales with the buyer's needs is critical for start-ups to build long-term relationships and increase revenue. By doing so, start-ups can create a customer-centric approach that meets the buyer's needs at every stage of the sales process.

Critical Points For Sustaining Sales

Start-ups need to sustain sales from day one for several reasons.[20] First and foremost, sales are the lifeblood of any business. Without sales, a start-up cannot generate revenue; without revenue, it cannot survive. Start-ups must generate sales from day one to cover operating costs, pay salaries, and invest in growth. Secondly, sustaining sales from day one helps start-ups establish their market position. The early stages of a start-up are critical for building brand recognition and customer trust. By generating sales early on, start-ups can establish a strong foothold in the market and differentiate themselves from competitors. It can also help start-ups attract investors and secure funding for growth. Thirdly, sustaining sales from day one allows start-ups to validate their business model. Start-ups need to prove that there is a market for their product or service and that they can generate revenue. By sustaining sales from day one, start-ups can demonstrate to potential investors and partners that they have a viable business model that can scale. Start-ups must understand that supporting sales from day one helps start-ups build momentum. Generating sales early on can create a snowball effect as satisfied customers become advocates and refer others to the business. It can lead to organic growth and help start-ups achieve their goals faster.

For any start-up, it is essential to focus on sustaining sales from the very beginning. With consistent sales, a start-up can generate revenue, attract investors, and grow its customer base. To sustain sales from the start, a start-up needs to clearly understand its target audience, its needs and preferences, and how its products or services can provide value and solve its problems. Start-ups must also develop effective marketing and sales strategies, including identifying the most effective channels to reach their target audience, creating compelling messaging and branding, and building solid customer relationships. Sustaining sales from day one helps start-ups manage risk. The early stages of a start-up are inherently risky, and generating sales can help mitigate some of that risk. By generating revenue early on, start-ups can diversify their revenue streams and reduce reliance on external funding sources. Sustaining sales from the inception is critical for start-ups to establish their market position, validate their business model, build momentum, and manage risk. By generating sales early on, start-ups can establish a strong foundation for growth and set themselves up for long-term success. I have talked about three ways to sustain sales - empowering your team, enhancing your sales' impact, and expanding your sales stack. The section below will give you more clarity regarding these, and you will be able to better implement these strategies in the operations of your new business.

Empower Your Team

Start-ups can empower their teams to drive maximum sales by creating a supportive and collaborative environment that fosters creativity, innovation, and continuous learning.[21] Start-ups should provide their sales teams with clear goals and objectives to work towards. It helps team members focus on what is essential and stay motivated. Clear goals also provide direction and help teams align with the company's mission and vision. Start-ups should provide their sales teams with ongoing training and development opportunities. It helps team members stay up-to-date with the latest industry trends and best practices, which can help them drive maximum sales. Start-ups can provide training sessions, workshops, and access to online resources to facilitate continuous learning. Start-ups should encourage collaboration among their sales teams. Team members should be encouraged to share their ideas, best practices, and success stories. It can help create a culture of innovation and lead to new and creative ways of driving sales. Start-ups can incentivize their sales teams to encourage them to drive maximum sales. It can include bonuses, commissions, and other rewards for achieving sales targets. Incentives can motivate team members to go above and beyond, leading to increased sales and revenue for the start-up.

Start-ups should also give their sales teams autonomy to make decisions and take ownership of the sales process. It empowers teams to make decisions, take calculated risks, and learn from mistakes. Start-ups should provide their sales teams with the necessary tools and resources to drive sales. It includes sales software, marketing materials, and customer data. By providing the resources needed, teams can work efficiently and effectively. They should create a supportive culture that encourages collaboration and communication. It involves making an open-door policy, providing feedback, and recognizing team members' efforts. Start-ups should foster professional development opportunities for their sales teams. It includes offering training programs, mentorship, and career advancement opportunities. By promoting professional development, start-ups can attract and retain top talent and drive maximum sales. Hence, empowering sales teams is essential for start-ups to drive high sales. By empowering their teams, start-ups can build a foundation for growth and set themselves up for long-term success.

Enhance The Impact Of Your Sales

All start-ups want to succeed. In doing so, they need to enhance the impact of their sales efforts.[22] To achieve this, they must focus on improving their sales strategy, tactics, and execution. Start-ups should focus on meeting customer needs and solving their problems. It involves understanding their pain points and tailoring solutions to meet their requirements. By focusing on customer needs, start-ups can differentiate themselves from competitors and build customer loyalty. Start-ups should align their sales and marketing teams to ensure they work towards the same goals. It involves creating a shared understanding of the target market, messaging, and sales processes. By aligning sales and marketing, start-ups can generate higher-quality leads, improve the lead-to-customer conversion rate, and increase revenue. Start-ups should also leverage technology to enhance their sales impact. It includes using customer relationship management (CRM) software, sales automation tools, and analytics to track and measure sales performance. Using technology, start-ups can streamline their sales processes, improve data accuracy, and gain insights into customer behavior.

Start-ups must emphasize following up with potential customers to increase their conversion rates. It involves promptly responding to inquiries, nurturing leads through the sales funnel, and following up with existing customers to maintain relationships. By emphasizing follow-up, start-ups can improve customer satisfaction and retention rates. Start-ups should focus on providing excellent customer service to differentiate themselves from competitors. It involves being responsive, providing value-added services, and resolving issues quickly. By offering excellent customer service, start-ups can increase customer loyalty and generate repeat business. Start-ups should establish sales metrics to track and measure their performance. It includes metrics such as lead generation, conversion rates, customer acquisition costs, and revenue per customer. By establishing sales metrics, start-ups can identify areas for improvement and optimize their sales processes. Hence, start-ups must enhance the impact of their sales efforts by focusing on the dimensions discussed above. By implementing these strategies, start-ups can differentiate themselves from competitors, increase revenue, and build a foundation for long-term success.

Expand Your Sales Stack

You might have heard a lot about sales stack. But what does sales stack mean? The sales stack includes all the tools, technologies, and processes that help businesses manage and grow their sales operations. For start-ups, expanding their sales stack can be critical to achieving growth and success. Start-ups should begin by identifying the gaps in their current sales stack. It involves evaluating their existing sales tools, processes, and workflows to determine where improvements can be made. By identifying these gaps, start-ups can decide which areas of their sales stack require the most attention. Once start-ups have identified the gaps in their sales stack, they can begin researching and evaluating new sales tools. It involves considering cost, ease of use, functionality, and compatibility with existing systems. By considering new tools, start-ups can determine which will best meet their needs and help them achieve their sales goals. After selecting new sales tools, start-ups should test and implement them. It involves training sales teams on using new tools, integrating them into existing workflows, and monitoring their impact on sales performance. By testing and implementing new tools, start-ups can ensure they get the most out of their sales stack.[23]

Start-ups should continuously monitor and improve their sales stack. It involves regularly evaluating sales performance metrics, gathering feedback from sales teams, and staying up-to-date with new sales technologies and best practices. By continuously monitoring and improving their sales stack, start-ups can adapt to changing market conditions and stay ahead of the competition. Start-ups may also consider outsourcing certain sales functions to third-party providers. It includes lead generation, appointment setting, and sales enablement. By outsourcing, start-ups can free up internal resources and focus on other business areas. Expanding the sales stack can help start-ups streamline their sales processes and workflows, enabling them to work more efficiently. By automating repetitive tasks, such as lead generation and data entry, sales teams can focus on higher-value activities, such as nurturing relationships with prospects and closing deals. A robust sales stack can help start-ups deliver a better customer experience. Using tools like chatbots, live chat, and email automation, start-ups can respond to customer inquiries more quickly and efficiently. Additionally, a CRM system can help sales teams track customer interactions and preferences, enabling them to personalize their sales approach and build stronger relationships with customers. As start-ups grow, they need sales processes and tools to scale. Expanding the sales stack can help start-ups achieve this scalability, enabling them to handle larger volumes of leads and deals without sacrificing quality or efficiency. By expanding their sales stack, start-ups can improve sales performance, increase revenue, and achieve long-term growth and success.

Companies That Inspire You To Excel At Sales

Learning from companies that successfully get their sales right is crucial as an entrepreneur. Sales are the lifeblood of any business; with them, the most innovative and well-executed ideas will succeed. Many successful companies have achieved their success by excelling at sales. They have relentlessly focused on improving their sales strategies and operations to drive growth and increase revenue. These companies have built strong sales teams, invested in the latest sales technologies, and continuously monitored and optimized their sales performance.[24] Getting the sales model right is essential for the success of any start-up. Start-ups must have a sales model that aligns with their target audience and business objectives. One key aspect of learning from successful companies is their sales strategies. For example, they identify and target their ideal customer, differentiate themselves from their competitors, create a sense of urgency for their products or services, and build strong customer relationships. Another aspect to consider is the importance of effective communication in sales. Successful companies have a clear, compelling message that resonates with their target audience. They can communicate that message effectively through various channels, such as advertising, social media, and email marketing. Furthermore, it is essential to analyze and optimize your sales approach constantly. Successful companies always experiment with new sales strategies and tactics, measure their effectiveness, and adjust as needed. This continuous improvement process allows them to stay ahead of the competition and maintain a steady stream of sales. Learning from successful companies that have mastered the art of sales can provide valuable insights and guidance for entrepreneurs looking to grow their businesses. Following are a few such companies that I have written about. Their stories will inspire you to figure out the sales model right and ensure progress for your new ventures.

Gumroad

Gumroad[25] is a digital marketplace that was founded in 2011 by Sahil Lavingia. The company is based in San Francisco, California, and provides a platform for creators to sell their digital products, such as e-books, music, videos, and software. Gumroad has become a popular platform for independent creators who want to sell their products online e-book and has helped many people earn a living from their creative work. One of the critical features of Gumroad is its simplicity and ease of use. The platform is designed to be user-friendly and intuitive, with a clean and minimalistic interface that makes it easy for creators to set up their online store and start selling their products. Gumroad handles all the technical details, such as payment processing and file hosting, so creators can focus on creating and marketing their products. It has helped the company to ensure higher sales. Another reason for this is their low fees. Unlike many other digital marketplaces that charge a percentage of the sale price, Gumroad only charges a small flat fee per transaction, which makes it an attractive option for creators who want to keep more of their earnings. This fee structure also means that Gumroad is more accessible to creators who are just starting and may not have a large following or high sales volume. In addition to its marketplace, Gumroad also offers a range of tools and services to help creators grow their businesses. These include analytics and reporting tools, email marketing integrations, and the ability to provide discounts and promotional codes to customers. Gumroad also has a community of creators who share tips and advice on succeeding on the platform. The company has thus become a valuable resource for independent creators who want to sell their digital products online. Their calculated approaches in terms of sales have helped them carve a position in the industry.

Company Name: Gumroad

Founded: 2011

Significant reason(s) for success: The company offers something that wasn't new in the industry. However, it has tapped into the growing demands and increased sales by being customer-centric in its business approaches.

Clockify

Clockify[26] is a time-tracking software company founded in 2017 by Nenad Milanovic. The company is based in Serbia and provides a free time tracking tool that helps individuals and businesses track their time spent on tasks and projects. Clockify has become a popular choice for remote workers, freelancers, and small businesses that need an easy and affordable way to track their time and improve their productivity. One of the significant features of Clockify that has helped to boost sales is its simplicity and ease of use. The platform is designed to be user-friendly and intuitive, with a clean and minimalistic interface that makes it easy for users to track their time and manage their projects. Clockify offers a wide range of features, including time tracking, project management, team management, and reporting tools, all designed to help users improve their productivity and track their progress. Clockify also offers a free plan, allowing users to track their time and manage their projects without paying fees. It makes it an attractive option for individuals and small businesses that may not have the budget to invest in more expensive time-tracking software, creating a scope for higher sales in the times to come. Clockify's free plan also includes a range of features, such as unlimited users, unlimited projects, and reporting tools, which means that users can get a lot of value from the platform without paying anything. Furthermore, Clockify offers a range of paid plans with more advanced features, such as invoicing, time off tracking, and integrations with other tools and services. Clockify's paid plans are also affordable and scalable, meaning users can upgrade their plans as their needs grow, and their business expands. They know how to master the sales model. And in doing so, Clockify has become a valuable resource for individuals and companies that need an easy and affordable way to track their time and manage their projects. As entrepreneurs, you have a lot to learn from companies like Clockify.

Company Name: Clockify

Founded: 2017

Significant reason(s) for success: The company has been catering to the increasing demand of customers. It offers a simple product but takes care of details, making it attractive for customers, thus generating more sales.

Manscaped

Manscaped[27] is a men's grooming company founded in 2016 by Paul Tran. The company is based in San Diego, California, and provides a range of grooming products designed specifically for men, including trimmers, razors, and skincare products. Manscaped has become a popular choice for men who want to look and have the best feeling about themselves and has helped to redefine the men's grooming industry. Manscaped has focused on men's grooming needs since the first day of its inception. The company recognizes that traditional grooming brands overlook men's unique needs. It has developed a range of products specifically designed to address these needs. Manscaped's products are designed to be effective, easy to use, and affordable, making them accessible to men of all ages and backgrounds. It has helped the company to ensure humongous sales. Manscaped also commits to quality and innovation. The company uses the latest technology and materials to develop its products and works closely with experts in the field to ensure that its products are effective and safe for use. Manscaped is also committed to sustainability and uses eco-friendly materials and packaging whenever possible. Manscaped has also become known for its marketing and branding, which has helped the company make more sales. The company uses humor and irreverence to promote its products and has developed a solid online presence through social media and influencer marketing. Manscaped's marketing campaigns are designed to appeal to a wide range of men and have helped the company to build a loyal and engaged customer base. Today, Manscaped is a leading player in the men's grooming industry, thanks to its focus on men's grooming needs and doing everything to connect to potential customers across the globe. The aspect of buyer persona and customer-centric sales stand true to companies like Manscaped.

Company Name: Manscaped

Founded: 2016

Significant reason(s) for success: The company has been offering products as per a significant user community that it targets. It has increased sales by leveraging on its exclusive product line globally.

StreamYard

StreamYard[28] is a live-streaming software company founded in 2018 by Geige Vandentop and Dan Briggs. The company is based in Vancouver, Canada. It provides a platform that allows individuals and businesses to create and stream live video content on various platforms, including YouTube, Facebook, and LinkedIn. StreamYard has become a popular choice for creators and companies that want to engage with their audience and expand their reach through live streaming. It has been able to master the art of sales by providing what the audience wants and providing it consistently. StreamYard is known for its ease of use. The platform is designed to be user-friendly and intuitive, with a clean and straightforward interface that makes it easy for users to set up and stream their content. StreamYard also offers many features, including customizable branding, live comments, and screen sharing, designed to help users create engaging and interactive live streams. StreamYard's sales have also seen a tremendous increase because of its scalability. The platform is designed to accommodate both small and large-scale live streams, making it an attractive option for creators and businesses of all sizes. StreamYard also offers a range of pricing plans, including a free plan that allows users to stream up to 20 hours per month and a range of paid plans that provide more advanced features and higher streaming limits. StreamYard provides a range of integrations with other tools and services, which allows users to streamline their workflow and improve their productivity. StreamYard's integrations also help users expand their reach by streaming their content on multiple platforms simultaneously. It is not surprising that StreamYard has been growing as a valuable resource for creators and businesses that want to engage with their audience and expand their reach through live streaming. With their commitment to offering the best for customers and designing their features for various audiences, they are already set to make it big even after their acquisition by Hopin.

Company Name: StreamYard

Founded: 2018 (acquired by Hopin in 2021)

Significant reason(s) for success: The company has been offering products by following the successful trends of the industry. It has increased sales by focusing on user interactions and customizations.

CoachHub

CoachHub[29] is a Germany-based company founded in 2018 by Yannis Niebelschütz and Matti Niebelschütz. The company provides an innovative coaching platform that connects employees with certified coaches to help them achieve their personal and professional goals. CoachHub has quickly become a leading player in the corporate coaching industry, assisting organizations in supporting and developing their employees through coaching. The central feature of CoachHub that has ensured regular sales is its accessibility. The platform is designed to be user-friendly, with a simple and intuitive interface. It makes it easy for employees to connect with coaches and start their coaching journey. CoachHub also offers a range of coaching formats, including one-on-one coaching, group coaching, and peer-to-peer coaching, which allows employees to choose the layout that best suits their needs and preferences. CoachHub is also known to focus on personalization. The platform uses a proprietary matching algorithm to pair employees with coaches best suited to their needs and goals based on personality, experience, and coaching style. This personalized approach ensures that employees receive coaching tailored to their specific needs and preferences and helps maximize the impact of coaching on their personal and professional development. CoachHub offers a range of tools and features to support the coaching process, including a goal-setting tool, progress tracking, and feedback and rating systems. These tools help employees stay motivated and engaged in their coaching journey and provide valuable insights into their client's progress and needs. Not only has CoachHub's sales boosted in recent times, but it has also become a valuable resource for organizations that want to support and develop their employees through coaching. If your start-up is in sync with this company's services, you must closely follow their growth story for your venture.

Company Name: CoachHub

Founded: 2018

Significant reason(s) for success: The company has been offering services as per the increasing needs of the industry. It has ensured outstanding sales by making the platform user-friendly.

Clumio

Clumio[30] is a cloud-based data protection and management company founded in 2017 by Poojan Kumar, Woon Jung, and Kaustubh Patil. The company provides a comprehensive suite of services that help businesses protect and manage their data in a hybrid cloud environment, enabling them to secure and control their information across various cloud platforms. Clumio has been doing incredibly well in the market because of its cloud-native approach. The company's platform is designed to work seamlessly with modern cloud platforms like Amazon Web Services (AWS), Microsoft Azure, and Google Cloud Platform (GCP), enabling businesses to protect and manage their data in a flexible and scalable manner. Clumio's platform also integrates with other cloud services, such as data analytics and machine learning tools, providing businesses with a comprehensive solution for their data management needs. Also, Clumio is known for its ease of use. The platform is designed to be simple and intuitive. It has a user-friendly interface makes it easy for businesses to set up and manage their data protection and management workflows. Clumio's platform also includes a range of automation and orchestration tools that help companies to streamline their data management processes, reducing the risk of errors and improving efficiency. Clumio places a strong emphasis on security and compliance. The platform incorporates advanced security features, such as encryption, multi-factor authentication, and role-based access control, to ensure that data is always protected. Clumio's platform also complies with various regulatory requirements, such as the General Data Protection Regulation (GDPR) and the Health Insurance Portability and Accountability Act (HIPAA), ensuring that businesses can maintain compliance with relevant regulations. Clumio has become a valuable resource for companies that want to protect and manage their data in a hybrid cloud environment. It has thus generated outstanding sales over the last few years.

Company Name: Clumio

Founded: 2017

Significant reason(s) for success: The company has been offering products as per the trends of the industry. It has increased sales by relying on its niche.

Conclusion

While some start-ups may have an easier time getting their sales right due to high demand or a lack of competition, others may need help with challenges such as a crowded market or a product requiring a longer sales cycle. That being said, it is vital for start-ups to have a well-defined sales strategy and to assess and optimize their approach continuously. It can involve identifying the target market and ideal customer, creating a compelling value proposition, building solid customer relationships, and leveraging various sales channels to reach and convert prospects. Additionally, it can be helpful for start-ups to seek guidance from experienced sales professionals, invest in sales training and resources, and leverage data and analytics to track and optimize their sales performance. While getting the sales right for a start-up may be challenging, it is achievable with the right strategy, approach, and resources. It may require persistence, experimentation, and a willingness to adapt and optimize as needed. Still, a successful sales strategy can ultimately be a crucial driver of growth and success for any start-up.

As an entrepreneur, you have the passion and drive to bring your vision to life. Entrepreneurship requires a high level of dedication, persistence, and willingness to take risks. You also need to be ready to make sacrifices. Without a strong sense of passion and drive, staying motivated and overcoming the many obstacles that come with starting and growing a business can be challenging. Passion is also critical because it helps to fuel creativity and innovation. When entrepreneurs are passionate about their ideas and believe in their ability to make a mark in the industry, they are likelier to develop unique solutions and approaches to set their businesses apart from the competition. By focusing on getting your sales right, you can make that vision a reality, creating a successful business that provides value to your customers, team, and community. So don't be discouraged by the challenges of getting your sales right. Embrace them as opportunities to learn, grow, and improve. With dedication, hard work, and a commitment to excellence, you can achieve your sales goals and build a thriving start-up that changes the world.

As I have done with the chapters before this one, I am laying the crux of this chapter in coherent pointers for you to refer to them whenever required. Hopefully, with the help of this chapter, you will be able to ace your start-up sales model.

1. Finding a suitable sales model for your business will help you go a long way.
2 There are different kinds of sales models; the most suitable one will depend exclusively on what you're offering as a company.

3. A successful model for one business does not necessarily guarantee success for another with a similar product or service offering.
4. Your business sales model will depend on your target audience and what kind of scalability you're looking for as a business.
5. It will also depend on the technology you're ready to explore and invest in as a start-up.
6. Continuous evaluation of sales is essential for all kinds of businesses, especially start-ups.
7. Maximizing sales is the next essential step for getting the sales model right.
8. It will influence your company's growth trajectory and market position.
9. Customer-centric sales will give you a better grip on the industry and offer products or services based on what is relevant for your customers.
10. Buyer's journey and persona are crucial for your company to have successful sales.
11. Aligning sales with the buyer's needs will give an edge to your start-up.
12. Sustaining sales is as essential as kickstarting or increasing them.
13. Empower your team to make sure that your sales are booming.
14. Enhance the impact of your sales for long-term prosperity.
15. Expand your sales stack to be ahead in the sales game.

References

1. Fuchs, J. (2022). The ultimate guide to start-up sales. Available at: https://blog.hubspot.com/sales/11-skills-startup-sales [Accessed 13 Mar. 2023].
2. Peddinti, S. (2021). *Three sales strategies to help you grow your business.* Available at: https://www.forbes.com/sites/forbesbusinesscouncil/2021/08/24/three-sales-strategies-to-help-you-grow-your-business/?sh=1b4bd4e95476 [Accessed 13 Mar. 2023].
3. Harvard Business Review (2016). *How one start-up developed a sales model that works in emerging markets.* Available at: https://hbr.org/2016/09/how-one-startup-developed-a-sales-model-that-works-in-emerging-markets [Accessed 13 Mar. 2023].

4. Santora, J. (2022). *6 tips to drive sustainable business growth.* Available at: https://www.entrepreneur.com/growing-a-business/6-tips-to-drive-sustainable-business-growth/427946 [Accessed 13 Mar. 2023].
5. Tarver, E. (2022). *What is inside sales? Definition, how it works, and advantages.* Available at: https://www.investopedia.com/terms/i/inside-sales.asp [Accessed 13 Mar. 2023].
6. Pereira, D. (2021). *How to develop an effective content strategy.* Available at: https://www.forbes.com/sites/forbesbusinesscouncil/2021/06/09/how-to-develop-an-effective-content-strategy/?sh=5112cf0f29f4 [Accessed 13 Mar. 2023].
7. Kenton, W. (2022). *What is a sales lead? How it works and factors affecting quality.* Available at: https://www.investopedia.com/terms/s/sales-lead.asp [Accessed 13 Mar. 2023].
8. Rose, M. (2017). *What is account-based marketing?* Available at: https://www.forbes.com/sites/forbesagencycouncil/2017/11/01/what-is-account-based-marketing/?sh=22e61ed23343 [Accessed 13 Mar. 2023].
9. ProductLed (2023). *Pros and cons of self-serve, sales-driven, and the hybrid model.* Available at: https://productled.com/blog/pros-and-cons-of-self-serve-sales-driven-hybrid-model [Accessed 13 Mar. 2023].
10. Forbes (2022). *16 tactics to retain customers while using a self-service option.* Available at: https://www.forbes.com/sites/forbescommunicationscouncil/2022/08/19/16-tactics-to-retain-customers-while-using-a-self-service-option/?sh=4549bc607a4f [Accessed 13 Mar. 2023].
11. Zwilling, M. (2013). *7 steps to outstanding sales growth for your startup.* Available at: https://www.forbes.com/sites/martinzwilling/2013/07/21/7-steps-to-outstanding-sales-growth-for-your-startup/?sh=4afaec5f2fea [Accessed 13 Mar. 2023].
12. HubSpot (n.d.). *Customer feedback strategy: The only guide you'll ever need.* Available at: https://www.hubspot.com/customer-feedback [Accessed 13 Mar. 2023].
13. Forbes (2022). *How customer-centric selling can help you close more leads.* Available at: https://www.forbes.com/sites/allbusiness/2022/07/18/how-customer-centric-selling-can-help-you-close-more-leads/?sh=5cbe33df7f32 [Accessed 13 Mar. 2023].
14. McKinsey (2020). *Understanding and shaping consumer behavior in the next normal.* Available at: https://www.mckinsey.com/capabilities/growth-marketing-and-sales/our-insights/understanding-and-shaping-consumer-behavior-in-the-next-normal [Accessed 13 Mar. 2023].

15. Ramich, A. (2022). *Council post: What is customer centricity?* Available at: https://www.forbes.com/sites/forbesagencycouncil/2022/01/20/what-is-customer-centricity/?sh=72310761ade9 [Accessed 13 Mar. 2023].
16. Burns, R. (2022). *Why buyer personas are more important than ever for Facebook advertisers.* Available at: https://www.forbes.com/sites/forbesagencycouncil/2021/12/02/why-buyer-personas-are-more-important-than-ever-for-facebook-advertisers/?sh=4c527648423c [Accessed 13 Mar. 2023].
17. Vaughan, P. (2022). *How to create detailed buyer personas for your business.* Available at: https://blog.hubspot.com/marketing/buyer-persona-research [Accessed 13 Mar. 2023].
18. Richardson (2019). *The importance of buyer journey alignment.* Available at: https://www.richardson.com/blog/the-importance-of-buyer-journey-alignment/ [Accessed 13 Mar. 2023].
19. Amaresan, S. (2022). *Why customer service is important: 16 data-backed facts to know.* Available at: https://blog.hubspot.com/service/importance-customer-service [Accessed 13 Mar. 2023].
20. Horn, B.A. (2017). *4 secrets to improve your start-up's sales.* Entrepreneur. Available at: https://www.entrepreneur.com/starting-a-business/4-secrets-to-improve-your-startups-sales/284057 [Accessed 13 Mar. 2023].
21. Fatemi, F. (2019). *3 tips to empower your sales team, inspired by top sales organizations.* Available at: https://www.forbes.com/sites/falonfatemi/2019/06/27/3-tips-to-empower-your-sales-team-inspired-by-top-sales-organizations/?sh=3faaf24f3ae4 [Accessed 13 Mar. 2023].
22. Harvard Business Review (2017). *How to improve your sales skills, even if you're not a salesperson.* Available at: https://hbr.org/2017/05/how-to-improve-your-sales-skills-even-if-youre-not-a-salesperson [Accessed 13 Mar. 2023].
23. Miller, L. (2022). *The sales stack: What it is, why it matters and how to build one.* Available at: https://www.entrepreneur.com/growing-a-business/the-sales-stack-what-it-is-why-it-matters-and-how-to/432334 [Accessed 13 Mar. 2023].
24. Tyre, D. (2021). *21 ways to improve individual and team sales performance.* Available at: https://blog.hubspot.com/sales/how-to-improve-sales-performance [Accessed 13 Mar. 2023].
25. Konrad, A. (2021). *Inside Gumroad's historic crowdfunding – and Sahil Lavingia's plans to turn customers into investors.* Available at: https://www.

forbes.com/sites/alexkonrad/2021/03/22/gumroad-crowdfunding-results-sahil-lavingia-investing/?sh=1cd092cd55d7 [Accessed 13 Mar. 2023].

26. Business (2023). *Clockify Review and pricing in 2023*. Available at: https://www.business.com/reviews/clockify/ [Accessed 13 Mar. 2023].
27. DeAcetis, J. (2020). *Find out how manscaped saw a gap in the space of male hygiene and Consumer Packaged Goods*. Available at: https://www.forbes.com/sites/josephdeacetis/2020/03/13/find-out-how-manscaped-saw-a-gap-in-the-space-of-male-hygiene-and-consumer-packaged-goods/?sh=7ed3a3df1a70 [Accessed 13 Mar. 2023].
28. Wilhelm, A. (2021). *Hopin buys livestreaming start-up streamyard for $250M as it looks to expand its product line-up*. Available at: https://techcrunch.com/2021/01/07/hopin-buys-livestreaming-startup-streamyard-for-250m-as-it-looks-to-expand-its-product-lineup/ [Accessed 13 Mar. 2023].
29. Butcher, M. (2021). *CoachHub raises $80m in series 'B2' round, as coaching goes digital in the pandemic*. Available at: https://techcrunch.com/2021/09/01/coachhub-raises-80m-in-series-b2-round-as-coaching-goes-digital-in-the-pandemic/ [Accessed 13 Mar. 2023].
30. Warren, J. (2019). *Clumio launches as enterprise backup-as-a-service with $51 million in funding*. Available at: https://www.forbes.com/sites/justinwarren/2019/08/14/clumio-launches-as-enterprise-backup-as-a-service-with-51-million-in-funding/?sh=5eaf49f95ff6 [Accessed 13 Mar. 2023].

CHAPTER 8
Right Partnering Model

The right partnering model is significant to ensure your business's success.[1] The right partnership has enabled many companies to prosper over the years. As discussed earlier, you could partner with an individual or an organization. As an entrepreneur, you need to understand the differences between these two models to choose the one that suits your needs best. For instance, if you are partnering with an organization, this will benefit both parties involved as they can share their resources and expertise. On the other hand, if you are partnering with an individual, they can provide valuable administrative support and mentoring assistance. Often, a company enters into a partnership with another company to create a new product or service that will benefit both companies. In other scenarios, companies choose to form an operational partnership when there is a need for expertise, products, or services that they do not have within their organization. An example would be McDonald's forming an operational partnership with local restaurants for them to increase sales through franchising. Furthermore, another kind of partnership is a marketing partnership involving two organizations. In such a case, one organization offers its customers special offers or discounts from the other organization through advertising campaigns or promotions. An example would be Tesco offering free delivery on orders over £10 from Asda or Argos, or John Lewis offering free delivery on all orders over £50 from Currys PC World.

A good partnership model[2] should have clear perspectives and be able to support both partners in their growth. It should also have a clear goal and vision to which both partners can commit. These are some key questions you should ask yourself when identifying a partner for your business: What is your business objective? Can both partners contribute to the purpose? What are the deliverables you can identify? Is this a long-term relationship? The answer to these questions depends on the business you want to establish and grow. For instance, if it is a service-based business, it is best suited as a long-term relationship as there will be no urgency in finding funding, new markets, etc. However, entering something short-term would make more sense if it's an enterprise-based business. This chapter will take you through everything significant for deciding the best business partnerships for entrepreneurs. It will give you insights into various dimensions of business partnerships and help you learn from partnerships that have worked well for certain businesses. Remember, as I always say, proper planning and relentless pursuit of goals are tips to stand out and be successful as a start-up entrepreneur.

Why You Need A Partnership

Many companies have provided their clients with a wide range of services and the best products owing to solid partnerships. Also, many companies have ideas about the right partnership and why one must need a partnership. It is, however, essential to remember that the partnership is only as good as the stakeholders involved. A good partnership works for both parties and should be based on mutual trust. The right partner can help your business grow, but it's also essential to ensure you're not being taken advantage of by a partner who doesn't share your goals or values. If you are in such a situation, let them know how strongly you feel about it before proceeding. Finding a partner for your business takes time. You need to know what you want in a business partner and what you are looking for in a partner. You must know what kind of company or individual you seek concerning a partnership. You should also be clear on what your aims are.[3]

It would be best if you had business partnerships for various reasons. When entrepreneurs join hands, they can magnify their presence across industries. With the help of a business partner, you can expand your reach and gain access to resources that might be unavailable to you on your own. You also have an opportunity to share knowledge and build new skills together. A business partnership is not just about sharing services or products; it's about sharing ideas and working together as a team. When entrepreneurs partner with brands, they get access to resources that can help them grow faster. They also get access to experts who can help them develop products and services that are in sync with the needs of their customers. A business partner gives you access to more people, which allows you to expand your network and reach more customers. A business partner enables you to market yourself by leveraging its resources. You may create a new product or service that takes off because it's promoted by someone else. Partnerships enable you to collaborate on projects at scale and make data-driven decisions quickly. Business partnerships are an excellent way for small businesses to grow and multiply. With the right partnership, you can increase your reach by partnering with others. You can also gain access to more customers and clients when you partner with other businesses in your industry or niche. You can diversify your product offerings and improve customer service by expanding your product line, services, or locations by adding other companies' products or services to your products or services. And when going for a business partnership, you can leverage the other person's knowledge and expertise. You get access to a broader network of markets, which can help you find more customers or partners as you move ahead. I have elaborated on three essential points here. Firstly, you need a partnership for ideas. A business partnership will yield ideas that you may not generate alone. Secondly, you need a partnership for investments. Investments are significant for all businesses, and the right partnership will probably guarantee suitable investments. Thirdly, you need a business partnership for insights. However much you might generate in terms of money if you have more profound insights into your business, you will go a long way.

For Ideas

What is the foremost reason an entrepreneur would want to have a business? The answer is simple: starting a business today is easier than ever.[4] With new technology and simplified processes, anyone can create a successful business online without prior experience or training in business management or salesmanship. Once you have made your website and social media profiles, you can market yourself as an entrepreneur who offers unique products or services at reasonable prices. However, one of the best ways to expand your business remains to find outstanding business partners. Your business partners will generate the best ideas. For this to happen, you must choose partners willing to work with you on your terms. Partnering with people who share ideas without any hesitation is vital. When a business person is trying to create a groundbreaking business idea, they need partners - for an added perspective, one that is not afraid to be blunt. When minds of an equal wavelength work together to make a business successful, there is no looking back after a point.

The right partnerships in business give way to splendid ideas. It is like your friends and family who want you to succeed. They want you to be happy, so they will support you when you are doing something new and exciting. You should also know that you need a good team to bring your ideas into reality, with the help of which your business will flourish and grow stronger daily. The ability to work together with others who share similar goals and visions is vital to success. It can be done through successful partnerships and alliances. The first step in establishing a partnership is determining what each party wants from the collaboration. Partnerships require both parties to be committed to the partnership's success, so both parties must be on board with the idea of working together. Once both sides have agreed upon what they want from each other, it's time to create your partnership agreement. If all these are in place, you are in for a reservoir of ideas due to your strong business partnerships. Some of the most incredible ideas exist because more extraordinary minds have worked on those together. Ideas fight ideas, and for you to take on a big company in the industry, you must have an idea that would take the world by storm.

For Investments

Another reason to join hands with the right partner is to ace investments. In many cases, business partnerships have led to solid investments. The best partnerships are often made by entrepreneurs who can identify good opportunities and make the right decisions at the right time. The key is knowing when to invest in a particular opportunity and when not to. You can't just cast a wide net and hope to find something that works out, or else you'll get nothing but bad deals. Regarding investments, you can't afford to do everything yourself. You need to find someone passionate about your product who can help you bring it to life. It would be best to have a partner who will work with you no matter what happens. As discussed earlier, you can expect two kinds of investments from a partnership. Firstly, joint ventures[5] and alliances, wherein two or more companies join together to create a new entity, often involve a profit division. Still, the individual companies do not own the joint entity. Secondly, Mergers and Acquisitions (M&A),[6] wherein one company buys another, often intending to take over its assets and business. When starting a business, thinking about the big picture and jumping headfirst into any promising venture is tempting. But if you're not careful, that can lead to big mistakes - like investing in companies with poor track records or signing up with partners who aren't suitable matches for your company.

Just identifying the investment type is not enough. How to go about finding the right partner for investment is equally significant. What kind of partnership do you want? How could you be sure of sealing the deal? These are the questions you must answer to decode the partnership mantra. Why is it important to consider multiple options before deciding on a partner? One option is to work together as equals. But if one partner has more experience than the other, it could be beneficial to have them handle more of the day-to-day operations so that they can focus on what they do best. Having compatible personalities will help keep your partnership running smoothly - but if there are issues between the two parties that can't be resolved, it could be time to look elsewhere for help. Business partners must get along well and trust each other enough to share critical information. If both parties feel comfortable sharing information concerning the business without hesitation, this could lead to a healthy business partnership. And this is true, especially in terms of investments.

For Insights

Businesses need to be agile and flexible to grow and succeed. They must also focus intensely on what matters most - customers, employees, shareholders, and clients. A company must be smart about innovating and developing new offerings in today's fast-paced world. The key to success is in aligning your business with the right partner or mentor who can help you achieve these goals. When you partner with the right firm or mentor for your business, you sign up for valuable insights. There are many ways to improve your business. You can hire more people or increase your sales. You can work harder, become more efficient, and practice better marketing techniques. You can even find a new job that's more rewarding and fun than your current one. But what about intangible things? What about the little things that make a big difference in how much money you earn and how happy you are? One of those is mentorship and business partnerships.[7]

The right business partners will help you grow faster than if you were trying to figure out everything independently. And they will help you avoid mistakes that can derail your progress toward success. You're also committing to putting in some extra time and effort. They can help you eliminate your bad habits and make good decisions. They can also help you develop new skills that will benefit your career and business long term. Furthermore, they can show you how to overcome challenges so you can grow and succeed as an entrepreneur. Your mentor can assist you with finding the right product and marketing strategy and even how to run a profitable business. The earlier in the process you begin looking for a partner, the more likely it will yield constructive results. Many entrepreneurs start by contacting the closest people they know and utilizing the situation best. While looking for a partner, try to find someone with experience doing what you want them to do for your company or project. They can help you create a successful plan and offer advice on what works best. Your new business partner will be able to help you navigate through unknown territory and make sure that you are on the right track. They can also help you avoid some common pitfalls entrepreneurs face when starting.

Aspects To Consider Before Partnering

Entrepreneurs often consider going for a business partnership to help achieve their goals. However, it's essential to understand that a successful business partnership takes work. Entrepreneurs should consider several vital factors before entering into a partnership. Compatibility between partners is crucial, ensuring they share the same vision for the business and can work together effectively. Trust is a critical element in any successful partnership. It's essential to have confidence in each other's honesty and integrity and to rely on each other to fulfill commitments. While entering a partnership, you must define and agree to each partner's roles and responsibilities within the business, ensuring that everyone understands their specific duties and that there is no confusion about who is responsible for what. Discussing the business finances is another significant aspect to consider - how it will be managed, including how much each partner will contribute, how profits will be split, and how expenses will be shared, is crucial to avoid financial conflicts.[8] Always having a written partnership agreement that outlines the terms of the partnership, including ownership percentages, decision-making processes, and what happens if one partner wants to leave the business, is essential to avoid any legal issues in the future. Another critical dimension I want to highlight is openness and honesty. Open and honest communication is crucial in any partnership. It sets the tone for many things in a business.

Finding the right business partner can be essential to building a successful business as an entrepreneur. A proper strategy for finding the right business partner can benefit entrepreneurs greatly. In that regard, identifying your needs is crucial to determining what skills, knowledge, and experience you need in a partner that can complement your strengths and weaknesses. As hinted earlier, networking is a great way to expand your reach and connect with potential partners. Attending industry events, conferences, and meetups can help you connect with individuals who share your interests and have the skills you seek. Reach out to colleagues, mentors, and other professionals in your industry to see if they know of any potential partners. Don't forget to conduct thorough research and due diligence on potential partners. Review their backgrounds, experience, qualifications, and any previous business ventures or partnerships they've participated in. Entrepreneurs can significantly increase their chances of building a successful and sustainable business with a proper strategy for finding the right business partner. I have discussed three aspects before going for a business partnership. Firstly, the vision of partners. Aligning your professional goals with your business partner's is vital for both parties. Secondly, I have written about the market and customers. These are of utmost importance and will either make or break the partnership for you. Thirdly, the outcome of your business partnership. You must be aware of the partnership in store for you to build a solid collaboration.

The Vision Of Partners

For a successful business partnership, understanding the partners' vision is essential.[9] The success of an organization depends upon its ability to get the best out of its employees and partners. A good partnership can be defined as one in which both partners have equal rights, responsibilities, and freedom to make decisions independently but with mutual understanding and respect for each other's position. The partners' vision helps define the objectives they want to work on together. It should be appropriate to the nature of business and mutually agreed upon by both parties before starting the deal. Understanding the vision will make it easier for them to work together effectively and efficiently. It will also help them know what each other expects from the partnership and what both parties need to do to ensure success. For example, suppose one partner wants to be the business's sole owner while another would prefer that he share ownership with someone else. In that case, they must develop a shared vision where both parties can feel comfortable about their role in the company. For instance, if one partner has more experience than another, both partners need to determine how much time should be dedicated toward learning new skills so that they can continue improving their skills as well as grow professionally together as part of this partnership.

The role of a business partner is to help you succeed. They are the closest thing to an authentic employee you will ever have. They are not only the stockholders of your business but also your partners. As a business owner, you need to be able to trust and rely on your business partners. If you don't have faith in them, it will affect your business's success. Vision is the most crucial thing in any business partnership. A successful business partnership depends on the vision of the partners. If you and your partner have different visions, it will be challenging to reach the milestones together and ensure all the goals are achieved. The vision should be clear enough to ensure you know where you are going and what you want to achieve. The vision is also an important tool to determine whether or not a partnership is working out as planned. If this is not something that interests you, then a partnership may not be suitable for you. For a partnership to work out, both parties need commitment and dedication. Understanding each other's vision and values is vital to a successful business partnership. It's also essential for making decisions together. If you can't agree on what your business is about, it will be hard for you to decide how best to achieve it.

The Market And Customers For The Partnership

The market and customers also play a significant role in ensuring success in business partnerships.[10] The market and customers are vital to ensure success in business partnerships. The partners should know the trends, the market, and the competition. They should also know what the potential of their business to grow is. The partners should clearly understand each other's strengths, weaknesses, and opportunities. They should also agree on how they will work together and ensure that both parties benefit from the partnership. The partners should establish their business plans based on market demand, customer needs, and other vital factors. While developing a partnership agreement that outlines how they will collaborate, the aspect of customers and markets is indispensable. The agreement should be clear about who is responsible for what tasks and how it will be done vis-a-vis customers and markets. The partners should also consider how they will share profits from their business relationship and any liabilities incurred during the partnership period.

We all know that the market is the buyers of products or services, and the customers are the people who buy a product or service. Both are important to ensure you are successful with your business partnerships. The market includes all buyers of your product and can be segmented into different categories, such as the general public, business buyers, and specific target markets. The general public comprises anyone with the right to buy or sell goods or services. Business buyers work in businesses that need to purchase products or services from suppliers. Specific target markets are small groups with similar needs and desires that differ from those of other groups within the same industry or industry groupings. When you have a strong market, the demand for your products or services will be high; hence, your revenues will also increase. However, when a market is weak, then there would be no one who would want to buy from you. Hence, your partnership based on these factors can bring you various rewards. A business partnership is a two-way relationship between two or more companies. This two-way relationship must be nurtured by both parties to ensure the best results for all stakeholders involved.[11]

The Outcome Of The Partnership

You must know the possible outcomes to know if your business partnership is worth your efforts. You must also understand the risks and rewards of each partner's role in the partnership.[12] For example, if one partner is responsible for revenue generation and another is responsible for profits, they will have different expectations from their roles. It may be that one partner is willing to work hard to make money but would like to keep it simple and not have to deal with day-to-day operations. The other partner may prefer working hard at making money and may want to take on a more hands-on role to provide their partner with more help and support when needed. Both partners must be willing to negotiate openly about how they want things done and their responsibilities going forward. One of the best ways to ensure success is by having regular meetings with both partners so that there's always clear communication between them about what needs to be done next or what needs improvement. If one partner wants to take over the business, but the other refuses, a compromise will likely have to be made. If both partners want the same things for their company and are willing to readjust them, then a good partnership can be formed. But if one partner wants to do everything their way and won't change their mind no matter what, then it's best not to get involved with them in the first place.

There are some outcomes that you may think of. Firstly, you have an opportunity to make money. If your idea is flourishing and you receive substantial profits, this is great for both parties. The investor gets his money back, and you can start a business independently. Secondly, you acquire a great asset. If other people want to work with you, then this means that their companies benefit from your skills, experience, and knowledge. You also get access to additional opportunities for profit. Thirdly, you gain substantially. If things turn out well for both parties and both parties benefit from their collaboration, they have made a good choice in choosing each other as partners. Business partnerships are a great way to get started in your own business, and they are also a great way to develop relationships with other people. However, if you don't plan or think about what will happen when it comes time to split up, you may regret it later. For this, you can be mindful of a few things to ensure your business partnership works out for the best. Firstly, keep track of all expenses. You need to keep an eye on the money spent by both parties so that all costs are accounted for, and no fraud occurs. It helps ensure that both parties share equally in any profits or losses incurred during the partnership. Secondly, make sure everyone has an equal say. When it comes time to divide up profits and losses, ensure everyone involved in the decision process has an equal say in how things will be handled from here on out. It includes ensuring that both parties have equal responsibility in managing day-to-day operations rather than just one person taking on too much work while leaving others behind without doing anything at all.

Why Is Partnership Important For Your Business

A partnership is an essential thing that you can opt for to help your business grow.[13] When you have a good partnership, you can focus on doing your job right and making money. A good partnership also enables you to keep your customers happy and loyal. Why is the right business partnership important for your business? A great business partnership makes you successful. It's what makes you grow and brings prosperity. A partnership is an agreement between two or more people, corporations, or other entities to carry out a task or accomplish a common goal. Partnerships can help with everything from sharing resources to coordinating actions. The most successful partnerships are mutually beneficial; both parties get something they want out of the arrangement. Partnerships are also essential for many businesses because they help companies avoid the costs of going it alone. A business partnership can allow you access to a broader range of customers and suppliers. A good partnership will help you to develop your skills, knowledge, and experience. It will also give you an extra pair of hands when it comes time to start your new venture or take on new projects.

The benefits of having a business partnership are endless, but having the right partner can make all the difference in the world.[14] A good business partnership is a mantra to success in any business. A successful partnership will help you get the most out of your business and fulfill your goals. Good partnerships are beneficial for both parties involved. A good partner understands your needs and will work with you to find solutions for both parties. A good partner also knows when to step in and take control of their part of the partnership. The right business partner is essential for your business because it helps you to increase your profit and improve your reputation. You can use the help of a business partner in many ways. For example, you can use their expertise in a particular area or task you cannot do alone. In addition, they can share their knowledge with you and help you to improve your skills in this area. A good business partnership also allows you to learn from someone who has already been through the same challenges you face now. It will enable you to avoid making mistakes at the beginning of your business journey that might eventually lead to failure. Finally, having a business partner who shares similar goals with yours will make working together more enjoyable and efficient in terms of time management. I have elaborated on three reasons why a business partnership is essential. Firstly, it establishes integrity for both parties. Integrity is vital for any business targeting to go a long way in the industry. Secondly, it delivers variety. When two or more stakeholders come together to form a business partnership, it yields more variety - be it for products, services, marketing strategies, or operations. Thirdly, it reaffirms the reputation of all the parties involved. It is true, especially when a start-up partners with a renowned company.

Establishes Integrity

The right business partnership establishes integrity among the partners and customers, who trust both brands more post-partnership.[15] The right business partnership is one in which the partners have agreed to work together and have yet to establish a collective identity. While there are many reasons why businesses should partner with each other, the most common reason is that they need each other's products or services. There are many benefits that companies can enjoy from partnerships. They both get access to a larger market, which gives them more resources and capabilities to compete with rivals; it helps them build their brand and attract new customers. They can sell products across borders without having to change prices or packaging. The right business partner is willing to work with you for the long term, not just the short term. It knows that it's not about how much you pay them but how much they can help your business grow and profit. A good partner understands and respects your brand and its values. A good partner will always be willing to invest their time and expertise in helping you achieve your goals.

The partnership is also supposed to create value for both parties involved. The value can be quantified in terms of money or goodwill. It is important to note that there are two types of value: financial and non-financial. You need to conduct a cost-benefit analysis to know what financial value your company can expect from a partnership with another company. It means that you should identify all costs involved in the deal and then determine how much money it will cost you to acquire the benefits of that deal. On the other hand, non-financial value refers not just to money but also includes intangible factors such as brand equity and customer loyalty. For instance, if one company has invested heavily in its brand image over time, it would be foolish not to get some benefit from another company's investments in its brand image as well. A business partnership is a long-term commitment between two or more companies. It helps both parties to grow their business, and it also benefits the customers. If done the right way, a business partnership can benefit both partners. It is particularly true for a brand that seeks to establish a new identity. A partnership can help a company establish its credibility and build trust with customers, suppliers, and other partners. A partnership also allows brands to communicate more effectively with each other and their customers. Starbucks and Seattle's Best Coffee are excellent examples of how this can work. Starbucks' partnership with Seattle's Best Coffee helped it become one of the world's leading independent coffee companies. Starbucks has since expanded its presence in other countries worldwide by using similar partnerships as part of its growth strategy.

Delivers Variety

An effective business partnership would mean variety in products or services for customers.[16] With various products and services, customers are likelier to choose you over the competition. The better your products or services are, the more likely you will succeed in any business. It is imperative to have a variety of products and services if you want to be successful in the business world. It would be best to offer what your customer wants rather than what you think. You can only succeed if you provide something new to your customers. It would also mean that the partners would work together to make the best decisions, even when they conflict. It is because it's hard always to please everyone, so your partner can help you with some of those tough decisions and ensure you're always creating a product or service that will delight your customers. A good partner would also be willing to help with marketing and advertising. For example, they could create ads for your product or service and run them in local newspapers and television stations. You could also use their contacts with other companies to get more exposure for your business.

Going ahead with variety would mean taking care of clients and expanding. A great partner is also willing to help you get new clients and grow your business in new ways. A great business partner brings their expertise and resources to the partnership and is ready to leverage their networks and relationships to help their partner's business grow. A well-connected partner in your industry or target market can introduce you to potential clients, partners, or investors who can help you expand your business in new ways. For example, suppose you have a store in a mall. In that case, they can get more customers from those areas by taking advantage of their existing relationships with the mall management and ensuring that the mall knows about your business. They may also have insights into new trends or opportunities you can leverage to gain a competitive advantage. Additionally, a business partner committed to your success will be invested in helping you achieve your goals. They may be willing to collaborate on marketing initiatives, offer feedback on your products or services, or provide guidance on navigating industry challenges. Ultimately, a great business partner shares your vision for success and is committed to helping you achieve it. They are willing to go above and beyond to support your business and help you realize your full potential.

Reaffirms Reputation

The relationship between two brands can be defined as a symbiotic relationship where one benefits from the other's resources. The partnership can be mutually beneficial, and mutually beneficial relationships will keep both partners on board for many years to come. It is important to note that partnerships are not all about money; they can also be about trust, loyalty, and reputation.[17] When your business establishes a partnership with a worthy company or individual, it helps reaffirm your brand's reputation. Reputation is built with much effort during partnerships, and it can be a great way to expand your reach. When you partner with another organization, you want to be sure you are working with someone with similar values. It also gives you access to a new audience, which can be invaluable in marketing and branding. If you have a good reputation, you'll be more likely to attract customers looking for quality products and services. When you partner with other companies or individuals, you're not just creating a new business relationship. You're building a lasting partnership between yourself and the other party.

Partnerships can help increase profits by leveraging each other's strengths and weaknesses.[18] For example, if you're a small business specializing in software development but need an established company's expertise in marketing, advertising, and sales, working together could help both sides achieve their goals more quickly and efficiently. Another example is when you partner with a quality restaurant or hotel, elevating the standard of your business. Partnering with a high-quality audio equipment provider gives your brand the credibility of the industry leader. When you partner with a quality organization, you can show that you are committed to giving back in community service. Partnerships also provide opportunities for innovation. For example, when one of your partners has something new that could improve what you already do, try it out first. It will help build trust between you and your partner and may lead to other opportunities. It is imperative if you are in a competitive industry and want to set yourself apart from other businesses. An excellent example is when Bill and Hillary Clinton's decision to collaborate with Apple (NASDAQ: AAPL) was initially met with skepticism. However, the partnership proved successful for both parties. By working with a company like Apple, Clinton had an opportunity to effectively communicate his message to consumers and help them understand who he was and what he stood for.

Partnerships That Are Exemplars For Every Start-Up

Entrepreneurs can learn many valuable lessons from the strategic business partnerships of start-ups that have become leading names in their industries. Strategic partnerships work best when each partner brings unique strengths to the table.[19] For example, the partnership between Uber and Spotify combined Uber's transportation services with Spotify's music streaming platform, offering customers a more enjoyable and personalized experience. Partnerships are most effective when both parties share a common vision and are committed to achieving shared goals. It was evident in the partnership between Airbnb and WeWork. It aimed to create a seamless travel experience for customers by combining Airbnb's home-sharing platform with WeWork's co-working spaces. Successful partnerships often leverage new technologies or approaches to disrupt existing markets. For example, the partnership between Square and Starbucks introduced mobile payments to the coffee chain's customers, making purchasing items faster and more convenient. Also, the best partnerships are adaptable and can evolve to meet changing market conditions or customer needs. The partnership between Apple and IBM has evolved over the years, with both companies working together to develop new enterprise applications and services for their customers. A focus on the customer is also critical for any successful partnership. For instance, the partnership between Warby Parker and Nordstrom allowed Warby Parker to expand its reach by offering its products through Nordstrom stores, providing customers with a more convenient way to shop for eyewear. By studying the strategic business partnerships of successful start-ups, entrepreneurs can gain insights into what works and what doesn't in partnership building. These lessons can help them develop successful partnerships and drive business growth. Following are some that I have compiled for your ready reference:

Casper And West Elm

Casper, a popular mattress start-up, partnered with West Elm, a furniture retailer, in 2017 to sell their mattresses in West Elm stores and on the West Elm website.[20] This partnership is a testimony to the power of effective collaboration. The partnership between Casper and West Elm made sense strategically, as both companies catered to a similar target market - young, urban consumers who valued design and comfort. West Elm is a well-established brand with a strong reputation for quality furniture and home goods. By partnering with West Elm, Casper gained credibility and exposure among West Elm's existing customer base. West Elm has an extensive distribution network of retail stores and an established e-commerce platform. Through this partnership, Casper was able to leverage West Elm's distribution channels and expand their reach. Furthermore, the partnership between Casper and West Elm was innovative and unique, as it combined a mattress start-up with a furniture retailer. This approach helped both companies differentiate themselves in the highly competitive retail landscape. The Casper-West Elm partnership was a win-win for both companies, allowing them to tap into new markets and expand their customer base.

Company Name: Casper; West Elm

Founded: 2014; 2002

Significant reason(s) for success: The companies attracted customers worldwide by offering necessary and durable products. Both companies have redefined the optics for each other by collaborating smartly and integrating their visions seamlessly across the industry.

BMA Group And Talentank

The business partnership between BMA Group and Talentank is commendable.[21] The two companies have formed a strong working relationship, developing beneficial services. The two companies sought to create a more efficient and effective way of hiring talent. Both organizations have invested in each other's businesses, creating a platform for growth and expansion. This is particularly true of Talentank's product range, which BMA Group has developed to provide training solutions for their clients. It has been a beneficial relationship for both companies, with both sides benefiting from the partnership. The two firms have entered into a Memorandum of Understanding (MOU) to create a joint venture that provides training, consulting, and mentoring services to clients in the healthcare, education, government, and non-profit sectors. The partnership was designed with the aim of these two companies expanding their offerings to address the needs of their respective clients. It demonstrates a commitment to accelerating innovation and supporting potential talent from both companies. The two companies are looking to work together to create a new type of business that will be more profitable for both parties and help the environment. The partnership between these two companies will enable them to contribute to the development of the workforce globally by allowing them to learn and improve their skills. The training programs that both parties are offering will be beneficial not only for their employees but also for their clients. This collaboration will help both parties maximize profits and make their business more competitive. It will also help them expand their business by offering new services and products that can better meet the needs of their clients and users.

Company Name: BMA Group; Talentank

Founded: 1997; 2009

Significant reason(s) for success: Providing extraordinary human resource and recruitment assistance. Both companies have taken great advantage of the partnership, ensuring growth in the industry.

Aurora And Toyota

In April 2022, Aurora announced the signing of a letter of intent with Toyota Motor Corporation to develop and deploy advanced automotive technologies that will be used to produce self-driven cars.[22] The deal is part of a broader investment collaboration between both companies, which also involves Aurora's partnership with Toyota on developing advanced self-driven vehicles. Toyota is a Japanese automotive manufacturer that was founded in 1937. The corporation has become one of the world's largest companies, with annual sales of over 10 million vehicles in 2016. Aurora and Toyota announced a partnership to develop self-driving taxis. The collaboration aimed to integrate Aurora's self-driving system with Toyota's vehicles, starting with the Toyota Sienna minivan. The partnership was seen as a significant boost for Aurora, which had previously partnered with several other automakers. In July 2020, it was reported that Aurora had paused testing of its self-driving vehicles due to the COVID-19 pandemic. However, the partnership with Toyota was said to be continuing, with both companies reportedly working on integrating Aurora's self-driving technology with Toyota's e-Palette autonomous vehicle platform. Overall, the collaboration between Aurora and Toyota has been seen as a positive development in autonomous driving. Both companies bring significant expertise and resources to the partnership, and their combined efforts could help accelerate the development of self-driving technology. Many are hopeful that this partnership will yield great results in the future.

Company Name: Aurora; Toyota

Founded: 2017; 1937

Significant reason(s) for success: Offering the best products and innovation in the industry. The partnership between these two companies is strategic, and both have utilized each other's strengths to create something that would go a long way.

Walgreens And Pager

The partnership between Walgreens and Pager, a virtual care and telehealth platform, provides several lessons and takeaways entrepreneurs must benefit from.[23] Choosing a partner that aligns with your business goals and values is essential when considering a partnership. Walgreens and Pager identified a mutual interest in expanding access to healthcare services, making the partnership a strategic fit. With the increasing reliance on technology, incorporating it into your business model can improve customer experience and streamline operations. It is precisely what these companies have done. Walgreens and Pager used technology to connect patients with healthcare providers in real-time, creating a seamless and convenient healthcare experience. This partnership also cements the belief that collaborating with other businesses can lead to innovative solutions and better outcomes. Walgreens and Pager combined their expertise to create a new way of delivering healthcare services, demonstrating the power of collaboration. Both companies agree that it is crucial to prioritize customer needs and satisfaction to succeed as businesses. And this partnership is a visible gesture in this regard. Walgreens and Pager focused on providing patients with a convenient and accessible healthcare experience, enhancing customer loyalty, and generating positive reviews and referrals. Walgreens and Pager also recognized the growing demand for virtual healthcare services and adapted their business model to meet this need. Adapting to changing market conditions and consumer preferences is necessary for a rapidly evolving industry. The partnership between Walgreens and Pager highlights the importance of strategic partnerships, technology, collaboration, customer focus, and adaptability in achieving business success. You can learn and apply these principles to your ventures to drive growth and innovation.

Company Name: Walgreens; Pager

Founded: 1901; 2014

Significant reason(s) for success: Prioritizing essential services for customers. Both companies have leveraged the partnership avenues and grown immensely ever since.

Louis Vuitton And BMW

Louis Vuitton and BMW are another fantastic business partnership with outstanding results.[24] The two brands have worked together for years and collaborated on several products, including leather goods and accessories. The two companies do not belong primarily to the same industry. They had different goals and visions for their businesses, but they were able to come together and collaborate on a project that brought them both successes. Louis Vuitton has always been an innovator in the luxury industry. Louis Vuitton partnered with BMW to design its next generation of bags. The designer's initials LV were embossed on the interior of each bag, along with a signature tag that reads "Louis Vuitton x BMW." It was an exciting idea because it showed that BMW was willing to create a product based on something else instead of creating its product. It is something that other companies should take note of when thinking about partnerships or collaborations with other brands in their industry. The best part about this partnership? The results speak for themselves, especially in terms of sales. Not only did this collaboration produce excellent results in sales numbers, but it also resulted in more brand awareness for both companies.

Company Name: Louis Vuitton; BMW

Founded: 1854; 1916

Significant reason(s) for success: Focusing on specific clientele and offering the best products. Both companies have benefited immensely from the collaboration and ensure the best quality in whatever they offer.

DeltaTrainer And Anytime Fitness

The business partnership between DeltaTrainer and Anytime Fitness is a solid collaboration.[25] It has several reasons. Many people talk about the benefits that this partnership offers to both companies. DeltaTrainer gains access to Anytime Fitness's large customer base, while Anytime Fitness can offer its customers a new service through DeltaTrainer's AI-powered fitness coaching. They would also achieve many milestones together, which they couldn't have achieved at that pace individually. DeltaTrainer and Anytime Fitness share the goal of helping people improve their health and fitness. This alignment of goals ensures that the partnership is focused on creating value for customers. The partnership is also essential vis-a-vis complementary services. DeltaTrainer's technology and AI-powered coaching complement Anytime Fitness's gym facilities, creating a comprehensive fitness solution for customers. Such a partnership ensures incredible scalability. Anytime Fitness has a significant global presence, making it easier for DeltaTrainer to expand its reach through the partnership. Many people are hopeful and enthusiastic about the kind of record this partnership will bring to both brands in the coming times. Anytime Fitness is a well-established brand with a successful track record in the fitness industry, which lends credibility to the partnership. Overall, the partnership between DeltaTrainer and Anytime Fitness appears to be a solid collaboration because it offers mutual benefits, aligns with shared goals, combines complementary services, provides scalability, and leverages a track record of success. These factors suggest that the partnership has the potential to be successful for both companies and their customers. And entrepreneurs must learn a great deal from this collaboration.

Company Name: DeltaTrainer; Anytime Fitness

Founded: 2019; 2002

Significant reason(s) for success: Offering the best fitness services and evolving with the requirements of changing times. Both companies have come forward to utilize the best practices of each other and make a difference in the industry.

Conclusion

In conclusion, a good business partnership can be a game-changer for your company.[26] It can provide much-needed support and expertise as you navigate the challenges of entrepreneurship. However, finding the right partner is critical. Take the time to assess your needs, values, and goals, and seek out potential partners who share them. Remember that a successful partnership requires open communication, trust, and a shared vision for the future. You can achieve great things with the right partner and take your business to new heights.

A successful partnership can be the key to significant growth for your business. By finding the right partner, you can tap into a wealth of skills, experience, and resources to accelerate your growth and increase your revenue and profitability. With two business partners working together, you can accomplish more in less time, focus on your strengths, and delegate tasks you may not enjoy or excel at. Additionally, a business partner can bring in new ideas and perspectives, expanding your market reach and helping you capitalize on new opportunities. By communicating openly and building trust, you and your partner can create a solid and successful business that is more incredible than the sum of its parts. The right approach to a meaningful business partnership will help in the long run, especially for start-ups. Collaborating with other businesses can offer a range of benefits, such as access to new markets, new customers, shared expertise, resources, and technology, and the ability to scale more quickly. When forming a partnership, it's crucial to approach it with a focus on creating mutual value and benefit. It means that both parties should clearly understand what they hope to achieve and what they can bring to the partnership. As I mentioned, communication is crucial to ensuring that both parties are aligned on goals and expectations. Choosing partners who share your values, vision, and commitment to success is equally important. It will help to ensure that the partnership is sustainable and can withstand any challenges that may arise. Meaningful business partnerships can be a great way to accelerate growth and achieve success in the long run. However, it's essential to approach them with the right mindset and take the time to build relationships based on mutual trust and respect.

Forming the right business partnership requires determination, hard work, and support. Starting a business and creating a partnership can be challenging and uncertain, and getting discouraged is easy. But by staying focused on your goals and working hard to achieve them, you can overcome obstacles and progress toward success. In addition to trusting in your plans and efforts, seeking support and guidance from others who can offer valuable insights and expertise is essential. It might include mentors, business partners, advisors, or other entrepreneurs who have been through similar experiences. By creating an environment of trust and transparency and seeking out the help and advice of others, you can increase your chances of success and build a thriving business over time.

Following are the brief takeaways from this chapter, which I have compiled for your easy reference. You must thoroughly study them and move ahead with conviction.

1. It would be best if you had a business partnership for ideas.
2. A partnership also helps with investments.
3. It gives you valuable insights that you may not gain as the only driving force of your business.
4. The vision of the partners will decide the fate of the partnership. Aligning visions also minimizes conflicts.
5. The market and customers are important factors for a successful collaboration.
6. It would be best if you were prepared for the outcome of partnerships. Visualizing this will give you clear ideas of whether to move ahead with the planned partnership.
7. Business partnerships help entrepreneurs establish integrity as far as their businesses, visions, and values are concerned.
8. You can deliver various products/services and operations with the right partnership.
9. The right partnership reaffirms your reputation as a start-up.

References

1. Forbes (2023). *12 tips to solidify 'win-win' Partnerships in business.* Available at: https://www.forbes.com/sites/forbesbusinessdevelopmentcouncil/2023/02/06/12-tips-to-solidify-win-win-partnerships-in-business/?sh=7dd2a49226d0 [Accessed 5 Mar. 2023].
2. Brown, S. *et al.* (2021). *Collaborations between corporates and start-ups.* Available at: https://www.mckinsey.com/capabilities/strategy-and-corporate-finance/our-insights/collaborations-between-corporates-and-start-ups [Accessed 5 Mar. 2023].
3. Forbes (2018). *Eight important elements of successful business partnerships.* Available at: https://www.forbes.com/sites/forbesbusinessdevelopmentcouncil/2018/12/18/eight-important-elements-of-successful-business-partnerships/?sh=3d7f48e6128d [Accessed 5 Mar. 2023].
4. HBS (2020). *10 characteristics of successful entrepreneurs.* Available at: https://online.hbs.edu/blog/post/characteristics-of-successful-entrepreneurs [Accessed 5 Mar. 2023].

5. Stott, A. (2022). *Partnerships and joint ventures: How can they benefit your business?* Available at: https://www.forbes.com/sites/forbescoachescouncil/2022/09/29/partnerships-and-joint-ventures-how-can-they-benefit-your-business/?sh=f8bec7e6828d [Accessed 5 Mar. 2023].
6. Harvard Business Review (2009). *Don't integrate your acquisitions, partner with them.* Available at: https://hbr.org/2009/12/dont-integrate-your-acquisitions-partner-with-them [Accessed 5 Mar. 2023].
7. CIO (2022). *A partnership approach for turning data into insights.* Available at: https://www.cio.com/article/304031/a-partnership-approach-for-turning-data-into-insights.html [Accessed 5 Mar. 2023].
8. Forbes (2022). *15 tips to realign and resolve conflict with your business partner.* Available at: https://www.forbes.com/sites/theyec/2021/11/01/15-tips-to-realign-and-resolve-conflict-with-your-business-partner/?sh=2396eefb23f0 [Accessed 5 Mar. 2023].
9. Watenpaugh, N. (2019). *Aligning your organization with your strategic partner relationships.* Available at: https://www.forbes.com/sites/forbessanfranciscocouncil/2019/01/07/aligning-your-organization-with-your-strategic-partner-relationships/?sh=da946f020be1 [Accessed 5 Mar. 2023].
10. Backer, R. D. & Rinaudo, E. K. (2019) *Improving the management of complex business partnerships.* Available at: https://www.mckinsey.com/capabilities/strategy-and-corporate-finance/our-insights/improving-the-management-of-complex-business-partnerships [Accessed 5 Mar. 2023].
11. Kopp, C. M. (2023). *Partnership: Definition, how it works, taxation, and types.* Available at: https://www.investopedia.com/terms/p/partnership.asp [Accessed 5 Mar. 2023].
12. Indeed (2022). *Guide to business partnership roles.* Available at: https://www.indeed.com/career-advice/career-development/partnership-roles [Accessed 5 Mar. 2023].
13. Business (2023). *Benefits of strategic partnerships.* Available at: https://www.business.com/articles/connor-blakley-strategic-partnerships/ [Accessed 5 Mar. 2023].
14. Forbes (2022). *Eight essential qualities of a successful business partner.* Available at: https://www.forbes.com/sites/theyec/2021/07/15/eight-essential-qualities-of-a-successful-business-partner/?sh=4ac641a2374f [Accessed 5 Mar. 2023].
15. GrowPartnerships (2022). *Everything you need to know about partnership marketing.* Available at: https://growpartnerships.medium.com/what-is-partnership-marketing-and-what-are-the-different-types-67da4b4d5cf3

[Accessed 5 Mar. 2023].

16. Yovanno, D. A. (2022). *Partnerships: A great way to establish trust and become more relevant with consumers.* Available at: https://www.forbes.com/sites/forbesagencycouncil/2022/06/23/partnerships-a-great-way-to-establish-trust-and-become-more-relevant-with-consumers/?sh=5b9b7fd04a46 [Accessed 5 Mar. 2023].
17. Bernazzani, S. (2022). *21 examples of successful co-branding Partnerships (and why they're so effective).* Available at: https://blog.hubspot.com/marketing/best-cobranding-partnerships [Accessed 5 Mar. 2023].
18. Inc. (2018). *6 steps to creating a partnership that drives strong business growth.* Available at: https://www.inc.com/marissa-levin/6-steps-to-creating-a-partnership-that-drives-strong-business-growth.html [Accessed 5 Mar. 2023].
19. Safoian, T. (2019). *How the right strategic partnerships can drive business growth.* Available at: https://www.forbes.com/sites/forbestechcouncil/2019/01/29/how-the-right-strategic-partnerships-can-drive-business-growth/?sh=7af3609a2c10 [Accessed 5 Mar. 2023].
20. Danziger, P. N. (2018). *Casper has figured out how to sell more mattresses: Sleep before you buy.* Available at: https://www.forbes.com/sites/pamdanziger/2018/07/12/casper-has-figured-out-how-to-sell-more-mattresses-let-em-sleep-on-it/?sh=2155292d2d48 [Accessed 5 Mar. 2023].
21. NimB (2017). *BMA Group to shake up recruiting with Unique Service.* Available at: https://newsismybusiness.com/recruiting-unique-service/ [Accessed 5 Mar. 2023].
22. Hirsch, J. (2022). *Toyota and Aurora craft deal to develop self-driving taxis, Forbes.* Forbes Magazine. Available at: https://www.forbes.com/wheels/news/toyota-aurora-deal-develop-self-driving-taxis/ [Accessed 5 Mar. 2023].
23. Baum, S. (2017). *Doctor-on-demand service pager gains national presence.* Available at: https://medcitynews.com/2015/10/doctor-on-demand-service-pagers-latest-deal-gives-it-national-presence/ [Accessed 5 Mar. 2023].
24. Binlot, A. (2017). *Quintessentially expands into marketing, PR and events in US with clients like BMW, LVMH.* Available at: https://www.forbes.com/sites/abinlot/2017/07/31/quintessentially-expands-into-marketing-pr-and-events-in-us-with-clients-like-bmw-lvmh/?sh=439500b53e46 [Accessed 5 Mar. 2023].
25. Mericle, J. (2021). DeltaTrainer partners with Anytime Fitness. Available at: https://www.bizjournals.com/pittsburgh/news/2021/02/23/

pittsburgh-startup-partners-with-anytime-fitness.html [Accessed 5 Mar. 2023].

26. Inc. (2014). *9 key things successful business partners always do*. Available at: https://www.inc.com/bill-murphy-jr/9-key-things-successful-business-partners-always-do.html [Accessed 5 Mar. 2023].

CHAPTER 9
Listening to the Customer

Start-ups are founded based on a great idea or innovation, but it takes more than that to succeed in the competitive business world. In the world of start-ups, it can be easy to focus on building a unique product or service and forget about the people who will ultimately use it. But in reality, listening to customers is crucial for the success of any business. Customer experience[1] plays a vital role in retention, and start-ups prioritizing their customers tend to achieve excellent results. This chapter focuses on listening to customers and their role in start-up success. This chapter emphasizes the significance of identifying and solving the right problems through customer feedback. Listening to customers gives start-ups valuable insights into their target market's preferences, pain points, and expectations. This information enables start-ups to develop products or services that meet customers' needs, resulting in higher customer satisfaction and loyalty. You must have read about examples of successful start-ups such as Zoomcar, Honk Mobile Inc., Tesla, and Black Girl Sunscreen in the Introduction section of this book. These were companies that all integrated customer feedback into their business strategies.

Ultimately, the success of a start-up hinges on its ability to solve the right problems, and listening to customers is a crucial component of this. By prioritizing customers and incorporating their feedback into their business strategies, start-ups can develop products and services that meet their customers' needs and exceed their expectations. This chapter will also discuss the role of technology in listening to customers, specifically social listening. By monitoring social media comments and employing social listening technology, start-ups can identify customer pain points, track customer calls, and incorporate customer sentiment into their marketing strategy. I have explored the "why" and "how" of listening to customers for start-ups. I will also discuss why listening to customers should be integral to a start-up's early days. After you finish reading this chapter, you will understand how customer feedback provides real-time data on their thinking about the company, enabling the organization to make informed decisions and develop a better product or service.

Why Do Start-Ups Need To Listen To Customers?

The success of any start-up depends on its ability to acknowledge and meet the needs of its target customers.[2] As a start-up founder, your vision and passion are crucial for your business. However, it is equally important to recognize that your customers are the driving forces of your business. With their support, your start-up will be able to survive. So, why do start-ups need to listen to customers? Firstly, customer feedback is essential for developing products or services that people want. You can gain insights into their pain points, preferences, and behaviors by soliciting customer feedback. You can use this information to guide product development, ensuring that you are creating something that meets the needs of your target audience. By understanding their pain points and preferences, you can create something that meets their needs rather than just assuming what they want. This approach saves time and money in the long run by avoiding developing products that don't resonate with your target audience. Furthermore, listening to your customers can help refine your business strategy. By understanding your customers' needs and behaviors, you can tailor your marketing efforts to sync with them. You can also identify new growth opportunities, whether expanding your product line or targeting new customer segments. Customer feedback can also help you to make informed decisions about pricing, packaging, and distribution strategies.

Customer feedback is essential for building brand loyalty and trust. When customers feel that their opinions and feedback are valued, they are more likely to feel invested in your brand. It can increase customer retention, word-of-mouth referrals, and positive online reviews. You can build strong brand loyalty by demonstrating that you are actively listening to your customers and considering their feedback. It can also help you to relook at your marketing strategy. As mentioned, you can customize how you connect to them to ensure healthy customer relationships. In short, listening to customers is critical for the success of any start-up. It allows you to develop products and services that meet the expectations of your target audience, refine your business strategy, and build strong relationships with your customers. By prioritizing customer feedback and making it an integral part of your decision-making process, you can position your start-up for long-term success. I have divided this section into three aspects. Understanding these will help you to see why you need to listen to your customers as a start-up entrepreneur. Firstly, I have talked about how listening to customers helps start-ups to offer what is relevant. Secondly, I have discussed how this process makes it easier for customers to participate in the business, which is crucial. Lastly, I have elaborated on how it helps you create a strong feedback loop, a critical business growth dimension.

To Offer What's Relevant

One of the most important reasons start-ups need to listen to their customers is to ensure they offer what's relevant. For example, consider the success of Airbnb. The company started as a platform for renting air mattresses in a spare room but quickly realized their customers were looking for more. By listening to their customers, they discovered that people wanted unique and authentic travel experiences. It led to the "Experiences" feature, which allows hosts to offer activities and tours that provide a more immersive travel experience. Another example is the meal kit delivery service, Blue Apron. The company launched with a standard subscription model but soon discovered that many customers were overwhelmed by the cooking involved. By listening to their customers, Blue Apron introduced "Knockouts," which offers pre-prepared and partially cooked meals that can be assembled in minutes. This change made the service more accessible to busy customers who still wanted the convenience of a meal kit delivery service. In both of these examples, listening to customers allowed these start-ups to pivot their offerings in a way that better met the needs of their target audience. By offering what's relevant, these companies were able to stay ahead of the competition and build strong, loyal customer bases. Start-ups that ignore customer feedback and fail to adapt their offerings to meet changing needs and preferences risk falling behind and becoming irrelevant.

Offering relevant products is critical for the success of start-ups for several reasons. First and foremost, relevant products or services are more likely to meet the needs and preferences of the target audience, which can lead to increased customer satisfaction and loyalty. By providing a solution that solves a specific problem or fulfills a particular desire, start-ups can differentiate themselves from competitors. It can help them establish themselves as leaders in their industry. Customers are more likely to go for products or services they perceive as relevant to their needs[3] and to recommend those products or services to others. It can increase sales and expand the customer base, positively impacting the bottom line. In addition, offering relevant products or services can increase revenue and profitability. Offering relevant products or services can also help start-ups to build a strong brand reputation. Customers who feel a start-up provides products or services tailored to their needs are more likely to trust and respect that company. It can lead to positive word-of-mouth marketing and a solid online presence, which can help start-ups to attract prospective customers and create brand awareness. As discussed earlier, offering relevant products or services can help start-ups to stay ahead of the competition. By constantly listening to customer feedback and adapting their offerings accordingly, start-ups can ensure that they are always meeting the evolving needs of their target audience. It can help them stay ahead of competitors who are slower to adapt or not as attuned to customer needs.

To Make It Easy For Customers To Participate In Businesses

Making it easy for customers to participate in businesses is crucial for start-up success. By removing barriers to participation, start-ups can increase customer engagement and build strong, loyal customer bases. It can increase sales, revenue, positive word-of-mouth marketing, and a solid online presence. One way start-ups can make it easy for customers to participate is by offering convenient and user-friendly platforms for purchasing and interacting with their products or services. For example,

Amazon has become known for its one-click ordering system, which makes it incredibly easy for customers to purchase products with just a few clicks. This system has helped Amazon to become the dominant player in the online retail space, with millions of customers around the world. Another way that start-ups can make it easy for customers to participate is by offering personalized and targeted marketing campaigns. By gathering customer preferences and behavior data, start-ups can create marketing campaigns tailored to individual customers. It can increase the relevance of marketing messages and make customers more likely to engage with the brand. A third way start-ups can make it easy for customers to participate is by offering flexible and convenient payment options.[4] For example, mobile payment options like Apple Pay and Google Wallet make it incredibly easy for customers to purchase on the go without needing cash or credit cards. It can increase customer convenience and make it more likely that they will make a purchase. Start-ups can make it easy for customers to participate by offering exceptional customer service. It can lead to positive word-of-mouth marketing and a reputation for excellent customer service. By providing timely and responsive customer support, start-ups can build strong customer relationships and foster loyalty.

Customer participation in business is integral for start-up success because it allows start-ups to understand and meet the preferences and needs of their target audience. When customers participate in a business, they become invested in the company's success. They are more likely to provide valuable feedback that can help the start-up to improve its products or services. It can come from online reviews, social media comments, or direct communication with customer service representatives. By considering customer feedback, start-ups can change their offerings tailored to their target audience's needs and preferences. It can lead to increased customer satisfaction and loyalty and a competitive advantage over other businesses that are slower to adapt to customer needs. As pointed out in many ways, customer participation can help start-ups to build a strong brand reputation. When customers feel that a business values and considers their opinions, they are likelier to trust and respect that company. It can lead to positive word-of-mouth marketing and a robust online presence, which can help start-ups attract new customers and build brand awareness. By providing opportunities for customers to participate in the business, such as by leaving reviews or participating in surveys, start-ups can gather valuable insights into customer preferences and behaviors. It can help them create more targeted and effective marketing campaigns and make changes to their offerings that are more likely to resonate with their target audience. Furthermore, customer participation can lead to increased sales and revenue for start-ups.

To Generate A Strong Feedback Loop

Generating a solid feedback loop is essential for start-up success.[5] By creating a system allowing open and honest customer feedback, start-ups can gain valuable insights into their target audience, improve their products or services, and build strong, loyal customer bases. As discussed earlier, one way to generate a strong feedback loop is by actively involving customers. By actively seeking feedback, start-ups can demonstrate that they value the opinions and experiences of their customers and create a culture of open communication. Another way to generate a strong feedback loop is by using analytics tools to track customer behavior and preferences. By gathering data on customer interactions with a website or product, start-ups can gain insights into what works well and what needs improvement. This data can then be used to make changes more likely to resonate with the target audience. You could also generate a strong feedback loop by creating a system of rewards and incentives for customers who provide feedback. It works wonders for many companies. For example, start-ups can offer discounts or exclusive access to new products or features for customers who leave reviews or participate in surveys. It can encourage customers to provide feedback and create a culture of engagement and participation. You must respond promptly and transparently to customer feedback to ensure a strong feedback loop. By addressing concerns and questions promptly and respectfully, start-ups can build trust and loyalty with their customers. It can lead to many avenues for your company in the future.

The benefits of generating a strong feedback loop for start-ups are multi-faceted and critical for long-term success. One of the most significant benefits is that it allows start-ups to gain valuable insights into the requirements of their target audience. By actively soliciting feedback and using analytics tools, start-ups can understand what works well and what needs improvement. This information can help start-ups to create better products or services, improve customer experiences, and make better strategic decisions. In addition, generating a solid feedback loop can help start-ups to build robust customer bases. Customers who feel that their feedback is valued continue doing business with that company. It can increase customer loyalty, positive word-of-mouth marketing, and a strong reputation for excellent customer service. By actively seeking feedback and responding promptly to customer concerns or complaints, start-ups can minimize the negative impact on their business and prevent issues from escalating. Furthermore, generating a solid feedback loop can help start-ups to identify and address problems quickly. It can lead to a more positive customer experience, increased customer retention, and improved brand reputation. Generating a solid feedback loop can also help start-ups to make more informed business decisions. By gathering data and insights from customer feedback, start-ups can make more informed decisions about product development, marketing strategies, and other essential aspects of their business. It can help start-ups to stay competitive, make better use of their resources, and ultimately, increase profitability.

How Does Listening To Customers Impact Start-Ups?

Listening to customers is crucial for start-ups looking to succeed in today's competitive business landscape. Start-ups that listen to their customers can gain valuable insights into their target audience and use this information to create better products or services, improve customer experiences, and make better strategic decisions. This approach has been successful for numerous start-ups, such as Square, which provides payment processing services. Square was founded in 2009 to help small businesses accept credit card payments. However, the company soon realized that many customers wanted more than payment processing services. They wanted additional features, such as inventory management and customer loyalty programs. Square listened to this feedback and added new features and services to its platform. Today, Square offers a wide range of services that help small businesses manage all aspects of their operations, from payments to inventory management. By listening to its customers, Square was able to identify new growth opportunities and improve its product offerings. It increased customer satisfaction and loyalty and helped the company multiply. Square's revenue has increased from around $200 million USD in 2012 to over $9 billion USD in 2020, making it one of the most successful start-ups in the payment processing industry. In addition to improving product development, listening to customers can help start-ups build robust and loyal customer bases. When customers feel that their feedback is valued and considered, they are likelier to continue doing business with that company. It can increase customer retention, positive word-of-mouth marketing, and a strong reputation for excellent customer service.

By listening to customers, start-ups can identify and address issues quickly.[6] When you seek feedback proactively, you minimize the damages and prevent problems from impacting your company. It can lead to a more positive customer experience, increased customer retention, and improved brand reputation. A fine example of a company that seeks customer feedback proactively is Warby Parker, an online eyewear retailer. Warby Parker allows customers to take a quiz to determine their ideal frame style, and they also offer a "Home Try-On" program where customers can select a few frames to try on at home before making a purchase. After customers purchase, Warby Parker sends a follow-up survey to gather feedback on the product and the overall customer experience. They use this feedback to continuously improve their product offerings, website functionality, and customer service. By proactively seeking feedback, Warby Parker has established a loyal customer base and maintained a strong brand reputation. From this, entrepreneurs must learn the importance of proactively prioritizing the customer experience and seeking feedback. By doing so, start-ups can improve their product offerings, website functionality, and customer service, leading to higher customer satisfaction and loyalty. Additionally, listening to customer feedback can help entrepreneurs identify issues quickly and prevent them from impacting their business negatively, thus building a solid brand reputation. I have elaborated on three dimensions regarding how listening to customers impacts businesses. I have discussed how customers feel valued, and what it leads to. The next dimension I have elaborated on is how listening to what increases your business sales. The final point of discussion is how all this can help you build a loyal and sustainable clientele.

Customers Feel Valued

When customers feel valued, they remain loyal to a brand,[7] provide repeat business and recommend the brand to others. It is why start-ups must listen to their customers and make them feel appreciated. Customers appreciate when companies walk the extra mile to accommodate their needs and preferences. One way to make customers feel valued is by providing personalized experiences. For example, Starbucks offers personalized drink recommendations based on customer purchase history and preferences. It makes customers feel like their choices are being heard and considered, which fosters brand loyalty. Another way to ensure customers feel valued is by incorporating their suggestions into business decisions. It shows that the start-up cares about what the customer says and is willing to make changes to meet their needs. For example, Uber frequently surveys its users to gather feedback on their experiences and uses it to change its app and services. It shows that Uber cares about what its customers say and is willing to make changes to meet their needs. Prompt and efficient customer service is also crucial to making customers feel valued. When customers have an issue or concern, they want it to be addressed quickly and effectively. Start-ups prioritizing customer service and responding promptly to customer inquiries or complaints can build trust and loyalty with their customers. Another example could be Zappos, an online shoe retailer, which has built its business on exceptional customer service. The company offers free shipping and returns, a 24/7 customer service hotline, and a 365-day return policy. This customer service commitment has helped Zappos build a loyal customer base and differentiate itself in a crowded market.

Another step to make customers feel valued is providing a seamless and hassle-free experience. It means removing unnecessary steps in the customer journey and ensuring everything runs smoothly. For example, start-ups could invest in user-friendly website design[8] or streamline their checkout process to make it as quick and easy as possible.

You must also proactively address their pain points. It could involve conducting market research, considering customer feedback, or using data analytics to identify areas for improvement. By taking customer concerns seriously and making changes accordingly, start-ups can demonstrate that they care about their customers and are committed to providing a better experience. Offering exclusive benefits or rewards to loyal customers can also make them feel valued and appreciated. It could include access to exclusive content or products, discounts on future purchases, or personalized offers. For example, Amazon Prime offers a range of benefits like free two-day shipping, access to streaming video and music, and discounts on select products. These benefits incentivize customers to continue doing business with Amazon and make them feel like their loyalty is being rewarded. Start-ups can also make customers feel valued by providing exceptional customer service. It means being available to customers when they need help, resolving issues quickly and efficiently, and going beyond to ensure customers are satisfied with their experience. By prioritizing customer service, start-ups can build trust with their customers and establish a positive reputation in the market.

Increase Sales

The next significant impact of listening to customers is that it can help start-ups increase their sales.[9] By understanding what customers want and need, start-ups can personalize their products and services to meet those needs better, growing sales. Listening to customers can increase sales by improving the relevance of a start-up's products or services. By using customer concerns and feedback to inform product development, start-ups can ensure that they offer products high in demand and meet the needs of their target market. For example, if a start-up sells fitness gear and notices that customers consistently ask for workout equipment that is easy to store, they could develop and market products that fit that need, potentially leading to increased sales. Another way you can ensure an increase in sales is by improving the overall customer experience. Furthermore, start-ups can also use customer feedback to inform their marketing and advertising strategies. By understanding what resonates with their target market, start-ups can develop more effective marketing campaigns and messaging that speak directly to their customer's needs and desires. It can lead to increased brand awareness, customer engagement, and sales.

Another impact of listening to customers that can help start-ups increase their sales is the ability to identify new opportunities and emerging trends in the market. By knowing what the market wants, start-ups can gain insights into changing consumer preferences and emerging market trends, which can help them stay ahead of the curve and capitalize on new opportunities. For example, a start-up that produces plant-based protein products might notice a growing demand for sustainable packaging among its customers. By paying attention to this demand and adapting their packaging to be more eco-friendly, the start-up could attract more customers interested in sustainable products, ultimately increasing sales. By understanding the needs and preferences of their customers, start-ups can identify opportunities to develop new products or services that complement existing offerings and appeal to their target market. Additionally, listening to customers can help start-ups identify potential areas for expansion or diversification. It can help start-ups to grow their customer base and increase their revenue streams over time. Finally, listening to customers can help start-ups differentiate themselves from their competitors. By ensuring excellent customer service, start-ups can develop a reputation for being customer-focused and responsive to their customers' needs. It can help them stand out in a crowded market and attract customers who value a personalized and responsive approach to business.

Sustainable Clientele

What good are your efforts of listening to customers if they cannot generate a long-term clientele? So, the next significant impact of listening to customers for start-ups is the ability to build a sustainable clientele. By addressing the needs and concerns of their customers, start-ups can build strong relationships with their clients. It, in turn, can help to create a loyal and dedicated customer base, which is crucial for long-term success in the market. For example, a start-up that produces natural skincare products might listen to customer feedback and create a loyalty program, rewarding customers for repeat purchases. It can encourage customers to continue buying from the start-up and attract new customers interested in the rewards program. Moreover, customers who feel valued and listened to are more likely to become regular customers and recommend the start-up to their friends and family. It can lead to increased sales and word-of-mouth marketing, which can be incredibly valuable for start-ups with limited budgets. By building a sustainable clientele, start-ups can reduce customer acquisition costs over time. This is because repeat customers are often more profitable than new customers, as they require less marketing and advertising to attract and are more likely to make larger purchases.

An added advantage of a substantial clientele could be building a solid brand reputation. Customers who feel valued and heard are more likely to have positive feelings toward the start-up and spread positive remarks about their experiences. One way start-ups can build a strong brand reputation by listening to customers is by addressing negative feedback and resolving issues promptly and satisfactorily.[10] By doing so, start-ups can show their customers that they care about their experiences and are committed to providing high-quality products or services. For example, a start-up that produces eco-friendly clothing might receive negative feedback from customers who are unhappy with the quality of their products. By actively addressing these concerns and offering refunds or exchanges, the start-up can demonstrate its commitment to customer satisfaction and improve its brand reputation in the eyes of its customers. Moreover, start-ups that actively listen to their customers can also identify trends and patterns in customer feedback that can help them improve their products or services. By addressing these issues, start-ups can create products or services that better meet the needs and desires of their customers, which can lead to increased customer satisfaction and loyalty. For example, a start-up that produces meal kits might notice customers consistently asking for more vegetarian or vegan options. By responding to this and offering more plant-based meal options, the start-up can cater to the needs of its customers and build a more substantial brand reputation. In addition to improving brand reputation and customer loyalty, listening to customers can help start-ups stay competitive in their respective markets. By understanding the needs and desires of their customers, start-ups can develop products or services that differentiate them from competitors and attract prospective customers. For example, a start-up that produces electric bikes might notice that customers are looking for bikes with longer battery life. By reciprocating this and developing bikes with longer battery life, the start-up can differentiate itself from competitors and attract new customers interested in its unique offering.

Is Listening To Customers Easy Or Difficult?

Listening to customers can be easy if businesses take the right approach. The first step is creating customer opportunities to provide feedback through surveys, focus groups, or social media interactions. By making it easy for customers to share their opinions and experiences, businesses can gain valuable insights into their customers' wants and needs. Another easy way to listen to customers is by analyzing data from customer interactions,[11] such as sales data or customer service interactions. Businesses can review this data to identify trends and patterns that inform their decision-making and product development. For example, a company may notice a high rate of returns for a particular product, which may indicate a need to improve the product's design or functionality. Businesses can also leverage social media platforms to listen to customer feedback. By monitoring social media conversations about their brand, companies can gain real-time customer feedback, identify potential issues, and address them quickly. For example, a company may receive negative feedback on social media about a recent product launch. By responding to this feedback and addressing the issue, the company can show its commitment to customer satisfaction and potentially turn a negative experience into a positive one.

Listening to customers can also be difficult for businesses, especially if they don't have a clear plan or strategy. One challenge is knowing which feedback to prioritize and act on. Not all customer feedback is created equal, and businesses may receive conflicting or unclear feedback that is difficult to act on. For example, a company may receive feedback that customers want a specific feature added to a product, but another group may prefer the product without that feature. Another challenge is effectively communicating with customers to gather feedback. If a business doesn't have a straightforward process for collecting feedback or responding to customers, it may miss out on valuable insights or fail to address customer concerns. Additionally, some customers may be hesitant to provide feedback or may not know how to provide constructive feedback, making it difficult for businesses to understand their customers' needs thoroughly. Finally, it can be difficult for businesses to act on customer feedback promptly and effectively. For example, a company may receive feedback that a particular product is too expensive, but reducing the price may hurt profitability or product quality. Implementing changes based on feedback may require significant time and resources, and businesses may struggle to balance customer demands with other priorities. However, we need to strike a balance here. I have written in detail about this section hereafter. Firstly, I have written about how easy it becomes if you are only customer-centric. Then, I have elaborated on how difficult it becomes if you focus only on the needs of your business. Finally, I have helped you understand why you should strike the right balance and how to do it as a start-up owner.

Easy If You Make It Customer-Centric

Listening to customers can make businesses easier if they adopt a customer-centric approach.[12] It means placing the customer at the center of all decision-making and prioritizing their needs and wants. By doing so, businesses can gather relevant and actionable feedback, improving products, services, and customer satisfaction. One way to make listening to customers simple is to create multiple channels for feedback. It includes online surveys, social media engagement, email communication, and in-person interactions. By making it easy for customers to share their thoughts and opinions, businesses can gather a wide range of feedback to inform decision-making. Another critical aspect of a customer-centric approach is prioritizing the most important concern. It means developing a system for categorizing and prioritizing concerns so that businesses can focus on the most pressing customer needs and concerns. For example, a company may prioritize product quality over branding or marketing concerns.

Businesses can gather valuable insights that drive growth and success by prioritizing the customer, creating multiple feedback channels, prioritizing important concerns, and regularly engaging with customers. Additionally, businesses can make it easier to listen to customers by understanding everything related to the business from the customer's perspective. Adopting a customer-centric approach can make listening to customers convenient and more effective for businesses. It means actively engaging with customers rather than waiting for them to contact you. By engaging with customers and building relationships, businesses can better understand their needs and inform product development and marketing strategies.

Difficult If You Make It Business-Centric

On the other hand, if a business is focused on its own goals and objectives rather than the needs and wants of its customers, listening to customers can be difficult.[13] This business-centric approach often results in a lack of understanding of the customer's needs and an inability to respond effectively. One challenge with a business-centric approach is that businesses may make assumptions about what their customers want or need rather than actively researching. It can lead to a disconnect between the company and its customers, offering products or services that do not meet customer expectations. As a result, customers may become dissatisfied and turn to competitors who are better aligned with their needs. Another challenge of a business-centric approach is that it can lead to a lack of prioritization of customer needs. If businesses are focused on their goals and objectives, they may not prioritize the customer, leading to missed opportunities for growth and improvement. For example, suppose a business is solely focused on increasing profits. In that case, it may ignore product quality or customer service feedback, ultimately decreasing sales and revenue. Additionally, a business-centric approach can result in a lack of transparency and communication with customers.

If businesses are not prioritizing customers, they may not be transparent about their decision-making process or how they incorporate customer requirements into their operations. It can lead to a loss of trust between the business and its customers, ultimately harming its reputation and bottom line.

When a start-up approaches customers from a business-centric perspective, it can lead to difficulties in effectively listening to and acting upon their needs. In such cases, the primary focus is often on the bottom line, and the goal is to increase profits and reduce costs. While this approach is not entirely wrong, it can often result in customers being ignored or dismissed if it doesn't align with the business's priorities. For instance, imagine a start-up that produces a new type of health drink that it believes to be nutritious and healthy. The business-centric approach would prioritize sales and profit and push marketing campaigns focusing on the drink's health benefits. However, if customers say their drink tastes bad or has a strange aftertaste, it may be ignored or downplayed as it doesn't align with the business's priorities. It can lead to a disconnect between the start-up and its customers, resulting in lower sales and reduced brand loyalty. Start-ups may prioritize the bottom line over customer satisfaction, leading to decisions that may negatively impact customer experience. For instance, a start-up may outsource customer service to reduce costs, resulting in longer wait times for customers and lower overall satisfaction levels. This business-centric approach may lead to customer dissatisfaction, resulting in lost business and a damaged reputation. Furthermore, a business-centric approach can often result in a lack of empathy towards customers.

Perfect If You Can Strike The Right Balance

Striking the right balance between customer-centric and business-centric approaches can lead to a perfect solution for start-ups.[14] It means that a start-up that can effectively listen to customers and incorporate their inputs into its business strategy while considering its goals and objectives can create a strong foundation for success. By being customer-centric, a start-up can gather valuable insights from its target market to inform its product development, marketing campaigns, and overall business strategy. This customer-centric approach can help start-ups identify and address pain points, preferences, and trends that can give them an edge in the market. Additionally, start-ups prioritizing customer needs and using them to shape their offerings are more likely to gain customer loyalty and trust, leading to sustainable growth. On the other hand, being solely business-centric can lead to a lack of understanding and consideration for the needs and wants of the customer. By ignoring or undervaluing customer requirements, start-ups may miss out on opportunities for progress. This approach can also make it difficult for start-ups to establish a sustainable client base, as they may not be meeting the needs of their target market. Therefore, by striking the right balance between these two approaches, start-ups can create a perfect solution considering customers' needs and business objectives. It requires an ongoing effort to listen to customers, evaluate their concerns and feedback, and incorporate that into business decisions while focusing on achieving business goals. Start-ups prioritizing this balance can create a strong foundation for long-term success, with a sustainable client base and a competitive edge in the market.

Slack[15] is an excellent example of a start-up that has found the right balance between being customer-centric and business-centric. Slack offers a simple, easy-to-use platform that allows teams to communicate and collaborate more efficiently. The company has always put its users first, listening to their needs and improving accordingly. By focusing on user experience, Slack has attracted a loyal user base, which has helped the company grow. However, Slack has also generated revenue and become a profitable business. The company offers a freemium model, where users can use the basic version of the platform for free but have to pay for advanced features. It has allowed Slack to cater to small and large businesses, generating revenue from both segments. Another example of a start-up that has struck the right balance is Shopify. The e-commerce platform has successfully empowered small business owners to start and grow their online stores. Shopify offers a variety of features and integrations that make it easy for anyone to set up an online store, regardless of their technical expertise. At the same time, Shopify has generated revenue through various means, such as transaction fees, subscription plans, and add-on services. The company has also built a robust ecosystem of developers and partners who create apps and services that integrate with Shopify. It has helped Shopify to cater to the needs of businesses of all sizes, from solopreneurs to large enterprises.

Companies That Listen Well To Customers

Entrepreneurs can learn a lot from companies with a reputation for listening to their customers. One way to do this is to study these companies' strategies and practices to gather and incorporate customer feedback. For example, businesses like Patagonia and Warby Parker have created strong customer communities by listening to customer feedback and combining it into their products and services. Similarly, Zappos is known for its exceptional customer service and for listening to its customers' needs to provide a personalized shopping experience. By studying the approaches of successful companies, entrepreneurs can gain insights into how to listen to their customers effectively. Additionally, entrepreneurs can seek out mentorship or advice from individuals who have experience in customer listening or attend workshops or conferences on the topic. By learning from the best, entrepreneurs can develop the skills and strategies they need to create products and services that meet the needs of their customers, ultimately leading to tremendous success and growth for their businesses.

ThredUp

ThredUp[16] is an online marketplace for second-hand clothing that has become a significant success story in the fashion industry. The company was founded in 2009 by James Reinhart, Chris Homer, and Oliver Lubin, who wanted to create a more sustainable and affordable way for people to buy and sell clothes. ThredUp has become one of the world's most extensive online thrift stores, with millions of customers. One reason for ThredUp's success is its innovative approach to the second-hand clothing market. ThredUp makes it easy for people to sell their clothes by sending them a clean-out kit, including a bag and a pre-paid shipping label. Once the dresses are received, ThredUp sorts them, photographs them, and lists them for sale on its website. This model has made it easy for people to declutter their closets and earn money from clothes they no longer wear. It also provides a more sustainable alternative to traditional clothing consumption. Another factor in ThredUp's success is its focus on customer experience. ThredUp has built a strong community of loyal customers by providing a seamless online shopping experience and excellent customer service. They have a 100% satisfaction guarantee, and customers can quickly return items they don't like. ThredUp also uses customer feedback to improve its business, adding new features like personal styling and clothing rentals based on customer demand. ThredUp has also successfully partnered with major brands and retailers, including Gap, J.C. Penney, and Walmart, to provide a platform for their unsold inventory. It has allowed ThredUp to expand its inventory and offer its customers a more comprehensive range of products while also helping reduce waste in the fashion industry.

Company Name: ThredUp

Founded: 2009

Significant reason(s) for success: The company's success can be credited to its innovative approach to the second-hand clothing market, its focus on customer experience, and its ability to forge partnerships with major brands and retailers. As the fashion industry grapples with sustainability and waste, it has positioned itself as a leader in the growing second-hand clothing market.

Depop

Depop[17] is a social shopping app, becoming a significant success story in the fashion industry, particularly among younger generations. The company was founded in 2011 by Simon Beckerman as a platform for buying and selling second-hand clothing but has since evolved into a vibrant community of fashion enthusiasts and creatives. One reason for Depop's success is its unique approach to social commerce. The app is designed to feel like a social media platform, with features like direct messaging and the ability to follow and like other users' profiles and items. It has made it easy for users to connect with others who share their interests and discover new trends and styles. Depop has become a platform for young people to express their style and explore new trends without the pressure to conform to traditional fashion standards. Depop has also successfully attracted a younger demographic of users, mainly Gen Z and millennials. These users are drawn to the app's focus on sustainability and its emphasis on individuality and self-expression. Another factor in Depop's success is its commitment to supporting small businesses and independent sellers. The app provides a platform for these sellers to reach a wider audience and grow their businesses while promoting sustainable fashion practices. Depop has also successfully forged partnerships with major brands, including Adidas, which has helped boost the app's credibility and appeal among a wider audience.

Company Name: Depop

Founded: 2011

Significant reason(s) for success: Its success can be attributed to its unique approach to social commerce, its focus on sustainability and individuality, and its commitment to supporting small businesses and independent sellers. It has positioned itself as a leader in the growing social shopping market and a champion of sustainable fashion practices.

Happy Money

Happy Money[18] is a financial technology company that has been making waves in the industry with its innovative approach to personal finance. The company was founded in 2009 by Scott Saunders, who wanted to create a financial institution that put people's happiness and well-being at the center of its mission. One reason for Happy Money's success is its focus on helping people pay off debt and achieve financial freedom. The company offers a range of debt consolidation and refinancing services and tools and resources to help people manage their finances more effectively. Happy Money's goal is to help people reduce their financial stress and improve overall well-being, which has resonated with many consumers who are struggling with debt and financial insecurity. Another factor in Happy Money's success is its commitment to social responsibility and sustainability. The company has partnered with several organizations and initiatives focused on social and environmental causes, including the Rainforest Action Network and the Surfrider Foundation. Happy Money also uses its platform to promote sustainable financial practices, such as reducing paper waste and promoting digital banking. Happy Money has also successfully created a strong brand identity and community. The company's name and branding reflect its mission to help people find happiness and well-being through financial freedom. Its messaging has resonated with many consumers looking for more socially responsible and purpose-driven financial solutions.

Company Name: Happy Money

Founded: 2009

Significant reason(s) for success: The company's success can be attributed to its innovative approach to personal finance, commitment to social responsibility and sustainability, and strong brand identity and community. As consumers demand more from their financial institutions, it has become a mark in the growing movement towards more socially responsible and sustainable financial solutions.

Honeybee Health

Honeybee Health[19] is a rapidly growing online pharmacy changing how people access and purchase prescription medications. The company was founded in 2017 by Dr. Jessica Nouhavandi and Dr. Ronak Manisha Doshi, who saw an opportunity to disrupt the traditional pharmaceutical industry and make healthcare more affordable and accessible for everyone. Honeybee Health's commitment to transparency and affordability is one reason for its success. The company offers a wide range of prescription medications at significantly lower prices than traditional pharmacies, attracting many customers. Honeybee Health can do this by sourcing medicines directly from manufacturers and passing on the savings to customers. Another factor in Honeybee Health's success is its user-friendly platform and exceptional customer service. The company's website is easy to navigate, and customers can easily search for and order their medications online. Honeybee Health also offers free shipping on all orders, and its customer service team is available to answer any questions or concerns. Honeybee Health has also successfully built a strong brand identity and community. The company's name and branding reflect its commitment to transparency, affordability, and accessibility. Its messaging has resonated with many consumers frustrated with the high cost of healthcare and prescription medications.

Company Name: Honeybee Health

Founded: 2017

Significant reason(s) for success: Its success can be attributed to its disruptive approach to the pharmaceutical industry, its commitment to transparency and affordability, and its strong brand identity and community. As the healthcare industry continues to evolve and adapt to changing consumer preferences, it has proven itself in the growing movement towards more affordable and accessible healthcare solutions.

Moesif

Moesif[20] is a rapidly growing API analytics platform that is helping companies gain deeper insights into their API usage and improve their API performance. The company was founded in 2013 by Derric Gilling and Xing Liu, who saw an opportunity to address the growing need for more sophisticated API analytics tools. One reason for Moesif's success is its innovative approach to API analytics. The company's platform uses machine learning algorithms to automatically identify and diagnose issues with API performance, making it easier for companies to identify and resolve problems quickly. Moesif also provides detailed insights into how APIs are used, allowing companies to optimize their APIs for better performance and user experience. Another factor in Moesif's success is its commitment to customer service and support. The company offers a range of resources and tools to help customers get the most out of its platform, including detailed documentation, online forums, and personalized support from its team of experts. Moesif has also been successful in building a solid brand identity and community. The company's name and branding reflect its mission to provide more sophisticated and intelligent API analytics tools. Its messaging resonated with many companies looking for more data-driven API development and management approaches.

Company Name: Moesif

Founded: 2017

Significant reason(s) for success: The company's success can be attributed to its innovative API analytics approach, commitment to customer service and support, and strong brand identity and community. As companies continue relying more heavily on APIs to power their digital experiences, it is considered a leader in the growing API analytics and management tools market.

SnatchBot

SnatchBot[21] is a fast-growing platform for building and deploying chatbots across various messaging channels. The company was founded in 2015 by Avi Ben Ezra and Henri Ben Ezra, who saw an opportunity to democratize access to chatbot technology and make it more accessible to businesses of all sizes. One reason for SnatchBot's success is its user-friendly platform, which makes it easy for businesses to build and deploy chatbots without requiring any coding knowledge. The platform offers a range of customizable templates and drag-and-drop tools, allowing users to create chatbots that can handle various tasks, from customer support to lead generation and more. Another factor in SnatchBot's success is its commitment to innovation and staying ahead of the curve in chatbot technology. The company constantly updates its platform with new features and integrations, ensuring users can access the latest and most sophisticated chatbot capabilities. SnatchBot has also been successful in building a solid brand identity and community. The company's name and branding reflect its mission to make chatbot technology more accessible and approachable. Its messaging has resonated with many businesses looking for more efficient and effective ways to communicate with their customers.

Company Name: SnatchBot

Founded: 2015

Significant reason(s) for success: Its success can be attributed to its user-friendly platform, commitment to innovation, and strong brand identity and community. As businesses adopt chatbot technology as a crucial part of their customer engagement strategies, it makes its mark in the growing chatbot platform and tool market.

Conclusion

As an emerging entrepreneur, it is critical to understand that being mindful[22] of your customers' needs and expectations is one of the most important things you can do for your business. By understanding your customers' needs, preferences, and pain points, you can develop products and services that meet their needs and provide a great customer experience. To effectively be mindful of your customers, you need to actively engage with them and take the time to understand their unique situations. It means asking questions and listening to their responses. It also means being open to feedback and criticism and using that feedback to improve your products and services. In addition to being mindful, there are several strategies that you can use to understand your customers better. These include conducting market research, creating customer personas, and monitoring social media and other online channels for customer feedback. Using these strategies,[23] you can better understand your customer's needs and preferences and use that knowledge to develop products and services that genuinely meet their needs.

Ultimately, the success of your start-up will depend on your ability to listen to your customers and respond to their needs effectively. By developing strong listening skills and effective strategies for understanding your customers, you can position your start-up for long-term success and growth.[24] So, to all emerging entrepreneurs, remember that listening to your customers is vital to building a successful business. Don't be afraid to ask for feedback; truly listen to what your customers tell you. Use that feedback to make improvements and provide them with the best possible customer experience. With dedication and hard work, you can build a successful start-up that genuinely meets your customers' needs and positively impacts the world.

Since the beginning of this book, my goal has been to motivate you and take you through a successful entrepreneurial journey. I am sure you have gained insights about listening to customers by reading this chapter. Like many other founders of companies, I hope your story will also turn into a success story in the times to come and inspire others to start their journey. Remember that every successful entrepreneur faces obstacles and challenges along their journey. The willingness to persevere and the determination never to give up will set you apart. You must focus on what you can control and trust what has worked for these outstanding founders. Embrace the inevitable bumps and use them as opportunities to learn, grow, and improve. Believe in yourself and your vision; let that belief fuel your passion and drive toward success. To sum up the chapter and give you a clear glimpse of the what, why, and how of listening to customers, follow the pointers below and keep them for ready-reference:

1. Listening to customers will give you more clarity of thought as an entrepreneur driving a start-up.
2. Listening to customers will help you to offer what's relevant.
3. You also need to listen to customers to make it easy for them to participate in the business.
4. You must listen to customers to generate a strong feedback loop for your company's continued progress.
5. The impact that listening to customers creates is crucial for your start-up to get the boost to conquer great business heights.
6. When you listen to customers, they feel valued.
7. It leads to an increase in sales.
8. It also helps you build a sustainable clientele that will take your business a long way.
9. Listening to customers can be both easy and difficult.
10. It is easy if you make it customer-centric since that will allow you to prioritize their needs.
11. It is difficult if you make it business-centric because customers will take a back seat in your list of priorities, which could backfire.

12. If you could strike the right balance between the two, it would be ideal for you as an entrepreneur.

References

1. Swinscoe, A. (2022). *7 customer-experience-related predictions for 2023.* Available at: https://www.forbes.com/sites/adrianswinscoe/2022/12/14/7-customer-experience-related-predictions-for-2023/?sh=66fb24242a15 [Accessed 1 May 2023].
2. Pineiro, F. A. (2023). *Customer needs: How to identify & meet them.* Available at: https://startups.co.uk/marketing/tips/customer-needs/ [Accessed 1 May 2023].
3. Nandwana, A. (2023). *The importance of a great customer experience for pharmaceutical companies.* Available at: https://www.forbes.com/sites/forbesbusinesscouncil/2023/04/03/the-importance-of-a-great-customer-experience-for-pharmaceutical-companies/?sh=44cfe27ac2fd [Accessed 1 May 2023].
4. Harvard Business Review (2023). *What do your customers want in 2023?* Available at: https://hbr.org/2023/01/what-do-your-customers-want-in-2023 [Accessed 1 May 2023].
5. Ciabarra, C. (2018). *How start-ups can close the feedback loop.* Available at: https://www.forbes.com/sites/forbestechcouncil/2016/10/28/how-startups-can-close-the-feedback-loop/?sh=4e84950f63ed [Accessed 1 May 2023].
6. Redbord, M. (2021). *12 critical customer service tips for start-ups & Small Businesses.* Available at: https://blog.hubspot.com/service/customer-service-startups [Accessed 1 May 2023].
7. Business News Daily (2023). *How to build customer loyalty.* Available at: https://www.businessnewsdaily.com/16017-build-customer-loyalty.html [Accessed 1 May 2023].
8. Kocher, G. (2021). *How website design can make or break the SEO for startups.* Available at: https://www.entrepreneur.com/growing-a-business/how-website-design-can-make-or-break-the-seo-for-startups/378160 [Accessed 1 May 2023].
9. Hyken, S. (2021). *Six ways listening improves the customer experience.* Available at: https://www.forbes.com/sites/shephyken/2017/04/29/six-ways-listening-improves-the-customer-experience/?sh=160444af72da [Accessed 1 May 2023].

10. Fallon N. (2023). *How to handle negative customer reviews.* Available at: https://www.businessnewsdaily.com/6503-negative-customer-reviews.html [Accessed 1 May 2023].
11. Acquire. (2021) *Customer analytics: Importance, types, and how to use them.* Available at: https://acquire.io/blog/customer-analytics [Accessed 1 May 2023].
12. Johnson, B. (2022). *8 tips for becoming a customer-centric organization.* Available at: https://blog.hubspot.com/service/customer-centric [Accessed 1 May 2023].
13. Ruhlin, J. (2017). *Being a 'boss' entrepreneur doesn't mean you have to be selfish.* Available at: https://www.entrepreneur.com/leadership/being-a-boss-entrepreneur-doesnt-mean-you-have-to-be/298813 [Accessed 1 May 2023].
14. Forbes (2022). *10 ways to balance what customers want with what's best for business.* Available at: https://www.forbes.com/sites/theyec/2022/04/13/10-ways-to-balance-what-customers-want-with-whats-best-for-business/?sh=38ed5a616e70 [Accessed 1 May 2023].
15. Butterfield, S. (2020). *The CEO of Slack on adapting in response to a global crisis.* Available at: https://hbr.org/2020/07/the-ceo-of-slack-on-adapting-in-response-to-a-global-crisis [Accessed 1 May 2023].
16. Segran, E. (2021). *How Thredup became a $184 million technology giant.* Available at: https://www.fastcompany.com/90619485/how-a-used-clothing-site-became-a-184-million-tech-giant [Accessed 1 May 2023].
17. Ogunshe, S. (2022). *The rise of Depop from a start-up to a billion-dollar company.* Available at: https://www.linkedin.com/pulse/rise-depop-from-startup-billion-dollar-company-samson-ogunshe/?trk=public_profile_article_view [Accessed 1 May 2023].
18. Money, H. (2022). *Happy money hits unicorn status and raises $50M series D-1, led by Anthemis Group.* Available at: https://www.prnewswire.com/news-releases/happy-money-hits-unicorn-status-and-raises-50m-series-d-1-led-by-anthemis-group-301477088.html [Accessed 1 May 2023].
19. Spirer, A. (2020). *Dr. Jessica Nouhavandi of Honeybee Health: "Why self-awareness is so critical".* Available at: https://medium.com/authority-magazine/dr-jessica-nouhavandi-of-honeybee-health-if-you-dont-know-who-you-are-what-you-care-about-8b1a0c4b99ad [Accessed 1 May 2023].
20. Hall, C. (2021). *Moesif secures $12M to provide user behavior insights on API usage.* Available at: https://techcrunch.com/2021/08/23/

moesif-secures-12m-to-provide-user-behavior-insights-on-api-usage/?guccounter=1&guce_referrer=aHR0cHM6Ly93d3cuZ29vZ2xlLmNvbS8&guce_referrer_sig=AQAAABa_ix0vKkhIYIxAiAHDiR3gHqwMOjGMQVlmLy4I1_AxaMfEKJflDeMy8-mtqfM3xO3_8Env4-FCtx5F9ep0XjmJ2OdSBma7n1TdmkapVJ_982xM_uIxOXULZgAqzYT55c07NsZYrsdruuxvTqHtDpKKr38z6IV9F2H5FM5TqDG4 [Accessed 1 May 2023].

21. SaaSworthy (2023). *Snatchbot*. Available at: https://www.saasworthy.com/product/snatchbot [Accessed 1 May 2023].
22. Freedman, M. (2023). *What it means to be an entrepreneur*. Available at: https://www.businessnewsdaily.com/7275-entrepreneurship-defined.html [Accessed 1 May 2023].
23. Lau, Y. (2022). *Council post: Tips for scaling customer success*. Available at: https://www.forbes.com/sites/forbeshumanresourcescouncil/2022/01/12/tips-for-scaling-customer-success/?sh=4d2c2002c08d [Accessed 1 May 2023].
24. Matteo Forgione, P. E. (2018). *Council post: Why listening is the foundation of Customer Service and success*. Available at: https://www.forbes.com/sites/forbesbostoncouncil/2018/05/22/why-listening-is-the-foundation-of-customer-service-and-success/?sh=421d6d04418e [Accessed 1 May 2023].

CHAPTER 10
Focus

Start-ups are exciting, dynamic, and full of possibilities. As a founder, you're the ship's captain, responsible for charting the course and navigating the rough waters of entrepreneurship. But with so many tasks to juggle and opportunities to pursue, it's easy to lose sight of your goals and get bogged down in the day-to-day operations. That's why, to succeed as a start-up, you need to master the art of focus. Focus is one of the essential traits that a start-up founder can possess.[1] Without it, you risk spreading yourself too thin, chasing after every shiny new opportunity, and losing sight of what matters. The less you say yes to, the more you can accomplish, and the more likely you are to succeed. But what does it mean to be focused, and how can you cultivate this trait as a start-up founder? This chapter will explore these questions in depth and examine the importance of focus for start-ups.

First and foremost, the focus is on setting priorities. As a founder, you have limited time and resources and must use them wisely. It means identifying the most critical tasks that need to be done and focusing your energy on completing them first. It also means saying no to distractions and opportunities that don't align with your vision for the company. However, the focus is more than just a matter of prioritization. It's also about maintaining a clear and consistent vision for your start-up. As you navigate the complex entrepreneurship landscape, you'll encounter countless obstacles and challenges, and getting sidetracked or discouraged is easy. But by staying true to your company vision and focused on your goals, you can weather the storm and emerge stronger on the other side. So, how can you stay focused as a start-up founder? One approach is to adopt a "one thing at a time" mentality. It means focusing all your energy and attention on a task or project until it's complete before moving on to the next one. This approach can help you avoid multitasking, which can harm productivity and focus. Another key to staying focused is to avoid distractions. In today's digital age, we're bombarded with information and notifications from all sides, and it's easy to get lost in the endless scroll of social media or the black hole of email. You must intentionally set boundaries and create a distraction-free workspace to stay focused. Of course, focus isn't just about the individual founder – it's also about building a culture of focus within your start-up. It means hiring team members who share your vision and values and are committed to working efficiently and effectively. It also means setting clear expectations and holding everyone accountable for meeting them. Ultimately, the key to focus is discipline. It takes discipline to stay on task when countless distractions await your attention. It takes discipline to say no to opportunities that don't align with your vision for the company. And it takes discipline to maintain a clear and consistent vision for your start-up in the face of uncertainty and adversity. In this chapter, we'll dive deeper into the topic of focus and explore the strategies and techniques that successful start-up founders use to stay on track and achieve their goals.

What Does It Mean To Focus On Start-Ups?

Focusing on specific goals is essential for a start-up's success. It allows the start-up to allocate resources towards achieving its goals, streamline decision-making, and create a strong brand identity. In this section, we will explore what it means to "focus" in more detail and include examples of companies (wherever possible) that emerged as successful start-ups by maintaining a laser-like focus. One of the key benefits of focus is that it allows start-ups to create a product or service that meets the specific needs of a niche market. By identifying a particular market segment, start-ups can tailor their product or service to meet the needs of that market.[2] It can lead to a more loyal customer base, as customers will appreciate the start-up's focus on meeting their needs. One example of a start-up that has been successful in maintaining focus is Zoom. The video conferencing company has focused on providing a seamless and reliable experience. This focus allowed Zoom to become the go-to platform for remote meetings quickly and has helped the company grow to a valuation of over $17 billion USD. Another benefit of focus is that it allows start-ups to streamline decision-making. When a start-up has a clear focus, it can quickly and easily evaluate potential opportunities or ideas. Start-ups that lack focus may find themselves pulled in different directions and need help deciding which opportunities to pursue. By maintaining a clear focus, start-ups can avoid wasting time and resources on opportunities that do not align with their goals.

Focusing on a specific market or product can help start-ups create a strong brand identity. By honing in on a specific niche, start-ups can create a brand that resonates with customers in that market. It can lead to an extensive customer base and help the start-up stand out from competitors. One example of a start-up that has successfully created a solid brand identity through focus is Peloton. The fitness equipment company has been focused on creating a connected fitness experience. Peloton has created a brand that resonates with customers who want a personalized and connected fitness experience by focusing on this market. This focus has helped Peloton become one of the fastest-growing companies in the fitness industry. Another example of a start-up that has successfully maintained focus is Wistia, a video hosting and analytics platform for businesses. Wistia has been focused on providing businesses with a customizable and brandable video hosting platform since its inception. This focus has allowed Wistia to quickly become the go-to platform for companies that want to use video to engage with customers. By clearly focusing on serving this market, Wistia has built a loyal customer base and has become a video hosting industry leader. I have divided this section (what it means to focus) into three dimensions. The first is to stay true to its mission and values. I have discussed why this is essential and how can start-ups ensure the same. The second dimension is prioritizing key activities and how they affect focus for start-ups. Thirdly, I have discussed aligning resources toward goals and the implications of the same.

Staying True To Mission/Values

Staying true to a start-up's mission and values is crucial. It helps maintain focus and guide decision-making.[3] A start-up's mission and values define its purpose and provide a framework for its strategy, product development, and overall operations. When a start-up's mission and values are clear and well-defined, it can act as a North Star that guides the company's decision-making. For example, suppose a start-up's mission is to create a more sustainable future. In that case, every decision the company makes should be evaluated in the context of whether it contributes to or detracts from that mission. Staying true to a start-up's mission and values can also help build a strong brand and a sustainable customer base. When a start-up has a clear mission and values that resonate with its target market, it can differentiate itself from competitors. It can build a following of customers who share those values. So, staying true to a start-up's mission and values is critical to maintaining focus. It requires the company to be clear about its purpose, goals, and the principles that guide its decision-making. A start-up can achieve several positive outcomes when it stays true to its mission and values.

A clear mission and set of values can create a strong identity and reputation for a start-up. This identity can help the company to lead the league and achieve a unique market position. A strong brand identity can also help attract and retain customers who share the start-up's values. By remaining true to its mission and values, a start-up can develop a brand that resonates with its target audience and sets the business benchmark high. Staying true to a start-up's mission and values can also attract and retain top talent. When a start-up has a clear mission and values that resonate with talented individuals, it can attract and retain top talent who are passionate about the company's purpose. It can lead to higher levels of employee engagement and productivity. Employees who share the company's values are more likely to be motivated and committed to achieving the company's goals, resulting in better performance and a more positive work environment. Staying true to a start-up's mission and values provides a framework for decision-making. It can help ensure that decisions align with the company's long-term goals and values rather than just focusing on short-term gains. A clear mission and values can also ensure that all stakeholders, including employees, customers, and investors, are aligned on the company's priorities. It can help a start-up make more informed decisions consistent with its overall strategy and purpose. When customers see that a start-up is committed to a particular cause or set of values, they are likelier to trust the company and be repeat customers. It can lead to increased customer retention and word-of-mouth referrals. By staying true to its mission and values, a start-up can build a reputation as a trustworthy and reliable partner, which can be a significant competitive advantage.

Prioritizing Key Activities

Prioritizing key activities is another critical aspect of focus for start-ups.[4] With limited resources, time, and money, start-ups need to be efficient in their operations and prioritize the activities that will significantly impact their success. By prioritizing key activities, start-ups can maximize their chances of achieving their goals and gaining a competitive advantage in their market. One of the first steps in prioritizing key activities is identifying the company's most critical goals. It could include increasing revenue, expanding the customer base, launching a new product or service, or building brand awareness. Once the company has identified its top priorities, it can focus its resources on the activities that will significantly impact achieving those goals. Next, start-ups must prioritize their tasks and projects based on their importance and urgency. Some tasks may be critical for achieving the company's goals, while others may be less important or have a longer timeline. By prioritizing tasks based on their importance and urgency, start-ups can ensure that they are focusing their resources on the most critical activities. The art of prioritizing can also improve company culture. When employees are aligned with the company's priorities, they will probably feel motivated and engaged at work. It can lead to a more positive work environment and better overall performance. A start-up that prioritizes its key activities creates a culture that encourages collaboration, innovation, and a commitment to excellence.

It's also important for start-ups to be disciplined in prioritizing key activities. It means setting clear goals, creating an action plan, and sticking to it. Start-ups must say no to distractions and opportunities that do not align with their goals or remove resources from critical activities. By being disciplined in their approach, start-ups can avoid wasting resources and ensure that they focus on the activities that will significantly impact their success. Prioritizing key activities also requires start-ups to be agile and adaptable. Priorities can change quickly in a start-up environment, and it's essential to pivot quickly when necessary. Start-ups need to be able to adjust their priorities based on changes in the market, customer feedback, or other external factors. By being agile and adaptable, start-ups can respond quickly to changes and maximize their chances of success. Thus, prioritizing key activities is something that helps to ensure focus for start-ups. By identifying their most critical goals, prioritizing tasks based on importance and urgency, being disciplined, and being agile and adaptable, start-ups can boost their company image and meet all business expectations. With limited resources, start-ups need to be efficient in their operations and prioritize the activities that will significantly impact their success. By focusing on key activities, start-ups can remain focused on their goals and increase their chances of success.

Aligning Resources Toward Goals

Aligning resources toward goals is another essential aspect of focus for start-ups. Start-ups typically have limited resources, so they must strategically allocate them to achieve their goals. By aligning resources toward goals, start-ups can ensure that they are maximizing the impact of their resources and focusing on the activities that will have the most significant impact on their success. One of the first steps in aligning resources toward goals is identifying the resources needed to achieve the company's goals. It could include financial resources, personnel, technology, or other resources necessary to achieve the company's objectives. Once the company has identified the resources needed, it can allocate them to the activities that will significantly impact achieving those goals. Start-ups also need to be strategic in how they allocate their resources. It means focusing their resources on the activities that will significantly impact achieving their goals. For example, if a start-up aims to increase revenue, it may need to invest in marketing and sales efforts to attract new customers and increase sales. By allocating resources to these critical activities, start-ups can maximize the impact of their resources and increase their chances of success.

It's also important for start-ups to be disciplined in allocating their resources. It means being mindful of their budget and avoiding unnecessary expenditures that do not align with their goals. Start-ups need to be able to prioritize their resources and allocate them efficiently to the activities that will guarantee achievement and success. Another important aspect of aligning resources toward goals is to ensure that the company's culture and values align with its goals. It means hiring employees who share the company's values and are committed to achieving its goals. By aligning the company's culture and values with its goals, start-ups can create a cohesive team focused on achieving its objectives. Aligning resources toward goals is a critical aspect of focus for start-ups.[5] By identifying the resources needed to achieve the company's goals, being strategic in how those resources are allocated, being disciplined in how resources are spent, and ensuring that the company's culture and values align with its goals, start-ups can maximize their chances of success. With limited resources, start-ups need to be efficient in their operations and align their resources toward the activities that must be taken up and completed on priority. By aligning resources toward goals, start-ups can remain focused and ensure that the output syncs with their requirements or expectations.

Why Is Focus Necessary For Start-Ups?

Focus is essential for start-ups to achieve their goals efficiently and effectively. By honing in on a specific niche or target market, start-ups can streamline their operations and direct their resources toward achieving their objectives. This approach ensures that their efforts are concentrated and effective, leading to better results in less time. One of the key advantages of focus for start-ups is increased efficiency. When start-ups concentrate on a particular area, they can optimize their resources, such as personnel, time, and funds, to achieve the greatest impact. With a clear focus, start-ups can avoid distractions and prioritize the most critical tasks, leading to more efficient operations. As a result, start-ups can achieve their goals with fewer resources, making their growth and development more sustainable. Another advantage of focus is that it enhances creativity. By honing in on a specific area, start-ups can develop a deep understanding of their target market or niche. This understanding can lead to innovative solutions that meet the unique needs of their customers. By focusing on a particular area, start-ups can develop expertise in that field and identify new opportunities for growth and expansion.

With a clear focus on specific goals, start-ups can channel their resources toward achieving them. It helps avoid waste and maximize the impact of the resources at hand.[6] Start-ups with a clear focus are more likely to make consistent progress toward their goals. They can measure their progress and adjust as needed by aligning their activities and resources toward achieving their goals. It helps ensure they are moving in the right direction and not getting sidetracked by distractions. Focus also helps start-ups to build a strong brand. By honing in on a specific area, start-ups can develop a clear brand identity and establish themselves as experts in their field. It can help build trust with existing and prospective customers, prove how they differ from competitors, and enhance brand positioning. A strong brand position can also help start-ups to attract and retain employees, sharing their values and vision.

The need to focus on start-ups is divided into three main aspects. First, the notion of the conservation of resources is directly linked to the notion of focus. Second, the aspect of staying competitive and relevant in the industry. Third, discipline and efficiency as a result of focus. The break-up of these ideas hereafter will give you more clarity.

Conserves Resources

Focusing on the right things can help companies conserve resources, which is particularly important for start-ups with limited funding and staff.[7] By prioritizing key activities and aligning resources toward goals, start-ups can make the most of their available resources and achieve their objectives more efficiently. It leads to resource conservation or achieving sustainability in terms of resources. One way that focusing on the right things can conserve resources is by reducing waste. When companies focus on activities and initiatives that align with their goals and mission, they are less likely to engage in activities not essential to their success. It means they can avoid wasting time, money, and other resources on activities that do not contribute to their bottom line. For example, suppose a start-up is focused on developing a new product. In that case, it may decide to forego attending a trade show that is not directly related to its industry or target market. Focusing on the right things can also help start-ups to avoid costly mistakes. When companies try to do too many things at once or pursue initiatives that are not well-aligned with their goals, they are more likely to make mistakes and encounter setbacks. These mistakes can be expensive to fix and consume valuable resources that could be better spent on activities directly related to achieving the company's objectives.

With a clear focus, start-ups can make better decisions. They can prioritize their targets and resources and make informed decisions about where to invest their time and money. Start-ups who remain focused on what they want to achieve rather than just looking at the business trends and blindly following them are more likely to succeed. By staying committed to their objectives, they can weather the ups and downs of the start-up journey and stay on course toward their goals. It can increase their chances of success and help them achieve their vision for the future. In addition, focusing on the right things can help start-ups to stay lean and agile. When companies are focused on achieving specific goals, they are more likely to adopt a "minimum viable product" approach to product development, which involves creating a product or service with only the essential features needed to meet customer needs. It can help start-ups conserve resources by avoiding unnecessary features and functions that can add cost and complexity to their offerings. This focus can also help start-ups build strong and efficient teams. With the resource conservation dimension in mind, companies can ensure hiring staff with the right skills and experience. It can help start-ups avoid over-staffing and reduce the risk of hiring staff not well-suited to their needs. Thus, focusing on the right things is essential for start-ups that want to efficiently conserve resources and achieve their objectives.

Stays Competitive

Focusing on the right things can significantly impact a start-up's ability to stay competitive in its respective market.[8] It is because focus allows a company to optimize its resources and prioritize key activities, improving efficiency and outcomes. By concentrating on specific objectives, a start-up can create a unique and valuable position in the market, making it harder for competitors to replicate. One significant advantage of focusing on the right things is that it helps a start-up stay ahead of the curve. Companies must adapt quickly to changing market conditions to remain relevant in today's fast-paced business environment. By prioritizing necessary operations and concentrating on essential objectives, start-ups can remain agile and responsive to changes in the market. It allows them to stay ahead of the competition and take advantage of new opportunities. Another way focusing on the right things can help a start-up stay competitive is by improving customer satisfaction. By identifying and prioritizing the most critical aspects of their business, start-ups can provide customers with the best possible experience. For example, a start-up that focuses on providing excellent customer service is likely to attract and retain more customers than a company that doesn't place the same emphasis on customer satisfaction. It will help the company to remain competitive and relevant.

Focusing on the right things can help start-ups optimize their resources, significantly impacting their industry position against the competition. By streamlining processes and cutting unnecessary expenses, start-ups can reduce operating costs, making them more cost-effective than their competitors. It can give start-ups an edge in the market and allow them to offer competitive pricing and better value to their customers. Focusing on the right things can help start-ups innovate and develop new products or services that meet the needs of their target audience. By understanding what customers want and need, start-ups can create unique solutions that differentiate them from their competitors. It can help them capture a larger market share and create a lasting competitive advantage. Finally, focusing on the right things can help start-ups build a solid brand image. By identifying their core values and mission and aligning all aspects of their business with them, start-ups can create a consistent brand image that resonates with their target audience. It can help them build a loyal customer base and establish themselves as a reputable player in their respective market.

Fosters Discipline And Efficiency

Focusing on the right things can help companies foster discipline and efficiency. When a start-up clearly understands what it wants to achieve, it can develop a streamlined process for achieving those goals. It means that everyone within the organization is working towards a common objective and understands the tasks required. With a clear focus, employees are less likely to get distracted by unimportant tasks or ideas that don't align with the company's goals. When a start-up is disciplined and efficient, it can accomplish more with fewer resources. Start-ups often operate on tight budgets and limited resources, so they must use them wisely. By focusing on the right things, start-ups can avoid wasting time and money on activities that won't generate a return on investment. It can include cutting back on unnecessary expenses and streamlining the hiring process to ensure that only the best candidates get through. One example of a start-up that has successfully fostered discipline and efficiency is Basecamp. The company, which offers project management software, has a clear mission to help people work together more effectively. The firm has developed a streamlined product focusing on project management essentials to achieve this. Basecamp also operates with a flat organizational structure that encourages autonomy and responsibility, which helps to foster a culture of discipline and efficiency.

A disciplined and efficient start-up is better equipped to adapt to changes in the market. By clearly understanding its goals and processes, a start-up can quickly pivot when necessary, without losing sight of its overall mission. This flexibility is especially important in today's fast-paced business environment, where start-ups must respond quickly to new challenges and opportunities.[9] One such example is Zapier, a start-up that provides business automation tools. The company has a clear focus on simplifying workflows and automating repetitive tasks. To achieve this, Zapier has developed a simple and easy-to-use platform that integrates with many other tools and services. The company also has a culture of discipline and efficiency, reflected in its commitment to remote work and its emphasis on documentation and standardization. Once you realize the power of being disciplined and efficient, you will become more mindful of being focused. The results matter, and once you witness remarkable results with simple rules that you stick to, building a company becomes more fulfilling as an entrepreneur.

Strategies To Maintain Focus In Start-Ups

Sustaining business focus is a crucial aspect of success for any start-up. While initially, it may be easy to stay focused due to the novelty of the idea and the excitement of starting a new venture, it is important to develop strategies to sustain this focus over time. Without proper strategies, it is easy to get sidetracked by the numerous challenges and distractions of building and growing a business. And solid strategies will always help you to achieve the company's goals and become successful. One way of having a proper strategy to sustain business focus is the ability to allocate resources effectively. When a start-up has a clear focus, it can more easily identify the necessary resources to achieve its goals.[10] It allows the company to allocate resources more efficiently, ensuring they are used to their fullest potential. It is important to use limited resources effectively; a clear focus helps with that. Another way is the ability to adapt to changes in the market. The business world is constantly evolving, and start-ups that cannot adapt to these changes will likely need help to survive. A clear focus allows start-ups to identify changes in the market that are relevant to their business and adapt accordingly. Without a proper strategy to sustain focus, start-ups may struggle to identify these changes and adapt on time.

The next strategy to sustain focus also helps start-ups to make better decisions. When a start-up has a clear focus, it can more easily identify which decisions align with its goals and which do not. It allows the company to make more informed decisions, leading to better outcomes. With the sheer number of decisions, a start-up has to make, having a clear focus can make the decision-making process more efficient and effective. Having a proper strategy to sustain focus also helps to maintain team alignment. When everyone is aligned toward the same goals, working together as a team and achieving success is easier. A clear focus helps to ensure that everyone is working towards the same objectives, minimizing distractions and potential conflicts. It helps to create a cohesive team culture, which is critical for the success of any start-up. Also, having a proper strategy to sustain focus can help your company go a long way. It also helps ensure all stakeholders are satisfied and trust you and your business. When a start-up wants to maintain focus, it must communicate its value proposition and stand out from other companies in the industry. It helps to build strong brand recognition. In strategies to maintain focus in start-ups, you must consider three important sub-points I have elaborated on hereafter. Firstly, I have written about delegation being appropriate and result-oriented. Secondly, I have discussed why it is important to review goals regularly. Thirdly, having clear expectations and accountability as a strategy.

Appropriate Delegation

To sustain a focused strategy, start-ups must ensure that the delegation of tasks is done appropriately. Effective delegation can help start-ups maximize productivity and ensure resources are utilized efficiently.[11] However, improper delegation can lead to confusion and disorganization. It can ultimately hinder the start-up's ability to stay focused. One of the most important aspects of appropriate delegation is to delegate tasks to the right people. The start-up should assign tasks to individuals with the necessary skills, expertise, and experience. By doing so, the start-up can ensure that tasks are completed efficiently, and the team members can achieve their goals more effectively. Delegating tasks to people with the right skills can also reduce the likelihood of errors, which can be costly for a start-up. Another important aspect of appropriate delegation is to ensure clear communication and understanding between the person delegating and the person to whom the task is being delegated. It is crucial for the person delegating to clearly communicate the expectations and goals to the person responsible for completing them. The person conducting the task should clearly understand what is expected of them, the timeline in which the task needs to be completed, and the resources available.

Appropriate delegation can also foster a culture of trust within the start-up. When team members feel trusted with essential tasks, they are more likely to take ownership and feel responsible for the start-up's success. It can lead to increased motivation and productivity, which ultimately helps the start-up to stay focused on its goals. Moreover, appropriate delegation can help to reduce the workload of the founder or CEO of the start-up, who can then focus on higher-level tasks such as developing business strategies and building relationships with potential clients or investors. By delegating tasks to the appropriate team members, the founder or CEO can also create more opportunities for team members to develop new skills and take on additional responsibilities. Hence, delegating tasks to the right people, ensuring clear communication and understanding, and fostering a culture of trust can help start-ups maximize productivity, reduce the workload of the founder or CEO, and ultimately stay focused on their goals. By delegating tasks with the right intent and efficacy, start-ups can maximize their employees and resources.

Regular Goal Review

The next key strategy for sustaining business focus is regular goal reviews. As a start-up grows, it's essential to ensure that everyone in the organization is aligned with the company's goals and objectives. Regular goal reviews keeps everyone on the same page and focused on the same priorities. It allows start-ups to track their progress, identify what's working and not, and make necessary adjustments to stay on course. Regular goal reviews help start-ups identify key areas for improvement and make necessary course corrections in a timely manner. It enables them to remain agile and respond quickly to market changes or new opportunities. Without regular goal reviews, start-ups may be drifting off course or missing significant opportunities altogether. Moreover, regular goal reviews helps improve transparency and communication within the organization. It allows everyone to share their perspectives and provide feedback on the progress toward the company's goals. It will enable start-ups to identify potential roadblocks or challenges early on and work collaboratively to find solutions. It also helps build a culture of accountability. Thus, everyone takes ownership of their role in achieving the company's goals.

Another advantage of regular goal reviews is that it helps set realistic expectations.[12] Start-ups often face a lot of pressure to grow quickly and achieve success in a short period. However, this can sometimes lead to unrealistic expectations and cause start-ups to lose focus on their core mission. Regular goal reviews helps set realistic goals and milestones and ensures that the company's priorities align with its mission and values. In addition, regular goal reviews helps in identifying and mitigating risks. As start-ups grow and evolve, they may face various risks, such as financial, operational, or legal risks. Regular goal reviews helps identify potential risks early on and develop strategies to mitigate or manage them. It allows start-ups to avoid potential pitfalls and maintain their focus on achieving their core objectives. For regular and effective goal reviews, it's crucial to establish clear metrics and Key Performance Indicators (KPIs) for measuring progress toward the company's goals. It ensures that everyone in the organization knows what they're working towards and can track their progress. It's also essential to establish a regular cadence for goal reviews, whether weekly, monthly, or quarterly, to ensure that the company is consistently reviewing and adjusting its priorities.

Clear Expectations And Accountability

In addition to what we discussed until now, setting clear expectations and establishing accountability is a crucial aspect of sustaining business focus for start-ups. Clear expectations and accountability help to ensure that every team member is aware of their responsibilities and understands the standards to which they will be held accountable. One of the main advantages of having clear expectations is that it allows employees to know what is expected of them and what goals they are working towards. This clarity can lead to better productivity, as employees will not waste time on tasks that do not align with the company's overall goals. It can also lead to better employee satisfaction, as employees will feel more confident knowing what is expected. Accountability is also important for sustaining business focus. It is important for employees to be accountable for their actions and to take ownership of their work. It can help ensure work is completed on time and to the required standard and promote a culture of responsibility within the company.[13]

Establishing clear expectations and accountability is not always easy. It requires effective communication and a willingness to hold oneself and others accountable. However, the benefits of doing so can be substantial. For example, if a team member fails to meet their responsibilities, clear expectations and accountability can help to identify the problem and take corrective action. It can prevent minor problems from becoming major issues and help keep the team focused on achieving its goals. To establish clear expectations and accountability, start-ups can begin by creating job descriptions that clearly outline the responsibilities of each team member. Regular performance reviews and check-ins can help ensure employees meet their goals and expectations. Additionally, start-ups can consider implementing a rewards system for employees who consistently meet or exceed their expectations while providing support and training for those needing additional help. Thus, by setting clear goals and expectations and holding oneself and others accountable for meeting them, start-ups can stay focused on achieving their long-term objectives and ultimately succeed in their industry.

Companies That Aced Their Start-Up Journeys With Focus

When it comes to start-ups, having a clear and focused strategy can make all the difference between success and failure. While the journey may be challenging, many start-ups have achieved remarkable success by staying laser-focused on their goals, prioritizing key activities, and aligning resources toward their objectives.[14] The success of a start-up largely depends on its ability to stay focused and prioritize its key activities toward achieving its goals. Numerous examples of start-ups have achieved tremendous success by staying true to their mission, prioritizing key activities, and aligning their resources toward their goals. These start-ups have successfully navigated various challenges and maintained their focus, resulting in significant growth and profitability. These companies have managed to identify their niche markets, build innovative solutions, and create a loyal customer base, all while navigating the challenges of a rapidly changing business landscape. By examining these companies, we can gain insight into the importance of focus in the start-up journey and how it can be leveraged to achieve long-term success. Let's look closely at some success stories and what we can learn from them.

The Nudge

The Nudge[15] is a start-up founded by John Peterson and Sarah Peterson that helps people make positive lifestyle changes. The company's mission is to empower individuals to live healthier, happier lives by providing them with the tools and support they need to make sustainable changes. The Nudge's focus on its mission and values has been a key factor in its success. One way The Nudge has stayed focused is by prioritizing key activities. The company has focused on developing a mobile app that allows users to come off their phones and take a break. The Nudge has built a loyal user base by focusing on the app's development and ensuring it meets users' needs. Another way The Nudge has maintained its focus is by aligning its resources towards its goals. The company has carefully allocated resources to support its mission and values. For example, The Nudge has invested in hiring top talent to ensure its team has the expertise to deliver high-quality products and services. The Nudge has also fostered discipline and efficiency within its organization. The company has established clear expectations and accountability for its team members, ensuring everyone is working towards the same goals. The Nudge's culture of discipline and efficiency has allowed it to operate efficiently and effectively, even as it has grown rapidly.

Company Name: The Nudge

Founded: 2017

Significant reason(s) for success: The company is true to its mission and values. It prioritizes key activities and output, building a successful business that positively impacts the lives of its users.

Goodr

Goodr[16] was founded by Jasmine Crowe in 2017, focusing on reducing food waste and hunger. The company provides an innovative solution by working with businesses to donate surplus food to those in need. Goodr tracks the food from the donation point to the final destination, ensuring the food is safe and delivered on time. One of the critical reasons for Goodr's success is its focus on its mission. The company's focus on this mission has allowed it to create a clear roadmap for achieving its goals, which has helped the company to stay focused and motivated. Goodr has also prioritized vital activities to accomplish its mission. The company has developed technology to track food donations and manage logistics, which has helped it to streamline its operations and reduce costs. Goodr has also focused on building solid partnerships with businesses, nonprofits, and government agencies to ensure a steady supply of food donations. In addition to this, Goodr has aligned its resources toward its goals. The company has a dedicated team of employees passionate about reducing food waste and hunger. The company's innovative approach to reducing food waste and hunger has helped it stand out from its competitors. Its focus on technology has allowed it to streamline operations and stay ahead of the curve. Another way in which Goodr has fostered discipline and efficiency is by implementing clear expectations and accountability. The company has set clear goals for reducing food waste and hunger and tracks its progress against these goals. Goodr's employees are held accountable for meeting their targets, and the company regularly reviews its performance to identify areas for improvement.

Company Name: Goodr

Founded: 2017

Significant reason(s) for success: The company aligns its resources toward its goals, fostering discipline and efficiency. It has significantly impacted the fight against food waste and hunger.

Farmstead

Farmstead[17] is a San Francisco-based start-up that provides an online grocery delivery service. The company was founded in 2016 by Pradeep Elankumaran and Kevin Li. Farmstead's mission is to make fresh, high-quality groceries accessible to everyone, regardless of location or how much they can afford to spend. Farmstead's focus on sustainability and efficiency distinguishes it from other online grocery delivery services. The company sources its products from local farmers and producers, which supports the local economy and reduces the carbon footprint associated with transportation. In addition, Farmstead uses artificial intelligence and predictive analytics to optimize its inventory and delivery routes, which minimizes food waste and reduces delivery times. Farmstead's commitment to sustainability and efficiency has been crucial to its success. By focusing on these values, the company has been able to attract a loyal customer base and secure partnerships with local farmers and producers. In addition, Farmstead's use of technology has allowed it to scale its operations quickly and efficiently, which has helped it to remain competitive in the crowded online grocery delivery market.

Company Name: Farmstead

Founded: 2016

Significant reason(s) for success: The company focuses on sustainability and efficiency. The company has grown rapidly and sustainably by staying true to its values and prioritizing key activities.

Snackpass

Snackpass[18] is a food ordering and delivery platform founded in 2017 by Kevin Tan, Jamie Marshall, and Jonathan Cameron. The platform was designed to make it easy for college students to order and pay for food from their favorite local restaurants. One key factor contributing to Snackpass's success is its unwavering focus on serving college students. From the beginning, the founders recognized that college students have unique needs and preferences regarding food ordering and delivery, and they have tailored the platform accordingly. For example, Snackpass allows users to split the cost of a meal with friends, and it also offers a loyalty program, rewarding frequent users with free meals. Snackpass's focus on its core mission has helped it to stand out in a crowded market and win over a loyal user base. By raising impressive funding, Snackpass has continued expanding to new markets and improving its offerings for college students. In addition to focusing on college students, Snackpass has prioritized building strong relationships with local restaurants. The company has worked closely with restaurant owners and managers to understand their needs and preferences. It has developed tools and features that help them better manage their orders and payments. It has helped Snackpass to win the trust and loyalty of restaurant partners, which has, in turn, helped to attract more users to the platform.

Company Name: Snackpass

Founded: 2017

Significant reason(s) for success: It focuses on a specific target audience and mission. It works closely with its users and partners, positively impacting the communities it serves.

Public Goods

Public Goods[19] is a direct-to-consumer company that offers high-quality and sustainable household essentials, personal care, and food products at affordable prices. The company was founded by Michael Ferchak and Morgan Hirsh in 2016, focusing on providing clean and healthy products that are good for people and the planet. Public Goods aims to make a healthy, sustainable lifestyle more accessible and affordable. To achieve this goal, the company uses a membership-based model that allows customers to purchase products directly from the company at wholesale prices. By cutting out intermediaries and reducing packaging waste, Public Goods can offer products at lower prices than traditional retail prices. One of the keys to Public Goods' success has been its laser focus on its core values of sustainability, transparency, and accessibility. The company is committed to using only high-quality and sustainable ingredients in its products. It provides detailed information about the sourcing and production of each item on its website. In addition to its focus on sustainability, Public Goods has also invested heavily in creating a seamless and enjoyable customer experience. The company's website is user-friendly and easy to navigate. It offers a range of features, such as auto-replenishment and customizable subscriptions that make it easy for customers to get the products they need when needed.

Company Name: Public Goods

Founded: 2016

Significant reason(s) for success: By focusing on its core values and prioritizing sustainability, transparency, and accessibility, it has established itself as a leader in the direct-to-consumer space.

Blueland

Blueland[20] is a sustainable cleaning products company founded in 2019 by John A. Mascari and Sarah Paiji Yoo. The company aims to eliminate the need for single-use plastic packaging by offering innovative, eco-friendly cleaning solutions. The company's products include cleaning tablets mixed with water in reusable bottles, significantly reducing plastic packaging use. Blueland has maintained a strong focus on sustainability and innovation, leading to its rapid growth and success. One of the main factors contributing to Blueland's success is its unwavering commitment to its core values. The company's dedication to sustainability is evident in every aspect of its business, from its products to its packaging and shipping practices. This clear focus has helped the company to differentiate itself from competitors and attract a growing customer base. Another critical aspect of Blueland's success is its focus on innovation. The company has developed unique and innovative solutions to everyday cleaning challenges, such as eliminating single-use plastic packaging. This focus on innovation has helped the company to stand out in a crowded market and appeal to consumers looking for new and eco-friendly products. In addition to focusing on sustainability and innovation, Blueland has prioritized building a strong team and company culture. The company has intentionally hired employees who share its values. It has created a workplace culture that fosters creativity, collaboration, and growth.

Company Name: Blueland

Founded: 2018

Significant reason(s) for success: The company focuses on core values and strategic goals. It has become successful by staying true to its mission of sustainability and innovation, differentiating itself in a crowded market.

Patch Plants

Patch Plants[21] is a London-based online plant delivery service founded in 2015 by Freddie Blackett. The company specializes in delivering indoor and outdoor plants and providing plant care advice. The idea behind Patch Plants is to make it easy for people to buy plants and have them delivered to their homes without worrying about the plant's quality and health. Patch Plants operates on the principle of simplicity and convenience. Customers can easily browse the company's website to choose from various plants that fit their needs, whether they're looking for indoor or outdoor plants, small or large plants, or plants that are easy to care for. The company also offers a plant subscription service, where customers receive new plants regularly. One of the reasons why Patch Plants has been successful is its focus on providing excellent customer service. The company offers customers a dedicated plant doctor who can answer questions and provide advice on plant care. Additionally, Patch Plants provides customers with detailed instructions on how to care for each plant, ensuring that the plants stay healthy and vibrant. Patch Plants has also been successful in its marketing strategy. The company has collaborated with famous influencers and publications to showcase its products and services, which has helped to increase brand awareness and drive sales. The company's focus on sustainability is another factor that differentiates it from other plant delivery services. Patch Plants works with eco-friendly suppliers and has taken steps to reduce its carbon footprint by using recycled packaging materials and minimizing transportation emissions.

Company Name: Patch Plants

Founded: 2015

Significant reason(s) for success: The company has achieved success by focusing on providing quality products, excellent customer service, commitment to sustainability, and the ability to adapt to changing market demands.

Conclusion

As I discussed in this chapter, focus is a critical element for the success of any start-up. With so many distractions and opportunities that can divert attention, focusing on the right things is essential to achieve the company's objectives. Many successful start-ups have demonstrated the power of focus in their journeys. Whether a small team of entrepreneurs or a growing organization, maintaining focus on their goals and mission sets them apart. These companies have demonstrated the importance of focus in their business models, operations, and growth strategies, contributing significantly to their success.

As an entrepreneur, there are several strategies you can adopt to maintain focus on your business. And I am sure you have gotten some insights by reading this chapter. Focus requires discipline, dedication, and strategic planning. Staying focused will enable you to navigate the complexities of the business world, make informed decisions, and achieve your objectives. Remember tips like having goals that are clear, attainable, and sustainable. Once you have defined your goals, you should break them down into smaller tasks and assign deadlines to each task. It will help you to stay on track and monitor your progress toward achieving your goals. Another important aspect to remember is eliminating distractions and focusing on what matters most for your business. Taking care of your physical and mental health and others in your company is also essential. As an entrepreneur running a start-up, getting caught up in work and neglecting your well-being can be easy. However, taking breaks, exercising regularly, eating healthily, and getting enough sleep is critical to maintaining focus and productivity. By adopting healthy habits, you will be better equipped to tackle the challenges of entrepreneurship and stay focused on achieving your business goals.

Remember that success is not always a linear journey, and facing challenges or setbacks along the way is okay. Remember to stay focused on your goals and keep pushing forward, even when it feels complicated or overwhelming. Take breaks, when necessary, but don't give up on your dreams. Believe in yourself and your abilities, and know that every step you take towards your goal is progress. As an entrepreneur, staying focused and committed to your goals is essential, even when faced with obstacles or distractions. Remember that the journey toward success is a process of growth and development, and the skills and knowledge you acquire will be invaluable in your personal and professional life. Don't be afraid to take risks and try new things, but stay mindful of your priorities and true to your vision. Keep learning, growing, and adapting to new challenges, and don't be afraid to seek help or guidance when you need it. With determination, hard work, and a willingness to learn, you can achieve great things and positively impact the world around you. So, stay undivided and keep pushing towards your dreams!

Now, it is time to recollect your learnings and understandings. I want you to have more clarity as you move ahead and act on the learnings you have gathered. Your knowledge, blended with calculations and guidance, will yield actionable outcomes. These will then impact your business and decide its course ahead. Like every chapter, this can also be summed up into minor points you can remember and note down for easy access. These are listed below:

1. The meaning of focus for different start-ups may be different, but it is essential to set some ground rules by looking at successful start-ups and their notions of the same.
2. The meaning of focus is directly proportional to staying true to the mission and values. It helps start-ups go a long way in their business journey.
3. Prioritizing key activities is another aspect that adds more substance and sense to the meaning of focus for start-ups.
4. The next aspect of this notion is aligning resources toward goals. It is an essential factor that decides the longevity of start-ups in various ways.
5. Focus is necessary for start-ups for many reasons. Without focus, a lot of operations and ideations may become blurred.
6. Focus helps conserve resources for start-ups, which is essential, especially for businesses with limited resources.
7. Focus also helps start-ups to stay competitive and relevant in the industry. After all, competition is necessary for business success.
8. Focus also fosters discipline and efficiency. With these dispositions, start-ups can make their presence in the market and stay ahead of their competitors.

9. There are many strategies to maintain focus in start-ups, and you must identify those that work for your business and sustain them once you identify them.
10. One strategy to stay focussed is to ensure appropriate delegation in the company. It helps in sustainably using resources and delivering the expected output.
11. Another strategy is regular goal reviews. With this as a priority, you can lead your company in the desired direction without any major crisis.
12. One more key strategy is ensuring clear expectations and accountability among employees, other leaders, and stakeholders.

References

1. Goldstein, G. (2018). *Staying in your lane: Why start-ups must stay focused.* Available at: https://www.entrepreneur.com/starting-a-business/staying-in-your-lane-why-startups-must-stay-focused/309236 [Accessed 4 May 2023].
2. Cote, C. (2022). *How to do market research for a start-up.* Available at: https://online.hbs.edu/blog/post/how-to-do-market-research-for-a-start-up [Accessed 4 May 2023].
3. Crawford, G. (2022). *Council post: Creating a modern vision and Mission for Your Organization: Part 2.* Available at: https://www.forbes.com/sites/forbesbusinesscouncil/2022/05/03/creating-a-modern-vision-and-mission-for-your-organization-part-2/?sh=7442a5f51523 [Accessed 4 May 2023].
4. Riani, A. (2021). *The key to prioritizing successfully in the early startup stages.* Available at: https://www.forbes.com/sites/abdoriani/2021/11/26/the-key-to-prioritizing-successfully-in-the-early-startup-stages/?sh=11d3c2462023 [Accessed 4 May 2023].
5. Piktochart (2016). *Managing Time & Resources: How start-ups deal with Productivity.* Available at: https://medium.com/piktochart/managing-time-resources-how-startups-deal-with-productivity-8c3e8c811cb8 [Accessed 4 May 2023].
6. Ghimire, S. (2022). *Innovative strategies to help small businesses maximize resources.* Available at: https://www.forbes.com/sites/forbesbusinesscouncil/2022/11/18/innovative-strategies-to-help-small-businesses-maximize-resources/?sh=22715ec2fc82 [Accessed 4 May 2023].

7. Forbes. (2019). *10 ways to save money as a start-up.* Available at: https://www.forbes.com/sites/theyec/2019/07/09/10-ways-to-save-money-as-a-startup/?sh=de8782c5c977 [Accessed 4 May 2023].
8. Harvard Business Review (2013). *How competition strengthens start-ups.* Available at: https://hbr.org/2013/03/how-competition-strengthens-start-ups [Accessed 4 May 2023].
9. Taparia, N. (2021). *5 ways for start-ups to take advantage of ai.* Available at: https://www.forbes.com/sites/nealtaparia/2021/02/11/5-ways-for-start-ups-to-take-advantage-of-ai/?sh=6bc2a6c51a57 [Accessed 4 May 2023].
10. Riani, A. (2020). *How to set smart start-up goals at the idea stage.* Available at: https://www.forbes.com/sites/abdoriani/2020/05/26/how-to-set-smart-startup-goals-at-the-idea-stage/?sh=120d7a2e56d2 [Accessed 4 May 2023].
11. Inc. (n.d.). *How to delegate as an entrepreneur: 7 tips for Success.* Available at: https://www.inc.com/young-entrepreneur-council/how-to-delegate-as-an-entrepreneur-7-tips-for-success.html [Accessed 4 May 2023].
12. Forbes (2019). *Setting and monitoring goals for your start-up.* Available at: https://www.forbes.com/sites/theyec/2019/02/20/setting-and-monitoring-goals-for-your-startup/?sh=2121a9f97711 [Accessed 4 May 2023].
13. Rendtslev, A. H. (2017). *Start-ups and accountability.* Available at: https://medium.com/aherforth/startups-and-accountability-7fd978c6f336 [Accessed 4 May 2023].
14. Techstars (2020). *Accountability 101: The entrepreneur's guide to accountability.* Available at: https://www.techstars.com/the-line/advice/accountability-101-the-entrepreneurs-guide-to-developing-an-accountable-organization [Accessed 4 May 2023].
15. Bastone, N. (2018). *This brother and sister duo have a growing startup that uses simple text messages to get you off your phone and off on real-life adventures.* Available at: https://www.businessinsider.in/tech/this-brother-and-sister-duo-have-a-growing-startup-that-uses-simple-text-messages-to-get-you-off-your-phone-and-off-on-real-life-adventures/articleshow/66490240.cms [Accessed 4 May 2023].
16. Locke, T. (2021). *Goodr CEO turned her passion into a multimillion-dollar business: 'I'm really motivated by all the naysayers'.* Available at: https://www.cnbc.com/2021/02/19/goodr-ceo-jasmine-crowes-advice-to-build-a-successful-business.html [Accessed 4 May 2023].
17. Ha, A. (2020). *Farmstead, a grocery start-up with a focus on software, raises $7.9M.* Available at: https://techcrunch.com/2020/11/18/farmstead-series-a/ [Accessed 4 May 2023].

18. Tan, M. (2023). *Report: Snackpass business breakdown & founding story.* Available at: https://research.contrary.com/reports/snackpass [Accessed 4 May 2023].
19. Knox, D. (2021). *How public goods became a one-stop shop for Healthy Everyday Essentials.* Available at: https://www.forbes.com/sites/dave-knox/2021/12/08/how-public-goods-became-a-one-stop-shop-for-healthy-everyday-essentials/?sh=7c31950c5b9f [Accessed 4 May 2023].
20. Decker, V. (2019). *Meet Blueland: Making single use plastics a thing of the past.* Available at: https://www.forbes.com/sites/viviennedeck-er/2019/04/30/meet-blueland-making-single-use-plastics-a-thing-of-the-past/?sh=22926ae162eb [Accessed 4 May 2023].
21. Reuter, D. (2020). *The head of marketing for a UK urban-gardening start-up explains how strong brand recognition helps him grow his team.* Available at: https://www.businessinsider.in/strategy/news/the-head-of-marketing-for-a-uk-urban-gardening-startup-explains-how-strong-brand-recogni-tion-helps-him-grow-his-team/articleshow/75070928.cms [Accessed 4 May 2023].

CHAPTER 11
Right Team

In entrepreneurship, success is not a solitary pursuit but a collective journey. As you embark on your entrepreneurial odyssey, the realization dawns that your vision can only be transformed into reality through the combined efforts of a capable and dedicated team.[1] When you have an idea brimming with promise, a collaborative team will be essential to bring it to fruition. As your venture's scope expands, so will the realization that outstanding achievements are seldom reached through solo efforts alone. The realm of start-ups will continue to emphasize the importance of assembling a team that shares your passion and embraces collective responsibility. In this future landscape, the journey toward success will undoubtedly be paved with the collaborative efforts of a dedicated and synergistic team. Warren Buffet, the iconic investor and business magnate, once imparted a powerful piece of wisdom: "Associate with people who are better than you." These words echo through the corridors of entrepreneurial insight, emphasizing the importance of assembling a team with diverse skills, experiences, and perspectives. The right team becomes the lifeblood of your start-up, breathing vitality and resilience into its very core.

Building the right team is a challenging feat. It requires a discerning eye, an acute understanding of human dynamics, and an unwavering commitment to finding individuals who complement your abilities and share a profound belief in your vision. As you navigate this complex process, you'll discover that the amalgamation of character traits, expertise, and unwavering dedication sets the right team apart. In the tumultuous world of start-ups, challenges loom at every turn. The ability to weather storms and stand firm in adversity is a defining characteristic of the right team. Resilience becomes their armor, fortifying your start-up against the forces that threaten to undermine its progress. With the right team by your side, you gain the confidence to tackle even the most daunting obstacles, secure in the knowledge that you have a collective strength to rely on.

Key Traits To Look For In Team Members

When assembling your team, seeking individuals with common key traits is essential. These traits bring many advantages that can significantly benefit entrepreneurs and start-ups on their path to success. One valuable trait to seek in team members is adaptability. In the dynamic and ever-evolving landscape of start-ups, adaptability is crucial for navigating challenges and seizing opportunities. Adaptable team members can embrace change, pivot strategies when necessary, and quickly learn and grow in response to new circumstances. Their flexibility allows the start-up to navigate uncertainty with agility, staying ahead of the curve and finding innovative solutions to possible obstacles. Having strong communication skills among team members is yet another advantageous trait. Effective communication fosters transparency, collaboration, and the efficient exchange of ideas and information. Team members who excel in communication can articulate their thoughts clearly, actively listen to others, and provide constructive feedback. It cultivates a culture of open dialogue where everyone feels valued and empowered to contribute their insights. Effective communication enhances teamwork and strengthens relationships with stakeholders, investors, and customers.

In addition to the unique skills and qualifications[2] that individuals bring to a team, the presence of certain common key traits among team members is essential for the success of any start-up. These traits are foundational elements that contribute to a cohesive and high-performing team dynamic. While each individual may possess a distinct combination of traits, the shared presence of these common key traits creates a harmonious and productive environment. They form the bedrock upon which effective teamwork, innovation, and problem-solving can flourish. These common key traits collectively lay the groundwork for a team that can navigate challenges, seize opportunities, and propel the start-up toward long-term success. In this section, I have elaborated on three main dimensions of key traits to look for in team members. Firstly,

I have written on passion and alignment and how these two enhance a team's performance. Secondly, I have described two more important aspects - adaptability and resilience. Many writers have written about these, but you must get added perspectives. Lastly, I have written about a collaborative mindset. An essential 21st-century skill, collaboration is the key to achieving many milestones, especially for start-ups.

Passion And Alignment

Passion[3] is a driving force that propels individuals to go above and beyond in their pursuit of excellence. When team members are deeply passionate about their work and aligned with the mission and vision of the start-up, remarkable things can happen. Passion ignites enthusiasm and a sense of purpose, infusing energy into the team and fueling their commitment to success. It sparks creativity and innovation, as passionate individuals are likelier to think outside the box, take risks, and push the boundaries of what is possible. Moreover, passion is contagious. When team members exude passion for their work, it inspires and motivates others, creating a ripple effect that elevates the entire team's performance. Passionate team members are driven by a genuine desire to make a meaningful impact, and this intrinsic motivation leads to a stronger work ethic, perseverance in the face of challenges, and a relentless pursuit of excellence. Ultimately, passion becomes the catalyst that transforms a start-up from a mere business venture into a fulfilling and purpose-driven journey. Passion ignites a fire within individuals that goes beyond sheer dedication or enthusiasm. It is a deep-rooted love and zeal for the work they do, the mission they pursue, and the impact they aim to make. Passionate team members are driven by an intrinsic motivation that goes beyond external rewards, allowing them to push through obstacles, overcome setbacks, and continuously strive for improvement. Their passion fuels their creativity, pushing them to think innovatively and find unique solutions. Moreover, passion transcends the boundaries of time and effort, as team members willingly invest extra hours and go the extra mile because their work is not just a job but a manifestation of their passion.

Alignment among team members is vital for a start-up to operate cohesively and effectively. When team members are aligned, they share a common understanding of the start-up's goals, values, and direction. This alignment enables everyone to pull in the same direction, fostering unity and synergy within the team. Aligned team members have a shared sense of purpose, which guides their decision-making and actions. This alignment enhances collaboration and streamlines processes, as team members are on the same page and can work towards common objectives with clarity and efficiency. Furthermore, alignment promotes effective communication and reduces misunderstandings or conflicts due to differing perspectives or goals. It fosters a supportive and inclusive environment where team members respect and value each other's contributions. In addition, alignment extends beyond internal team dynamics and influences interactions with external stakeholders, such as investors and customers. When the team is aligned, it exudes a sense of unity and coherence, creating a positive impression and instilling confidence in the start-up's potential for success. Overall, alignment among team members strengthens cohesion, boosts productivity, and enhances the start-up's ability to navigate challenges and seize opportunities with a unified vision.

Adaptability And Resilience

In the ever-evolving landscape of start-ups, adaptability is a trait that can make a significant difference in the success and survival of a venture. By embracing adaptability, start-ups can stay nimble, proactively respond to market shifts, and seize new avenues for growth. Start-ups often encounter unexpected challenges, rapidly changing market conditions, and the need to pivot strategies. Team members who possess adaptability are invaluable assets as they can navigate through uncertainty with agility and ease. They embrace change as an opportunity for growth rather than a setback, readily adjusting their approaches, plans, and mindsets to align with new circumstances. Adaptable team members are willing to learn, unlearn, and relearn, staying ahead of the curve and capitalizing on emerging trends or opportunities. Their flexibility and open-mindedness foster resilience and innovation, enabling them to think on their feet, take calculated risks, and find creative solutions to problems.

Resilience[4] is a vital trait that can empower individuals and teams to bounce back from setbacks, navigate challenges, and continue moving forward with determination. In the context of a start-up, where uncertainties and obstacles are part of the journey, resilient team members become pillars of strength. They possess the mental fortitude to face adversity, learn from failures, and persevere despite setbacks. Resilient individuals view obstacles as opportunities for growth, drawing valuable lessons from each experience and using them to refine their strategies and approaches. They maintain a positive outlook, staying focused on the long-term vision and goals of the start-up even when faced with short-term difficulties. Resilient team members inspire and motivate others, fostering a can-do attitude and creating a culture of perseverance and tenacity. Their ability to adapt, recover, and thrive amidst challenges gives the start-up a competitive edge, allowing it to navigate turbulent waters and emerge stronger than before. With resilience as a guiding trait, start-ups can weather storms, overcome hurdles, and achieve sustainable success.

Collaborative Mindset

A collaborative mindset[5] is a powerful trait that fuels effective teamwork, fosters innovation, and propels the success of start-ups. Team members with a collaborative mindset recognize the value of collective intelligence and actively seek opportunities to collaborate and cooperate with their peers. They understand that collaboration brings together diverse perspectives, experiences, and skill sets, leading to more problem-solving and robust decision-making. These individuals prioritize open communication, actively listen to other's ideas, and encourage contributions from all team members. Promoting a collaborative culture creates an environment where everyone feels valued, empowered, and motivated to contribute their best. In a start-up setting, a collaborative mindset becomes even more crucial as it facilitates the exchange of knowledge and expertise, driving innovation and creativity. Team members with this mindset willingly share their knowledge and insights, collaborate on projects, and leverage each other's strengths to achieve common goals. They value teamwork over individual achievements and understand that by working together, the team can accomplish more than any individual can achieve alone.

A collaborative mindset fosters trust and psychological safety within the team, where everyone feels comfortable sharing ideas, challenging assumptions, and providing constructive feedback. This collaborative environment fosters continuous learning and improvement as team members leverage each other's expertise to solve complex problems and seize opportunities. Moreover, a collaborative mindset extends beyond internal team dynamics to external collaborations with partners, customers, and stakeholders. Start-ups prioritizing collaboration build solid networks and strategic alliances that enhance their market presence and broaden their reach. They actively seek partnerships that complement their strengths, allowing them to tap into additional resources, knowledge, and market opportunities. By embracing collaboration, start-ups can leverage the collective power of a broader ecosystem, accelerating their growth and success.

Ways To Ensure Effective Team Communication

Ensuring effective team communication[6] is crucial for the success of start-ups as it offers numerous advantages that contribute to productivity, cohesion, and overall performance. When team members communicate effectively, they can align their efforts, share information, and collaborate seamlessly. Transparent and clear communication channels foster a shared understanding of goals, expectations, and responsibilities, ensuring everyone is on the same page. This alignment promotes efficiency, minimizes duplication of efforts, and maximizes productivity as team members can work together towards a common purpose. Effective communication also enhances problem-solving and decision-making processes within start-ups. When team members can openly express ideas, concerns, and perspectives, it promotes healthy discussions and critical thinking. Through active listening and constructive dialogue, team members can identify potential obstacles, explore solutions, and collectively make informed decisions. The exchange of diverse viewpoints not only enriches the quality of decision-making but also encourages innovation and creativity. When individuals feel heard and valued, they are more likely to contribute their unique insights and ideas, leading to more robust solutions and fostering a culture of continuous improvement.

Effective team communication nurtures a positive and supportive work environment. Regular and open communication allows team members to build trust, establish strong relationships, and foster a sense of belonging. When individuals feel comfortable expressing their thoughts and concerns, it promotes psychological safety, encouraging risk-taking, creativity, and collaboration. Effective communication also helps resolve conflicts and address issues promptly, preventing misunderstandings or tensions from escalating. A positive work environment boosts morale, motivation, and job satisfaction, increasing productivity and retaining talented team members. To make it clearer, I have talked about a few important aspects related to ways to ensure effective team communication. Firstly, I have written about creating clear and open channels and how these impact communication within your start-up team. Secondly, I have written about the importance of active listening and why you need to create an environment of openness for your team members. Thirdly, I have written about the importance of regular team meetings and how these add to your start-up's success.

Clear And Open Channels

Creating clear and open communication channels is essential for fostering effective collaboration and ensuring that information flows seamlessly within a start-up. Here, two key aspects of establishing such communication channels are crucial: transparency and accessibility. Transparent communication[7] is a cornerstone of a successful start-up. When team members have access to relevant information, understand the company's goals and strategies, and are kept informed about important updates, it creates a sense of trust and empowerment. Transparency cultivates a culture of openness and honesty, where everyone feels valued and included in decision-making. It involves sharing relevant information about the company's progress, challenges, and milestones, enabling team members to align their efforts and make informed decisions. Transparent communication also extends to addressing concerns and providing constructive feedback. When feedback flows freely, it enables continuous improvement and growth. By fostering transparency, start-ups empower their team members to contribute effectively, collaborate efficiently, and take ownership of their work.

Accessibility[8] of communication channels is vital for ensuring that information reaches all team members on time. Start-ups need to establish accessible platforms and tools that facilitate communication, collaboration, and knowledge sharing. It includes utilizing project management software, instant messaging applications, shared document repositories, and video conferencing tools. By leveraging these technologies, team members can communicate effectively, regardless of their physical location or time zone. Accessibility also involves creating an environment where communication is encouraged and valued. Start-ups should promote open-door policies, where team members feel comfortable approaching leaders and sharing their ideas, concerns, and feedback. Creating a supportive and inclusive atmosphere encourages active participation and engagement, leading to a more cohesive and productive team.

Active Listening

Active listening[9] is a vital skill that entrepreneurs must cultivate to build strong relationships, foster effective teamwork, and drive the success of their start-ups. Active listening allows entrepreneurs to better understand their team members, stakeholders, and customers. Entrepreneurs can develop empathy and form meaningful connections by attentively listening to their perspectives, concerns, and aspirations. This empathetic understanding helps entrepreneurs tailor their communication and decision-making processes to address the needs and interests of their stakeholders. It enables them to build trust, establish rapport, and forge mutually beneficial partnerships. Through active listening, entrepreneurs can identify opportunities, anticipate challenges, and make informed decisions that align with the expectations of their team members and stakeholders. Start-ups thrive when they understand their customers' needs and deliver products or services that meet those needs effectively. Active listening is pivotal in gaining valuable insights into the target audience. Entrepreneurs can actively listen to customer feedback and uncover pain points, preferences, and emerging trends. This information helps them refine their offerings, enhance customer experiences, and build solid and long-lasting relationships with their target market.

Entrepreneurs face numerous challenges and obstacles on their journey. Active listening equips them with valuable insights and diverse perspectives to tackle these hurdles effectively. Entrepreneurs can tap into a wealth of knowledge and expertise by attentively listening to the input and ideas of their team members and collaborators. This collaborative problem-solving approach fosters innovation, creativity, and better decision-making. By encouraging open dialogue and actively seeking input, entrepreneurs can leverage their team's collective intelligence, identifying innovative solutions and overcoming obstacles that may have seemed impossible. Active listening also enables entrepreneurs to identify potential roadblocks early on, mitigating risks and ensuring smoother execution of their plans.

Regular Team Meetings

Regular team meetings[10] are fundamental to effective team communication and collaboration within start-ups. There are some advantages of conducting regular team meetings and the benefits they bring to entrepreneurs and their start-up ventures. Regular team meetings provide a platform for entrepreneurs to align their team members' efforts with the start-up's overall vision, goals, and strategies. These meetings offer an opportunity to communicate updates, share progress, and discuss any changes or adjustments in direction. By fostering alignment, entrepreneurs ensure everyone is on the same page, working towards a common purpose. Regular team meetings promote clarity, minimize miscommunication, and enable team members to understand how their contributions add to the broader objectives of the start-up. Through these meetings, entrepreneurs can reinforce the start-up's values, motivate their team members, and foster a sense of shared ownership.

Team meetings facilitate collaboration and foster a culture of collective problem-solving within start-ups. They provide a dedicated space for team members to share ideas, offer feedback, and engage in productive discussions. Entrepreneurs can leverage their team members' diverse expertise and perspectives to explore new opportunities, address challenges, and develop innovative solutions. Regular team meetings promote synergy, creativity, and a sense of camaraderie among team members. By encouraging active participation and creating an inclusive environment, entrepreneurs can harness their team's collective intelligence and experience, resulting in more robust outcomes and a stronger start-up. Team meetings serve as a platform for effective decision-making within start-ups. By bringing team members together, entrepreneurs can leverage their insights, expertise, and diverse viewpoints to make informed choices. These meetings enable entrepreneurs to discuss various options, evaluate risks and benefits, and make consensus-based decisions. Regular team meetings also facilitate the delegation of responsibilities, ensuring that everyone understands their roles and contributions to the overall success of the start-up. Efficient decision-making in team meetings helps entrepreneurs navigate challenges, seize opportunities, and propel their start-ups forward with agility and confidence.

Empowering Team Members To Make Decisions

Empowering team members to make decisions[11] is key to fostering a culture of autonomy, ownership, and innovation within start-ups. When leaders empower their team members, it positively impacts them and their start-up ventures. When team members are empowered to make decisions, they feel a sense of ownership and accountability for their work. This heightened sense of responsibility fuels their motivation and engagement, as they are actively involved in shaping the outcomes and success of the start-up. Empowered team members are likelier to take the initiative, display creativity, and go the extra mile to achieve exceptional results. By giving team members the autonomy to make decisions, entrepreneurs create an environment that fosters intrinsic motivation, encourages growth, and cultivates a high-performance culture. Empowering team members to make decisions enables faster and more agile decision-making within start-ups. As entrepreneurs delegate decision-making authority to their team members, it reduces bottlenecks and eliminates the need for constant approval from higher levels of management. It allows for quicker response times, adaptability to changing circumstances, and the ability to capitalize on emerging opportunities. Empowered team members can make informed decisions in their respective areas of expertise, leveraging their knowledge and experience to drive progress and innovation. This decentralized decision-making approach enhances the start-up's ability to navigate challenges swiftly, seize market opportunities, and stay ahead of the competition.

Empowering team members to make decisions fosters a culture of progress and continuous learning within start-ups. When individuals can explore new ideas, experiment with different approaches, and take calculated risks, it sparks creativity and drives progress. Empowered team members feel encouraged to contribute their unique perspectives and suggest improvements, leading to the development of innovative solutions and processes. This culture of empowerment also promotes a growth mindset, as team members learn from successes and failures. By encouraging learning and innovation, entrepreneurs position their start-ups as a hub of creativity, attracting talented individuals who thrive in an environment that values their ideas and contributions. It would not be beneficial to tell you about empowering your team members to make decisions and not tell you how. So, I have discussed this in detail hereafter. I have written about the power of encouraging independent thinking and how it helps in your entrepreneurial journey. I have also discussed setting measurable goals and why it is crucial for your team members to do so. Lastly, I have written about establishing accountability systems, which is considered inevitable by companies, new and established alike. A strong sense of accountability takes the company way forward.

Encouraging Independent Thinking

Encouraging independent thinking[12] is a fundamental aspect of empowering team members within start-ups. Entrepreneurs create an environment that fosters creativity, critical thinking, and innovation by promoting independent thinking. There are many benefits of encouraging independent thinking in a company. When team members are encouraged to think independently, they are more likely to generate creative and innovative ideas. Independent thinking allows individuals to break free from conventional patterns, explore new possibilities, and propose unique solutions to challenges. By embracing diverse perspectives and encouraging team members to think outside the box, entrepreneurs create an environment that nurtures creativity and fosters innovation. Infusing fresh ideas and alternative viewpoints can lead to breakthrough innovations, positioning the start-up at the forefront of its industry. Encouraging independent thinking signals trust and confidence in team members' abilities. When entrepreneurs empower their team members to think independently, they convey that their input and ideas are valued and respected. This trust and confidence cultivate a positive and empowering work culture where team members feel encouraged to take ownership of their work and confidently make decisions. Building trust and confidence through independent thinking leads to greater job satisfaction, higher levels of engagement, and a stronger commitment to the start-up's success.

Independent thinking empowers team members to take the initiative, seek out opportunities, and proactively respond to challenges. When encouraged to think independently, individuals develop a growth mindset and become more adaptable to change. They are willing to explore new strategies, embrace innovation, and navigate uncertainties with resilience. This ability to adapt and grow fuels the start-up's agility and positions it for long-term success in a dynamic business landscape. Independent thinking encourages team members to take ownership of their decisions and actions. When individuals are free to think independently, they feel accountable for the outcomes and results they generate. This ownership mindset drives a higher level of commitment and responsibility, as team members understand that their decisions directly impact the start-up's success. By promoting independent thinking, entrepreneurs foster a culture of accountability, where team members actively contribute to the growth and achievement of the start-up's goals.

Setting Measurable Goals

Setting measurable goals is critical to empowering team members and driving success within start-ups. Setting measurable goals provides clarity and focus for both individual team members and the start-up as a whole. When goals are Specific, Measurable, Achievable, Relevant, and Time-bound (SMART), they provide a clear roadmap for success. Team members understand what is expected of them and can align their efforts toward achieving those goals. This clarity and focus eliminate ambiguity, minimize distractions, and maximize productivity, ensuring everyone is working towards the same objectives. Measurable goals serve as benchmarks for performance evaluation and accountability. When goals are clearly defined and measurable, team members can track their progress and measure their achievements. This transparency allows individuals to assess their performance, identify areas for improvement, and take proactive steps to meet or exceed their targets. The existence of measurable goals also fosters a sense of accountability, as team members take responsibility for their contributions towards achieving those goals.

Setting measurable goals[13] impacts team members' motivation and engagement. Challenging yet attainable goals can inspire individuals to stretch their capabilities and strive for excellence. Clear benchmarks and milestones give team members a sense of progress and achievement as they work towards their goals. This motivation and engagement contribute to a positive work environment where individuals feel energized and enthusiastic about their work, increasing job satisfaction and overall team performance. Measurable goals facilitate alignment and coordination within the start-up. When goals are set at the team or organizational level, they create a shared sense of purpose and direction. Team members understand how their individual goals contribute to the larger goals of the start-up, fostering collaboration and synergy. The alignment of goals ensures that everyone is working towards a shared vision, avoiding silos and promoting cross-functional cooperation. Measurable goals enable effective communication and coordination, as team members can track progress, share updates, and provide support where needed.

Establishing Accountability Systems

Establishing accountability systems[14] is crucial to fostering a high-performance culture within start-ups. Accountability systems ensure that clear expectations and responsibilities are communicated to team members. By defining roles, tasks, and performance standards, entrepreneurs provide team members with a clear understanding of their responsibilities. This clarity eliminates confusion and ambiguity, enabling individuals to align their efforts toward achieving the start-up's goals. When team members know what is expected of them, they can take ownership of their work and be held accountable for their performance. Accountability systems drive improved performance and results within start-ups. When team members know their performance will be evaluated and measured, they are more likely to strive for excellence. Establishing performance metrics, key performance indicators (KPIs), and regular performance evaluations ensures that individuals are held accountable for their contributions. This focus on accountability encourages individuals to consistently deliver high-quality work, improving productivity, efficiency, and overall business performance.

Accountability systems promote transparency and trust within the start-up.[15] When performance expectations and evaluation criteria are communicated, team members have a transparent view of how their contributions are assessed. This transparency builds trust between team members and entrepreneurs, as everyone knows the standards and measures used to evaluate performance. Trust is essential for effective collaboration and teamwork, fostering an environment where individuals can rely on each other and work towards common goals. Accountability systems provide opportunities for learning and growth. Through regular feedback, performance evaluations, and accountability discussions, team members can identify areas for improvement and development. Constructive feedback and coaching help individuals refine their skills, enhance their knowledge, and address performance gaps. This focus on continuous learning and growth benefits individual team members and contributes to the start-up's overall growth and development. Accountability systems ensure alignment between individual and organizational goals. By establishing systems that track and evaluate progress, entrepreneurs can ensure that individual efforts are aligned with the start-up's strategic objectives. This alignment enhances the overall efficiency and effectiveness of the start-up, as everyone is working towards the same vision. Accountability systems create a shared understanding of the importance of individual contributions in driving the start-up's success.

Companies That Got The Team Right

In the vast landscape of start-ups, remarkable companies have truly embraced the principles we have discussed throughout this chapter on building the right team. These companies are inspiring examples of what can be achieved when the right team comes together with a shared vision, common values, and a relentless pursuit of excellence.[15] Their stories illuminate the transformative power of assembling a talented and cohesive team, demonstrating how it can propel a start-up from mere ideas to groundbreaking innovations and remarkable success. These companies serve as beacons of inspiration, reminding us that behind every great start-up is a group of individuals who believe in a shared dream and bring their diverse skills, experiences, and perspectives to the table. They embody the entrepreneurial spirit, pushing boundaries, defying conventions, and disrupting industries. Their stories testify that success is not achieved in isolation but through the collaborative efforts of a passionate and capable team. As you delve into the stories of these exceptional companies, you will witness the impact of a strong team that possesses the key traits we have explored – passion, alignment, adaptability, resilience, a collaborative mindset, effective communication, empowerment, and accountability. These traits have propelled these companies to new heights, enabling them to overcome challenges, seize opportunities, and create a lasting impact in their respective fields. Through the lens of these companies, you will discover the real-world applications of the principles we have discussed. Their journeys will inspire you to reflect on your start-up and the team you are building.

Iterable

Iterable[16] is a leading customer engagement platform that empowers companies to create personalized marketing campaigns across various channels. With its robust features and intuitive interface, Iterable enables businesses to deliver relevant and timely messages to their customers, driving engagement and enhancing the overall customer experience. The company's powerful automation capabilities, flexible workflows, and deep integrations with popular marketing tools make it a preferred choice for many organizations seeking to build strong customer relationships and drive revenue growth. What sets Iterable apart is its focus on enabling marketers to orchestrate highly targeted and personalized campaigns at scale. Businesses can tailor their messaging to individual customer preferences, behaviors, and lifecycle stages by leveraging data-driven insights and segmentation capabilities. This level of personalization fosters stronger connections, increases customer loyalty, and drives higher conversion rates. Iterable's dedication to innovation and continuous improvement has positioned it as a trusted partner for numerous well-known brands across various industries. Through its user-friendly platform, comprehensive analytics, and advanced automation capabilities, Iterable empowers marketers to optimize their campaigns, experiment with different strategies, and achieve measurable results. With Iterable, companies can unlock the full potential of their customer engagement strategies, delivering impactful experiences that resonate with their target audience. By leveraging the power of this cutting-edge platform, businesses can foster long-term customer relationships, drive brand advocacy, and propel their growth in today's competitive market.

Company Name: Iterable

Founded: 2013

Significant reason(s) for success: Its focus is on assembling a team that combines technical expertise with a deep understanding of marketing and customer engagement. This interdisciplinary approach has allowed them to create a powerful platform that meets the evolving needs of their clients.

Plume

Plume[17] is a pioneering company that is revolutionizing the home Wi-Fi experience. With a focus on delivering reliable, fast, and secure internet connectivity, Plume has developed an innovative whole-home Wi-Fi solution that optimizes network performance and ensures seamless connectivity in every corner of the house. Plume's approach to home Wi-Fi centers around "Adaptive Wi-Fi." By leveraging artificial intelligence and machine learning algorithms, the Plume system continuously analyzes network conditions, device behavior, and user patterns to adapt and optimize Wi-Fi performance intelligently. This dynamic optimization ensures that devices are always connected to the best available signal, resulting in faster speeds, reduced latency, and enhanced online experience for users. One of the key advantages of Plume's solution is its ease of use and intuitive setup. The Plume app provides a user-friendly interface, allowing homeowners to easily manage their Wi-Fi network, monitor connected devices, and troubleshoot any issues. With features like parental controls and guest access management, Plume empowers users to fully control their home network and customize it to suit their needs. Furthermore, Plume's commitment to cybersecurity and data privacy sets it apart in the industry. The company prioritizes the security of its users' data, employing robust encryption protocols and implementing advanced threat detection mechanisms to safeguard against potential cyber threats. This focus on security ensures users enjoy a worry-free online experience without compromising their privacy. Plume's innovative approach to home Wi-Fi has garnered recognition and partnerships with leading service providers and technology companies worldwide. By offering a comprehensive solution combining intelligent network optimization, user-friendly management, and robust security measures, Plume is reshaping how people experience Wi-Fi connectivity at home, creating a seamless and reliable internet environment for households everywhere.

Company Name: Plume

Founded: 2015

Significant reason(s) for success: Its ability to build a team that brings together experienced professionals from the telecommunications and technology sectors. This diverse team has enabled Plume to develop innovative solutions that revolutionize the sector.

Hopper

Hopper[18] is a trailblazing travel technology company transforming how people plan and book their trips. With its advanced algorithms and data-driven approach, Hopper provides travelers personalized recommendations, real-time insights, and predictive pricing to help them find the best deals and make informed travel decisions. One of Hopper's standout features is its powerful flight prediction and price monitoring capabilities. By analyzing vast amounts of historical and current flight data, Hopper can accurately forecast future prices and advise users on the optimal time to book their flights. It empowers travelers to save money by securing the best fares and avoiding unnecessary price fluctuations. In addition to flight predictions, Hopper also offers hotel booking services, providing users with a seamless end-to-end travel planning experience. The platform presents travelers with personalized hotel recommendations based on their preferences and budget, simplifying the search process and ensuring a tailored selection of accommodations. Hopper's commitment to transparency and customer satisfaction sets it apart in the travel industry. The platform provides users with detailed breakdowns of flight and hotel prices, highlighting any additional fees or charges that may apply. This level of transparency allows travelers to make well-informed decisions and eliminates surprises during the booking process. Furthermore, Hopper's user-friendly mobile app offers a streamlined and intuitive interface, making it easy for travelers to search, book, and manage their trips. The app also provides real-time notifications and alerts, informing users about price changes, travel advisories, and other relevant updates. With its innovative technology and customer-centric approach, Hopper has gained recognition as a trusted platform for millions of travelers worldwide. By leveraging data insights, predictive analytics, and a commitment to transparency, Hopper empowers travelers to optimize their travel plans, save money, and have a seamless and enjoyable travel experience from start to finish.

Company Name: Hopper

Founded: 2007

Significant reason(s) for success: Its exceptional data science and engineering team. By leveraging advanced algorithms and machine learning techniques, they have created a platform that accurately predicts flight and hotel prices, helping travelers save money.

TripActions

TripActions[19] is a leading corporate travel and expense management platform transforming how businesses manage and optimize their travel programs. With a comprehensive suite of tools and services, TripActions enables companies to streamline their travel processes, improve cost control, and enhance the overall travel experience for their employees. One of the key advantages of TripActions is its user-friendly interface and intuitive booking platform. The platform provides employees with a seamless and efficient way to search and book flights, accommodations, and other travel-related services. With its vast inventory of options and integration with major travel providers, TripActions ensures that employees can access a wide range of choices to suit their preferences and needs. Beyond its booking capabilities, TripActions offers robust travel policy management, expense tracking, and reporting features. Companies can easily define and enforce travel policies, ensuring compliance and cost control. Additionally, the platform provides real-time expense tracking and reporting, allowing businesses to gain insights into their travel spend and make data-driven decisions to optimize their travel programs. One of the standout features of TripActions is its dedication to providing exceptional customer support. The platform offers 24/7 assistance to travelers, ensuring they have access to support and guidance whenever needed. This commitment to customer service helps alleviate travel-related issues and enhances employee experience, fostering greater satisfaction and productivity. Furthermore, TripActions leverages technology and data analytics to provide businesses with valuable insights and recommendations for improving travel programs. The platform offers comprehensive reporting and analytics, allowing companies to identify cost-saving opportunities, negotiate better deals with travel suppliers, and make strategic decisions to optimize travel spending.

Company Name: TripActions

Founded: 2015

Significant reason(s) for success: Its team's deep domain knowledge and expertise in travel and technology. By assembling a team that understands the pain points of business travel and has the technical skills to build a user-friendly platform, TripActions has disrupted the corporate travel industry and gained widespread adoption among companies and travelers.

BetterUp

BetterUp[20] is a leading professional coaching platform that empowers individuals and organizations to reach their full potential. Through its innovative technology and network of certified coaches, BetterUp delivers personalized coaching experiences to help individuals unlock their growth, improve their well-being, and achieve their professional goals. One of the key advantages of BetterUp is its focus on holistic development. The platform goes beyond traditional coaching models by incorporating various elements, including behavioral science, positive psychology, and mindfulness practices. This comprehensive approach allows individuals to develop their professional skills, emotional intelligence, resilience, and overall well-being. BetterUp's personalized coaching programs are tailored to meet each individual's unique needs and aspirations. Through one-on-one coaching sessions, individuals work closely with their dedicated coach to identify their strengths, set meaningful goals, overcome challenges, and develop strategies for success. The ongoing support and guidance provided by the coaches help individuals stay accountable, motivated, and on track toward their desired outcomes. Another significant advantage of BetterUp is its convenient and flexible delivery model. The platform leverages digital technology to enable coaching sessions to take place remotely, eliminating geographical constraints and making coaching accessible to individuals worldwide. This flexibility allows busy professionals to schedule coaching sessions conveniently, maximizing their time and productivity. Furthermore, BetterUp utilizes data analytics and insights to drive continuous improvement and measure the impact of coaching. The platform collects data on individual progress, engagement levels, and outcomes, providing individuals and organizations with valuable feedback and actionable insights. This data-driven approach helps individuals track their growth, identify areas for development, and make informed decisions to optimize their personal and professional development journeys.

Company Name: BetterUp

Founded: 2013

Significant reason(s) for success: Its focus on building a team of renowned experts in coaching, psychology, and organizational development. By combining technology with human-centered approaches, they have created a platform that offers personalized coaching and professional development to individuals and organizations.

Airtable

Airtable[21] is a powerful collaboration platform that combines a spreadsheet's flexibility with a database's functionalities. It allows individuals and teams to organize, track, and manage their work in a highly customizable and intuitive manner. With its versatile features and user-friendly interface, Airtable provides numerous advantages for businesses across various industries. One of the key advantages of Airtable is its ability to adapt to different workflows and processes. The platform offers a wide range of templates and pre-built apps that can be customized to meet specific needs. Whether it's project management, content planning, customer relationship management, or inventory tracking, Airtable provides the flexibility to design and tailor databases and workflows that align with the unique requirements of any team or project. Collaboration is another major strength of Airtable. The platform allows teams to collaborate in real-time, providing a centralized hub where members can view, edit, and comment on data. It enhances communication, transparency, and productivity, as team members can easily collaborate, share updates, and track progress on shared projects. With its built-in commenting and notification features, Airtable keeps everyone on the same page and fosters seamless collaboration. Additionally, Airtable offers powerful automation features that help streamline repetitive tasks and save time. With its automation capabilities, users can set up rules, triggers, and actions to automate various processes and workflows. It reduces manual effort, minimizes the chances of errors, and ensures consistency in data management and operations. Another advantage of Airtable is its integration capabilities with other popular tools and platforms. It seamlessly integrates with third-party apps and services like Zapier, Slack, Google Drive, and more, allowing users to connect their existing tools and create efficient workflows. This integration capability further enhances productivity and efficiency by combining data and functionalities from multiple sources into a single, unified platform.

Company Name: Airtable

Founded: 2012

Significant reason(s) for success: Its ability to assemble a team that blends creativity, design, and engineering expertise. Its team has developed a flexible and intuitive no-code platform for building custom databases and applications, empowering individuals and teams to organize and collaborate effectively.

Webflow

Webflow[22] is a cutting-edge web design and development platform that enables individuals and businesses to create stunning, custom websites without coding or technical expertise. With its intuitive visual interface and powerful design tools, Webflow offers several advantages for professional designers and those new to web development. One of the key advantages of Webflow is its ability to provide complete design control. The platform offers a wide range of pre-designed templates and components, which can be customized to suit individual preferences and branding requirements. Users can easily drag and drop elements, adjust layouts, and style every aspect of their website with precision. This level of design control allows users to create unique and visually appealing websites that align with specific business goals and target audience needs. Webflow also offers a responsive design feature, ensuring that websites automatically adapt and look great on various devices, including desktops, tablets, and mobile phones. This responsiveness is crucial in today's mobile-first era, as it allows businesses to provide a seamless user experience across different screen sizes and devices. With Webflow, designers can confidently create websites optimized for various devices, enhancing user engagement and satisfaction. Another advantage of Webflow is its robust content management system (CMS) capabilities. The platform allows users to easily manage and update website content, such as blog posts, product listings, and media assets, without complex coding or reliance on third-party systems. This flexibility and control over content enable businesses to keep their websites fresh, relevant, and up-to-date, fostering better engagement and driving more conversions. Webflow also offers powerful e-commerce functionality, allowing businesses to create and manage online stores. Users can set up product catalogs, customize shopping cart functionality, and handle transactions securely, all within the Webflow platform. This e-commerce integration streamlines launching and managing an online store, providing businesses with the tools to sell products or services directly from their websites.

Company Name: Webflow

Founded: 2013

Significant reason(s) for success: Its team's deep understanding of design, development, and user experience. Their team's commitment to simplicity and empowerment has fueled Webflow's growth and popularity among professionals in the web design industry.

Conclusion

The success of a start-up heavily relies on assembling the right team.[23] Throughout this chapter, we have explored the advantages of team members possessing key traits such as passion, alignment, adaptability, resilience, a collaborative mindset, effective communication, and empowered decision-making. These traits benefit the growth and sustainability of a start-up and contribute to a positive and productive work environment. When team members are passionate about their work, they bring unparalleled dedication and enthusiasm. Their unwavering commitment fuels creativity, innovation, and the drive to overcome challenges. By aligning team members' goals and values with the start-up's vision, everyone is united under a common purpose, working together towards a shared objective.

Adapting to dynamic circumstances and bouncing back from setbacks is crucial in the fast-paced and dynamic world of start-ups. Resilient team members can navigate uncertainties, learn from failures, and pivot when necessary, ensuring the start-up remains agile and responsive to market demands. Additionally, fostering a collaborative mindset and promoting effective team communication enhances synergy, encourages creativity, and leads to more vital problem-solving capabilities. Empowering team members to make decisions and take ownership of their work fosters a sense of autonomy and accountability. When individuals are encouraged to think independently, set measurable goals, and establish transparent accountability systems, they become more proactive and invested in the start-up's success. It fosters a culture of perpetual improvement, where team members strive to exceed expectations and drive the start-up toward its full potential.

As you embark on your start-up journey, remember that building the right team is not just about finding individuals with impressive resumes or specific skill sets. It is about cultivating a culture that values all the traits I discussed in this chapter. Surround yourself with individuals who share your vision, complement your strengths, and inspire you to push the boundaries of what is possible. So, leap with confidence, assemble your dream team, and set out to conquer new horizons. With the right team by your side, there is no limit to your achievements. Embrace the challenges, learn from every experience, and continue to nurture and develop your team as you work towards transforming your start-up into a thriving venture.

The following bullet points summarize the crucial points covered in this chapter, providing a concise reference for quick understanding and recall:

1. Look for several key traits in team members and remember that these traits collectively will bring progress and success to your business.
2. Passion and alignment are the first traits you should look for, which will take your company a long way.

3. Adaptability and resilience are also important for your team's success. Many companies have built empires based on these.
4. A collaborative mindset is the next trait you should prioritize while looking for the right team members. The collaboration will bring to the table what individual efforts cannot.
5. There are many ways to ensure effective team communication, and you should stick to the ones that suit your business context. The clarity in all of these is crucial.
6. Clear and open channels are necessary for your business progress and to sustain your achievements.
7. Active listening is something companies should prioritize from day one. A culture of active listening would mean that your team members speak without hesitation, creating a culture of results.
8. Some may consider Regular team meetings unnecessary, but these are vital. I am not suggesting long, boring meetings. Regularity should be interpreted as an uninterrupted bridge of communication rather than an exhaustive regular exercise.
9. You must empower your team members to make decisions, if you want results and progress.
10. You can do so by encouraging independent thinking, which calls for alertness and proactiveness on your team's part. If you create the scope for this, your team members will only further it.
11. Setting measurable goals for everyone is essential - for you as a leader and your team. Your team will achieve only when it knows what to achieve, when, why, and how.
12. Make sure that you establish accountability systems for all. It is a healthy way of ensuring that people are appreciated for their value addition and take greater ownership of their output.

References

1. FasterCapital (2023). *The importance of team development for startups.* Available at: https://fastercapital.com/content/The-Importance-of-Team-Development-for-Startups.html [Accessed 23 May 2023].
2. Forbes (2020). *10 critical qualities every start-up hire should have.* Available at: https://www.forbes.com/sites/theyec/2020/12/02/10-critical-qual-

ities-every-startup-hire-should-have/?sh=3f580ed34ba7 [Accessed 23 May 2023].
3. Deeb, G. (2014). *The top 4 reasons passion drives start-up success.* Available at: https://www.forbes.com/sites/georgedeeb/2014/12/04/the-top-4-reasons-passion-drives-startup-success/?sh=5059271f1f16 [Accessed 23 May 2023].
4. Constable, A. (2021). *How to build resilience as a start-up founder.* Available at: https://www.forbes.com/sites/forbescoachescouncil/2021/02/16/how-to-build-resilience-as-a-startup-founder/?sh=229df16662dd [Accessed 23 May 2023].
5. Jude, D. (2021). *How to develop a mindset for collaboration.* Available at: https://www.forbes.com/sites/forbesbusinesscouncil/2021/02/16/how-to-develop-a-mindset-for-collaboration/?sh=29fabce5525c [Accessed 23 May 2023].
6. Datta, S. (2021). *Effective communication in a start-up: A doorway to business success.* Available at: https://blog.scalefusion.com/effective-communication-in-a-startup/ [Accessed 23 May 2023].
7. Panel, E. (2021). *Council post: Nine ways to maintain clear, transparent communication at your growing company, Forbes.* Available at: https://www.forbes.com/sites/theyec/2021/08/24/nine-ways-to-maintain-clear-transparent-communication-at-your-growing-company/?sh=1b7b76ac1396 [Accessed 23 May 2023].
8. StartupResources (2021). *11 tips for choosing the best communication channels for your business.* Available at: https://startupresources.io/best-communication-channels/ [Accessed 23 May 2023].
9. D'Angelo, M. (2021). *Listening to employees yields management rewards.* Available at: https://www.businessnewsdaily.com/1934-leadership-listening-employee-input-initiative.html [Accessed 23 May 2023].
10. Wolfe, M. (2022). *The meeting that can make your start-up.* Available at: https://medium.com/point-nine-news/the-meeting-that-can-make-your-startup-509d09856f38 [Accessed 23 May 2023].
11. Smet, A. D., Hewes, C. & Weiss, L. (2020). *For smarter decisions, empower your employees.* Available at: https://www.mckinsey.com/capabilities/people-and-organizational-performance/our-insights/for-smarter-decisions-empower-your-employees [Accessed 23 May 2023].
12. Seppala, E., Emma Schootstra, D. D. & Claman, P. (2019). *How to encourage entrepreneurial thinking on your team.* Available at: https://hbr.

org/2018/12/how-to-encourage-entrepreneurial-thinking-on-your-team [Accessed 23 May 2023].

13. Leonard, K. (2022). *The Ultimate Guide to S.M.A.R.T. goals.* Available at: https://www.forbes.com/advisor/business/smart-goals/ [Accessed 23 May 2023].
14. Leighton, N. (2022). *Here's how to foster a culture of accountability at your business.* Available at: https://www.entrepreneur.com/leadership/heres-how-to-foster-a-culture-of-accountability-at-your/433785 [Accessed 23 May 2023].
15. Tengblad, M. (2023). *Five tips for building a successful start-up team.* Available at: https://www.forbes.com/sites/forbesbusinesscouncil/2023/01/04/five-tips-for-building-a-successful-startup-team/ [Accessed 23 May 2023].
16. Swant, M. (2021). *After raising $200 million before CEO ouster, Marketing Automation Startup Iterable announces $2 billion valuation.* Available at: https://www.forbes.com/sites/martyswant/2021/06/15/marketing-automation-startup-iterable-raises-200-million-reaches-2-billion-valuation-a-month-after-ceos-ouster/?sh=611eafc5368e [Accessed 23 May 2023].
17. Rogers, B. (2021). *Fahri Diner builds plume as the world's first SAAS experience platform for CSPS and their subscribers.* Available at: https://www.forbes.com/sites/brucerogers/2021/08/05/farhi-diner-builds-plume-as-the-worlds-first-saas-experience-platform-for-csps-and-their-subscribers/?sh=30b04be21494 [Accessed 23 May 2023].
18. Rogers, B. (2019). *Hopper out to disrupt $800 billion global online travel market.* Available at: https://www.forbes.com/sites/brucerogers/2019/03/25/hopper-out-to-disrupt-800-billion-global-online-travel-market/?sh=2eb-1359b456e [Accessed 23 May 2023].
19. Jeans, D. (2020). *Covid-19 nearly killed $4 billion corporate travel startup tripactions. Now it has a $125 million lifeline.* Available at: https://www.forbes.com/sites/davidjeans/2020/06/15/covid-19-tripactions-funding/?sh=3bf219104abb [Accessed 23 May 2023].
20. Kaufman, J. (2023). *Mindset matters: How Betterup is providing clarity to the mission of human transformation.* Available at: https://www.forbes.com/sites/jonathankaufman/2023/04/06/mindset-matters-how-betterup-is-providing-clarity-to-the-mission-of-human-transformation/?sh=53e3229230b7 [Accessed 23 May 2023].
21. Iwuozor, J. (2023). *Airtable Review 2023: Features, pricing, pros & cons.* Available at: https://www.forbes.com/advisor/business/software/airtable-review/ [Accessed 23 May 2023].

22. Cai, K. (2022). *Website builder Webflow hits $4 billion valuation as it nears $100 million revenue.* Available at: https://www.forbes.com/sites/kenrick-cai/2022/03/16/webflow-series-c-4-billion-valuation-100-million-revenue/?sh=65b5a9ce71e1 [Accessed 23 May 2023].
23. Srivastava, P. (2018). *How to assemble the right team when starting a business.* Available at: https://www.forbes.com/sites/forbeschicagocouncil/2018/11/07/how-to-assemble-the-right-team-when-starting-a-business/?sh=2877c1ea3e05 [Accessed 23 May 2023].

CHAPTER 12
Passion

Passion, the fuel that ignites the human spirit, has an extraordinary power to transform our lives and the world around us. When our deepest passions are harnessed and channeled into our work, something remarkable happens – it no longer feels like work. This chapter delves into the enchanting realm of passion[1] and its pivotal role in creating thriving and monetized start-ups. Steve Jobs once proclaimed, "The only way to do great work is to love what you do." This sentiment resonates profoundly with those who have embarked on entrepreneurial journeys driven by their unwavering ardor for a particular subject or pursuit. Just like the individuals behind Humans of New York, Rent the Runway, and Patagonia, who transformed their passions into thriving ventures, this chapter explores the pathways that can help you monetize your fervor. As we venture into this chapter, we enter a world where passion catalyzes entrepreneurial success. Countless individuals have embarked on extraordinary journeys, fusing their unwavering devotion with astute business acumen to create thriving start-ups. Like beacons of inspiration, these stories remind us that the fusion of passion and enterprise can lead to remarkable achievements.

Consider the tale of an individual captivated by the art of gastronomy who transforms their love for food into a thriving culinary venture, reshaping how people experience flavors. Or envision an entrepreneur who combines their deep appreciation for technology and sustainability, forging a green-tech start-up that revolutionizes energy consumption. The possibilities are as diverse as the passions that fuel them. Whether you aspire to create innovative products, offer transformative services, or reshape entire industries, understanding how to blend passion with business acumen effectively is the mantra that unlocks the doors to remarkable possibilities. This chapter explores the profound connection between passion and the pursuit of entrepreneurial success. We unravel the principles, strategies, and mindset required to harness the true potential of your passions and convert them into sustainable and prosperous ventures.

Nurturing Your Inner Entrepreneurial Drive

Nurturing your inner entrepreneurial drive[2] can provide numerous advantages as you embark on your start-up journey. Passion ignites the entrepreneurial spirit and propels you forward, even with obstacles and setbacks. When you cultivate and nurture your inner drive, remarkable things can happen. One of the primary advantages of nurturing your inner entrepreneurial drive is the unwavering commitment and determination it brings. Passion is the driving force behind the pursuit of your start-up idea. It fuels your persistence, enabling you to push through challenges, overcome hurdles, and stay motivated during difficult times. It gives you the resilience to bounce back from failures and setbacks, learning and growing stronger with each experience. As an entrepreneur, nurturing your inner entrepreneurial drive cultivates a sense of purpose and fulfillment. When you are genuinely passionate about your start-up, it becomes more than just a business venture. It becomes a reflection of your values, your aspirations, and your vision for making a positive impact on the world. This sense of purpose infuses every aspect of your work, making it more meaningful and fulfilling. It allows you to derive satisfaction from building your start-up, not just the eventual outcomes.

Another advantage of nurturing your inner entrepreneurial drive is the boundless energy and creativity it unlocks. When you are genuinely passionate about your work, you are immersed in constant curiosity and enthusiasm. This energy fuels your creativity, enabling you to generate innovative ideas, think beyond the box, and find unique solutions to problems. Your passion becomes contagious, inspiring and motivating those around you, including your team members, investors, and customers. Nurturing your inner entrepreneurial drive also provides a sense of personal growth and self-actualization. As you passionately pursue your start-up goals, you embark on continuous learning and self-improvement. You develop new skills, expand your knowledge, and gain valuable experiences. This personal growth benefits your start-up and enriches your own life as you become a better version of yourself through the pursuit of your passion. I have written elaborately on this by highlighting the three most important dimensions. Firstly, identify your passion and how it helps in the long run. Secondly, I have written about cultivating a growth mindset and enabling your employees to improve. Thirdly, embrace challenges and risks and how this could benefit you.

Identifying Your Passion

Identifying your passion[3] is a crucial step in nurturing your inner entrepreneurial drive. It involves exploring your interests, values, and personal experiences to discover the areas that ignite your enthusiasm and align with your vision. Understanding and pinpointing your passion lays the foundation for building a start-up that resonates with your authentic self and brings you immense fulfillment. To identify your passion, reflect on your experiences and the activities that bring you joy and a sense of purpose. Consider the moments when time seems to fly by when you feel fully engaged and energized. These are often indicators of your true passions. Think about the topics, industries, or problems that interest and inspire you. Ask yourself what you would pursue even if you weren't concerned about financial rewards or external validation. Engage in self-exploration and introspection. Take the time to assess your skills, strengths, and areas where you excel. Consider how you can leverage these abilities in pursuing your passion. Seek feedback from others who know you well, as they may offer insights into your unique qualities and potential avenues for passion-driven pursuits.

It's important to remember that your passion may evolve and change over time, and that's normal. The key is to stay open to new experiences and be willing to explore different paths. Be curious and embrace a growth mindset, as it allows you to learn and adapt along your entrepreneurial journey continuously. Once you have identified your passion, it's time to align it with a viable start-up idea. Look for opportunities within your passion with market demand and sustainable growth potential. Conduct market research, analyze industry trends, and assess the competitive landscape to ensure your start-up idea has a unique value proposition and a viable market position. Remember, identifying your passion is not just about finding what you love but also about discovering how to channel that passion into a meaningful and successful entrepreneurial endeavor. Embrace the process of self-discovery, take the time to explore your interests, and be open to new possibilities. By identifying your passion and aligning it with a viable start-up idea, you lay a solid foundation for nurturing your inner entrepreneurial drive and building a personally fulfilling and commercially feasible start-up.

Cultivating A Growth Mindset

Cultivating a growth mindset is the belief that your abilities and intelligence can be developed with dedication, effort, and continuous learning. By embracing a growth mindset,[4] you are to new possibilities, overcome challenges with resilience and unlock your potential as an entrepreneur. One of the critical advantages of cultivating a growth mindset is the ability to see setbacks and failures as opportunities for growth. Instead of being discouraged by obstacles, you view them as valuable learning experiences. You understand that failure is not a reflection of your worth or potential but a stepping stone to success. This mindset empowers you to persist in facing challenges, learn from mistakes, and adapt your strategies to achieve better outcomes. Cultivating a growth mindset also enhances your willingness to take risks and step out of your comfort zone. You embrace the idea that growth and progress come from pushing the boundaries of what is familiar and comfortable. By embracing challenges and seeking out new experiences, you expand your skills, knowledge, and perspectives. This willingness to embrace discomfort and the unknown is essential for entrepreneurial success, as it allows you to innovate, experiment, and seize opportunities that others may shy away from. A growth mindset fosters a passion for learning and continuous improvement. You recognize that the entrepreneurial journey is constantly learning and evolving. You actively seek knowledge, seek feedback, and invest in your personal and professional development. This thirst for learning enables you to stay ahead of industry trends, adapt to changing market conditions, and cultivate the skills needed to navigate the complexities of entrepreneurship.

Cultivating a growth mindset enhances your ability to collaborate and build strong relationships within your team. With a growth mindset, you embrace the power of collaboration and value the diverse perspectives and ideas that others bring to the table. You see feedback as an opportunity for growth and actively seek input from team members and stakeholders. This collaborative mindset fosters a culture of innovation, trust, and continuous learning within your start-up, leading to increased creativity, problem-solving abilities, and business success. Cultivating a growth mindset involves adopting specific strategies and practices to foster a philosophy of continuous growth and development. It starts with embracing challenges as opportunities for learning and reframing failures as stepping stones to success. Developing a habit of seeking out new experiences, learning from feedback, and being open to constructive criticism helps expand one's knowledge and skills. Also, setting goals, creating a supportive network, and practicing self-reflection and self-awareness are essential in cultivating a growth mindset. By consistently applying these strategies, individuals can develop a mindset that embraces lifelong learning, resilience, and a passion for personal and professional growth.

Embracing Challenges And Risks

Embracing challenges and risks is a fundamental aspect of cultivating a growth mindset as an entrepreneur. By facing challenges and taking calculated risks, you can push the boundaries of the possible and unlock new opportunities for growth and success. Embracing challenges and risks allows you to step out of your comfort zone, expand your skills and knowledge, and drive innovation within your start-up. One of the key advantages of embracing challenges and risks is the opportunity for personal and professional growth. By willingly tackling difficult situations, you build resilience, develop problem-solving abilities, and strengthen your capacity to overcome obstacles. Each challenge you encounter provides a chance to learn, adapt, and acquire valuable experience that can benefit your entrepreneurial journey. Embracing challenges helps you develop the confidence and self-assurance to navigate uncertainties and thrive in a dynamic business environment. Embracing risks is also essential for entrepreneurial success. It involves taking calculated and strategic risks that have significant rewards.

Risk-taking[5] allows you to seize opportunities, explore new markets, and innovate within your industry. It enables you to stay ahead of the competition and adapt to changing market conditions. By embracing risks, you are willing to step outside conventional boundaries and explore new possibilities that can lead to breakthrough ideas, increased market share, and business growth. To embrace challenges and risks effectively, you must adopt a mindset that reframes failure as a learning opportunity and approaches challenges with a problem-solving mindset. Embrace a mindset of curiosity and view challenges as chances to discover new solutions, learn from setbacks, and improve your strategies. Develop a strategic approach to risk-taking by conducting thorough research, analyzing potential outcomes, and evaluating the potential rewards against the associated risks. Surround yourself with a supportive network of mentors, advisors, and like-minded entrepreneurs who can provide guidance, insights, and encouragement as you navigate challenges and risks.

Igniting Passion In Your Team

Igniting passion in your team[6] brings numerous advantages and benefits that significantly contribute to the success of your start-up. One of the primary advantages is increased motivation. When team members are genuinely passionate about their work, they are intrinsically motivated to go above and beyond their responsibilities. They are driven by a deep sense of purpose and enthusiasm, which fuels their commitment to achieving the company's goals. A heightened motivation leads to higher levels of engagement, productivity, and a willingness to take on challenges with a positive attitude. Another significant benefit of igniting passion in your team is enhanced creativity and innovation. Passionate individuals are more likely to think outside the box, challenge conventional wisdom, and develop innovative ideas. Their enthusiasm and genuine interest in their field of work ignite a spark of creativity that can lead to breakthrough solutions and unique approaches to problem-solving. By fostering an environment that encourages passion, you create a breeding ground for creative thinking, fostering a culture of innovation within your start-up.

Passion also drives continuous learning and development. When team members are passionate about their work, they are naturally inclined to seek opportunities for growth and improvement. They desire to expand their knowledge, develop new skills, and stay current with industry trends. Passionate individuals actively seek learning opportunities through professional development programs, attending conferences, or pursuing additional certifications. This continuous learning mindset benefits the individual team members and enriches the collective knowledge and expertise within your start-up. Passion also plays a pivotal role in building strong and cohesive teams. When team members share a common passion for the company's mission and vision, it creates a sense of unity and shared purpose. They are more likely to collaborate effectively, support one another, and work towards a common goal. Passionate team members inspire and motivate their colleagues, fostering a positive and energizing work environment. This sense of camaraderie and shared passion fosters a strong team spirit, leading to increased collaboration, synergy, and, ultimately, the success of your start-up. You can ignite passion in your team by following three simple strategies I have elaborated hereafter. Firstly, you must communicate your passionate vision to the rest of the organization so that everyone is on the same page. Secondly, you must paint a compelling future for everyone to believe in your passion and become equal partakers. Thirdly, it is about engaging and enrolling team members in your vision for sustained results.

Communicating Your Passionate Vision

Communicating your passionate vision is crucial in igniting the same level of passion in your team. When team members are aligned with your vision and understand the purpose behind their work, it fuels their sense of passion and commitment. And how can you effectively convey your passionate vision? Well, first and foremost, paint a clear and compelling picture of your vision. Use powerful and inspiring language to describe the future you envision for the company. Clearly articulate the impact your start-up can make in the industry or society. Help your team members visualize the possibilities and the positive change your company can bring. When team members see and understand the bigger picture, they become more motivated and inspired to contribute their best efforts. In addition to verbal communication, leverage visual aids and storytelling techniques to convey your vision. Use visuals, such as presentations, videos, or infographics, to bring your ideas to life. Share stories and examples that illustrate the real-world implications of your vision. By appealing to your team members' logical and emotional aspects, you can create a deeper connection and foster a stronger sense of passion for the shared goal.

As a leader, be authentic and passionate when communicating your vision.[7] Your enthusiasm and belief in the vision will naturally influence and inspire others. Show genuine excitement and confidence in what you're trying to achieve. Share personal anecdotes and experiences shaping your passion and commitment to the vision. When team members see your genuine dedication and enthusiasm, it creates a ripple effect and encourages them to embrace the same passion and dedication. Lastly, encourage open dialogue and create a safe space for team members to share their thoughts and ideas about the vision. Actively listen to their perspectives and feedback and incorporate their insights into the overall vision whenever possible. When your employees feel valued and heard, they become more invested in the vision and are more likely to contribute their unique skills and ideas toward its realization.

Painting A Compelling Future Picture

Painting a compelling future picture is a powerful way to ignite passion in your team and inspire them to work towards a shared goal. Envision the future you want to craft for your start-up. Visualize the possibilities and imagine your company's impact on its customers, industry, or society. Consider how your product or service can solve problems, improve lives, or disrupt the market. Let your imagination soar and think big. Having a clear vision of the future can convey a sense of purpose and direction to your team. Once you have a clear vision, articulate it in a way that captures the hearts and minds of your team members. Use descriptive and inspiring language to paint a vivid picture of the future when your start-up achieves its goals. Describe the benefits and positive outcomes that your customers or users will experience. Help your team members see the value and impact of their work. To make the future picture even more compelling, connect it to the values and aspirations of your team members. Show them how their contributions align with the larger vision and how their efforts are essential to making it a reality. Help them see the personal growth and fulfillment they can achieve by being part of this journey. When team members can see themselves playing a meaningful role in the future you paint, it fuels their passion and commitment.

As an entrepreneur, use visual aids and storytelling techniques to enhance the impact of your future picture. Create visual representations[8] like diagrams, charts, or mock-ups to help your team members visualize the result. Share success stories and testimonials from customers or users who have benefited from your product or service. Use real-life examples to make the future picture tangible and relatable. Lastly, regularly revisit and reinforce the future picture with your team. Incorporate it into team meetings, presentations, and discussions. Continuously remind your team members of the vision and the progress being made towards it. Celebrate milestones and achievements along the way, keeping the future picture alive and inspiring.

Engaging And Enrolling Team Members In Your Vision

Engaging and enrolling team members in your vision[9] is essential for igniting passion and creating a cohesive and dedicated team. Communicate your vision to your team. Share your start-up's purpose, values, and goals in a compelling and authentic manner. Explain how your vision aligns with their personal and professional aspirations. Help them see the bigger picture and the meaningful impact they can make by being part of your journey. When team members understand and connect with the vision, they are more likely to be engaged and motivated. It would help if you fostered open and transparent communication. Create a culture where team members feel comfortable expressing their thoughts, ideas, and concerns. Actively listen to their input and feedback, and genuinely consider their perspectives. Encourage collaboration and invite team members to participate in decision-making processes actively. By involving them in the decision-making and problem-solving processes, you demonstrate that their voices are valued, which fosters a sense of ownership and commitment.

As a leader, provide opportunities for personal and professional growth. Support and invest in developing your team member's skills and talents. Offer training programs, workshops, or mentorship opportunities that align with their individual goals and aspirations. Show that you are invested in their success and advancement. When team members feel they are growing and progressing in their careers, they become more engaged and passionate about their work. You must recognize and appreciate the contributions of your team members. Celebrate their achievements and acknowledge their hard work and dedication. Provide regular feedback and praise for their accomplishments. Create an inclusive work environment where everyone feels valued and recognized for their unique strengths and contributions. When team members feel appreciated and valued, their motivation and passion naturally increase. Lastly, lead by example. Demonstrate your passion and dedication toward the vision. Be an authentic and inspiring leader who embodies the values and principles of your start-up. Show resilience and determination in times of challenge. Lead with empathy and understanding, fostering a supportive and collaborative team culture. Your enthusiasm and commitment will be contagious, inspiring team members to share your passion and actively contribute to realizing the vision.

Fueling Your Passion Across Your Business

Fueling your passion across your business is vital for sustained growth and success. Passion serves as a driving force and a source of intrinsic motivation. When deeply passionate about your business, your unwavering commitment and enthusiasm propel you forward. It fuels your determination to overcome obstacles and persevere during difficult times. Passion keeps you focused, resilient, and dedicated to achieving your goals, which is crucial for long-term success. Passion[10] also inspires and influences others. When your passion is evident in every aspect of your business, it becomes contagious and has a ripple effect on your team members, customers, and stakeholders. Your genuine enthusiasm and belief in what you're doing inspire others to believe in your vision and join you on your journey. Passionate leaders can attract top talent, build strong customer relationships, and create a positive and dynamic work culture. It would help if you also remembered that passion drives innovation and creativity. When truly passionate about your business, you constantly seek ways to improve, innovate, and disrupt the status quo. Your passion compels you to think outside the box, explore new possibilities, and challenge conventional wisdom. This entrepreneurial spirit fuels a culture of innovation within your team, leading to the development of groundbreaking products or services that can differentiate your start-up in the market.

Passion also fosters customer engagement and loyalty. When genuinely passionate about what you offer, it resonates with your customers. Your enthusiasm and dedication shine through every interaction, creating a memorable and positive customer experience. Passionate entrepreneurs can connect with their target audience emotionally, building trust and loyalty that can drive repeat business and positive word-of-mouth referrals. Remember that passion cultivates a positive work culture and employee satisfaction. When you foster a culture that celebrates and encourages passion, you create an environment where employees are motivated, engaged, and fulfilled. They feel a sense of purpose and alignment with the company's mission, which leads to higher job satisfaction and productivity. Passionate work culture also attracts and retains top talent,[11] as individuals are drawn to organizations that embody their values and passions. You can fuel your passion across your business if you are strategic and if you work with dedication from day one. I have focussed on three important aspects here. Firstly, it provides opportunities for growth and development and ensures outstanding results. Secondly, it is about recognizing and celebrating the achievements of your employees so that they feel valued and consider the company's passion as their driving force. Thirdly, promoting work-life integration is essential. If you encourage your employee to undertake a healthy approach to the company, their efforts will multiply, and they will have a greater sense of accountability.

Providing Opportunities For Growth And Development

Providing opportunities for growth and development[12] is essential for harnessing the full potential of your team members and ensuring their continued engagement and satisfaction. Foster a culture of continuous learning and skill development. Encourage your team members to expand their knowledge and acquire new skills through training programs, workshops, and educational resources. Provide them with opportunities to attend conferences, industry events, and seminars to stay updated with the latest trends and advancements in your field. By investing in their professional growth, you enhance their capabilities and demonstrate your commitment to their long-term success. You must also create clear career pathways and progression opportunities. Establish a framework that outlines your start-up's various roles, responsibilities, and growth opportunities. Work with each team member to identify their strengths, aspirations, and areas for development. Set clear goals and milestones for their career progression and provide them with the necessary support, guidance, and feedback to help them reach their full potential. By aligning their personal goals with the growth of your start-up, you foster a sense of ownership and commitment. As a leader, encourage mentorship and peer learning. Facilitate opportunities for team members to learn from each other, share experiences, and collaborate on projects. Establish mentorship programs where experienced team members can guide and support junior colleagues, fostering a knowledge exchange and growth culture. Encourage cross-functional collaboration and create regular interaction and idea-sharing platforms to stimulate creativity and innovation.

You must provide challenging and meaningful assignments. Assign team members projects and tasks that stretch their capabilities and allow them to apply and develop new skills. Offer them opportunities to take on leadership roles or spearhead initiatives that align with their interests and aspirations. Providing challenging and meaningful work keeps team members engaged and fosters their personal and professional growth as they tackle new and exciting challenges. As a leader, you must offer regular performance feedback and recognition. Create a feedback-rich culture where constructive feedback is provided promptly to help team members identify areas for improvement and celebrate their successes. Recognize and appreciate their contributions and achievements, reinforcing a positive and supportive work environment. Acknowledging their efforts and providing feedback inspires them to strive for continuous improvement and growth.

Recognizing And Celebrating Achievements

Recognizing and celebrating achievements is crucial to fostering a positive and motivating work environment within your start-up. Establish a culture of appreciation and recognition.[13] Make it a regular practice to acknowledge and celebrate individual and team achievements. It can be done through various means like team meetings, newsletters, or dedicated recognition programs. Encourage team members to recognize and appreciate each other's contributions, creating a peer-to-peer recognition culture. You must personalize the recognition. Tailor the recognition of the individual preferences and interests of your team members. Some may appreciate public recognition in team meetings or company-wide announcements, while others may prefer more private acknowledgments such as a personalized note or one-on-one conversation. By recognizing achievements in a way that resonates with each team member, you demonstrate that their contributions are valued and appreciated. As an entrepreneur, highlight the impact and significance of the achievements. When recognizing accomplishments, emphasize the positive outcomes and the value they bring to the team, the company, clients, and customers. By showcasing the tangible results and benefits of their work, you validate their efforts and inspire and motivate others to strive for excellence.

You must offer tangible rewards or incentives. Consider implementing a rewards program or offering incentives such as bonuses, additional time off, or professional development opportunities. These rewards can serve as tokens of appreciation and motivate team members to continue performing at their best. As an employer, create opportunities for team celebrations. Organize team-building activities, social events, or outings to celebrate major milestones, project completions, or exceptional achievements. These events recognize individual and collective efforts, foster camaraderie, strengthen team bonds, and create a sense of shared accomplishment. Lastly, encourage continuous improvement and growth. While celebrating achievements is important, it's equally crucial to encourage team members to reflect on their accomplishments and identify areas for further development. Foster a growth mindset by encouraging them to set new goals and challenges that align with their aspirations and the overall objectives of your start-up. This continuous focus on growth and improvement helps maintain motivation and keeps team members engaged and striving for further success.

Promoting Work-Life Integration

Promoting work-life integration is essential for creating a healthy and balanced environment within your start-up. Encourage flexible work arrangements.[14] Allow team members to control their schedules and provide options such as remote work, flexible hours, or compressed workweeks. This flexibility enables them to manage their responsibilities and commitments better while meeting work requirements. You must lead by example. As an entrepreneur, demonstrate a healthy work-life integration by setting boundaries and caring for your well-being. Encourage open discussions about work-life balance and ensure team members feel comfortable and supported in prioritizing their personal lives and work responsibilities. As an entrepreneur, promote a results-oriented work culture. Focus on outcomes rather than hours worked or face time. Encourage team members to manage their time effectively, set realistic goals, and measure success based on the quality of work and achievements rather than solely on the number of hours spent in the office.

Wellness programs and initiatives are also crucial for promoting work-life integration. Implement wellness programs that support your team members' physical, mental, and emotional well-being. It can include providing access to fitness facilities, organizing wellness challenges or workshops, or offering mental health resources and counseling services. As an employer, encourage breaks and time off. Emphasize the importance of taking regular breaks throughout the workday and utilizing vacation or personal days to recharge and rejuvenate. Discourage a culture of constant overwork and stress by promoting a healthy work-life balance.[15] You must also foster open communication and support. Create an environment where others are comfortable discussing their work-life challenges and seeking support when needed. Encourage open dialogue about balancing personal and professional responsibilities and provide resources or guidance to help team members navigate these challenges. Lastly, promote self-care and well-being. Encourage team members to prioritize self-care activities such as exercise, hobbies, relaxation techniques, and quality time with family and friends. By valuing and supporting their well-being, you contribute to their work-life integration and help prevent burnout.

Companies That Are Driven By Passion

Passion is a powerful driving force that propels individuals and organizations to achieve remarkable feats. When passion is infused into the DNA of a company, it becomes a driving factor in its success and growth.[16] Passionate companies go beyond the ordinary and create extraordinary experiences, products, and services. They inspire and ignite a spark in their customers, employees, and the industry. In this section, we will explore a selection of companies that embody the spirit of passion and have leveraged it to achieve remarkable results. These companies have harnessed the power of passion to fuel their innovation, driving their teams and shaping their unique identities. They are driven by a deep love for what they do and a genuine desire to impact the world positively. Each company has a compelling story showcasing passion's transformative potential in entrepreneurship. From disruptive start-ups to established industry leaders, these companies have carved their niche by infusing passion into every aspect of their operations. They have found a way to align their purpose with their work, creating a powerful synergy that drives their success. Through their unwavering commitment, they have redefined industries, disrupted markets, and inspired others to follow in their footsteps. These stories will help us uncover the common threads that tie them together. We will explore how their passion has shaped their vision, guided their decisions, and propelled them forward in the face of challenges. These companies testify to the transformative power of passion in entrepreneurship and offer valuable insights for aspiring entrepreneurs looking to ignite their ventures. So, let us embark on a journey to discover the stories behind these passionate companies and draw inspiration from their extraordinary achievements. By exploring their experiences, we can learn valuable lessons about the role of passion in building successful businesses and how it can be harnessed to create a lasting impact.

Stellar Energy

Stellar Energy[17] emerges as a prominent international provider of groundbreaking power augmentation and energy solutions, dedicated to assisting power generation and utility markets in preparing for future energy demands. With an incredible passion for making positive change, the company has successfully established itself as a trailblazer in the industry. The company's portfolio boasts an impressive range of cutting-edge solutions designed to address the diverse needs of power generators. From innovative evaporative cooling and mechanical inlet air chilling technologies to thermal energy storage and the groundbreaking hybrid direct contact air chilling technology, Stellar Energy offers a comprehensive suite of solutions that empower power generators to recapture lost megawatts and elevate combustion gas turbines beyond their nameplate capacities. In addition to its prowess in power augmentation, Stellar Energy specializes in industrial cooling, data center cooling, and district energy and district cooling technologies. With a deep understanding of the unique requirements of these sectors, the company delivers tailored solutions that optimize energy efficiency, enhance operational performance, and reduce environmental impact. The remarkable success of Stellar Energy is reflected in its extensive track record, spanning over 125 projects across 14 countries. It has augmented over 3,000 megawatts and generated over 1.2 million tons of refrigeration. The company's contributions have significantly met evolving energy demands worldwide. With 400+ modular units fabricated and an impeccable track record of 100% performance test success, Stellar Energy has established itself as a trusted partner in delivering reliable and efficient energy solutions. The company's commitment to excellence and customer satisfaction is evident in its revenue of $34.8 million USD. This financial success is a testament to the trust and confidence placed in Stellar Energy by its clientele, who recognize the company as a leading provider of transformative energy solutions.

Company Name: Stellar Energy

Founded: 1999

Significant reason(s) for success: Its unwavering dedication to driving sustainable change in the power generation and utility markets sets it apart from its competitors. By combining innovative technologies with a passion for making a difference, the company has positioned itself as a driving force in shaping the future of energy.

DreamScape Immersive

DreamScape[18] is a captivating example of a company fueled by passion for virtual reality (VR) entertainment. With a deep-rooted love for immersive experiences and a vision to revolutionize entertainment, DreamScape Immersive has carved a niche for itself in the VR industry. The company's talented artists, designers, and technologists are driven by their shared passion for creating breathtaking virtual worlds and transporting audiences into extraordinary realms of imagination. At the core of DreamScape's success is its unwavering belief in the power of VR to redefine storytelling and entertainment. Their passion for pushing the boundaries of what is possible in virtual reality drives them to develop cutting-edge technology and craft awe-inspiring experiences that captivate audiences. From thrilling adventures to fantastical journeys, DreamScape Immersive brings dreams to life and enables people to immerse themselves in extraordinary narratives. DreamScape's commitment to passion goes beyond just creating mind-bending VR experiences. They actively engage with their audience, seeking to evoke emotions, spark imagination, and leave a lasting impact on each participant. By infusing their creations with passion and attention to detail, DreamScape Immersive creates a sense of wonder and transports people to worlds they could only dream of. Entrepreneurs can draw inspiration from DreamScape's story by recognizing the power of passion in driving their ventures. By embracing their unique passion and tapping into the transformative potential of emerging technologies like VR, entrepreneurs can create remarkable experiences that resonate with audiences on a profound level. DreamScape Immersive serves as a reminder that passion, combined with creativity and innovation, can unlock new realms of entertainment and inspire others to dream big.

Company Name: DreamScape Immersive

Founded: 2016

Significant reason(s) for success: The dedication to pursue their passion relentlessly and sharing it with the world. By doing so, the company has created unforgettable experiences and paved the way for the future of immersive entertainment.

Zephyr AI

Zephyr AI[19] is a shining example of a company driven by passion for artificial intelligence (AI) and machine learning. Founded by a team of brilliant minds with a shared love for AI and its potential to transform industries, Zephyr AI is at the forefront of developing innovative AI solutions that address complex challenges. Passion permeates every aspect of Zephyr AI's work. Their team is deeply passionate about exploring the frontiers of AI research and pushing the boundaries of what is possible. With a relentless drive to advance the field, they dedicate themselves to developing sophisticated algorithms, models, and systems that can make a meaningful impact in various domains. At Zephyr AI, passion translates into a deep commitment to excellence. The team's unwavering dedication to their craft enables them to tackle intricate problems and find ingenious solutions. They continuously refine and enhance their AI models, leveraging their passion for driving innovation and delivering cutting-edge technology that surpasses expectations. Beyond their technical expertise, Zephyr AI understands the importance of applying AI in a socially responsible and ethical manner. Their passion for making a positive difference is evident in their commitment to developing AI solutions prioritizing fairness, transparency, and accountability. By infusing their work with purpose, Zephyr AI demonstrates that passion and ethics coexist, leading to societal advancements. Entrepreneurs can draw inspiration from Zephyr AI's journey by recognizing the power of passion in driving their own AI ventures. By immersing themselves in the field, staying curious, and fostering a genuine love for AI, entrepreneurs can fuel their innovative ideas and create AI solutions that have a meaningful impact. Zephyr AI serves as a testament to the transformative potential of passion in driving AI advancements and shaping the future of technology.

Company Name: Zephyr AI

Founded: 2020

Significant reason(s) for success: Its unwavering dedication, commitment to excellence, and ethical approach pave the way for AI-driven solutions that address complex challenges and improve lives.

InnoSpark

InnoSpark Ventures[20] is a remarkable company driven by passion, innovation, and relentlessly pursuing groundbreaking ideas. With a vision to create transformative solutions, InnoSpark Ventures ignites the entrepreneurial spirit within its team and fosters an environment that encourages bold thinking and boundless creativity. Passion is at the core of InnoSpark's DNA. Every team member is fueled by a genuine love for innovation and a deep desire to make a positive impact in their respective fields. This shared passion creates a vibrant and dynamic atmosphere where ideas flourish and breakthroughs are born. It drives individuals to challenge the status quo, think outside the box, and push the boundaries of what is possible. At InnoSpark Ventures, innovation is not just a buzzword but a way of life. The company's commitment to fostering a culture of innovation is evident in its emphasis on continuous learning, experimentation, and exploration. They encourage team members to embrace curiosity, take risks, and pursue unconventional ideas. This freedom to innovate empowers individuals to unleash their creativity and create solutions that have the potential to revolutionize industries.

InnoSpark Ventures understands that innovation thrives in collaboration. They actively cultivate a collaborative mindset within their team, fostering an environment where diverse perspectives and expertise intersect. By promoting cross-functional collaboration and creating opportunities for knowledge sharing, InnoSpark Ventures harnesses the collective power of its team members to drive innovation forward. The impact of InnoSpark's passion-driven approach extends beyond the company itself. Their innovative solutions can disrupt markets, improve lives, and create positive change. By nurturing an environment where passion is embraced, and innovation is celebrated, InnoSpark Ventures inspires other entrepreneurs to tap into their passions, ignite their creative spark, and embark on a journey of innovation and entrepreneurship.

Company Name: InnoSpark Ventures

Founded: 2012

Significant reason(s) for success: By cultivating a culture of passion, nurturing a spirit of innovation, and fostering collaboration, it sets a compelling example for entrepreneurs seeking to make a lasting impact.

EdgeX Foundry

EdgeX Foundry[21] is a great company driven by a deep passion for cutting-edge technology and a relentless pursuit of pushing the boundaries of what is possible. With a mission to revolutionize the world of edge computing, EdgeX Foundry embodies the spirit of innovation, collaboration, and forward-thinking. Passion is the driving force behind EdgeX Foundry's success. Every team member is fueled by an unwavering enthusiasm for technology and a genuine belief in the transformative power of edge computing. This shared passion creates a vibrant, dynamic work environment where ideas thrive and creativity flourishes. It fuels individuals to continuously explore new possibilities, challenge traditional paradigms, and drive innovation. At EdgeX Foundry, innovation is ingrained in the company's DNA. They have built a culture encouraging curiosity, experimentation, and a willingness to take calculated risks. The company embraces emerging technologies and actively explores uncharted territories to create groundbreaking solutions. By fostering a culture of innovation, EdgeX Foundry empowers its team members to think outside the box, embrace disruptive ideas, and pioneer advancements in edge computing. Collaboration lies at the heart of EdgeX Foundry's approach. The company recognizes that true innovation is often a result of diverse perspectives, collective expertise, and collaborative efforts. They foster a collaborative mindset within their team, encouraging open communication, knowledge sharing, and cross-functional collaboration. By leveraging its team members' collective intelligence and creativity, EdgeX Foundry can tackle complex challenges, drive breakthrough innovations, and deliver exceptional results. EdgeX Foundry's passion-driven approach propels the company forward and inspires others in the technology and entrepreneurial space. Their groundbreaking solutions and thought leadership catalyze innovation and encourage entrepreneurs to pursue their passion-driven ventures. EdgeX Foundry's journey is a testament to the power of passion, innovation, and collaboration in driving meaningful change and shaping the future of edge computing.

Company Name: EdgeX Foundry

Founded: 2017

Significant reason(s) for success: Its dedication to revolutionizing the field of edge computing, unwavering passion, and commitment to innovation worldwide.

Brightseed

Brightseed[22] is a shining example of a company driven by an unwavering passion for scientific discovery and a profound belief in the power of nature. With a mission to unlock the potential of plant compounds for human health, Brightseed embodies the spirit of innovation, sustainability, and transformative impact. Passion is the fuel that drives every member of the Brightseed team. They are deeply passionate about exploring the vast potential of plant compounds and their effects on human well-being. This shared passion creates a vibrant and purpose-driven work culture where individuals are inspired to push boundaries, challenge conventional thinking, and make groundbreaking discoveries. It fuels their relentless pursuit of scientific excellence and commitment to making a positive difference in the world. Innovation is at the core of Brightseed's DNA. They constantly push the boundaries of scientific research, leveraging cutting-edge technologies and multidisciplinary approaches to uncover the hidden treasures within nature. Brightseed embraces a culture of innovation that encourages curiosity, fosters collaboration, and supports risk-taking. It enables their team members to explore uncharted territories, make novel connections, and drive advancements in plant-based therapeutics. Collaboration is a fundamental pillar of Brightseed's success. They recognize that solving complex health challenges requires a collective effort and diverse expertise. Brightseed cultivates a collaborative environment where scientists, researchers, and industry experts share knowledge, exchange ideas, and work toward a common goal. Through cross-functional collaboration, they harness their team's collective intelligence and expertise, enabling them to accelerate scientific discoveries and bring innovative solutions to the market. Brightseed's passion-driven approach fuels its success and inspires others in the scientific and entrepreneurial community. Their groundbreaking research and commitment to sustainable, nature-inspired solutions are a beacon of hope and inspiration. They ignite a spark in entrepreneurs, scientists, and health enthusiasts, encouraging them to explore the incredible potential of nature and embark on their passion-driven quests for innovation and impact.

Company Name: Brightseed

Founded: 2017

Significant reason(s) for success: Its efforts to unlock the secrets of nature and pioneer breakthroughs in plant-based therapeutics; its passion and focus on innovation inspire entrepreneurs worldwide.

Astera Labs

Astera Labs is a company driven by a deep passion for redefining the data center interconnects and unlocking the full potential of high-performance computing. With a vision to revolutionize connectivity solutions, Astera Labs[23] is dedicated to delivering innovative technologies that enhance data transfer efficiency, reliability, and scalability. Passion fuels every aspect of Astera Labs' operations. Their team is passionate about pushing the boundaries of what's possible in data center interconnects. They are driven by a relentless desire to solve complex challenges and improve the performance of data-intensive applications. This shared passion creates a dynamic and motivated work culture where individuals are inspired to think outside the box, explore new technologies, and drive advancements in high-speed connectivity. Innovation is at the heart of Astera Labs' mission. They constantly strive to develop cutting-edge solutions that address the evolving needs of the data center industry. Astera Labs embraces a culture of innovation, encouraging its team members to challenge the status quo, experiment with new ideas, and pioneer transformative technologies. By fostering an environment that encourages creativity and risk-taking, they empower their team to drive industry-leading innovations in data center connectivity. Collaboration is a key ingredient in Astera Labs' success. They recognize that solving complex technological problems requires a collaborative approach. Astera Labs actively engages with industry partners, customers, and research institutions to foster collaboration and knowledge exchange. By bringing together diverse expertise and perspectives, they can tackle complex challenges and deliver comprehensive solutions that meet the needs of their customers and the industry. Astera Labs' passion for innovation and commitment to collaboration inspires entrepreneurs and technologists worldwide. Their breakthrough technologies and dedication to advancing data center connectivity catalyze transformative change in the industry. Astera Labs' story motivates and empowers individuals to pursue their entrepreneurial dreams, embrace technological innovation, and make a significant impact in high-performance computing.

Company Name: Astera Labs

Founded: 2017

Significant reason(s) for success: Its perpetual will to drive advancements in data center interconnects, innovative mindset, and collaborative spirit.

Conclusion

Throughout this chapter, we have explored the power and significance of passion in driving the success of start-ups. We have seen how entrepreneurs who nurture their inner drive, identify their passions, and cultivate a growth mindset can unlock their full potential. Passion fuels the individual entrepreneur and permeates the entire team, creating a contagious energy that propels the start-up toward greatness. Having a passionate team brings numerous advantages. It fosters dedication, commitment, and a sense of purpose beyond monetary gains. Passionate individuals are driven to excel, willing to go the extra mile, and consistently seek innovative solutions to overcome challenges. They have an unwavering belief in the vision, and their enthusiasm becomes a magnet attracting like-minded individuals, investors, and customers.

In start-ups, passion is the secret ingredient that fuels resilience, adaptability, and the ability to embrace risks and challenges. It infuses every aspect of the start-up journey with unparalleled drive and determination. Passionate entrepreneurs inspire and motivate their team members, empowering them to unleash their full potential. They create a culture of innovation, collaboration, and celebration, where everyone is encouraged to contribute their unique talents and ideas. Let passion be your guiding light as you embark on your entrepreneurial journey. Embrace your inner drive, identify your passions, and foster a growth mindset. Surround yourself with a team that shares your passion and belief in the vision. Nurture a culture of innovation, collaboration, and celebration where everyone is empowered to make a meaningful impact. Remember, the path of entrepreneurship may be challenging, but with passion as your driving force, you can turn your dreams into reality.

Stay committed to your vision, and always remember why you started this journey. Believe in yourself, trust your abilities, and let your passion shine through every aspect of your start-up. With passion as your foundation, you have the power to transform your dreams into a thriving reality. Embrace the journey, embrace the passion, and write your success story. To keep your learnings of this chapter handy, I have compiled them into pointers listed below:

1. Nurturing your inner entrepreneurial drive is essential for finding your passion and those associated with your start-up.
2. Identifying your passion cannot be done in isolation. You have to take care of the larger picture of your vision while doing so.
3. Cultivating a growth mindset will allow you to stay ahead in your entrepreneurial journey and help your team to enhance its skills and performance.
4. Embracing challenges and risks is the key to moving ahead with confidence and assurance that your company will go a long way.
5. Igniting your team's passion will help you boost your start-up's progress in many ways.
6. Communicating your passionate vision will help in this regard. The clarity in communication can help you and your team to understand what needs to be done and how to ensure repeated success for your business.
7. Painting a compelling future picture is also something you can look at. Visualization is a vital tool that acts as an excellent reinforcement for your team.
8. Engaging and enrolling team members in your vision will deliver results quicker and more intensely for your start-up.
9. Fueling your passion across the business is another crucial aspect of cementing your start-up's passion.
10 You can do so by providing opportunities for growth and development across the organization.
11. Recognizing and celebrating achievements helps leaders make sure that team members put in more effort for the company's progress.
12. Promoting work-life integration is a milestone you should strive to achieve in your entrepreneurial journey to sustain the passion you have identified for your business.

References

1. Forbes (2019). *The importance of passion as a business leader.* Available at: https://www.forbes.com/sites/theyec/2019/07/08/the-importance-of-passion-as-a-business-leader/?sh=17a861b021d1 [Accessed 26 May 2023].
2. Schramm, S. (2018). *How to bring an entrepreneurial spirit to your work.* Available at: https://today.duke.edu/2018/04/how-bring-entrepreneurial-spirit-your-work [Accessed 26 May 2023].
3. Guo, C. (2021). *How to find your calling as an entrepreneur.* Available at: https://www.entrepreneur.com/leadership/how-to-find-your-calling-as-an-entrepreneur/376032 [Accessed 26 May 2023].
4. Bauer, K. (2022). *4 ways to harness a growth mindset to set yourself up for success in 2023.* Available at: https://www.entrepreneur.com/leadership/4-ways-to-harness-a-growth-mindset-to-set-yourself-up-for/440692 [Accessed 26 May 2023].
5. Riani, A. (2022). *Why risk-taking is the biggest influencer of business growth.* Available at: https://www.forbes.com/sites/abdoriani/2022/03/01/why-risk-taking-is-the-biggest-influencer-of-business-growth/ [Accessed 26 May 2023].
6. Bacon, D. (2016). *4 leadership strategies to ignite passion in the workplace.* Available at: https://www.linkedin.com/pulse/4-leadership-strategies-ignite-passion-workplace-doug-bacon/ [Accessed 26 May 2023].
7. Forbes. (2023). *How to effectively communicate company goals with your employees.* Available at: https://www.forbes.com/sites/forbesbusinesscouncil/2023/01/10/how-to-effectively-communicate-company-goals-with-your-employees/?sh=23422d2429f7 [Accessed 26 May 2023].
8. Doyle, L. (2020). *Easelly – how to highlight your company's vision with Infographics.* Available at: https://www.easel.ly/blog/highlight-companys-vision-infographics/ [Accessed 26 May 2023].
9. Lavoie, A. (2017). *How to engage employees through your company vision statement.* Available at: https://www.entrepreneur.com/leadership/how-to-engage-employees-through-your-company-vision/290803 [Accessed 26 May 2023].
10. Herrity, J. (2023). *19 tips to become an influential leader for your team.* Available at: https://www.indeed.com/career-advice/career-development/influencing-leaders [Accessed 26 May 2023].

11. Forbes (2023). *15 ways to showcase employees to help attract and retain talent.* Available at: https://www.forbes.com/sites/forbescommunicationscouncil/2023/05/08/15-ways-to-showcase-employees-to-help-attract-and-retain-talent/?sh=30cca9627960 [Accessed 26 May 2023].
12. Grossman, D. (2023). *7 employee growth and development ideas for leaders.* Available at: https://www.yourthoughtpartner.com/blog/bid/73916/6-tips-to-help-employees-grow-and-develop [Accessed 26 May 2023].
13. Forbes (2017). *Council post: Seven ways to build a culture of employee recognition.* Available at: https://www.forbes.com/sites/theyec/2017/02/02/seven-ways-to-build-a-culture-of-employee-recognition/?sh=e800e9d1aaab [Accessed 26 May 2023].
14. Bushnell, M. (2023). *Flexible work policies to attract top talent.* Available at: https://www.businessnewsdaily.com/5466-successful-flex-work-program.html [Accessed 26 May 2023].
15. Hall, J. (2023). *How entrepreneurs can really achieve work-life balance.* Available at: https://www.forbes.com/sites/johnhall/2023/04/23/how-entrepreneurs-can-really-achieve-work-life-balance/?sh=4a52d7396e4f [Accessed 26 May 2023].
16. Miker, S. (2022). *4 reasons following your passion leads to Success.* Available at: https://www.entrepreneur.com/leadership/4-reasons-following-your-passion-leads-to-success/419610 [Accessed 26 May 2023].
17. Growjo (2013). *Stellar Energy Revenue and competitors.* Available at: https://growjo.com/company/Stellar_Energy [Accessed 26 May 2023].
18. PR Newswire (2018). *Dreamscape immersive closes $30M series B.* Available at: https://www.prnewswire.com/news-releases/dreamscape-immersive-closes-30m-series-b-300570490.html [Accessed 26 May 2023].
19. Business Wire (2022). *Zephyr AI raises $18.5 million in seed funding led by Lerner and M-cor.* Available at: https://www.businesswire.com/news/home/20220328005872/en/Zephyr-AI-Raises-18.5-Million-in-Seed-Funding-Led-by-Lerner-and-M-Cor [Accessed 26 May 2023].
20. PitchBook (n.d.). *Innospark Ventures Investor Profile: Portfolio & Exits.* Available at: https://pitchbook.com/profiles/investor/233966-71#overview [Accessed 26 May 2023].
21. LF Edge (2021). *EDGEX foundry reaches four years!* Available at: https://www.lfedge.org/2021/05/05/edgex-foundry-reaches-four-years/ [Accessed 26 May 2023].

22. Yakowicz, W. (2022). *With a $120 million war chest, Brightseed is unlocking the fat-fighting power of Hemp.* Available at: https://www.forbes.com/sites/willyakowicz/2022/05/09/with-a-115-million-war-chest-brightseed-is-unlocking-the-fat-fighting-power-of-hemp/?sh=296e41712fdd [Accessed 26 May 2023].
23. Feldman, A. (2022). *With data centers expanding, semiconductor start-up Astera Labs is on track for $100 million in revenue this year.* Available at: https://www.forbes.com/sites/amyfeldman/2022/08/16/with-data-centers-expanding-semiconductor-startup-astera-labs-is-on-track-for-100-million-in-revenue-this-year/?sh=33f08d903a10 [Accessed 26 May 2023].

CHAPTER 13
Seek the Right Advice from the Right Places

Even the most successful entrepreneurs and business moguls have relied on guidance and advice throughout their journeys.[1] Contrary to popular belief, they didn't possess some magical formula for success. Instead, they understood the value of seeking advice from the right places. Consider the mentorship between Warren Buffet and Bill Gates or how Bill Campbell coached the likes of Larry Page, Sergey Brin, Eric Schmidt, Sundar Pichai, Marissa Meyer, and Jeff Bezos. These legends, who have shaped the landscape of modern business, all shared a common trait: they recognized the importance of receiving guidance and coaching. Shouldn't this realization prompt us to consider how the right direction at the right time could have propelled them to become the remarkable individuals they are today? Entrepreneurs often underestimate the power of a few focused minutes of advice. It could come from a mentor, an angel investor, a personal relationship, or even a chance encounter with a stranger on the street. These fleeting moments have the potential to ignite a spark within entrepreneurs, leaving them feeling more encouraged and optimistic about their work. By seeking advice from the right sources, you open yourself up to discovering new perspectives that can lead your start-up on a more lucrative and fulfilling path. As an entrepreneur, it's crucial to acknowledge that it is difficult to fully understand every aspect of a company. Recognizing this fact and accepting help from mentors is a fundamental step toward guiding the growth of your start-up. However, it is equally important to exercise caution, as wrong advice has the potential to wreak havoc on your entrepreneurial journey.

By delving into the intricacies of seeking advice and mastering the art of filtering the good ideas from the lousy ones, you will gain valuable insights to navigate the complex world of entrepreneurship with confidence and clarity. Throughout this chapter, we will explore real-life anecdotes, case studies, and expert advice to shed light on adequate strategies and principles behind seeking wise advice. From identifying trustworthy mentors to leveraging personal networks and unexpected encounters, we will delve into the diverse avenues entrepreneurs can access invaluable guidance. Moreover, we will discuss the vital role of timing and discernment in extracting the most value from the advice received. As you progress through this chapter, you will gain a profound understanding of the immense impact that seeking the right advice can have on the success of your start-up.[2] By learning from the experiences of industry giants and drawing upon the wisdom of those who have paved the way before you, you will be better equipped to make informed decisions and chart a path toward entrepreneurial triumph. Remember, even the most accomplished entrepreneurs have relied on the guidance of others to shape their journeys. By seeking the right advice from the right places, you will position yourself on a trajectory that propels your start-up toward success and nurtures your personal growth as an entrepreneur. Get ready to explore the transformative power of advice and discover how it can unlock the full potential of your entrepreneurial aspirations.

Identifying The Need For Advice And Mentoring

Embarking on launching a start-up is an exciting and challenging endeavor. As an entrepreneur, you possess the vision, passion, and drive to bring your innovative ideas to life. However, even with the best intentions and a robust skill set, there are bound to be areas where you could benefit from outside advice and mentoring. Identifying the need for advice and mentoring in your entrepreneurial journey is the key.[3] One of the first steps in recognizing the need for advice and mentoring is to acknowledge that, as an entrepreneur, you can only possess expertise in some business areas. The entrepreneurial landscape is diverse and complex, with various facets that require specialized knowledge and skills. Handling everything without any support can quickly become overwhelming and may lead to costly mistakes. Therefore, taking stock of your strengths and weaknesses is crucial, and determining which aspects of your start-up could benefit from external guidance. Self-evaluation is also essential in identifying your knowledge gaps and areas where you may require assistance. Reflect on your abilities and experience, and be honest about areas where you may lack expertise. Consider the different functions within your start-up, such as marketing, finance, operations, and legal aspects. Assess your level of knowledge and competence in each area. This evaluation will help you pinpoint the specific areas where seeking advice and mentoring is crucial.

What may have worked for one entrepreneur or start-up in the past may not necessarily apply to your unique circumstances, which I have discussed previously in a few other chapters. The business landscape is ever-changing, influenced by technological advancements, consumer trends, and economic shifts. Staying abreast of these changes and adapting your strategies can be daunting. Seeking advice and mentoring can provide valuable insights and perspectives from seasoned professionals who have navigated similar challenges. Mentors, in particular, can offer guidance based on their experiences, sharing their successes and failures. This real-world wisdom can help you make more informed decisions, avoid common pitfalls, and accelerate your learning curve. Additionally, mentors can provide a sounding board for your ideas, challenge your assumptions, and offer constructive feedback. Another benefit of seeking advice and mentoring is expanding your professional network. Engaging with mentors and advisors opens doors to new connections and opportunities. They may introduce you to industry experts, potential investors, or strategic partners who can contribute to the growth and success of your start-up. Elaborating on this section, I have written about the value of seeking guidance. I have also written about sources of advice and mentorship and why you should focus on varied sources. Further, you will read about the impact of advice on start-up growth, which will convince you to prioritize the aspect of advice.

The Value Of Seeking Guidance

Seeking guidance and advice plays a pivotal role in the success of start-ups, offering a range of valuable benefits.[4] One of the primary advantages is the opportunity to gain valuable insights and expertise from experienced professionals. Mentors and advisors possess a wealth of knowledge and industry-specific expertise that can be invaluable in navigating your business's complexities. These seasoned professionals have likely encountered similar challenges and hurdles throughout their careers, allowing them to offer valuable guidance based on their experiences. By tapping into their knowledge, you can better understand best practices, industry trends, and potential pitfalls to avoid. Their insights can help you make more informed decisions, develop effective strategies, and optimize your operations. Moreover, seeking guidance provides a fresh and external perspective on your business. As an entrepreneur, it's easy to become immersed in regular operations and lose sight of the bigger picture. Mentors and advisors can offer a different vantage point, challenging your assumptions and providing objective feedback. This outside perspective can help you identify blind spots, uncover untapped opportunities, and refine your business strategy.

In addition to insights and perspectives, seeking guidance offers access to a valuable network of contacts and resources. Mentors and advisors often have extensive professional networks built over their years of experience. By connecting with them, you gain access to potential partners, investors, industry experts, and other valuable contacts who can contribute to the growth of your start-up. These connections can open doors to new opportunities, collaborations, and practical insights that may not have been accessible otherwise. Seeking guidance fosters personal and professional growth. Interacting with mentors and advisors allows you to learn from their successes and failures, expanding your knowledge and skill set. Through their guidance, you can develop critical entrepreneurial competencies, such as decision-making, problem-solving, and leadership. The mentor-mentee relationship provides a supportive environment for learning and growth, enabling you to enhance your entrepreneurial capabilities. When you seek guidance, you demonstrate humility and a willingness to learn. It is a proactive approach to self-improvement and recognizing that no one can achieve success alone. By seeking advice and mentoring, you show a commitment to continuous learning and an openness to different perspectives.

Sources Of Advice And Mentorship

Entrepreneurs can access a wide range of sources for advice and mentorship. These sources provide valuable perspectives, expertise, and guidance. Firstly, industry experts and professionals with extensive experience in your specific field or sector can be an invaluable sources of advice and mentorship. These individuals deeply understand the industry's dynamics, trends, and best practices. Their insights can help you navigate industry-specific challenges and make informed decisions. Engaging with industry experts and professionals can provide you with valuable connections, access to industry networks, and opportunities for collaboration. You could also reach out to entrepreneurial networks and communities offering a wealth of start-up resources, including advice and mentorship. These networks can be found through local business organizations, industry-specific associations, or online communities. Engaging with fellow entrepreneurs allows you to learn from their experiences, share knowledge, and access a supportive ecosystem. These networks often organize events, workshops, and mentorship programs that facilitate connections with experienced entrepreneurs willing to share their insights and guide you on your entrepreneurial journey.

Professional consultants and coaches with expertise in marketing, finance, operations, or strategy can offer specialized advice and mentorship.[5] These professionals possess tips and understanding that can provide targeted guidance to address specific challenges in your start-up. Engaging with consultants or coaches on a project basis can help you develop effective strategies, refine your business model, or enhance specific aspects of your operations. Their external perspective and specialized skills can complement your expertise and contribute to your start-up's success. The next source of advice and mentorship is that universities and entrepreneurship centers often have resources and programs to support start-ups. These institutions offer access to research, academic expertise, and mentoring programs. Professors, researchers, and alums with entrepreneurial experience can provide valuable advice and mentorship based on their academic and practical knowledge. Collaborating with educational institutions and entrepreneurship centers can offer a unique blend of theoretical knowledge, real-world experience, and a supportive community.

The Impact Of Advice On Start-Up Growth

Seeking advice and mentorship can profoundly impact the growth and success of start-ups. The guidance and insights gained from experienced mentors will go a long way in your business journey. One way how advice can positively impact the growth of your start-up is through strategic decision-making. Mentors and advisors bring a wealth of experience and industry knowledge, enabling them to offer valuable insights into market trends, competitive analysis, and growth opportunities. Their guidance can help you navigate complex strategic choices like market entry strategies, product development roadmaps, and expansion plans. By leveraging their advice, you can make more informed decisions that maximize your start-up's growth potential. Another significant benefit of seeking advice is the ability to avoid costly mistakes. Experienced mentors and advisors have likely encountered similar challenges and pitfalls in their entrepreneurial journeys. By sharing their experiences, they can help you avoid common mistakes that could be costly or detrimental to your start-up. Their guidance can save you time, resources, and potential setbacks.[6]

Seeking advice provides access to valuable networks and resources. Mentors and advisors often have extensive networks in the industry, providing invaluable opportunities for collaboration, partnerships, and access to potential investors or customers. These networks can open doors to new markets, strategic alliances, and additional resources that can fuel the growth of your start-up. By tapping into these networks through mentorship, you can leverage the expertise and connections of experienced professionals to propel your start-up's growth. You should also know that advice and mentorship offer a fresh and external perspective on your business. As an entrepreneur, it's easy to become immersed in the day-to-day operations and lose sight of the bigger picture. Mentors and advisors can provide a different vantage point, challenging your assumptions and providing objective feedback. By incorporating diverse perspectives into your decision-making process, you can make more well-rounded and informed choices that contribute to the growth and success of your start-up.

Seeking The Right Advice

For seeking advice for your start-up, it is crucial to seek the right advice.[7] Not all advice is created equal, and receiving guidance that aligns with your specific needs and goals is essential. Before seeking advice, it is crucial to define your needs and goals clearly. Each start-up has unique challenges and requirements, and understanding what you want to achieve will help you identify the type of advice you require. Are you seeking guidance on market entry strategies, product development, funding options, or scaling your operations? By clearly articulating your needs and goals, you can narrow your search for advisors or mentors with expertise in those areas. When seeking advice, prioritize individuals with industry-specific expertise and experience. Industry experts can provide insights and guidance tailored to your particular sector's nuances and dynamics. Their knowledge of market trends, customer preferences, and industry best practices can prove invaluable to your journey. Look for advisors or mentors with a track record of success within your industry who can offer relevant insights and strategies aligning with your start-up's objectives.

The stage of your start-up is an essential factor to consider when seeking advice. Different stages of growth require different types of guidance. For instance, in the early stages, you may need advice on validating your business idea, securing funding, and developing a minimum viable product (MVP). As your start-up matures, you may require advice on scaling operations, expanding into new markets, or optimizing your business processes. Finding advisors or mentors with experience working with start-ups at your specific stage can provide targeted guidance aligned with your current needs. Evaluating the credibility of potential advisors or mentors before seeking advice is essential. Seek out recommendations and testimonials from other entrepreneurs who have worked with them. By evaluating their credibility, you can ensure that the advice you receive is from trusted sources with a history of delivering value. Seek individuals who share your values and are genuinely interested in your success. To further focus on the dimension of seeking the right advice, I have written about establishing criteria for reliable advice, followed by identifying and engaging with mentors. Both these factors are equally important. I have emphasized another aspect following these - leveraging unexpected sources of advice.

Establishing Criteria For Reliable Advice

Establishing criteria for reliable advice is crucial when seeking guidance for your start-up. One key consideration is the expertise and experience of the individuals providing the advice. Look for advisors or mentors with excellent skill sets. They should possess deep knowledge and experience relevant to your start-up's industry or specific challenges. Assess their qualifications, professional background, and achievements to ensure their expertise meets your needs. Another important criterion is reputation and credibility. Reliable sources of advice often have a strong reputation within the industry or entrepreneurial community. While doing so, learn about their impact on other start-ups. Consider recommendations from entrepreneurs who have worked with them to gauge their reliability. Compatibility and alignment with your start-up's values and goals should also be considered. Establishing a solid rapport and shared vision with your advisors or mentors is crucial for effective collaboration. Seek individuals who understand how to lead and have done so in the past. Assess their communication style, willingness to listen, and ability to provide constructive feedback.

Additionally, consider the ability of potential advisors or mentors to provide a fresh and objective perspective.[8] Reliable advice often comes from individuals who can offer unbiased viewpoints and challenge your assumptions. Look for mentors or advisors who can provide a balanced assessment of your start-up's strengths, weaknesses, and opportunities. They should encourage critical thinking and offer alternative perspectives that broaden your understanding and enhance decision-making. Different mentors or advisors can bring varied experiences, approaches, and insights. Engaging with individuals from diverse backgrounds, industries, or skill sets can help you gain a broader understanding of the challenges and opportunities your start-up faces. By considering multiple perspectives, you can make more well-rounded decisions and develop innovative strategies that set you apart from the competition. Availability and accessibility are also important factors to consider. Reliable advisors or mentors should be accessible and willing to dedicate time and effort to support your start-up's growth. Assess their availability for meetings, discussions, and follow-up sessions. Understand their commitment level and ensure they can provide the guidance and support you need within your desired timeframe.

Identifying And Engaging With Mentors

Mentors play a crucial role in the growth and development of start-ups. They provide guidance, support, and knowledge based on their experiences. Identifying and engaging with mentors who can provide valuable insights and advice is essential for the success of your start-up. There are certain strategies for identifying and engaging with mentors effectively. Before identifying potential mentors, it is important to define your mentorship needs. Determine the areas where you require guidance, such as strategy, marketing, fundraising, or leadership. Assess your strengths and weaknesses, and identify the gaps in your knowledge or skill set. By understanding your needs, you can seek mentors with expertise and experience in the areas where you require support. A clear definition of your mentorship needs will guide you in selecting mentors who can provide targeted and relevant advice. Tap into your existing networks to identify potential mentors. Reach out to professional contacts, industry associations, or entrepreneurial communities you are a part of. Alum networks, business organizations, or networking events can also be valuable sources for finding mentors. Leverage online platforms and social media to connect with industry professionals or entrepreneurs who inspire you. Engaging with individuals who share similar interests and values can lead to fruitful mentorship opportunities.

In this process, you must find individuals with experience in your industry. Industry-specific mentors can provide valuable insights and guidance that are directly applicable to the challenges and dynamics of your sector. They can offer unique perspectives, share industry-specific best practices, and help you navigate the intricacies of your market. Once you have identified potential mentors, conduct thorough research and evaluation. Review their professional backgrounds, achievements, and contributions to the industry.[9] Seek out information about their previous mentorship experiences, if any. When engaging with potential mentors, focus on building a genuine connection. Reach out to them with a personalized message expressing your admiration for their work and explaining why you believe they would be a valuable mentor for your start-up. Highlight the specific areas where you believe their guidance can benefit you. Demonstrate your passion, commitment, and willingness to learn. Attending industry events, conferences, or workshops where potential mentors are present can also provide opportunities to establish face-to-face connections. Once you have established a mentor-mentee relationship, it is essential to nurture and maintain it. Treat your mentor's time and advice respectfully, and seek their guidance proactively.

Leveraging Unexpected Sources Of Advice

When seeking advice for your start-up, it's important to consider that valuable insights can come from unexpected sources. While mentors and industry experts are traditional avenues for guidance, other sources can provide unique perspectives and ideas. There are numerous benefits of leveraging unexpected sources of advice and how they can contribute to the success of your start-up. One valuable source of advice is cross-industry inspiration. Look beyond your immediate industry and seek insights from diverse sectors.[10] Different industries often face similar challenges, and solutions that have worked in one industry may apply to your start-up. By exploring case studies, attending conferences or events outside your field, or engaging in conversations with professionals from diverse backgrounds, you can gain fresh perspectives and innovative ideas that can be adapted to your specific context. Your customers can be an unexpected source of valuable advice. Actively seek customer feedback and consider their needs, preferences, and pain points. Analyze customer reviews, conduct surveys, or engage in direct conversations to understand their experiences with your product or service. This feedback can provide insights into areas where you may need to improve or innovate, helping you better align your offerings with customer expectations and driving the growth of your start-up. Engaging with other entrepreneurs and start-up founders through peer-to-peer networks can be a rich source of advice.

Your own employees and team members can provide unexpected sources of advice. They possess unique perspectives and insights derived from their roles and responsibilities within your start-up. Encourage open communication and create a culture where ideas and suggestions are valued. Regularly engage with your team members to understand their observations, suggestions, and concerns. Their feedback can uncover untapped opportunities, improve internal processes, and contribute to the overall success of your start-up. Collaborating with non-competitive businesses or organizations can offer fresh insights and advice. Identify potential partners whose expertise, resources, or customer base complement your start-up. By collaborating on joint projects, sharing knowledge, or exploring co-marketing opportunities, you can benefit from the advice and perspectives of professionals outside your immediate industry. These collaborations can lead to mutually beneficial relationships, expanded networks, and innovative solutions that propel your start-up forward. Stay updated on the latest trends, research, and thought-provoking ideas these individuals share.

Evaluating And Applying Advice

Once you have sought advice and received guidance from various sources, the next critical step is to evaluate and apply that advice effectively.[11] Not all advice will be equally applicable or beneficial to your start-up, and it is essential to assess the advice received to make informed decisions. You must know the strategies for evaluating and applying advice to maximize its impact on your start-up's growth. When evaluating advice, it is important to consider the context in which it was given. Recognize that every start-up is unique, with its circumstances, challenges, and goals. Therefore, it is crucial to contextualize the advice within your start-up's specific needs and characteristics. Consider factors such as your industry, market conditions, stage of growth, available resources, and the advice-givers' understanding of your start-up's context. By doing so, you can better assess the relevance and applicability of the advice to your specific situation. Evaluate the credibility of the individuals providing the advice. Look for consistency in their advice, and determine if their recommendations align with established best practices or industry standards. Remember, while individual perspectives can be valuable, weighing them against the broader industry's collective wisdom and expertise is important.

Listen to differing opinions and constructive criticism, and be open to challenging your assumptions and beliefs. Gathering diverse viewpoints can enrich your understanding and lead to more robust decision-making. Prioritize the advice based on its potential impact and urgency. Not all advice will be equally important or timely for your start-up. Consider the advice's alignment with your immediate priorities and objectives. Identify the advice that addresses critical challenges or opportunities your start-up is currently facing. Focus on actionable advice to implement within your available resources and timeframe. Remember that you can always revisit and evaluate other advice as your start-up progresses and evolves. When applying advice, ensure clear communication and alignment within your team. Share the relevant advice with key stakeholders and facilitate discussions to ensure a shared understanding and consensus. Define roles and responsibilities and establish a clear action plan for implementing the advice. To give you a better understanding of evaluating and applying advice, I have written about filtering good ideas and why this is important. After that, I wrote about the timing and relevance of advice, which will either make or break the deal for you. I have ended this section by incorporating advice into decision-making, which is equally vital.

Filtering Good Ideas

When seeking advice for your start-up, you will inevitably come across many ideas and suggestions. However, not all ideas are created equal, and it is crucial to filter and identify the good ones that have the potential to impact your start-up's growth positively. There are numerous strategies for filtering good ideas effectively. One of the critical criteria for filtering good ideas is assessing their alignment with your start-up's vision and goals. Consider whether the idea supports and furthers your overarching mission. Evaluate how the idea fits into your long-term strategic plan and whether it helps you achieve specific objectives. Good ideas should align with your start-up's core values, business model, and target market. By filtering out ideas that do not align with your vision and goals, you can focus on those most likely to contribute to your start-up's success. Filtering good ideas also requires evaluating their feasibility and practicality. Assess whether the idea can be realistically implemented within your available resources, budget, and timeframe. Consider the technical, operational, and logistical aspects of executing the idea. Evaluate the potential risks, challenges, and barriers to implementation. Good ideas should be actionable and achievable, considering the constraints and limitations of your start-up.

Consider conducting small-scale experiments or pilot projects to test the idea's feasibility and gather real-world data.[12] Good ideas should be supported by evidence and insights collected through market validation. Filtering good ideas can also involve considering their consistency with expert advice received. Evaluate whether the idea aligns with the recommendations of trusted mentors, industry experts, or successful entrepreneurs who deeply understand your start-up's industry and market. Consider their track record and the credibility of their advice. While being open to new ideas is important, good ideas should be consistent with sound advice and best practices. You can make more informed decisions by filtering out ideas that contradict or deviate from expert advice. In filtering good ideas, it is crucial to prioritize and focus on a select few. Recognize that resources, time, and attention are limited, and spreading yourself too thin by pursuing too many ideas can dilute your efforts and hinder progress. By filtering and focusing on a smaller set of good ideas, you can allocate resources effectively and increase the likelihood of successful implementation.

Timing And Relevance Of Advice

Timing and relevance are crucial factors to consider when evaluating the advice received for your start-up. The timing of advice refers to when it is given and whether it aligns with the current stage of your start-up's development. Relevance, on the other hand, pertains to how applicable and useful the advice is to your specific circumstances and challenges.[13] The stage of your start-up's development plays a significant role in determining the relevance and impact of advice. Different stages of the start-up journey present unique challenges and require distinct strategies. For example, product development and market validation advice may be more relevant during the early stages. At the same time, guidance on scaling operations and securing funding becomes critical as your start-up grows. Evaluate whether the advice received is tailored to your current stage and addresses your specific challenges and opportunities. Consider the ever-changing dynamics of your industry and market when evaluating the relevance of advice. Industries evolve at different paces, and market trends and customer preferences can shift rapidly. Advice that may have been relevant in the past may no longer hold or be effective in the current context.

Regularly evaluate the outcomes and impact of the advice you have implemented and gather feedback from stakeholders, customers, and team members. Reflect on the lessons learned and adjust your strategies and actions accordingly. Continuously iterating and refining your approach ensures that the advice remains relevant and aligned with your evolving needs. While seeking advice, consider the importance of customization and personalization. Recognize that generic advice may not always directly apply to your unique situation. Seek advisors, mentors, or experts who can provide customized guidance based on a deep understanding of your start-up's context, challenges, and goals. Customized advice can offer specific insights and strategies tailored to your industry, market, and competitive landscape. Personalizing the advice received can enhance its relevance and increase its potential impact. It is valuable to balance multiple perspectives when evaluating advice for timing and relevance. Seek diverse viewpoints from trusted mentors, advisors, industry experts, and your team members. Consider the various insights and experiences they bring to the table.

Incorporating Advice Into Decision-Making

In building and growing your start-up, receiving advice from various sources is valuable, but it is equally important to incorporate that advice into your decision-making process effectively. Integrating advice into your decision-making ensures that you leverage the wisdom and insights shared by others while staying true to your start-up's vision and goals. Before incorporating advice into your decision-making, it is crucial to clarify your decision-making criteria. Identify the key factors and considerations that guide your decision-making process. These criteria may include financial implications, market potential, customer impact, feasibility, and alignment with your start-up's vision and values. By establishing clear decision-making criteria, you can objectively evaluate the advice received and align it with your decision-making process. When incorporating advice, it is important to assess the source and credibility of the advice-giver. Consider the expertise, experience, and track record of the individual or organization providing the advice. Evaluate the pros and cons of the advice before incorporating it into your decision-making.

Assess the alignment of the advice with your start-up's vision and goals. Evaluate whether incorporating the advice supports your long-term strategic direction and contributes to achieving your start-up's objectives.[14] Consider how the advice fits into your business model, target market, and core values. Ensure that the advice aligns with your start-up's unique identity and mission. Incorporating advice in harmony with your vision and goals ensures consistency and coherence in decision-making. Perform a cost-benefit analysis to evaluate the potential impact of incorporating the advice. Assess the resources, time, and effort required to implement the advice against the expected benefits and returns. Consider the advice's short-term and long-term implications on your start-up's growth and success. By conducting a cost-benefit analysis, you can make informed decisions that maximize the value and impact of incorporating the advice. While incorporating advice, trusting your intuition and instincts as a founder is essential.

Companies That Have Prioritized Guidance

In the fast-paced and complex business landscape, many successful companies recognize the importance of seeking guidance and incorporating it into their strategies. By prioritizing guidance, these companies leverage external expertise and insights to navigate challenges, make informed decisions, and drive growth.[15] Companies that prioritize guidance understand the value of seeking diverse perspectives. They actively engage with various stakeholders, including mentors, industry experts, advisors, and consultants. By tapping into this diverse pool of knowledge, companies gain fresh insights, alternative viewpoints, and expertise from different domains. It helps broaden their understanding, challenge assumptions, and identify innovative solutions to complex problems. Guidance-seeking companies recognize the need for specialized expertise in specific areas. They proactively seek experts with in-depth knowledge and experience relevant to the industry, market, or particular challenges they face. These experts provide valuable guidance tailored to the company's unique circumstances, helping them navigate complexities, seize opportunities, and avoid potential pitfalls. They understand that seeking advice is an ongoing process that keeps them updated on industry trends, emerging technologies, and best practices. These companies actively engage in industry events, conferences, workshops, and training programs to expand their knowledge base and stay ahead of the curve.[16] Continuous learning and development ensure that companies remain agile, adaptable, and innovative in a rapidly changing business environment. I have written about some of these companies below:

Stripe

Stripe[17] is a highly successful start-up that has significantly impacted the online payment industry. Founded in 2010 by Irish brothers John and Patrick Collison, Stripe has revolutionized how businesses handle online transactions. With a focus on simplifying the payment process and providing robust infrastructure, Stripe has experienced remarkable growth and success. One of the key factors contributing to Stripe's growth is its relentless focus on customer experience. By developing an intuitive and developer-friendly platform, Stripe has attracted many businesses, from small e-commerce stores to large enterprises. The company's dedication to user-friendly design, seamless integration, and transparent pricing has made it a go-to choice for businesses seeking reliable and efficient payment solutions. Stripe's commitment to innovation and continuous improvement has also played a significant role in its success. The company has consistently introduced new features and capabilities to meet the evolving needs of its customers. For instance, Stripe has expanded beyond traditional online payments to include support for subscriptions, marketplaces, and mobile commerce. By staying at the forefront of technological advancements and anticipating market trends, Stripe has remained a leader in the industry. Another factor contributing to Stripe's growth is its global expansion strategy. The company has successfully expanded its presence to numerous countries, offering businesses worldwide access to its payment services. This expansion has been accompanied by strategic partnerships with financial institutions and technology companies, enabling Stripe to establish a robust global network.

Company Name: Stripe

Founded: 2010

Significant reason(s) for success: The company has focused on innovation and global expansion. It has been able to do so by making the advice of the market a part of its decision-making process.

Miro

Miro[18] is a collaborative online whiteboarding platform that has gained significant attention and has experienced remarkable growth in recent years. Founded in 2011, Miro has transformed how teams work together, enabling remote collaboration, ideation, and visual communication. One of the key factors contributing to Miro's growth is its focus on addressing the needs of remote and distributed teams. As remote work becomes increasingly prevalent, Miro's digital whiteboarding capabilities provide a virtual space for teams to brainstorm, plan projects, and visualize ideas in real-time. The platform offers a range of tools, including sticky notes, diagrams, wireframes, and mind maps, allowing teams to collaborate visually and overcome the challenges of distance and time zones. Miro's emphasis on user-friendly design and intuitive interface has also contributed to its success. The platform offers a seamless and interactive experience, making it easy for individuals and teams to adopt and integrate into their workflows. With features like real-time collaboration, video conferencing integration, and extensive template libraries, Miro provides a comprehensive solution for visual collaboration that enhances productivity and fosters creativity. The company has regularly introduced new integrations based on user feedback and emerging industry trends. For example, Miro has expanded its capabilities to support Agile methodologies, design thinking processes, and remote workshops. By staying agile and responsive to customer needs, Miro has positioned itself as a versatile tool for various industries and use cases. Another factor contributing to Miro's success is its vibrant and engaged community of users. Miro has cultivated a strong user community that shares best practices, templates, and ideas.

Company Name: Miro

Founded: 2011

Significant reason(s) for success: The company has been working on offering user-friendly designs and continuous innovation. It has been able to streamline its goals and work on the same without losing out on advice from the community.

Peloton

Peloton[19] has emerged as a trailblazer in the fitness industry, transforming how people exercise and stay motivated. Founded in 2012, Peloton has gained widespread recognition for its innovative approach to connected fitness, combining high-quality equipment, immersive content, and a vibrant community. One of the critical factors behind Peloton's success is its focus on bringing the studio experience to the comfort of users' homes. The company's flagship product, the Peloton Bike, offers a state-of-the-art indoor cycling experience with a large touchscreen display that streams live and on-demand classes led by world-class instructors. Peloton has created a compelling and convenient solution for individuals seeking an engaging workout experience from home by replicating the energy and excitement of a group fitness class. Peloton's emphasis on content and community has also played a pivotal role in its growth. The platform offers many workouts, including cycling, running, strength training, yoga, and more. Users can choose from various classes based on preferences, fitness levels, and goals. The interactive nature of Peloton's platform allows users to engage with instructors and fellow participants, fostering a sense of connection and accountability. The strong community motivates users to push themselves, celebrate milestones, and share their fitness journey, creating a supportive and inspiring environment. Furthermore, Peloton's use of technology to enhance the fitness experience has been instrumental in its success. Integrating real-time performance metrics, leaderboards, and personalized recommendations adds a gamified element to workouts, motivating users to challenge themselves and track their progress. The seamless data synchronization with the Peloton app allows users to monitor their fitness journey, set goals, and celebrate achievements.

Company Name: Peloton

Founded: 2012

Significant reason(s) for success: The company has been able to foster brand advocacy centered around its mission of bringing accessible and immersive fitness experiences to individuals worldwide. It shows the importance of filtering good advice and setting priorities right.

HashiCorp

HashiCorp[20] is a software company that has significantly revolutionized infrastructure automation and cloud provisioning. Founded in 2012 by Mitchell Hashimoto and Armon Dadgar, HashiCorp has emerged as a leader in the DevOps and cloud infrastructure management space, providing innovative tools that streamline application deployment, management, and scaling. One of the key factors contributing to HashiCorp's success is its suite of open-source tools, known as the HashiCorp Infrastructure Automation Platform. This platform includes popular tools such as Terraform, Consul, Vault, and Nomad, each addressing a specific aspect of infrastructure management. These tools provide developers and operations teams with a unified, scalable, and efficient solution for managing infrastructure across multiple cloud providers and on-premises environments. Terraform, HashiCorp's flagship product, has transformed how organizations provision and manage infrastructure. With Terraform, users can define their infrastructure as code, allowing consistent and reproducible infrastructure deployments. The tool supports multiple cloud providers and infrastructure technologies, enabling teams to adopt a multi-cloud or hybrid cloud strategy. Terraform's declarative syntax and a robust ecosystem of providers have made it a popular choice for automating infrastructure provisioning and management. Consul and Vault, two other vital tools in HashiCorp's suite, address the challenges of service discovery, networking, and security in distributed systems.

Company Name: HashiCorp

Founded: 2012

Significant reason(s) for success: The company has demonstrated a keen understanding of market trends and the evolving needs of its users. These could be counted as unexpected sources from which entrepreneurs can extract advice.

Patreon

Patreon[21] is a platform that has revolutionized how creators and artists monetize their work and connect with their audience. Founded in 2013 by Jack Conte and Sam Yam, Patreon has become a leading membership platform that enables creators to receive recurring payments from their fans, fostering a sustainable income stream and supporting their creative endeavors. One of the key factors contributing to Patreon's success is its focus on empowering creators. By providing a platform for creators to offer exclusive content, rewards, and experiences to their fans, Patreon enables a direct and meaningful connection between creators and their most dedicated supporters. This direct connection eliminates the traditional gatekeepers and allows creators to maintain creative control while cultivating a loyal community. Patreon's approach to monetization goes beyond simple one-time transactions or ad-based revenue models. Instead, it emphasizes the importance of ongoing patronage, encouraging fans to become long-term supporters of the creators they love. Through the platform, fans can contribute a set amount of money per creation or monthly, giving creators a more predictable and sustainable income stream. The success of Patreon can also be attributed to its ability to nurture a sense of community and belonging. The platform facilitates direct communication and engagement between creators and their patrons, fostering a closer relationship and allowing creators to understand better and cater to their fans' preferences. This sense of community creates a mutually beneficial ecosystem where creators receive financial support, and patrons access exclusive content, behind-the-scenes insights, and a deeper connection with the creators they support.

Company Name: Patreon

Founded: 2013

Significant reason(s) for success: The company has been able to give the required freedom to users and utilize indirect advice on improving the sector by focusing on its requirements.

Gong

Gong[22] is a sales enablement platform that has transformed how organizations analyze and optimize their sales processes. Founded in 2015 by Amit Bendov and Eilon Reshef, Gong has become a leading provider of revenue intelligence software, leveraging Artificial Intelligence (AI) and Machine Learning (ML) to unlock valuable insights from sales conversations. One of the key factors contributing to Gong's success is its focus on improving sales effectiveness and efficiency. The platform uses AI-powered conversation analytics to capture and analyze sales calls, meetings, and demos. By automatically transcribing, analyzing, and summarizing these interactions, Gong provides sales teams unprecedented visibility into customer conversations. This visibility helps identify best practices, uncover coaching opportunities, and deeply understand customer needs. Gong's revenue intelligence capabilities go beyond simple call recording and transcription. The platform applies advanced natural language processing and ML algorithms to extract valuable insights from sales conversations. These insights include sentiment analysis, keyword identification, talk-to-listen ratios, and objection-handling effectiveness. By analyzing large volumes of sales data, Gong enables organizations to make data-driven decisions, identify trends, and optimize their sales strategies for better outcomes. Another critical factor in Gong's success is its focus on improving sales coaching and skill development. The platform provides sales managers with detailed analytics and reports highlighting coaching opportunities for their team members. By identifying areas for improvement and providing specific recommendations, Gong helps sales managers deliver targeted coaching and training to their sales reps. This personalized approach to skill development enhances the performance and effectiveness of sales teams, resulting in improved sales outcomes.

Company Name: Gong

Founded: 2015

Significant reason(s) for success: The company has been able to build strong partnerships and establish itself as a trusted player, which would not have been possible without leveraging advice at various levels.

Asana

Asana[23] is a leading work management platform that has revolutionized how teams organize and execute their projects. Founded in 2008 by Dustin Moskovitz and Justin Rosenstein, Asana provides a comprehensive suite of tools and features designed to enhance productivity, streamline communication, and facilitate collaboration. One of the key factors contributing to Asana's success is its focus on simplifying workflow management. The platform offers a visual interface where teams can create tasks, assign responsibilities, set deadlines, and track progress. By providing a centralized hub for project management, Asana enables teams to have a clear overview of their tasks, dependencies, and milestones, promoting better coordination and alignment within the organization. The platform also offers a range of features that facilitate team collaboration, such as file sharing, commenting, and real-time updates. These features enable teams to have transparent and contextual conversations within the context of their tasks, reducing the need for excessive emails and meetings. As a result, teams can work more efficiently and make faster decisions. Another critical factor in Asana's success is its flexibility and scalability. The platform caters to teams of all sizes and across various industries, from small start-ups to large enterprises. Asana offers customizable workflows, allowing teams to adapt the platform to their specific processes and needs. Whether agile project management, marketing campaigns, product launches, or any other type of project, Asana provides the flexibility to tailor the platform to suit different workflows and methodologies.

Company Name: Asana

Founded: 2008

Significant reason(s) for success: The companies recognized the aspect of advice and focused on workflow management, collaboration, flexibility, scalability, and continuous improvement, among other factors.

Conclusion

By recognizing the value of seeking guidance, entrepreneurs can tap into a vast pool of knowledge, experience, and expertise that can propel their ventures forward. Whether through mentorship programs, industry networks, or unexpected sources of advice, the insights gained from others can provide invaluable direction and support. Identifying the need for advice and mentoring is the first step toward building a solid foundation for success. By acknowledging that no one has all the answers and that seeking guidance is a sign of strength, entrepreneurs open themselves up to new possibilities and opportunities for growth. The value of seeking advice lies in the fresh perspectives, alternative viewpoints, and tested strategies that can be gained, helping start-ups navigate challenges and make informed decisions. However, it's not just about seeking advice from any source. Establishing criteria for reliable advice and carefully selecting mentors is crucial.[24]

Evaluating and applying advice is equally important. Filtering good ideas, considering timing and relevance, and incorporating advice into decision-making processes are vital to extracting value from the guidance received. Entrepreneurs must strike a balance between staying true to their vision and remaining open to new insights that can contribute to their start-up's growth and success. Remember, the journey of entrepreneurship is not meant to be traveled alone. By seeking guidance, entrepreneurs can tap into a wealth of knowledge, avoid common pitfalls, and gain the confidence to overcome challenges. The stories of successful start-ups that have prioritized guidance demonstrate the transformative power of seeking advice from the right sources. These companies have harnessed the collective wisdom and experience of mentors, communities, and unexpected sources, propelling them toward remarkable achievements. As you embark on your start-up journey, remember that seeking the right advice is a testament to your commitment to growth and success.

Below are the essential pointers you must remember from this chapter while you embark on your entrepreneurial journey:

1. Identify the need for advice and mentoring because it will help you be on track and decide a long course of progress for your company.
2. Understand the value of seeking guidance and be proactive while doing so.
3. There are numerous sources of advice and mentorship; do not hesitate to explore them as you advance with your business.
4. The impact of advice on start-up growth is often underestimated, but know that it is powerful. We often look at its statistics and disregard advice from real people who have made it big in the industry.
5. Seeking the right advice will always help you advance in the league. It will help you surpass those companies that do not seek advice, as they may see many others only as competitors.
6. Establishing criteria for reliable advice will enable you to be focused on your entrepreneurial journey and eliminate distractions.
7. Identifying and engaging with mentors will allow you to learn from mistakes and success stories faster.

8. Leveraging unexpected sources of advice is one of the most important strategies to remember. With the changing business scenarios and technology, you might get the best benefits from sources completely away from your assumptions.
9. Evaluating and applying advice is crucial since all advice is contextual, and your business goals and vision will guide such applications.
10. Filtering good ideas is essential to ensure your team understands the strategies your company decides to incorporate. While these strategies will mostly come from instances of success in the industry, be doubly sure before applying them in your business.
11. The timing and relevance of advice can never be ignored. The when and why are equally relevant, and such a focus will enable you to stand out in the competitive industry.
12. It all comes down to incorporating advice into decision-making. Everything is of good use if it translates to actions. Your actions will decide the course of your company's future. So, take the right actions and take them today!

References

1. Quora (2022). *Should start-ups bring on advisors?* Available at: https://www.forbes.com/sites/quora/2021/12/09/should-startups-bring-on-advisors/?sh=204a9b9c20d3 [Accessed 26 May 2023].
2. Harroch, R. (2022). *The complete 35-step guide for entrepreneurs starting a business.* Available at: https://www.forbes.com/sites/allbusiness/2018/07/15/35-step-guide-entrepreneurs-starting-a-business/?sh=7b6c77ee184b [Accessed 25 Jun. 2023].
3. Lucanus, A. (2021). *Council post: Five reasons why every business owner needs a mentor, no matter how successful they are.* Available at: https://www.forbes.com/sites/forbesbusinesscouncil/2021/09/16/five-reasons-why-every-business-owner-needs-a-mentor-no-matter-how-successful-they-are/ [Accessed 25 Jun. 2023].
4. FasterCapital (2023). *The importance of advice and support for startups - FasterCapital.* Available at: https://fastercapital.com/content/The-importance-of-advice-and-support-for-startups.html [Accessed 25 Jun. 2023].

5. Faith, K. (2023). *Entrepreneurship mentoring: Definition, types, importance, and tips*. Available at: https://superscaling.com/blog/entrepreneurship-mentoring/ [Accessed 25 Jun. 2023].
6. Dunne, D. (2019). *How a mentor can help your entrepreneurial career*. Available at: https://smallbusinessbc.ca/article/mentor-can-help-entrepreneurial-career/#:~:text=A%20mentor%20will%20help%20you,tangible%20ways%20with%20business%20advice [Accessed 25 Jun. 2023].
7. Basel Area (2023). Mentoring for startups (complete guide 2023). Available at: https://baselarea.swiss/knowledge-hub/mentoring-for-startups/#:~:text=One%20of%20the%20most%20accessible,within%20your%20current%20professional%20network [Accessed 25 Jun. 2023].
8. Krach, K. (2016). *5 points on the importance of mentors for entrepreneurs*. Available at: https://medium.com/@KeithKrach/5-points-on-the-importance-of-mentors-for-entrepreneurs-a14736e7d7a9 [Accessed 25 Jun. 2023].
9. Morris, R. (2015). *Mentors are the secret weapons of successful startups*. Available at: https://techcrunch.com/2015/03/22/mentors-are-the-secret-weapons-of-successful-startups/ [Accessed 25 Jun. 2023].
10. Forbes (2020). *Council post: 10 entrepreneurs share the best advice they've heard about starting a business*. Available at: https://www.forbes.com/sites/theyec/2020/03/10/10-entrepreneurs-share-the-best-advice-theyve-heard-about-starting-a-business/?sh=3a278ba078e5 [Accessed 25 Jun. 2023].
11. Greenberg, R. (2021). *7 pieces of terrible advice aspiring entrepreneurs blindly believe*. Available at: https://entrepreneurshandbook.co/7-pieces-of-terrible-advice-aspiring-entrepreneurs-blindly-believe-9b89bcc7db6c [Accessed 25 Jun. 2023].
12. Harvard Business Review (2021). *How to scale a successful pilot project*. Available at: https://hbr.org/2021/01/how-to-scale-a-successful-pilot-project [Accessed 25 Jun. 2023].
13. Forbes (2020). *Council post: Three inspiring failure-to-success stories you may not have heard before*. Available at: https://www.forbes.com/sites/theyec/2020/11/11/three-inspiring-failure-to-success-stories-you-may-not-have-heard-before/?sh=126b7569f65c [Accessed 25 Jun. 2023].
14. LinkedIn (2021). *5 rules to follow when seeking expert advice for your startup*. Available at: https://www.linkedin.com/pulse/5-rules-follow-when-seeking-expert-advice-your-startup-ibrahim [Accessed 25 Jun. 2023].
15. Entrepreneur Beginnings (2021). *Why do entrepreneurs have to seek ad-*

vice from professionals?. Available at: https://entrepreneurbeginnings.com/why-do-entrepreneurs-have-to-seek-advice-from-professionals/ [Accessed 25 Jun. 2023].

16. Riani, A. (2022). *Why mentors are vital for new startup founders.* Available at: https://www.forbes.com/sites/abdoriani/2022/08/29/why-mentors-are-vital-for-new-startup-founders/?sh=3160170b4b5e [Accessed 25 Jun. 2023].
17. Armstrong, S. (2018). *The untold story of stripe, the secretive $20bn start-up driving Apple, Amazon and Facebook.* Available at: https://www.wired.co.uk/article/stripe-payments-apple-amazon-facebook [Accessed 25 Jun. 2023].
18. Wenzel, M. (2021). *Miro's explosive success: A case study in intuitive design and product-led growth.* Available at: https://uxdesign.cc/miros-explosive-success-a-case-study-in-intuitive-design-and-product-led-growth-4e91b5179f56 [Accessed 25 Jun. 2023].
19. Hartmans, A. (2023). *Peloton's massive recall of 2.1 million bikes is the latest blow as the company struggles to turn things around. here's how the fitness leader went from a pandemic-era success story to losing money and slashing workers.* Available at: https://www.businessinsider.in/retail/news/peloton-went-from-a-pandemic-era-success-story-worth-50-billion-to-laying-off-20-of-its-workforce-heres-how-the-companys-meteoric-rise-turned-into-an-equally-swift-fall-/articleshow/89530545.cms [Accessed 25 Jun. 2023].
20. Mayfield (2023). *The Hashicorp journey: The rise of a cloud powerhouse.* Available at: https://www.mayfield.com/the-hashicorp-journey-the-rise-of-a-cloud-powerhouse/ [Accessed 25 Jun. 2023].
21. Contrary Research (2023). *Patreon* . Available at: https://research.contrary.com/reports/patreon [Accessed 25 Jun. 2023].
22. Contrary Research (2023). *Gong.* Available at: https://research.contrary.com/reports/gong (Accessed: 25 June 2023).
23. Kindig, B. (2021). *Hybrid work is here to stay and asana will be a key beneficiary.* Available at: https://www.forbes.com/sites/bethkindig/2021/12/17/hybrid-work-is-here-to-stay-and-asana-will-be-a-key-beneficiary/?sh=1fa952257d57 [Accessed 25 Jun. 2023].
24. Aggarwal, G. (2022). *Why mentorship is as important as funding in the process of becoming a successful start-up.* Available at: https://www.entrepreneur.com/en-in/leadership/why-mentorship-is-as-important-as-funding-in-the-process-of/424020 [Accessed 25 Jun. 2023].

CHAPTER 14
The Importance of Energy in a Start-up and Maintaining that Energy

An intangible yet palpable force permeates successful start-ups—a soul, an energy, a presence that captivates the company's spirit.[1] Founders can inject this energy, while employees and customers, in turn, feel its resonance deep within themselves. This energy inspires individuals to contribute to the organization's success, propelling it forward with unwavering enthusiasm. Engagement soars as long as the dynamism remains and the start-up maintains its agility. If this energy wane, the once vibrant and unique qualities that define the venture may gradually dissipate. In essence, the effectiveness of a start-up is intricately linked to the collective human energy it harnesses. In their illuminating book, "The Positive Leader: How Energy and Happiness Fuel Top-Performing Teams," Jan Mühlfeit and Melina Costi assert that to lead by example and rally those under your guidance, you must embody the role of the energetic entrepreneur within the organization. By assuming this pivotal position, you can effectively manage your energy and your team's. Recognizing the signs of exhaustion as the workweek draws to a close or witnessing the early stages of burnout among board members are crucial indications that it is time to pace the team for a marathon rather than a sprint.

In start-ups, energy[2] is the lifeblood that fuels progress, ignites innovation, and fosters a sense of purpose among all stakeholders. The driving force propels entrepreneurs and employees to surpass their limits, push boundaries, and chart new territories. The energy within a start-up breathes life into its vision, shaping the culture and attracting like-minded individuals who share the passion and commitment to realize its goals. Yet, the road to success is challenging; sustaining this energy becomes paramount. As an energetic entrepreneur, you safeguard and cultivate your start-up's collective spirit. You can ensure sustained engagement, motivation, and dedication by proactively managing your energy levels and your team's. Through strategic planning, effective communication, and fostering a positive work environment, you can create a virtuous cycle that nourishes the energy within your start-up, leading to continued growth and prosperity. The following chapter will explore the various dimensions of energy within a start-up and uncover the fundamental principles and practices that facilitate its cultivation. From harnessing the power of purpose-driven leadership to promoting employee well-being and resilience, we will delve into the strategies and insights that successful start-ups employ to maintain their energy and create a thriving organizational ecosystem. In this chapter, we invite you on a transformative journey where you will discover the significance of energy in the start-up landscape and gain invaluable insights into the art of maintaining and nurturing this elusive yet essential force. By understanding energy dynamics, you will be equipped with the tools and knowledge to become an energetic entrepreneur, leading your start-up to unparalleled heights of success, innovation, and lasting impact. Get ready to unlock the power within your start-up and embark on a path of boundless energy and endless possibilities.

The Essence Of Energy In Start-Ups

In the fast-paced and highly competitive world of start-ups, energy is a driving force that propels entrepreneurs to overcome challenges, seize opportunities, and succeed. In the context of start-ups, energy refers to the enthusiasm, passion, and motivation permeating every aspect of the entrepreneurial journey. It is the vital ingredient that fuels innovation, resilience, and the ability to navigate the unpredictable nature of the start-up landscape. The significance of energy in start-ups and how it contributes to their growth and ultimate triumph cannot be understated. Start-ups are often born out of a spark—an initial burst of energy that ignites the entrepreneurial journey. This spark can be fueled by various factors, such as a compelling vision, a problem worth solving, or a passion for disrupting the status quo. An unwavering belief in their ideas drives entrepreneurs with this initial energy and the determination to see them through. This spark sets them on a path of exploration, innovation, and building something meaningful. Energy is not solely an individual attribute but also a collective force that permeates the start-up culture.[3] Cultivating a positive work environment is crucial for sustaining energy levels within the team. When entrepreneurs foster a supportive atmosphere where employees feel valued, empowered, and encouraged to take risks, it creates an ecosystem that fuels energy and fosters creativity.

The importance of energy in start-ups lies in its ability to fuel entrepreneurial resilience. Start-ups are no strangers to challenges and obstacles. They face a myriad of uncertainties, from funding constraints to market volatility. The ability to weather storms, bounce back from failure, and adapt to changing circumstances requires a reservoir of energy and resilience. Entrepreneurs with high energy levels exhibit a tenacious spirit that enables them to view setbacks as opportunities for growth and learning. They use their energy to fuel determination, persistence, and the ability to pivot when necessary. Energy is also closely intertwined with passion. Passionate entrepreneurs infuse their start-ups with a contagious enthusiasm that attracts investors, employees, and customers alike. This energy and passion are powerful driving forces that propel the start-up forward. It creates a sense of purpose, a shared belief in the mission, and a compelling story that resonates with stakeholders. This emotional connection formed through energy and passion can be the differentiating factor that propels a start-up from mediocrity to success. Maintaining energy in a start-up is equally essential as igniting it. Entrepreneurs must take proactive measures to sustain their energy levels. I have elaborated based on three aspects - unleashing the start-up energy, where you will read about how to get started. It is followed by inspiring engagement and contribution, which you must regard as essential to getting the right energy. I have also written about the pitfalls of energy drain, which will help you understand why there are better solutions than overdoing.

Unleashing The Start-Up Energy

Start-up energy is a powerful force that drives entrepreneurs to reach new heights and achieve extraordinary results.[4] This energy fuels innovation, propels growth, and sets start-ups apart. However, unleashing and harnessing this energy requires deliberate actions and strategies. One of the primary ways to unleash start-up energy is by establishing a clear and compelling vision. A visionary leader who can articulate a bold and inspiring vision creates a sense of purpose that energizes the entire team. The vision should not only focus on the start-up's mission but also outline the impact it aims to make in the world. When team members can connect their work to a larger purpose and see the positive change they drive, it ignites a sense of passion and fuels their energy. Another crucial aspect of unleashing start-up energy is fostering an environment that encourages autonomy and ownership. When entrepreneurs empower their team members to make decisions, take risks, and contribute their unique ideas, it instills a sense of ownership and autonomy. This autonomy allows individuals to tap into their creativity, take the initiative, and fully utilize their skills and expertise. This sense of ownership and empowerment fuels their energy and commitment to the start-up's success.

To further unleash start-up energy, fostering a culture of continuous learning and experimentation is essential. Start-ups thrive on innovation, which requires a mindset that embraces learning from successes and failures. Entrepreneurs should encourage their team members to experiment, try new approaches, and not fear failure. When mistakes are seen as valuable learning opportunities rather than reasons for punishment, it creates an environment where energy is channeled toward growth and improvement. Creating a sense of camaraderie and a shared sense of purpose is also crucial to unleashing start-up energy. Entrepreneurs should foster a collaborative and supportive culture where team members feel connected and aligned with the start-up's goals. Regular team-building activities, open communication channels, and celebrating milestones help build a sense of belonging and create a positive energy within the start-up. Establishing a feedback loop is also crucial for unleashing start-up energy. Regular and constructive feedback helps individuals understand their strengths and areas for improvement and align their efforts with the start-up's goals. Additionally, seeking feedback from team members and incorporating their ideas and suggestions fosters a sense of empowerment and shows that their input is valued, leading to increased energy and engagement. Celebrating big and small successes is also a powerful way to unleash start-up energy.

Inspiring Engagement And Contribution

In start-ups, engagement and contribution from team members are vital for driving innovation, achieving goals, and maintaining the momentum needed for success. When individuals feel engaged and valued, their energy and enthusiasm catalyze growth and progress. There are numerous strategies entrepreneurs can employ to inspire engagement and foster a culture of contribution within their start-ups. One of the key drivers of engagement is effective leadership. Entrepreneurs must lead by example, demonstrating a genuine passion for the start-up's mission and values. By embodying these values and consistently displaying enthusiasm, entrepreneurs create an environment that inspires team members to contribute their best efforts. Leaders should actively communicate the start-up's purpose and encourage open dialogue, ensuring that team members feel connected to the overall vision and have a voice in shaping its direction. Building trust is another crucial factor in inspiring engagement and contribution. Entrepreneurs must create an environment where team members feel safe to take risks, share ideas, and collaborate without fear of judgment or retribution. Transparent communication, active listening, and fostering an inclusive culture are essential for establishing trust within the start-up.

Entrepreneurs should also emphasize the importance of individual growth and development to inspire engagement.[5] Providing opportunities for skill-building, training, and professional advancement shows team members that their personal growth is valued. By investing in their development, entrepreneurs demonstrate their commitment to their employees' long-term success, which in turn fosters a sense of loyalty and engagement. When individuals feel supported in their growth journey, they are more likely to contribute their skills, knowledge, and energy to propel the start-up forward. Creating a culture of recognition and appreciation plays a significant role in inspiring engagement and contribution. Entrepreneurs should actively acknowledge and celebrate the efforts and achievements of team members. Regularly expressing gratitude, publicly recognizing accomplishments, and implementing reward and recognition programs instill a sense of pride and motivation among employees. Feeling appreciated and valued for their contributions boosts morale, encourages continued engagement, and fuels the overall energy within the start-up. By promoting collaboration and inclusion, entrepreneurs tap into their team members' collective energy and expertise, fostering a culture of contribution. Giving team members autonomy and the opportunity to take on meaningful responsibilities inspires engagement and contribution, which are crucial steps.

The Pitfalls Of Energy Drain

While energy is a valuable asset in start-ups, entrepreneurs must be aware of the potential pitfalls that can lead to energy drain.[6] Significant depletion of motivation, enthusiasm, and passion decreases productivity and hinders progress. Some pitfalls that can drain energy within start-ups are not unusual, and certain strategies can help you mitigate their impact. One of the primary causes of energy drain is burnout. Start-up entrepreneurs often work long hours, face high stress levels, and experience intense pressure to succeed. It can lead to exhaustion and a lack of work-life balance, ultimately draining their energy. To prevent burnout, entrepreneurs should prioritize self-care and well-being. Taking breaks, maintaining a healthy lifestyle, and setting boundaries between work and personal life are crucial for preserving energy and preventing burnout. Additionally, delegating tasks, seeking support from the team, and practicing effective time management can alleviate the workload and avoid energy depletion. A lack of alignment with the start-up's mission and values can lead to an energy drain. When individuals feel disconnected from the purpose and values of the start-up, their motivation and energy suffer. Entrepreneurs should regularly communicate the start-up's mission, reinforce its values, and ensure that team members understand the larger vision.

Another common pitfall is a negative work environment. Toxic cultures, micromanagement, and lack of recognition can drain the energy and motivation of individuals within a start-up. Entrepreneurs should foster a positive work environment with open communication, mutual respect, and a culture of appreciation. Regularly recognizing and celebrating achievements, providing constructive feedback, and promoting a healthy work-life balance contribute to a positive atmosphere that energizes team members and enhances their productivity. Unclear goals and lack of direction can also contribute to energy drain. When individuals don't determine what they are working towards or how their efforts contribute to the larger picture, their motivation can dwindle. Inadequate resources and support can also drain energy within start-ups. When team members need more tools, training, or support to perform their tasks effectively, frustration and energy drain can occur. Entrepreneurs should invest in providing the resources and support needed for success. It can include training programs, mentorship opportunities, and access to technology or software streamlining workflows. By equipping their team members with the necessary resources, entrepreneurs can empower them to perform at their best and maintain their energy levels. A lack of work-life balance also significantly contributes to energy drain.

Becoming An Energetic Entrepreneur

Being an energetic entrepreneur[7] is fundamental to driving success and growth within a start-up. The energy and passion entrepreneurs bring to their work fuel their motivation and energize their team members. Entrepreneurs who cultivate certain qualities and strategies can become energetic leaders and create a positive and energizing environment within their start-ups. One of the core qualities of an energetic entrepreneur is self-motivation. Successful entrepreneurs possess an innate drive and determination to relentlessly overcome obstacles and pursue their goals. They are driven by a deep sense of purpose and a belief in their vision, which enhances their zeal and commitment. Energetic entrepreneurs proactively seek out challenges, view setbacks as opportunities for growth, and maintain a resilient mindset. Their unwavering self-motivation catalyzes inspiring and energizing their team members. Another crucial quality is a relentless focus on personal growth and development. Energetic entrepreneurs understand the importance of continuous learning and self-improvement. They actively seek new knowledge, skills, and perspectives to enhance their leadership abilities. By investing in their growth, they expand their expertise and broaden their horizons, energizing their problem-solving and decision-making approach. Energetic entrepreneurs also prioritize their physical and mental well-being, recognizing that maintaining their energy levels is essential for leading effectively.

Effective communication is also a crucial strategy energetic entrepreneurs employ to create an energizing environment within their start-ups. Energetic entrepreneurs actively listen to their team members, value their input, and encourage open dialogue. They communicate expectations, provide feedback, and offer guidance in a constructive and inspiring manner. By fostering open and transparent communication, energetic entrepreneurs create a sense of trust, engagement, and collaboration within their teams. Building a strong and cohesive team is another essential aspect of becoming an energetic entrepreneur. Energetic entrepreneurs recognize the value of surrounding themselves with talented individuals who share their vision and passion. They hire team members with diverse perspectives and skills, creating a dynamic and energizing workforce. They also empower their team members to take ownership of their work. Energetic entrepreneurs are also adept at setting clear goals and maintaining a laser-like focus on achieving them. They understand the importance of defining challenging yet attainable objectives, and they communicate these goals effectively to their team members. Energetic entrepreneurs break down larger goals into smaller, actionable steps, creating a sense of progress and momentum. They regularly monitor progress, celebrate milestones, and adjust strategies as needed. To help you become an energetic entrepreneur, I have written about embracing the role of the energetic entrepreneur, managing team energy, and pacing for the marathon, not the sprint. Reading these will enable you to design your role as an energetic entrepreneur to fruition.

Embracing The Role Of The Energetic Entrepreneur

As an entrepreneur, embracing[8] the role of the energetic entrepreneur is essential for driving success and creating a positive and motivating environment within a start-up. First and foremost, embracing the energetic entrepreneur's role requires a deep passion and enthusiasm for the start-up's mission and goals. Energetic entrepreneurs genuinely believe in what they are building and are fueled by a burning desire to make a difference. Their infectious passion energizes them and inspires their team members to share that excitement. By embodying the vision and values of the start-up, they create a sense of purpose and ignite a collective drive for success. In addition to passion, energetic entrepreneurs are driven by a strong work ethic and a relentless commitment to achieving their goals. Their behavior should reflect their principles, demonstrating a willingness to put in the time, effort, and dedication required to succeed. Energetic entrepreneurs understand that their actions speak louder than words, and their undeterred commitment motivates their team members to match their level of dedication. By consistently displaying a strong work ethic, they create a culture of excellence and inspire their team members to go above and beyond. Embracing the role of the energetic entrepreneur also involves embracing the responsibility of leading and guiding a team and being compassionate. It is more about understanding than it is about power.

Embracing the role of the energetic entrepreneur also requires adaptability and a willingness to embrace change. Start-ups operate in dynamic and rapidly evolving environments, and energetic entrepreneurs understand the importance of staying agile and responsive to market trends and customer needs. They proactively seek new opportunities, embrace innovation, and are unafraid to take calculated risks. By encouraging a culture of adaptability and embracing change, energetic entrepreneurs create an environment responsive to challenges and primed for growth. Embracing the role of the energetic entrepreneur also involves effective communication and collaboration. Energetic entrepreneurs understand the power of effective communication. They are skilled communicators who can articulate their ideas, provide clear direction, and actively listen to their team members' input. Energetic entrepreneurs understand that the journey of a start-up is not without its obstacles and failures. However, they maintain a positive mindset and view setbacks as opportunities for growth and learning. They bounce back from adversity quickly, adapt their strategies, and inspire their team members to do the same.

Managing Team Energy

Managing team energy is a critical responsibility for entrepreneurs in ensuring a start-up's overall productivity, engagement, and success. Key mantras include identifying and implementing effective strategies and practices for managing team energy and creating a positive and energizing work environment. One of the primary strategies for managing team energy is fostering a positive and supportive work culture. Entrepreneurs should strive to create an environment where team members feel valued, respected, and motivated. It also involves providing opportunities for personal and professional growth. By creating a positive work culture, entrepreneurs can cultivate a sense of belonging and satisfaction among team members, directly contributing to their energy levels and overall engagement. Undertaking clear goal-understanding exercises is another important aspect of managing team energy. Monitoring progress, providing feedback, and celebrating achievements are crucial for maintaining high team energy levels and motivation. Effective delegation is a critical practice in managing team energy. Entrepreneurs should empower their team members by delegating tasks and responsibilities that align with their strengths and interests. Delegation helps distribute the workload and allows team members to feel a sense of ownership and autonomy in their work.

Recognizing and rewarding team members' contributions[9] is essential for managing team energy. Entrepreneurs should establish a culture of appreciation and acknowledgment where team members' efforts and successes are regularly recognized. Striking a balance of perspectives in the business is also crucial. Listening to what everyone has to say and collectively deciding the business's best interest are important strategies to consider. Entrepreneurs should also encourage their team members to prioritize self-care and well-being. It may involve implementing flexible work arrangements, encouraging breaks and vacations, and promoting healthy work-life integration. Recognizing that burnout and exhaustion can drain team members' energy, entrepreneurs should support a healthy balance between work and personal life, ultimately contributing to higher productivity and sustained energy levels. Regular team-building activities and social interactions can also play a significant role in managing team energy. Entrepreneurs should create opportunities for team members to connect and bond outside of their daily work tasks. Entrepreneurs can create positive team dynamics by fostering camaraderie and building strong relationships within the team. Furthermore, effective conflict resolution is crucial for managing team energy.

Pacing For The Marathon, Not The Sprint

One of the most critical aspects of entrepreneurial success is understanding the importance of pacing for the marathon, not the sprint.[10] Start-ups are often associated with a fast-paced and high-pressure environment, which can lead to burnout and diminished energy levels if not managed properly. It would be best if you always embraced the significance of pacing and maintaining sustainable energy throughout your entrepreneurial journey. In this regard, entrepreneurs must recognize that building a successful start-up is a long-term endeavor. It requires consistent effort and perseverance over an extended period. While initial bursts of energy and enthusiasm are essential, it is equally crucial to pace oneself and maintain a sustainable energy level throughout the journey. It means avoiding the temptation to push too hard in the early stages and understanding that success is achieved through incremental progress and continuous learning. Taking breaks and allowing oneself to recharge is not a sign of weakness but a necessary part of maintaining long-term energy. By caring for their well-being, entrepreneurs can lead by example and encourage their team members to prioritize self-care. Time management and prioritization are also essential for maintaining sustainable energy. Entrepreneurs should focus on high-impact tasks and avoid getting overwhelmed by trying to do everything simultaneously.

Delegating tasks and leveraging team members' strengths is another crucial aspect of pacing for the marathon. Entrepreneurs should recognize that they cannot do everything themselves and that empowering others to take on responsibilities is vital to preserving energy. By effectively delegating tasks and trusting their team members, entrepreneurs can free up their time and create a sense of ownership and empowerment among their employees. Delegation allows for a more balanced workload, prevents burnout, and keeps the team's energy levels high. Embracing a growth mindset is essential when pacing for the long run. Entrepreneurs should view setbacks and challenges as opportunities for learning and growth rather than roadblocks. This mindset shift allows them to maintain their energy and motivation even in the face of adversity. Rather than becoming discouraged by failures, entrepreneurs with a growth mindset see them as valuable lessons contributing to their personal and professional development. This resilience and ability to adapt to changing circumstances are vital for maintaining sustained energy levels over time. Another strategy for pacing effectively is to create a support network. Engaging in networking events, joining entrepreneurial communities, and seeking mentorship allow entrepreneurs to gain insights, learn from others' experiences, and find inspiration.

Cultivating And Sustaining Energy In Start-Ups

Cultivating and sustaining energy[11] in start-ups is crucial to driving success, maintaining motivation, and fostering a positive work environment. I have written about some key strategies and practices entrepreneurs can employ to cultivate and sustain energy within their start-ups. One of the fundamental strategies for cultivating and sustaining energy is creating a clear and compelling vision for the start-up. A strong vision provides a sense of purpose and direction, driving the energy and motivation of the entire team. Entrepreneurs should communicate the vision effectively, ensuring every team member understands and aligns with the overarching goals and objectives. By connecting the work of each individual to the bigger picture, entrepreneurs can create a sense of shared purpose and ignite a collective energy that propels the start-up forward. Building a strong and cohesive team is another critical factor in cultivating and sustaining energy. Entrepreneurs should invest time and effort in hiring individuals with the necessary skills and expertise that align with the start-up's values and culture. A diverse team with complementary strengths and a shared commitment to the mission creates a dynamic and energizing work environment.

Continuous learning and innovation are vital in cultivating and sustaining energy within a start-up. Entrepreneurs should promote a culture of curiosity, experimentation, and learning from failures. Encouraging team members to acquire new skills, explore innovative ideas, and challenge the status quo not only keeps the energy levels high but also drives the growth and competitiveness of the start-up. By fostering a learning mindset, entrepreneurs create an environment that thrives on innovation, adaptability, and continuous improvement, leading to sustained energy and progress. Effective communication is a cornerstone of cultivating and sustaining energy in start-ups. Entrepreneurs should establish open and transparent communication channels, ensuring that information flows freely and team members feel heard and valued. Regularly sharing updates, providing feedback, and actively listening to the ideas and concerns of team members fosters a sense of belonging and trust. By facilitating effective communication, entrepreneurs can build strong relationships, enhance collaboration, and maintain high energy and engagement within the start-up. I have divided this section further into three important dimensions. These are purpose-driven leadership and energy, innovation, and adaptability as energy catalysts and strategies for energizing the organizational ecosystem. You must read these elaborations with a focus to enhance your understanding of the underlying theme of this chapter.

Purpose-Driven Leadership And Energy

Purpose-driven leadership[12] is pivotal in cultivating and sustaining energy within a start-up. Entrepreneurs who lead with a clear purpose inspire and motivate their team members to invest their energy and effort into the collective vision. There is a deep connection between purpose-driven leadership and energy and how entrepreneurs can effectively harness purpose to drive motivation and engagement. A purpose-driven leader deeply understands and communicates the "why" behind the start-up's existence. They can articulate a compelling vision and mission that resonates with the team members. By connecting the start-up's work to a higher purpose, entrepreneurs infuse it with meaning and create a sense of shared values and passion. This alignment between individual and organizational purpose ignites a powerful energy that fuels motivation and commitment. When entrepreneurs embody purpose in their leadership, they inspire their team members to find meaning and fulfillment in their work. By emphasizing the impact and value that the start-up brings to the world, purpose-driven leaders tap into the intrinsic motivation of their team members. When individuals can connect their daily tasks and responsibilities to a larger purpose, their energy and enthusiasm naturally increase. They feel fulfilled and proud to contribute to something meaningful, fueling their commitment and dedication.

Purpose-driven leaders also foster a culture of autonomy and empowerment within the start-up. They allow their team members to make decisions, take risks, and pursue innovative ideas. Purpose-driven leaders value each individual's unique contributions and expertise by trusting their team and delegating responsibilities. This empowerment enhances team members' energy and motivation and promotes a sense of ownership and accountability. Moreover, purpose-driven leaders lead by example and demonstrate their unwavering commitment to the start-up's purpose. They show up with enthusiasm, resilience, and a strong work ethic, inspiring their team members to do the same. When team members witness the dedication and passion of their leader, it creates a ripple effect throughout the organization. Purpose-driven leaders inspire others through their actions, modeling the behavior and mindset necessary to sustain high energy and engagement levels. Effective communication is a critical component of purpose-driven leadership. Entrepreneurs must consistently and transparently communicate the start-up's purpose, vision, and progress to their team members. Purpose-driven leaders ensure energy is directed toward the right goals and objectives by keeping everyone informed and connected to the bigger picture.

Innovation And Adaptability As Energy Catalysts

Innovation and adaptability are essential energy catalysts within a start-up environment. As entrepreneurs navigate the dynamic and ever-changing business landscape, the ability to innovate and adapt becomes crucial for sustaining energy and driving success. Innovation is the fuel that propels start-ups forward. It involves generating new ideas, developing creative solutions, and challenging the status quo. Entrepreneurs who foster a culture of innovation inspire their team members to think outside the box and continuously seek improvement. By encouraging experimentation, risk-taking, and learning from failures, they create an environment energized by curiosity and a thirst for progress. Entrepreneurs can cultivate innovation by promoting an open, inclusive atmosphere where ideas are valued and encouraged. They can establish platforms for idea sharing, such as brainstorming sessions, innovation challenges, or designated time for exploration and research. By providing resources, support, and recognition for innovative thinking, entrepreneurs create a sense of empowerment and ownership among team members, which fuels their energy and enthusiasm. Innovation is closely intertwined with adaptability. In a fast-paced and ever-evolving business landscape, start-ups must be able to adapt quickly to changing circumstances, customer needs, and market trends.

Adaptability requires entrepreneurs to encourage a growth mindset among their team members. This mindset fosters a belief that challenges can be overcome and that individuals can develop new skills and capabilities. By promoting a culture of continuous learning[13] and personal development, entrepreneurs create an environment where team members feel energized by the prospect of tackling new challenges and embracing change. Entrepreneurs can also promote adaptability by fostering cross-functional collaboration and communication. By breaking down silos and encouraging knowledge sharing, team members gain exposure to diverse perspectives and experiences. This exposure enhances their ability to adapt and respond to new situations by drawing on the collective knowledge and expertise of the team. Collaboration also fosters camaraderie, boosting energy levels and strengthening the start-up's ability to adapt to change. To cultivate innovation and adaptability as energy catalysts, entrepreneurs should create a safe space for experimentation and risk-taking. Team members must feel empowered to explore new ideas without fear of judgment or failure. Entrepreneurs can establish innovation frameworks or processes that encourage idea generation and provide support for testing and implementing new concepts.

Strategies For Energizing The Organizational Ecosystem

Energizing the organizational ecosystem[14] is essential for creating a vibrant and thriving start-up. Entrepreneurs must employ effective strategies that enhance collaboration, communication, and overall engagement within the company. Fostering a culture of trust and psychological safety is essential. Trust is the foundation of a healthy and energized organizational ecosystem. Entrepreneurs should prioritize building trust among team members by encouraging open communication, active listening, and mutual respect. Creating a psychologically safe environment allows individuals to express their ideas, take risks, and learn from failures without fear of judgment or retribution. When team members feel safe and supported, they are more likely to contribute their energy and creativity to the start-up's success. Promoting collaboration and inclusive interaction is also vital. Collaboration fuels energy and innovation within a start-up. Entrepreneurs should create opportunities for healthy and inclusive collaboration, breaking down silos and encouraging knowledge sharing. By fostering a culture of collaboration, entrepreneurs facilitate the exchange of diverse perspectives, ideas, and expertise.

Entrepreneurs should also encourage autonomy and ownership, as I mentioned earlier. Empowering team members with autonomy and ownership over their work is a powerful energy driver. Entrepreneurs should delegate responsibilities and empower individuals to make decisions within their areas of expertise. Providing autonomy allows team members to take ownership of their work, fostering a sense of accountability and motivation. Entrepreneurs should provide support and resources while offering guidance and feedback to ensure alignment with the overall business mission. Prioritizing the perfect balance is crucial in this regard. Maintaining high energy levels requires attention to employee needs. Entrepreneurs should create a supportive work environment that promotes satisfaction. Embracing continuous learning and growth has become the key. Entrepreneurs should foster a culture of lifelong learning and growth within the organization.[15] Encouraging team members to pursue professional development opportunities, providing access to resources and training programs, and creating a learning-oriented environment energizes the workforce. When individuals have the opportunity to expand their skills and knowledge, they feel engaged, challenged, and motivated.

Companies That Have Decoded The Power Of Energy

Companies that have decoded the power of energy are often led by visionary leaders who possess a clear and inspiring vision for the future. These leaders effectively communicate the company's purpose and mission, aligning their team members' efforts with a collective sense of purpose. They exhibit passion, enthusiasm, and a relentless drive to achieve their goals, inspiring and energizing their workforce. These companies strongly emphasize core values and foster a positive and inclusive culture. They have well-defined values that guide decision-making and behavior throughout the organization. It creates a sense of identity and belonging among team members, promoting a cohesive and energized workforce. The company culture is often characterized by open communication, collaboration, and a focus on continuous learning and improvement. Companies that have mastered the power of energy empower their employees and actively engage them in the decision-making process. They provide opportunities for individuals to contribute their ideas, take ownership of their work, and make a meaningful impact. These companies foster a sense of autonomy, trust, and accountability, allowing employees to channel their energy and creativity into their roles.[16] These organizations are unafraid to challenge the status quo and explore new ideas, products, or processes. Following are some companies that will inspire you as an entrepreneur looking forward to bringing and sustaining the required energy in business.

Root Insurance

Root Insurance[17] is a company that has experienced remarkable growth and success in the insurance industry. Founded in 2015, Root Insurance has disrupted the traditional insurance model by leveraging technology and data analytics to offer its customers personalized and affordable car insurance. The company's unique approach and commitment to innovation and customer-centricity have propelled it to become a major player in the insurance market. One of the key factors contributing to Root Insurance's growth and success is its innovative use of telematics and data-driven underwriting. Unlike traditional insurance companies that rely on demographic factors and historical data, Root Insurance utilizes smartphone technology and telematics devices to gather real-time customer driving data. This data includes factors such as speed, braking patterns, and driving behavior, allowing the company to assess risk more accurately and provide tailored insurance coverage. By leveraging data analytics and machine learning algorithms, Root Insurance can offer customized policies and competitive rates based on individual driving habits, attracting customers who value transparency and fairness in insurance pricing. Root Insurance offers a mobile app that allows customers to obtain a personalized quote by downloading the app and completing a test drive. The app tracks driving behavior, eliminating the need for physical inspections or long questionnaires. The company aims to simplify the insurance experience by providing clear and jargon-free policy documents, offering 24/7 support, and handling claims efficiently.

Company Name: Root Insurance

Founded: 2015

Significant reason(s) for success: The company has been improving its services and features since inception, driving its energy feedback from industries and customers.

Postmates

Postmates[18] is a renowned on-demand delivery platform with significant traction and success in the food and goods delivery industry. Established in 2011, Postmates has revolutionized how people get their favorite meals, groceries, and other products delivered to their doorsteps. The company's innovative approach, commitment to convenience, and a vast network of delivery drivers have played a crucial role in its growth and success. One of the key factors contributing to Postmates' popularity is its user-friendly and intuitive mobile app. The app allows customers to browse various local restaurants and stores, place orders, and track their deliveries in real-time. The seamless and hassle-free ordering process appeals to busy individuals who seek convenience and time-saving solutions. Postmates' app also offers personalized recommendations, order history, and flexible payment options, enhancing the user experience. Postmates has also established a vast network of delivery drivers, often called "Postmates." These drivers, who are independent contractors, play a pivotal role in the company's success. Postmates' platform enables individuals to earn income by delivering orders using vehicles or even bicycles in some cities. This flexible employment model has attracted many drivers, allowing Postmates to provide efficient and reliable delivery services across a wide geographic area. Furthermore, Postmates has cultivated partnerships with various local restaurants, popular chains, and retail stores, broadening its range of offerings for customers. By collaborating with a diverse array of merchants, Postmates can provide a comprehensive selection of food and products to meet the needs and preferences of its customers.

Company Name: Postmates

Founded: 2011

Significant reason(s) for success: The company relies on ensuring that its energy, in terms of relevance, thrives and sustains.

Nubank

Nubank, also known as Nu Pagamentos S.A., is a prominent fintech company based in Brazil that has experienced remarkable growth and success in the financial services industry. Established in 2013, Nubank[19] has disrupted traditional banking by offering innovative and customer-centric digital banking solutions. The company's commitment to simplicity, transparency, and convenience has positioned it as one of the leading fintech unicorns globally. One of the key factors contributing to Nubank's popularity is its flagship product, the Nubank Credit Card. Unlike traditional banks that often impose high fees and complex processes, Nubank provides a no-annual-fee credit card with transparent terms and conditions. The company leverages technology to simplify the application process, allowing customers to apply for a credit card through a user-friendly mobile app. This streamlined approach resonates with individuals who value convenience and transparency in their financial transactions. Additionally, Nubank has capitalized on the growing adoption of mobile banking and digital payments. The company's mobile app is a digital banking platform offering features such as account management, bill payments, money transfers, and investment options. By providing a comprehensive suite of digital banking services, Nubank meets the evolving needs of its customers, who prefer to manage their finances through their smartphones. Nubank has also prioritized customer experience and satisfaction. The company has implemented a customer-centric approach by offering responsive and personalized customer support through various channels, including in-app chat and social media platforms. Nubank values feedback from its users, actively engaging with them to address queries, concerns, and suggestions. This commitment to exceptional customer service has fostered trust and loyalty among its user base.

Company Name: Nubank

Founded: 2013

Significant reason(s) for success: The company considers customers as the energy source, making their operations successful.

Betterment

Betterment is a leading robo-advisory platform that has gained significant recognition and success in the investment industry. Founded in 2008, Betterment[20] has revolutionized how individuals invest and manage their portfolios by leveraging technology and providing personalized investment solutions. The company's commitment to simplicity, low costs, and transparency has positioned it as a prominent player in the fintech space. One of the key factors contributing to Betterment's popularity is its user-friendly and intuitive platform. Betterment offers a seamless digital experience, allowing investors to easily set up an account, define their financial goals, and select an appropriate investment strategy. The platform utilizes advanced algorithms and data-driven insights to provide customized investment recommendations based on an individual's risk tolerance, time horizon, and financial objectives. This approach appeals to novice and experienced investors seeking a hassle-free and accessible investment solution. Another aspect that has contributed to Betterment's success is its emphasis on low-cost investing. The company pioneered the concept of low-cost automated investment management, commonly known as robo-advisory services. By leveraging technology, Betterment has significantly reduced operational costs, enabling it to offer competitive fees compared to traditional investment advisors. This cost advantage has made investment services more accessible to a broader range of investors, democratizing wealth management and financial planning. Betterment has also prioritized transparency in its operations. Through its online dashboard, investors can easily track their portfolios, review historical performance, and access detailed breakdowns of their holdings. This level of transparency instills confidence in investors, allowing them to make informed decisions and monitor their investments effectively.

Company Name: Betterment

Founded: 2009

Significant reason(s) for success: The company has maintained its transparency across operations. Transparency acts as a catalyst for maintaining energy across any business.

Lime

Lime is a prominent transportation company that has significantly impacted urban mobility. Founded in 2017, Lime offers electric scooters, electric bikes, and electric mopeds as convenient and eco-friendly alternatives for short-distance transportation. The company's focus on sustainability, accessibility, and innovation has contributed to its growth and success. One key characteristic that sets Lime apart is its commitment to sustainability. Lime[21] aims to reduce carbon emissions and alleviate traffic congestion in urban areas by providing electric-powered vehicles. Electric scooters and bikes offer a clean and efficient mode of transportation, helping to promote environmental stewardship and support the transition to sustainable mobility options. Lime has also established itself as a pioneer in the sharing economy. The company's platform allows users to locate, rent, and ride its electric vehicles through a mobile app. This convenient and on-demand approach aligns with the changing preferences and behaviors of urban dwellers who seek flexible transportation solutions. Lime's intuitive app interface and seamless unlocking and payment process have made it easy for users to access and utilize their vehicles. Moreover, Lime has focused on making its services accessible to many users. The company operates in numerous cities worldwide, allowing people to access its vehicles in their communities conveniently. Lime's presence in densely populated areas and strategic partnerships with cities and municipalities have helped expand its reach and increase accessibility to its transportation options. This accessibility is particularly beneficial for individuals who do not own personal vehicles or prefer alternative modes of transportation.

Company Name: Lime

Founded: 2017

Significant reason(s) for success: The company has grown significantly by maintaining employees' energy, thus making every initiative hassle-free.

Glossier

Glossier[22] is a highly successful beauty and skincare brand that has garnered a significant following and disrupted the traditional beauty industry. Founded in 2014 by Emily Weiss, Glossier has gained popularity for its minimalist approach to beauty, emphasis on inclusivity, and strong engagement with its community of customers. One key characteristic defining Glossier is its focus on natural, effortless beauty. The brand embraces a less-is-more philosophy, encouraging individuals to enhance their natural features rather than mask them. Glossier's product lineup consists of simple, high-quality skincare and makeup essentials designed to enhance and nourish the skin, providing a fresh and dewy look. This approach resonates with consumers who prefer a more natural and understated beauty aesthetic. Glossier has also become known for its commitment to inclusivity. The brand recognizes the diversity of its customer base and aims to create products that cater to a wide range of skin types, tones, and textures. Glossier's inclusive approach extends beyond product formulation to marketing and brand representation. The company features diverse models and embraces real and relatable individuals in its advertising campaigns, challenging conventional beauty standards and promoting a sense of inclusivity and acceptance. Furthermore, Glossier has fostered a strong sense of community and connection with its customers. The brand engages with its audience through social media platforms, inviting them to share their experiences, reviews, and beauty routines. Glossier's online community, often called the "Glossier fandom," has become a space for beauty enthusiasts to connect, share tips, and celebrate the brand's products.

Company Name: Glossier

Founded: 2014

Significant reason(s) for success: The company has maintained energy in the company and outside of it by listening to customers and giving then what they want.

Brex

Brex is a financial technology company that provides innovative financial solutions tailored for start-ups and small businesses. Founded in 2017, Brex aims to address entrepreneurs' unique financial challenges and help them navigate the complexities of managing their business finances. One of the critical characteristics of Brex is its focus on simplifying and streamlining financial processes for start-ups. The company offers a range of financial products and services, including corporate credit cards, expense management software, cash management accounts, and business rewards programs. These solutions give start-ups greater control and visibility over their finances, allowing them to make more informed decisions and manage their cash flow effectively. One of the standout features of Brex[23] is its corporate credit card offering. Unlike traditional credit cards, Brex offers credit cards specifically designed for start-ups, with features and benefits that cater to their unique needs. Start-ups can obtain a Brex credit card without requiring a personal guarantee or a credit history. Instead, Brex relies on alternative data sources and technology to underwrite credit limits, making it more accessible for early-stage companies to access credit and manage their expenses. In addition to credit cards, Brex provides an integrated expense management software that simplifies the tracking and reconciliation of business expenses. The platform allows businesses to capture receipts, categorize expenses, and generate real-time reports, reducing the administrative burden and providing greater visibility into spending patterns. This streamlined expense management process helps start-ups save time and ensure compliance with accounting and tax requirements. Brex also offers cash management accounts that give start-ups a centralized platform to manage their funds. These accounts include high-yield interest rates, unlimited transfers, and intuitive online banking interfaces. By consolidating their banking needs within Brex's cash management accounts, start-ups can streamline their financial operations and optimize their cash utilization.

Company Name: Brex

Founded: 2017

Significant reason(s) for success: The company is known for its unique visibility and expense management feature integration. Brex listens to customers, thus enabling the business to sustain the growth energy throughout.

Conclusion

The essence of energy in a start-up cannot be overstated. As entrepreneurs embark on their journey to build and grow their businesses, it is crucial to recognize that energy is the lifeblood that fuels innovation, resilience, and success. From unleashing the start-up energy within oneself to inspiring engagement and contribution from team members, and from embracing the role of an energetic entrepreneur to cultivating and sustaining energy throughout the organization, the commitment to maintaining a high level of energy becomes the driving force behind breakthrough ideas, relentless pursuit of goals, and unwavering determination in the face of challenges. The pitfalls of energy drain are ever-present, but by understanding and addressing these challenges head-on, entrepreneurs can navigate the obstacles and safeguard the vitality of their start-ups. Pacing oneself for the marathon, not the sprint, enables entrepreneurs to sustain their energy and avoid burnout while maintaining a clear sense of purpose and prioritizing self-care. The examples set by companies that have decoded the power of energy serve as inspirations, demonstrating that a strategic focus on energy can lead to remarkable achievements, disruptive innovations, and exceptional growth. As entrepreneurs reflect on the insights shared within this chapter, they are encouraged to embrace the importance of energy in their start-ups and commit to maintaining and nurturing it throughout their entrepreneurial journey.

An energetic entrepreneur sets the tone and leads by example, inspiring and motivating team members to bring their best selves to the table. The infectious energy permeates the company culture, fostering a sense of enthusiasm, collaboration, and a shared commitment to success. This dynamic and vibrant environment attracts top talent and cultivates a supportive ecosystem where everyone feels valued and empowered to contribute their unique skills and ideas. Let the flame of energy burn bright, and may it illuminate how entrepreneurs build thriving start-ups that leave a lasting legacy. I have summed up the most crucial points of this chapter below to help you keep referring to them as and when required:

1. Understand the essence of energy in start-ups before you set out to get it right.
2. Unleashing the start-up energy is essential for your entrepreneurial success, especially in the longer run.
3. Inspiring engagement and contribution of people around you will help you realize your vision with lesser challenges.
4. You must be aware of the pitfalls of an energy drain so as to not lose focus on aspects that require your undeterred attention.

5. Demonstrating the short-term traits of an energetic entrepreneur is easy, but sustaining this energy is more important.
6. If you know why you wish to embrace the role of the energetic entrepreneur, you will make long-term progress.
7. Managing team energy is as crucial as prioritizing your own energy. If the team around you is in the right spirit, then your job will be hassle-free.
8. Go for the marathon and not for the sprint. I have emphasized this point enough throughout the book. Long-term priorities for any entrepreneur are more beneficial than short-term hits that do not last.
9. Cultivating and sustaining energy in start-ups cannot be done by an individual; this requires persistent collective effort and dedication.
10. Purpose-driven leadership and energy will give way to an impact that will be enduring in terms of achievements and progress.
11. Innovation and adaptability are the right energy catalysts.
12. You must focus on strategies for energizing the organizational ecosystem. These will increase the productivity of your business and empower your employees to safeguard the energy built.

References

1. Smith, J. (2013). *How to keep your entrepreneurial spirit alive as the company you work for grows, Forbes.* Available at: https://www.forbes.com/sites/jacquelynsmith/2013/10/22/how-to-keep-your-entrepreneurial-spirit-alive-as-the-company-you-work-for-grows/?sh=2569f4ddc0d4 [Accessed 2 Jul. 2023].
2. Remley, M. (2020). *Council post: Maintaining a strong start-up culture in a remote work environment.* Available at: https://www.forbes.com/sites/forbestechcouncil/2020/12/21/maintaining-a-strong-startup-culture-in-a-remote-work-environment/?sh=3c9b6a54c2f7 [Accessed 2 Jul. 2023].
3. FasterCapital (2023). *The importance of start-up team.* Available at: https://fastercapital.com/content/The-Importance-Of-Startup-Team.html [Accessed 2 Jul. 2023].

4. Muehl, S. (2019). *How to get the team excited about your next release.* Available at: https://medium.com/agileinsider/how-to-get-the-team-excited-about-your-next-release-8293bcadef01 [Accessed 2 Jul. 2023].
5. Zwilling, M. (2011). *Ten steps to build real start-up team engagement.* Available at: https://www.forbes.com/sites/martinzwilling/2011/04/09/ten-steps-to-build-real-startup-team-engagement/?sh=1d6e7d966655 [Accessed 2 Jul. 2023].
6. Kumar, D. (2021). *How to make unicorns and stop the start-up drain.* Available at: https://indianexpress.com/article/opinion/startups-india-economy-7194625/ [Accessed 2 Jul. 2023].
7. Patel, D. (2018). *14 effective ways for entrepreneurs to boost their energy throughout the day.* Available at: https://www.entrepreneur.com/living/14-effective-ways-for-entrepreneurs-to-boost-their-energy/319788 [Accessed 2 Jul. 2023].
8. Michail, J. (2023). *How your entrepreneurial spirit can lead the way in crisis.* Available at: https://www.entrepreneur.com/leadership/how-your-entrepreneurial-spirit-can-lead-the-way-in-crisis/450397 [Accessed 2 Jul. 2023].
9. Matz, N. (2022). *4 ways to motivate your start-up team and get major results.* Available at: https://www.entrepreneur.com/leadership/4-ways-to-motivate-your-startup-team-and-get-major-results/403631 [Accessed 2 Jul. 2023].
10. Wong, K. (2014). *Start-ups are a marathon, not a sprint: Run at your own pace.* Available at: https://www.forbes.com/sites/kylewong/2014/11/12/startups-are-a-marathon-not-a-sprint-run-at-your-own-pace/?sh=162f2b16c105 [Accessed 2 Jul. 2023].
11. *Harvard Business Review* (2021). *The soul of a start-up.* Available at: https://hbr.org/2019/07/the-soul-of-a-start-up [Accessed 2 Jul. 2023].
12. Forbes (2020). *Council post: 15 top tips for creating a purpose-driven business.* Available at: https://www.forbes.com/sites/forbesbusinesscouncil/2020/12/18/15-top-tips-for-creating-a-purpose-driven-business/?sh=10a4dd086925 [Accessed 2 Jul. 2023].
13. Rabha, M. (2022). *Why continuous learning is important in this era.* Available at: https://blog.vantagecircle.com/continuous-learning/ [Accessed 2 Jul. 2023].
14. Paulson, M. (2021). *Council post: How to build a start-up ecosystem organization from scratch.* Available at: https://www.forbes.com/sites/forbesbusinesscouncil/2021/06/23/how-to-build-a-startup-ecosystem-organization-from-scratch/?sh=51169ef9117b [Accessed 2 Jul. 2023].

15. Council, Y. E. (2017). *Council post: Top benefits of focusing on internal growth for your small business.* Available at: https://www.forbes.com/sites/theyec/2017/11/22/top-benefits-of-focusing-on-internal-growth-for-your-small-business/?sh=38a78ca625a2 [Accessed 2 Jul. 2023].
16. Mawer, R. (2022). *Creativity is the backbone of your business. Here's why.* Available at: https://www.entrepreneur.com/starting-a-business/creativity-is-the-backbone-of-your-business-heres-why/440370 [Accessed 2 Jul. 2023].
17. Philip, R. (2021). *Is the root insurance IPO worth investing in?* Available at: https://www.renjitphilip.com/root-insurance-business-model-teardown [Accessed 2 Jul. 2023].
18. *Startup Grind (n.d.) 5 years to overnight success, post-mates nears $500M valuation & 1M deliveries/month.* Available at: https://www.startupgrind.com/blog/5-years-to-overnight-success-postmates-nears-500m-valuation-1m-deliveriesmonth/ [Accessed 2 Jul. 2023].
19. Reich, G. (2022). *How Nubank became one of the world's biggest digital banks.* Available at: https://thefinancialbrand.com/news/fintech-banking/how-nubank-became-the-worlds-biggest-digital-bank-131658/ [Accessed 2 Jul. 2023].
20. Hudson, H. (2022). *3 lessons from betterment on building a customer-centric financial service.* Available at: https://www.zendesk.com/in/blog/3-lessons-betterment-building-customer-centric-financial-service/ [Accessed 2 Jul. 2023].
21. *The SlideTeam Blog* (2022). *Lime company profile, valuation, investors, and original pitch deck included.* Available at: https://www.slideteam.net/blog/lime-company-profile-valuation-investors-and-original-pitch-deck-included [Accessed 2 Jul. 2023].
22. Danziger, P. N. (2022). *5 reasons that Glossier is so successful.* Available at: https://www.forbes.com/sites/pamdanziger/2018/11/07/5-keys-to-beauty-brand-glossiers-success/?sh=6d4ef57c417d [Accessed 2 Jul. 2023].
23. *Contrary Research* (2022). *Report: Brex business breakdown & founding story.* Available at: https://research.contrary.com/reports/brex [Accessed 2 Jul. 2023].

CHAPTER 15
Right Timing for Your Product

In the fast-paced world of start-ups, timing can make or break a company's success. It is not enough to have a groundbreaking idea or a revolutionary product; you must also consider the perfect moment to unveil it to the world.[1] This chapter delves into the importance of timing in the start-up ecosystem, emphasizing its critical role in determining whether your venture thrives or flounders. Imagine your favorite possession, something you cherish and rely on daily, like your smartphone. Now, transport yourself back a couple of decades. Would there have been a market for your beloved device's advanced features and capabilities? Perhaps the technology landscape and consumer expectations would have been vastly different. This extreme example serves as a reminder that to succeed, you must align the launch of your product or service with the prevailing technological advancements, societal attitudes, and customer expectations. Consider the stories of other industry disruptors that harnessed the power of perfect timing. Take the case of Netflix, which revolutionized the way we consume entertainment. In the early 2000s, when the company moved from a DVD-by-mail rental service to a streaming platform, it was met with skepticism. However, as broadband internet became more prevalent and the demand for on-demand content soared, Netflix's timing proved impeccable. By foreseeing the shift towards digital streaming and investing in the right technologies, they positioned themselves as the leader in a new era of home entertainment.

Another example is the success of Peloton, the fitness technology company that offers connected exercise equipment and virtual workout classes. Peloton entered the market when the demand for convenient at-home fitness options steadily increased, and advancements in technology made immersive and interactive workout experiences possible. By tapping into the growing desire for personalized and engaging fitness solutions, Peloton created a loyal following and established itself as a leader in the industry. This chapter explores the art of identifying the right timing for your start-up. We delve into the factors contributing to an opportune moment and provide practical strategies for assessing the market landscape, evaluating technological advancements, and understanding the evolving customer mindset. Timing is an intricate dance between intuition, analysis, and adaptability, and mastering it can significantly enhance your start-up's chances of success. So, join us as we embark on this journey to uncover timing secrets in the start-up world. By the end of this chapter, you will be equipped with the tools and insights needed to navigate the complex interplay of external factors, seize the right moment, and position your venture for long-term triumph. Remember, timing can turn an ordinary start-up into an extraordinary success story.

Assessing Market Landscape

In start-ups, one of the most crucial steps toward success is assessing the market landscape thoroughly.[2] Before launching a product or service, it is essential to gain a comprehensive understanding of the market dynamics, potential competitors, and target audience. This section focuses on the significance of market research and analysis, guiding entrepreneurs through effective market research to gain a competitive advantage and increase their chances of success. Market research plays a pivotal role in the success of any start-up. It gives entrepreneurs the necessary insights to make informed decisions, identify opportunities, and avoid pitfalls. By conducting thorough research, start-ups can uncover valuable data about their industry, target market, and competition, which becomes the bedrock of their business strategy. Knowledge truly is power in start-ups, and market research is the key to unlocking this power. Understanding the market landscape requires entrepreneurs to gather and analyze vast amounts of data, helping them make data-driven decisions instead of relying solely on intuition or gut feelings. By leveraging market research, start-ups can stay ahead of their competition and anticipate shifts in consumer behavior, industry trends, and emerging technologies.

Market research enables start-ups to identify potential challenges and opportunities, minimizing risks and maximizing investment returns. Entrepreneurs with the right information can allocate resources more efficiently, avoiding wasteful spending and directing their efforts towards areas that promise the highest return on investment. Furthermore, the insights gained from market research allow start-ups to tailor their products or services to meet their target audience's specific needs and preferences, leading to increased customer satisfaction and loyalty. At the heart of successful start-ups is the ability to effectively address customer pain points. Market research is instrumental in understanding consumers' pain points in their daily lives or within specific industries. By identifying these pain points, start-ups can develop innovative solutions that cater directly to the needs of their target market. Customer pain points can vary significantly, ranging from common inconveniences to critical problems that have yet to be adequately addressed by existing products or services. Conducting in-depth market research allows entrepreneurs to uncover these pain points, enabling them to develop unique value propositions that resonate deeply with their potential customers. By crafting solutions that alleviate or solve these pain points, start-ups position themselves as problem-solvers and build a loyal customer base. I have elaborated on this and other key points by focusing on three aspects. Firstly, I have written about industry trends and emerging technologies. I have then highlighted the aspect of competitive analysis and market readiness. Lastly, I have written about customer insights and needs.

Industry Trends And Emerging Technologies

In the world of start-ups, staying attuned to industry trends and emerging technologies is paramount. As markets evolve and consumer preferences change, entrepreneurs must proactively identify shifts that can impact their business. Here, I have focused on the significance of monitoring industry trends and emerging technologies and how it can be a game-changer for start-ups seeking the right timing for their products.

Industry trends encompass the collective shifts and developments that shape a particular market or sector. These trends can include changes in consumer behavior, technological advancements, regulatory updates, and shifts in market demand. As a start-up, knowing and analyzing industry trends is crucial for making strategic decisions that can put you ahead of the curve. Monitoring industry trends provides start-ups with insights into potential market opportunities and threats. Recognizing early signs of a growing market segment allows entrepreneurs to effectively position their products or services to meet emerging demands. On the other hand, identifying declining trends enables start-ups to pivot and adapt before it's too late. Ignoring industry trends can lead to missed opportunities and the risk of developing products that become outdated.

Innovation is the lifeblood of successful start-ups, and staying ahead often requires embracing emerging technologies.[3] These technologies are transformative and disruptive and can create entirely new markets. Recognizing and harnessing the power of emerging technologies can give start-ups a competitive edge and propel them to the forefront of their industry. Identifying emerging technologies demands a forward-thinking approach and a willingness to explore beyond the status quo. Start-ups must actively engage with industry forums, tech conferences, and research publications to stay informed about technological advancements. Keeping an eye on early adopters and tech enthusiasts can provide valuable clues about which technologies are gaining momentum and which are mere novelties. Industry trends and emerging technologies often go hand in hand with disruption. Start-ups that actively embrace disruption and leverage it to their advantage can rapidly disrupt established markets and gain a significant market share. Iconic start-ups like Uber, Airbnb, and Netflix exemplify the power of embracing disruptive trends and technologies. The key to leveraging disruption lies in understanding customer needs and pain points and providing innovative solutions that address them more efficiently than traditional offerings. Disruptive start-ups redefine the game's rules, challenging existing norms and pushing the boundaries of what is possible. While embracing disruption carries risks, it also opens the door to unparalleled opportunities for growth and success.

Competitive Analysis And Market Readiness

Assessing the competitive landscape and gauging market readiness are crucial components of a comprehensive market analysis. For start-ups to succeed, they must thoroughly understand their competitors, strengths, weaknesses, and market positioning. Additionally, they need to assess whether the market is ripe for their product or service. Industry competitive analysis thoroughly evaluates existing and potential competitors in the market. It allows start-ups to identify their competition, understand their offerings, and uncover gaps or opportunities that can be leveraged to gain a competitive advantage. One of the primary goals of competitive analysis is to assess the strengths and weaknesses of competitors. By identifying what makes competitors successful and what areas they struggle with, start-ups can devise strategies that play to their strengths and capitalize on the weaknesses of others. Additionally, competitive analysis helps start-ups uncover unique selling propositions (USPs) that set them apart from competitors and appeal to their target audience. Analyzing the competitive landscape also offers insights into pricing strategies, marketing approaches, and customer feedback of competitors.[4] Understanding how competitors price their products or services enables start-ups to position themselves effectively in the market. By evaluating competitors' marketing efforts and customer feedback, entrepreneurs can discover opportunities for differentiation and address pain points the competition does not address.

Market readiness refers to the state of the market in terms of its preparedness to embrace a new product or service. For a start-up, launching a product too early when the market is not ready may result in poor sales or limited interest. Conversely, launching too late may mean missing a golden opportunity and losing the first-mover advantage. There are several factors to consider when assessing market readiness. Customer awareness is crucial; if potential customers are unaware of a problem or the availability of a solution, the market might not be ready. Additionally, the level of competition, regulatory environment, and cultural acceptance of the product can all influence market readiness. Market research plays a significant role in determining market readiness. Surveys, focus groups, and pilot tests can help gauge customer interest and demand for the product. Analyzing industry reports and trends can provide insights into the overall market environment and help entrepreneurs identify favorable conditions for their product launches. Timing the market entry is a delicate balancing act that can make or break a start-up's success. Entrepreneurs must carefully assess the insights gained from competitive analysis and market readiness assessments to determine the optimal moment for launching their products. Entering the market too early may mean facing a lack of demand or skepticism from potential customers. In contrast, entering too late may lead to intense competition and difficulty in establishing a foothold. It is essential to balance being a pioneer and waiting for the market to mature.

Customer Insights And Needs

Customers are the lifeblood of any successful start-up.[5] Understanding their needs, preferences, and pain points is paramount to developing products that resonate with the target audience. Here, I delve into the significance of gaining customer insights and understanding their needs, how to obtain valuable feedback, and the role it plays in identifying the right timing for product launch. Customer insights are the in-depth understandings that entrepreneurs gather about their target audience. These insights provide valuable information about customer behaviors, motivations, and expectations. By gaining customer insights, start-ups can create products that genuinely address customer needs and desires, increasing the chances of product success. There are several methods to gather customer insights. Conducting surveys, interviews, and focus groups allows entrepreneurs to interact directly with potential customers, asking questions and understanding their pain points and aspirations. Analyzing online data, such as social media interactions and customer reviews, provides valuable feedback on customer sentiment and preferences. Furthermore, tracking website analytics and user behavior can offer insights into how customers engage with the start-up's online platforms.

The process of understanding customer needs demands a customer-centric approach. It requires active listening, putting oneself in the customer's shoes, and asking the right questions to reach their pain points' core. Start-ups should strive beyond surface-level desires and explore the emotions and motivations driving their target audience's purchasing decisions. By deeply understanding customer needs, start-ups can develop products that are not only innovative but also provide tangible value to customers. Addressing these needs enables the start-up to establish a meaningful connection with its target audience and fosters long-lasting customer loyalty. Customer insights and needs are crucial in the iterative product development process. Start-ups often release minimum viable products (MVPs) to gather feedback from early adopters and users. This feedback loop allows entrepreneurs to continuously improve their products based on real-world usage and customer input. By actively involving customers in product development, start-ups can build more effective products that meet customer expectations. Customers feel valued and heard when their feedback is incorporated, leading to increased brand loyalty and positive word-of-mouth.

Technological Considerations

In today's digital age, technological considerations are integral to the success of start-ups.[6] Embracing the right technologies can streamline operations, enhance product development, and enable efficient customer adoption. Here, I delve into the significance of technological considerations for start-ups and how leveraging the right technologies can impact their journey toward successful customer adoption. Technology plays a pivotal role in the product development process. Start-ups can leverage various tools and software to design, prototype, and test their products more efficiently. For instance, computer-aided design (CAD) software allows entrepreneurs to create detailed product blueprints and simulate real-world scenarios before investing in physical prototypes. Rapid prototyping technologies like 3D printing enable start-ups to iterate quickly and validate product designs. By harnessing these technologies, start-ups can reduce time-to-market, minimize development costs, and improve product quality. Customer experience is a critical factor in achieving successful customer adoption. Technological considerations play a significant role in optimizing customer experience at every touchpoint. Websites, mobile applications, and online platforms are essential for interacting with customers and delivering seamless experiences. Start-ups should invest in user-friendly interfaces, responsive design, and intuitive navigation to enhance customer interactions.

Data analytics and insights are invaluable tools for start-ups seeking customer adoption. By collecting and analyzing data from various sources, including customer interactions, website traffic, and social media engagements, start-ups can derive valuable insights into customer behavior and preferences. Data analytics enables start-ups to make informed decisions, identify trends, and predict customer needs. Start-ups can use this information to optimize their marketing strategies, tailor product offerings, and enhance customer engagement, ultimately driving successful customer adoption. Scalability is a critical consideration for start-ups aiming for rapid growth. Cloud computing offers scalable solutions that enable start-ups to adjust their resources based on demand. The cloud-based infrastructure allows flexibility, cost-efficiency, and the ability to quickly scale up or down without significant upfront investments. By leveraging cloud computing, start-ups can ensure that their technological infrastructure grows alongside their business, supporting increased customer adoption and business expansion. As start-ups rely more on technology, they must prioritize cybersecurity and data protection. Ensuring the security and confidentiality of customer data is essential to build trust and credibility with customers. Start-ups should implement robust cybersecurity measures, including encryption, firewalls, and regular security audits. Complying with data protection regulations is also crucial to avoid potential legal and reputational consequences. This section is further elaborated into three sub-sections. I have written about technological infrastructure and scalability, followed by a sub-section on development and testing. I have also elaborated on intellectual property and patents.

Technological Infrastructure And Scalability

Technological infrastructure and scalability are foundational considerations for start-ups aiming for successful customer adoption and sustainable growth. Establishing a robust and scalable technological foundation is crucial for supporting the increasing demands of customers and the evolving needs of the business. Here, I explore the significance of technological infrastructure and scalability and how they contribute to achieving customer adoption and long-term success. A robust technological infrastructure forms the backbone of a start-up's operations. It encompasses hardware, software, networks, and systems to support the organization's daily functions and product development. For start-ups, investing in reliable and high-performance hardware and equipment ensures that day-to-day operations run smoothly. Utilizing state-of-the-art software tools like project management platforms and communication applications streamlines internal collaboration and enhances productivity. Additionally, start-ups should consider leveraging cloud computing services that offer scalability and flexibility. Cloud-based infrastructure enables start-ups to access computing resources on demand, scale their operations seamlessly, and reduce the need for significant upfront investments in hardware and servers.

Scalability is the ability of a start-up's technological infrastructure to adapt and expand seamlessly as the business grows.[7] It involves anticipating future needs and designing systems that handle increased demand and data volumes without significant disruptions or performance issues. When start-ups experience rapid growth, their technological infrastructure must be prepared to handle increased website traffic, customer interactions, and data processing. Scalable systems can accommodate these surges without compromising the user experience or operational efficiency. By investing in scalable technologies from the outset, start-ups avoid the need for costly and time-consuming infrastructure overhauls as the business expands. Scalability ensures that the start-up can respond quickly to increasing customer demand, capitalize on opportunities, and maintain a competitive edge. Cloud computing is a powerful enabler of scalability for start-ups. Cloud service providers offer a range of resources, including computing power, storage, and networking, that can be adjusted on-demand to meet changing requirements. Through cloud computing, start-ups can scale their operations up or down as needed, paying only for the resources they use. This flexibility optimizes cost efficiency and allows start-ups to adapt quickly to market fluctuations and customer demand.

Development And Testing

Development and testing are crucial phases in the technological considerations of start-ups.[8] Building a high-quality product and ensuring its reliability is essential for successful customer adoption. It is vital to explore the significance of development and testing in the context of technological considerations and how they contribute to the overall customer adoption journey. Product development is the process of transforming ideas into tangible solutions that address customer needs. For start-ups seeking successful customer adoption, finding the right balance between speed and quality is essential. While speed is crucial for gaining a competitive edge and responding to market demands, it should not come at the expense of product quality. Rushing the development process can lead to critical errors, subpar performance, and dissatisfied customers. Conversely, overly long development cycles can result in missed opportunities and delayed market entry. To strike the right balance, start-ups can adopt an agile development approach. Agile development emphasizes iterative and incremental progress, allowing teams to continuously build and refine the product based on real-world feedback. Start-ups can maintain speed and quality by breaking down the development process into smaller, manageable increments.

Testing and quality assurance are essential components of the development process. They ensure that the product meets high standards and performs as intended before it is released to customers. Various testing methodologies, such as unit testing, integration testing, and user acceptance testing, are employed to identify and fix issues at different stages of development. Comprehensive testing helps uncover bugs, inconsistencies, and usability problems, enabling start-ups to address them before customers encounter them. Quality assurance goes beyond testing the product; it involves evaluating the entire development process to ensure that best practices and quality standards are followed. Implementing quality assurance measures helps build a culture of excellence within the start-up and ensures that the product delivered meets customers' expectations. User experience (UX) testing is critical to product development, especially for customer adoption. UX testing involves evaluating the product's usability, user interface, and overall user satisfaction. By involving potential customers in UX testing, start-ups can gain valuable insights into how users interact with the product and whether it fulfills their needs.

Intellectual Property And Patents

Intellectual property (IP) and patents are critical considerations for start-ups seeking to protect their innovative ideas and technological advancements. Safeguarding intellectual property rights can provide a competitive advantage, attract investors, and facilitate successful customer adoption. This part explores the significance of intellectual property and patents for start-ups and how they contribute to business success. Intellectual property refers to creations of the mind, such as inventions, designs, literary and artistic works, symbols, names, and images used in commerce. For start-ups, protecting their intellectual property is essential. It is to prevent others from using, reproducing, or profiting from their innovative ideas and original works. The most common forms of intellectual property protection include patents, trademarks, copyrights, and trade secrets. Each type of protection serves a specific purpose and offers distinct advantages to start-ups. Patents are a crucial form of intellectual property protection for start-ups with innovative technological solutions. A patent grants the inventor exclusive rights to their invention for a limited period, typically 20 years from the filing date. During this period, the start-up can prevent others from making, using, selling, or importing the patented invention without permission.

Obtaining a patent can provide several advantages for start-ups seeking customer adoption.[9] A patent grants the start-up a competitive advantage by providing a monopoly over the patented technology. This exclusivity can make the product more attractive to customers and differentiate it from competitors' offerings. Patents can be valuable assets that attract investors and venture capitalists. Investors are more likely to fund start-ups with protected intellectual property, as it reduces the risk of competitors replicating the technology. Start-ups can monetize their patented technology by licensing it to other companies. Licensing agreements can generate additional revenue streams and expand the start-up's market reach. If a competitor infringes on the start-up's patent, the start-up has legal grounds to enforce its rights through litigation. This legal protection can deter potential infringers and safeguard the start-up's market position. The patent process can be complex and time-consuming, requiring a thorough understanding of patent laws and regulations. Start-ups should work with patent attorneys or intellectual property experts to navigate the process successfully. The first step is conducting a thorough patent search to determine if the invention is novel and not already protected by existing patents. Once the novelty is confirmed, the start-up can file a patent application with the relevant office. The application process involves providing detailed descriptions and diagrams of the invention and demonstrating its uniqueness and utility. The patent office examines the application to ensure that it meets all requirements for patentability. Start-ups should know that the patent process can take several years to complete, and not all applications are approved. However, once granted, a patent can provide significant benefits and protection for the start-up's innovative technology.

Customer Adoption And Timing Strategies

Customer adoption is pivotal when a start-up's product or service gains traction in the market. It marks the transition from an innovative idea to a viable business.[10] However, achieving customer adoption requires careful planning and strategic timing. This section delves into the intricacies of customer adoption and explores timing strategies that can significantly impact a start-up's success. Customer adoption is the ultimate validation of a start-up's value proposition. It is the point where potential customers become paying users, indicating that the product or service addresses a genuine need in the market. Customer adoption is not just about acquiring new customers; it's about building a loyal customer base that continues to use and advocate for the product. For start-ups, customer adoption is a critical milestone that can attract investors, boost revenue, and lead to sustainable growth. It provides social proof that the product delivers on its promises, encouraging others to try it. Customer adoption generates valuable feedback, allowing entrepreneurs to improve their offerings based on real-world usage and customer insights. Timing is an essential factor in achieving successful customer adoption. Launching too early may result in a lack of readiness from the market, while launching too late can mean missed opportunities and increased competition.

Start-ups must employ strategic timing strategies to optimize their chances of successful customer adoption. The MVP approach involves releasing a basic product version with essential features to gather early user feedback. It allows start-ups to validate their value proposition and make necessary improvements based on real customer insights. By iteratively improving the product based on feedback, start-ups increase the likelihood of successful adoption. Targeting early adopters who are eager to try new solutions can be an effective strategy for gaining initial traction. Early adopters often have a higher tolerance for potential issues and are willing to provide valuable feedback. Satisfied early adopters can also become evangelists, spreading positive word-of-mouth and driving more significant adoption in the early stages. Timing the product launch in response to market trends and competitive forces can be critical. By understanding the competitive landscape and identifying gaps or weaknesses, start-ups can strategically time their entry to gain a competitive advantage. Launching when market demand is high can lead to faster customer adoption. Utilizing tactics that create a sense of urgency or scarcity can prompt potential customers to take action. Limited-time offers, exclusive access, or early-bird discounts can incentivize customers to adopt the product quickly, leading to more rapid uptake. Brand reputation and recognition can significantly influence customer adoption. You will have more clarity on this section by reading the three dimensions I have written about hereafter. Firstly, I have elaborated on early adopters and beta testing. I have then written about market entry and timing strategies. Finally, I have written about continuous monitoring and adaptation.

Early Adopters And Beta Testing

Early adopters and beta testing play a pivotal role in the success of a start-up's product or service. These strategies allow entrepreneurs to gain valuable feedback, build a loyal customer base, and refine their offerings before wider market release. This sub-section explores the significance of early adopters and the benefits of beta testing in achieving successful customer adoption. Early adopters are adventurous and forward-thinking individuals or businesses who eagerly embrace new products or technologies. They are willing to take a risk on unproven solutions and are typically among the first to try out innovative offerings. Engaging early adopters is essential for start-ups, as they can provide valuable feedback and become evangelists for the product. Early adopters are crucial for gaining initial traction and generating word-of-mouth marketing. They act as a bridge between the start-up and the early majority of customers, who may be more risk-averse and wait for the product to gain traction before trying it themselves. Satisfying early adopters can lead to positive reviews, testimonials, and recommendations that can significantly influence customer adoption in the later stages of a start-up. To attract early adopters, start-ups must create a value proposition that appeals to this unique segment. Early adopters are drawn to products that offer innovation, solve pressing problems, or provide a competitive advantage. Start-ups should communicate how their offering differs and why it is worth trying. Providing exclusive access or special benefits to early adopters can also be a powerful incentive. Early adopters like to feel part of something special and enjoy being ahead of the curve. Offering limited-time discounts, early access to new features, or access to a dedicated support channel can entice early adopters to jump on board.

Beta testing is a crucial phase in product development where a select group of users gets early access to the product before its official release.[11] This process helps start-ups identify bugs, gather user feedback, and understand how the product performs in real-world scenarios. Beta testing involves engaging with diverse users, including early adopters, willing to provide honest feedback. Start-ups should actively seek input from beta testers, encouraging them to report any issues, suggest improvements, and share their overall experience with the product. The insights from beta testing are invaluable for refining the product and ensuring it meets customer expectations. Beta testers essentially act as real-world representatives of the target audience, offering perspectives that may not have been considered during development. Early adopters and beta testers offer valuable feedback that helps identify and address issues, bugs, and areas for improvement. This iterative process allows start-ups to make necessary adjustments and refine the product based on real-world usage. Having satisfied early adopters and positive beta testing results provides proof that the product delivers on its promises. This validation can boost confidence in potential customers and encourage them to adopt the product. Early adopters who have positive experiences with the product can become enthusiastic advocates.

Market Entry And Timing Strategies

Market entry and timing strategies are vital for start-ups seeking successful customer adoption. Deciding when and how to enter the market can significantly impact a start-up's chances of gaining traction and securing a competitive advantage.[12] This sub-section explores the significance of market entry and timing strategies in achieving customer adoption and long-term success. Market entry introduces a start-up's product or service to the target market. It involves making decisions about the target audience, distribution channels, pricing, and marketing strategies. Strategic market entry ensures that the start-up is well-prepared to address customer needs effectively and compete in the market. When entering the market, start-ups should clearly understand their unique value proposition and how it addresses customer pain points. They must define their target audience and tailor their messaging to resonate with potential customers. Additionally, selecting the right distribution channels and pricing strategies is crucial for reaching the intended audience and creating a competitive offering. Timing is a critical factor in market entry. Launching too early may result in a lack of customer readiness or market acceptance, while launching too late can lead to missed opportunities and increased competition. Identifying the right timing requires thorough market research, understanding industry trends, and monitoring customer preferences.

When considering market entry timing, start-ups often face a strategic decision between being a first-mover or a follower. Being a first-mover means entering the market with an innovative product or service ahead of competitors. It can offer advantages such as brand recognition, customer loyalty, and the ability to set industry standards. However, being a first-mover also carries risks, as it involves uncertainty and potential resistance from early adopters. If the market is not yet ready for the product or if there are unforeseen challenges, being a first-mover can be a disadvantage. On the other hand, a follower strategy involves observing the successes and failures of early entrants and entering the market after the concept has been validated. This approach allows start-ups to learn from others' experiences and avoid some risks associated with being a first-mover. Ultimately, the decision between a first-mover and a follower strategy depends on the nature of the product, the competitive landscape, and the start-up's risk appetite. Market entry is not a one-time event but an ongoing process requiring adaptability and flexibility. Start-ups should embrace an iterative approach to market entry, continuously refining their strategies based on customer feedback and market dynamics. Feedback from early adopters, beta testing, and initial market responses should inform subsequent iterations of market entry strategies. Start-ups should be open to pivoting their approach based on new information and market trends, which you will learn in detail in the next chapter.

Continuous Monitoring And Adaptation

In the ever-changing world of start-ups, continuous monitoring and adaptation are essential for achieving successful customer adoption and sustaining long-term growth. Here, I explore the significance of continuously monitoring market trends, customer feedback, and industry developments and how start-ups can adapt their strategies to stay ahead of the competition and meet evolving customer needs. Continuous monitoring involves tracking and analyzing various market aspects, customer behavior, and industry trends. By staying vigilant and proactive, start-ups can gain valuable insights that inform their decision-making and product development processes. Monitoring market trends allows start-ups to identify emerging opportunities and potential threats. By keeping abreast of changing customer preferences and needs, entrepreneurs can pivot their strategies to align with evolving demands. Additionally, tracking competitor activities enables start-ups to benchmark their performance and identify areas for improvement. Customer feedback is a goldmine of valuable information that start-ups should actively seek and embrace. By soliciting and incorporating customer feedback into product development, start-ups can create solutions that better cater to customer needs and expectations. Iterative improvement based on customer feedback is a hallmark of successful start-ups.

Industries are dynamic and subject to continuous change due to technological advancements, regulatory updates, and shifting consumer behaviors.[13] Start-ups must adapt their strategies to stay relevant in the ever-changing landscape. Being open to change and quickly adapting is essential for start-ups seeking customer adoption. By embracing industry shifts and new opportunities, start-ups can position themselves as innovators and disruptors, gaining a competitive edge in the market. Flexibility and agility are key traits that enable start-ups to respond rapidly to market changes and customer needs. Start-ups must foster a culture that embraces experimentation and accepts failures as opportunities to learn and improve. Having an agile approach allows start-ups to seize opportunities and address challenges swiftly. Start-up founders and teams should be prepared to adjust their strategies and pivot when necessary to achieve customer adoption and success. Continuous monitoring and adaptation are most effective when supported by data-driven decision-making processes. Start-ups should invest in data collection and analysis tools to derive valuable insights from various data sources, including customer interactions, website analytics, and market research.

Companies That Acknowledged The Right Time For Their Product

Companies that master the right timing for their products keenly understand emerging trends and market readiness. By closely monitoring industry developments and customer behavior, these companies can identify opportune moments to introduce their innovations. They capitalize on shifts in customer preferences, economic conditions, and technological advancements to align their product launches with the market's demands. Furthermore, successful companies embrace a forward-thinking approach that allows them to foresee potential disruptions and customer needs in advance. They invest in research and development, anticipating future challenges and opportunities. By staying ahead of the curve, these companies can adapt their strategies and offerings, ensuring that their products are relevant and groundbreaking when they hit the market. The ability to sense the right timing for their product launch gives these companies a competitive edge, enabling them to establish themselves as industry leaders and gain widespread customer adoption.

Rappi

Rappi, a Colombian start-up founded in 2015, has quickly become a leading player in the on-demand delivery industry in Latin America. The company offers a mobile app that allows users to order a wide range of products and services, including groceries, meals, medications, and even cash withdrawals from ATMs, all delivered to their doorstep. Rappi's success can be attributed to its exceptional timing and strategic approach to tapping into a rapidly growing market. One of the key factors that contributed to Rappi's success was its recognition of the rising demand for on-demand services in Latin America. The region witnessed significant urbanization, increased smartphone penetration, and a growing middle class seeking convenient and efficient solutions for daily needs. Rappi[14] seized this opportunity to establish its on-demand delivery platform, providing a one-stop shop for diverse products and services. Moreover, Rappi's ability to adapt and expand its services at the right time played a crucial role in its success. While the company initially focused on food delivery, it quickly recognized the potential to provide a broader range of services, such as grocery delivery and pharmacy products. By diversifying its offerings and expanding its market presence, Rappi positioned itself as a comprehensive on-demand delivery platform, meeting various customer needs and gaining a competitive advantage over other regional players. Rappi's success also stems from its efficient use of technology to optimize its delivery operations. The company implemented advanced algorithms to match orders with available couriers in real time, ensuring speedy and reliable deliveries. This emphasis on operational efficiency and customer satisfaction further strengthened Rappi's position in the market.

Company Name: Rappi

Founded: 2015

Significant reason(s) for success: The company's remarkable success has been possible due to its astute timing in tapping into the burgeoning demand for on-demand delivery services in Latin America.

Duolingo

Duolingo,[15] a language-learning platform founded in 2011, has emerged as a global leader in the education technology space. The company offers a user-friendly app and website that enables users to learn various languages through interactive lessons, exercises, and gamified experiences. Duolingo's success can be attributed to its astute timing and innovative approach to meeting the growing demand for accessible and effective language learning tools. One of the key factors that contributed to Duolingo's success was its recognition of the increasing interest in language learning driven by globalization and the rise of international communication. As people worldwide sought to expand their language skills for travel, work, and personal enrichment, Duolingo capitalized on this trend by offering a convenient and affordable language learning platform accessible to anyone with a smartphone or computer. By tapping into this growing demand, Duolingo positioned itself as a go-to solution for language learners of all ages and backgrounds. Furthermore, Duolingo's gamified approach to language learning was a game-changer. Leveraging the power of gamification, the platform turned language learning into an engaging and enjoyable experience. Users earn virtual rewards and progress through levels as they master new skills, creating a sense of achievement and motivation to continue learning. This unique approach attracted language learners and helped retain users over time, enhancing Duolingo's competitive edge in the language learning market. Duolingo also recognized the importance of mobile technology and the growing use of smartphones worldwide. By launching its app on iOS and Android platforms, the company tapped into a massive user base that could access language learning conveniently on the go. This mobile-first approach was crucial in reaching a wider audience and making language learning accessible to millions globally.

Company Name: Duolingo

Founded: 2011

Significant reason(s) for success: The company's success can be attributed to its timely entry into the language learning market and its innovative approach to making language learning accessible, engaging, and enjoyable.

Affirm

Affirm[16] is a financial technology company founded in 2012. It has emerged as a leading player in the fintech industry, providing innovative and consumer-friendly financial products. The company offers a "buy now, pay later" service, allowing consumers to make purchases and spread the cost over time with transparent, easy-to-understand terms. Affirm's success can be attributed to its pioneering timing and strategic approach to addressing evolving consumer preferences and needs in the digital era. One of the key factors that contributed to Affirm's success was its recognition of a changing consumer mindset toward credit and financing. As the digital age ushered in a generation of tech-savvy consumers, traditional credit cards and complex financing options became less appealing. Affirm seized this opportunity to disrupt the consumer lending landscape by providing a more transparent and user-friendly alternative. By introducing a straightforward "buy now, pay later" option that aligns with the preferences of the modern consumer, the company was able to carve a niche in the fintech market. Furthermore, Affirm's focus on promoting financial transparency and responsibility resonated with consumers seeking a more predictable and manageable way to finance their purchases. Affirm's platform allows users to see the total purchase cost upfront, avoiding hidden fees or confusing terms often associated with credit cards. This transparency helped build trust with consumers and empowered them to make informed financial decisions, fostering a positive customer experience and loyalty. Affirm's strategic partnerships with various merchants and e-commerce platforms were also instrumental in its success. By integrating its "buy now, pay later" service with online retailers. Affirm expanded its reach and accessibility to a broader customer base. These partnerships facilitated customer adoption and provided merchants with a competitive advantage by offering flexible payment options to attract more customers.

Company Name: Affirm

Founded: 2012

Significant reason(s) for success: The company pioneered the right timing by recognizing the demand for transparent and user-friendly financing solutions in the digital era.

Lalamove

Lalamove,[17] a Hong Kong-based start-up founded in 2013, has rapidly grown into a prominent player in the on-demand delivery and logistics industry. The company provides a platform that connects customers with delivery drivers, enabling fast and efficient delivery of goods and parcels. Lalamove's success can be attributed to its impeccable timing and strategic approach in tapping into the surging demand for on-demand delivery services. One of the key factors that contributed to Lalamove's success was its recognition of the rising demand for fast and reliable delivery services in urban centers. As urbanization and e-commerce continued to expand, consumers and businesses sought faster and more convenient delivery options. Lalamove seized this opportunity by providing an easy-to-use platform that connects customers with a network of drivers ready to deliver goods swiftly and efficiently within cities. By addressing this unmet need in the market, Lalamove positioned itself as a critical solution for businesses and individuals requiring on-demand logistics services. Furthermore, Lalamove's emphasis on localized services and real time tracking played a crucial role in its success. The company understood the importance of hyper-localized services in densely populated cities, where delivery distances can be short but time-sensitive. Lalamove's platform allows customers to access nearby drivers quickly, reducing delivery times and providing a competitive edge in crowded urban markets. The real time tracking feature enhances customer confidence, as they can monitor their deliveries every step of the way. Lalamove's strategic expansion into multiple markets also contributed to its success. The company recognized the global trend of urbanization and the potential for on-demand delivery services in various regions. Lalamove capitalized on the increasing demand for efficient logistics solutions in diverse markets by expanding its services to different cities and countries.

Company Name: Lalamove

Founded: 2013

Significant reason(s) for success: The company nailed the perfect timing in meeting the growing demand for fast, reliable, and localized logistics solutions.

Cazoo

Cazoo, a British start-up founded in 2018, has rapidly emerged as a disruptive force in the used car market, revolutionizing how people buy and sell pre-owned vehicles. The company operates an online platform that allows customers to browse, purchase, and have used cars delivered directly to their doorstep. Cazoo's success can be attributed to its strategic timing and innovative approach to addressing the automotive industry's evolving consumer preferences and needs. One of the key factors that contributed to Cazoo's success was its recognition of the changing consumer behavior and preferences in the used car market. Consumers increasingly sought convenient and transparent online purchasing experiences as the digital age transformed various industries. Cazoo[18] seized this opportunity to bring the traditional used car buying process into the digital realm, offering a seamless and hassle-free online platform. By addressing consumer pain points, such as time-consuming dealership visits and lack of transparency in the buying process, Cazoo positioned itself as a modern and customer-centric solution for used car purchases. Furthermore, Cazoo's emphasis on quality and transparency played a crucial role in its success. The company thoroughly inspects and certifies each vehicle before listing it on the platform, providing customers with the assurance of buying a high-quality and reliable used car. Additionally, Cazoo offers comprehensive vehicle information, including detailed images, specifications, and vehicle history reports, allowing customers to make informed decisions. This focus on transparency-built trust with customers and differentiated Cazoo from traditional used car dealerships. Cazoo's strategic timing in entering the market was also significant. The used car industry had been relatively untouched by digital transformation until Cazoo's entry. As other industries had successfully embraced e-commerce and online platforms, the used car market was ripe for disruption.

Company Name: Cazoo

Founded: 2018

Significant reason(s) for success: The company's success in the used car market can be attributed to its strategic approach in emphasizing transparency and quality and expanding its reach.

Klarna

Klarna, a Swedish fintech company founded in 2005, has emerged as a major player in the global payment industry, offering innovative payment solutions for online and offline transactions. The company provides a "buy now, pay later" service that allows consumers to make purchases and spread the cost over time. Klarna's success can be attributed to its strategic timing and revolutionary approach to meeting the changing demands of modern consumers and retailers. One of the key factors that contributed to Klarna's success was its recognition of the evolving consumer behavior and the growing demand for flexible payment options. As e-commerce and online shopping gained popularity, consumers sought more convenient and frictionless purchasing methods. Klarna[19] seized this opportunity by introducing its "buy now, pay later" service, allowing consumers to defer payment for their purchases or split the cost into interest-free installments. By addressing the changing needs of consumers, Klarna positioned itself as a convenient and user-friendly payment solution for online shoppers. Furthermore, Klarna's strategic partnerships with retailers and e-commerce platforms played a crucial role in its success. The company collaborated with numerous merchants to integrate its payment solution into its checkout process, providing customers with a seamless and efficient payment experience. This strategic expansion of its merchant network allowed Klarna to reach a broader customer base and gain widespread adoption among online retailers. Klarna's timing in disrupting the payment industry was also vital to its growth. As the digital revolution transformed various industries, the traditional payment landscape was ripe for disruption. Klarna's entry into the market coincided with the increasing trend of online shopping and the demand for simpler, more secure, and flexible payment methods. By offering a modern payment solution that met the needs of consumers and retailers, Klarna quickly gained traction and became a trusted payment partner for millions of customers and merchants worldwide.

Company Name: Klarna

Founded: 2005

Significant reason(s) for success: The company recognized the changing preferences of online shoppers and strategically partnered with merchants. It focused on user experience, technology innovation, and flexibility.

Calm

Calm,[20] a meditation and sleep app founded in 2012, has become a prominent name in the wellness and mental health industry, offering guided meditation, sleep stories, and relaxation techniques. The app's success can be attributed to its strategic timing and innovative approach to addressing the growing demand for mental well-being and stress reduction solutions. One of the key factors that contributed to Calm's success was its recognition of the increasing awareness and importance of mental health and self-care. The demand for mindfulness and stress reduction solutions soared as the fast-paced and digitally connected world took a toll on people's mental well-being. Calm seized this opportunity by providing an easy-to-use app with guided meditation sessions, calming music, and sleep stories to help users unwind and relax. By addressing the changing needs of individuals seeking moments of tranquility and peace amidst the chaos, Calm positioned itself as a go-to platform for mental well-being. Furthermore, Calm's focus on content diversity and quality was crucial to its success. The app offers a vast library of meditation sessions, sleep stories narrated by well-known personalities, nature sounds, and music to cater to various preferences and needs. This commitment to delivering high-quality and engaging content has attracted millions of users seeking personalized, immersive experiences to improve their mental health. Calm's timing in entering the meditation and sleep app market was impeccable. The growing emphasis on self-care and the cultural shift towards mindfulness and meditation made Calm's launch well-aligned with the evolving consumer behavior. The app's entry coincided with the increasing trend of wellness and mental health becoming mainstream topics, ensuring a receptive audience eager to adopt new relaxation and stress reduction tools.

Company Name: Calm

Founded: 2012

Significant reason(s) for success: The company's success can be attributed to its strategic timing and innovative approach to meeting the growing demand for mental well-being solutions.

Conclusion

As we conclude this chapter on "Right Timing for Your Product," we have explored the critical role timing plays in the success of start-ups and how strategic decision-making can lead to significant achievements. Understanding the market landscape, consumer needs, and emerging trends are key components in mastering the right timing for your product launch. By delving into case studies of successful companies, we have seen how astute timing can transform an idea into a thriving business. Armed with valuable insights, you might be inspired to embark on your own start-up journey. Remember that every successful entrepreneur starts with a vision, a passion, and the determination to take action. The path to success may have challenges, but with the right mindset, approach, and timing, you can overcome obstacles and turn your ideas into reality.

First and foremost, believe in yourself and your idea. Passion is the driving force that fuels start-ups and keeps entrepreneurs going during difficult times. Identify and leverage your unique strengths to create a product that stands out in the market. Embrace failures as learning opportunities and remain adaptable to continuously refine your offering. Next, surround yourself with a strong support network. Collaborate with like-minded individuals who share your vision and complement your skillset. Building a team that aligns with your goals will enhance your product's development and provide emotional and professional support during challenging phases. Timing is essential, but it's equally important to take action. Don't wait for the perfect moment; start laying the groundwork for your start-up today.

I have summarized the chapter's takeaways into actionable items for clarity and easy-to-refer notes. These are listed below:

1. Assessing the market landscape will help you make informed decisions about the right timing for your product.
2. Industry trends and emerging technologies contribute significantly in this regard.
3. Competitive analysis and market readiness will be valuable when identifying the timing suitable for your product launch.
4. Customer insights and needs are often overlooked, but these are essential if you wish to hit the nail on its head regarding the right timing for your product.
5. Technological considerations are of utmost significance in deciding the timing for your start-up product, especially today.
6. Technological infrastructure and scalability will determine how much you will leverage the right timing for your product.

7. Development and testing are essential to maximize the right time for your product launch and expansion.
8. Intellectual property and patents are requisite you cannot ignore if you wish to ensure expansion and sustainability for your product.
9. Many top companies, which were once start-ups, use customer adoption and timing strategies.
10. Early adopters and beta testing are other dimensions you should consider to achieve the best results for your start-up product.
11. Market entry and timing strategies are other essentials you must take care of to ensure a better growth trajectory for your product.
12. Continuous monitoring and adaptation have become more crucial due to the rapid development of businesses and the unprecedented rise of the relevance of technology.

References

1. Five Echelon (2023). *Determining the right timing for a product launch.* Available at: https://fiveechelon.com/determining-the-right-timing-for-a-product-launch/ [Accessed 26 Jul. 2023].
2. Capital, V. (2023). *How do you assess the competitive landscape and the potential threats to a start-up?.* Available at: https://www.linkedin.com/advice/3/how-do-you-assess-competitive-landscape-potential [Accessed 26 Jul. 2023].
3. Marr, B. (2023). *How to drive corporate innovation and outpace start-ups.* Available at: https://www.forbes.com/sites/bernardmarr/2023/03/09/how-to-drive-corporate-innovation-and-outpace-startups/?sh=6738c5cb7093 [Accessed 26 Jul. 2023].
4. Faster Capital (2023). *The ultimate guide to competitor analysis for start-ups.* Available at: https://fastercapital.com/content/The-ultimate-guide-to-competitor-analysis-for-startups.html [Accessed 26 Jul. 2023].
5. Inc. (2017). *Customer service is the lifeblood of your business.* Available at: https://www.inc.com/christina-nicholson/customer-service-is-the-lifeblood-of-your-business-here-are-7-ways-to-do-it-bett.html [Accessed 26 Jul. 2023].
6. Solaris Technologies. (2021) *Technology and the problems faced by start-ups.* Available at: https://www.solaristek.com/technology-and-the-problems-faced-by-start-ups/ [Accessed 26 Jul. 2023].

7. Altaf, Y. (2023). *7 crucial ways to scale your start-up or business.* Available at: https://www.entrepreneur.com/growing-a-business/7-crucial-ways-to-scale-your-startup-or-business/443794 [Accessed 26 Jul. 2023].
8. Purnama, A. P. (2022). *Council post: Testing for start-ups: How unit test is the enemy of start-up's agility and how you can fix it.* Available at: https://www.forbes.com/sites/forbestechcouncil/2022/10/05/testing-for-startups-how-unit-test-is-the-enemy-of-startups-agility-and-how-you-can-fix-it/?sh=742dd81856e4 [Accessed 26 Jul. 2023].
9. Herpy, J. (2020). *Council Post: A guide to modern intellectual property protection for start-ups.* Available at: https://www.forbes.com/sites/forbesbusinesscouncil/2020/08/11/a-guide-to-modern-intellectual-property-protection-for-startups/?sh=88ecb8a6b9e1 [Accessed 26 Jul. 2023].
10. Scout, H. (2023). *6 user adoption strategies for growing SAAS businesses.* Available at: https://www.helpscout.com/blog/user-adoption-strategies/ [Accessed 26 Jul. 2023].
11. Cloudways (2021). *How start-up beta testing can be a viral marketing success.* Available at: https://www.cloudways.com/blog/beta-testing-for-startups-viral-marketing-success/ [Accessed 26 Jul. 2023].
12. Cuofano, G. (2023). *Context-based market entry strategies for start-ups.* Available at: https://fourweekmba.com/market-entry-strategies/ [Accessed 26 Jul. 2023].
13. Golden, J. (2018). *Changing consumer behavior is the key to unlocking billion-dollar businesses.* Available at: https://techcrunch.com/2018/12/12/changing-consumer-behavior-is-the-key-to-unlocking-billion-dollar-businesses/ [Accessed 26 Jul. 2023].
14. Foggin, S. *et al.* (2022). *Rappi Mafia: How a delivery start-up took over Colombia's tech scene.* Available at: https://restofworld.org/2022/rappi-mafia-delivery-startup-colombia-tech-scene/ [Accessed 26 Jul. 2023].
15. Adams, S. (2019). *Game of tongues: How Duolingo built a $700 million business with its addictive language-learning app.* Available at: https://www.forbes.com/sites/susanadams/2019/07/16/game-of-tongues-how-duolingo-built-a-700-million-business-with-its-addictive-language-learning-app/?sh=5413856f3463 [Accessed 26 Jul. 2023].
16. Goel, S. (2022). *How does affirm make money: Business model.* Available at: https://thestrategystory.com/2022/02/26/how-does-affirm-make-money-business-model/ [Accessed 26 Jul. 2023].
17. Shu, C. (2020). *On-demand logistics company Lalamove gets $515 million series E.* Available at: https://techcrunch.com/2020/12/22/

on-demand-logistics-company-lalamove-gets-515-million-series-e/ [Accessed 26 Jul. 2023].

18. Martin, I. (2022). *British car start-up Cazoo raises $1 billion from SPAC merger*. Available at: https://www.forbes.com/sites/iainmartin/2021/08/27/british-car-startup-cazoo-raises-1-billion-from-spac-merger/?sh=54458363260e [Accessed 26 Jul. 2023].
19. FinTech (2020). *Four reasons why Klarna is the biggest fintech in Europe*. Available at: https://fintechmagazine.com/venture-capital/four-reasons-why-klarna-biggest-fintech-europe [Accessed 26 Jul. 2023].
20. Lynley, M. (2018). *Meditation app calm hits a $250m valuation amid an explosion of interest in mindfulness apps*. Available at: https://techcrunch.com/2018/06/20/meditation-app-calm-hits-a-250m-valuation-amid-an-explosion-of-interest-in-mindfulness-apps/ [Accessed 26 Jul. 2023].

CHAPTER 16
Pivoting at the Right Time

In the ever-evolving landscape of entrepreneurship, timing is everything.[1] While launching your product or service at the right time can be crucial, it is equally important to recognize when it's necessary to pivot to stay ahead of the curve. Throughout the history of successful start-ups, numerous examples of companies that have not only weathered the storm but also emerged as leaders in their respective industries by making timely pivots. This chapter delves into the art of pivoting at the right time and explores the critical factors distinguishing successful pivots from their less fortunate counterparts. Consider the stories of Twitter, Instagram, PayPal, Starbucks, and others that stood out in fiercely competitive markets. They faced rivals within the same space, yet they rose above and became frontrunners. So, what set them apart? What did they do right that other companies, who also attempted to pivot, did wrong? These questions lie at the heart of understanding the pivotal role of timing in the success of start-ups. One of the most striking examples of successful pivoting is Western Union. Once a thriving telegram service, it began to decline with the advent of telephones. However, the company recognized the need to adapt instead of accepting defeat and pivoted towards offering money transfer services. This strategic move breathed new life into Western Union and positioned it as a leading player in the financial services industry, a status it still holds. Similarly, once a dominant personal computing market, IBM faced the challenge of emerging competitors offering more affordable products. Realizing the need to reinvent itself, IBM shifted gears and transitioned into providing consultancy services for other large organizations, solidifying its position as a key player in the technology consulting space.

Sometimes, a successful pivot arises from an unexpected discovery. Take the Play-Doh company, for instance. Originally manufactured as a product to clean soot near coal heaters on walls, Play-Doh faced declining sales with the decline of coal heaters and the rise of oil and gas heaters. However, a stroke of luck came when the company learned that one of their sisters-in-law was using the product to teach a kindergarten class. This serendipitous revelation led to a new niche market for Play-Doh as an educational tool, reinvigorating its sales and securing its place as a beloved children's toy. This chapter delves into the fascinating world of pivoting at the right time. We examine the pivotal moments in the success stories of various start-ups, dissecting the strategies that propelled them forward and exploring the pitfalls that hindered their competitors. By understanding the principles and nuances of strategic pivoting, entrepreneurs can gain valuable insights into recognizing the signs that necessitate a change in direction, evaluating potential pivots, and executing them effectively. Whether you are a budding entrepreneur, a start-up founder, or an established business leader, understanding the art of pivoting at the right time is a skill that can make all the difference in the success of your venture. Get ready as we unravel the secrets behind successful pivots, drawing inspiration from the stories of companies that dared to embrace change and emerged triumphant in the face of adversity.

Recognizing The Need To Pivot

In the fast-paced and dynamic world of entrepreneurship, the ability to pivot can be a game-changer for start-ups facing challenges or seeking new opportunities. Pivoting refers to the strategic shift in a company's business model, product, or overall direction to adapt to changing market conditions or to better align with customer needs.[2] Recognizing the need to pivot is a crucial skill distinguishing successful entrepreneurs from those who falter in adversity. One of the primary reasons a start-up may need to pivot is when the initial product or business model fails to gain traction in the market. Despite careful planning and market research, unforeseen factors or competitive pressures can lead to less-than-desired results. In such instances, being open to recognizing the signs of stagnation and the need for change is essential. Market feedback, declining sales, or a lack of customer interest may indicate that adjustments are necessary to stay relevant and competitive. Moreover, market dynamics or industry trends changes can also necessitate a pivot. In a rapidly evolving landscape, start-ups must closely monitor external factors that could impact their business. Emerging technologies, shifts in consumer behavior, or regulatory environment changes can present challenges and opportunities. Recognizing these external influences early on and adapting your approach can lead your start-up to success.

Another crucial aspect in recognizing the need to pivot is the ability to listen to your customers. Customer feedback can provide invaluable insights into pain points, preferences, and unmet needs. By actively seeking and analyzing feedback, entrepreneurs can uncover areas for improvement and identify potential directions for pivoting. Listening to your customers' voices can be the key to unlocking untapped market segments and finding innovative solutions that resonate with your target audience. Furthermore, internal factors within the start-up, such as team dynamics and resource allocation, can also play a role in recognizing the need to pivot. A cohesive and adaptable team that embraces a culture of innovation is more likely to identify opportunities for improvement and navigate challenging times. Evaluating your team's strengths and weaknesses and fostering a culture that encourages constructive feedback can empower your start-up to make timely and informed decisions. I have expanded this section on three dimensions. Firstly, I have written about the signs of a necessary pivot and the importance of these in your start-up journey. Secondly, I have written about evaluating potential pivots since it will help you make an informed decision. Lastly, I have written about deciding to pivot. It is a big step but often proves necessary when done at the right time and in the right ways.

Signs Of A Necessary Pivot

For every entrepreneur, building a start-up is a rollercoaster of highs and lows.[3] While initial excitement and enthusiasm may drive the early stages, challenges and setbacks are an inherent part of the entrepreneurial experience. Recognizing the signs of a necessary pivot is crucial for start-ups to navigate rough waters and emerge stronger and more resilient. One of the key signs that a pivot may be necessary is when a start-up's initial product or business model fails to gain traction in the market. Despite thorough planning and meticulous research, unforeseen circumstances or changing market dynamics can impact the reception of a product. Low customer adoption, lackluster sales, or difficulty acquiring users may indicate that the current approach does not resonate with the intended audience. In such cases, entrepreneurs must accept the reality and acknowledge the need for a strategic shift. Another significant indicator of a necessary pivot is feedback from customers and users. Start-ups that actively seek and value customer feedback are better equipped to identify improvement areas and spot potential innovation opportunities. Unaddressed pain points or consistent requests for additional features or functionalities may point toward unmet customer needs. Embracing customer feedback as a valuable resource can provide a roadmap for pivoting in a direction that aligns more closely with customer desires.

Market trends and competitive pressures can also serve as compelling signs that a pivot may be warranted. Start-ups operating in rapidly evolving industries must keep a vigilant eye on market dynamics. Emerging technologies, changes in consumer behavior, or shifts in regulatory environments can create challenges or present new avenues for growth. Entrepreneurs who proactively recognize and respond to these external factors are better positioned to pivot their strategies and capitalize on emerging opportunities. Additionally, internal factors within the start-up can serve as a critical guide in determining the need for a pivot. Evaluating team dynamics, resource allocation, and overall efficiency can reveal insights into the company's adaptability and resilience. A cohesive and agile team that embraces innovation and open communication will likely recognize signs of stagnation and be receptive to necessary changes. Entrepreneurs should foster a culture that encourages constructive criticism and encourages employees to share their perspectives on areas that may require improvement or strategic realignment.

Evaluating Potential Pivots

Once the signs of a necessary pivot have been recognized, the next crucial step for start-ups is to thoroughly evaluate potential pivot options. Pivoting is not a decision to be taken lightly, as it can significantly impact the direction and future of the company. An informed and strategic evaluation process is essential to identify the most viable and promising pivot opportunities. The first step in evaluating potential pivots is comprehensively analyzing the market landscape and industry trends. Start-ups must thoroughly research their target market, competitors, and potential customer segments to understand current dynamics and emerging opportunities. This research-driven approach enables entrepreneurs to identify gaps in the market, unmet customer needs, and areas with the potential for high growth. Customer feedback and insights play a central role in the evaluation process. Engaging in open conversations with existing and potential customers can provide invaluable input into their preferences, pain points, and desires. Entrepreneurs should listen actively and attentively to customer perspectives to gain insights that can shape the direction of the pivot. This customer-centric approach ensures that the pivot aligns with actual market demands and increases the chances of successful customer adoption.

Financial analysis is another critical aspect in evaluating potential pivots. Start-ups must assess the financial implications of each pivot option, considering the costs involved, expected return on investment, and potential revenue streams.[4] This analysis will help entrepreneurs determine each pivot opportunity's financial feasibility and sustainability. Moreover, understanding the potential impact on the company's cash flow and progress is essential in making well-informed decisions to safeguard the financial health of the start-up. The capabilities and resources of the start-up also play a significant role in evaluating potential pivots. Entrepreneurs must assess whether the company has the necessary skills, infrastructure, and resources to execute the chosen pivot successfully. Entrepreneurs should identify strategies to acquire the required resources if gaps exist through hiring, partnerships, or collaborations. Understanding the existing capabilities and potential for growth is crucial in aligning the pivot with the company's core strengths. Risk assessment is an integral part of evaluating potential pivots. Every pivot involves inherent risks, and entrepreneurs must evaluate each option's potential downside and implications. Conducting a risk-benefit analysis helps entrepreneurs weigh the potential rewards against the risks involved, enabling them to make informed decisions that minimize potential pitfalls.

Making The Decision To Pivot

Once potential pivot options have been thoroughly evaluated, entrepreneurs face the critical moment of pivoting. This stage requires careful consideration, conviction, and the courage to embrace change. The decision-making process is pivotal in steering the start-up toward a new direction that aligns with market demands and capitalizes on growth opportunities. A data-driven approach is fundamental in deciding to pivot. Analyzing market research, customer feedback, financial projections, and risk assessments provides a foundation of objective insights. Entrepreneurs must rely on tangible data and empirical evidence rather than gut feelings or personal biases. This disciplined approach ensures that the decision is grounded in reality and minimizes the influence of emotional factors that might cloud judgment. A key consideration in the decision-making process is the alignment of the pivot with the company's core values and long-term vision. The pivot should not be a deviation from the start-up's mission but a strategic evolution that complements its purpose. Entrepreneurs must assess whether the pivot supports the start-up's core values and whether it advances the overall vision for the company. Maintaining alignment with the company's essence ensures that the pivot remains authentic and resonates with existing and potential customers.[5]

The involvement of key stakeholders is vital in deciding to pivot. Entrepreneurs should engage with their team, board members, advisors, and investors to gather diverse perspectives and insights. Collaborative decision-making enables entrepreneurs to comprehensively view the pivot's potential impacts, risks, and benefits. Engaging stakeholders fosters a sense of ownership and shared responsibility for the pivot's success. Timing is another critical factor in deciding to pivot. While some pivots may need to happen swiftly in response to immediate challenges, others may require more deliberate planning and execution. Entrepreneurs must consider the external market conditions, the start-up's financial position, and the readiness of the team to implement the pivot effectively. A well-timed pivot can create momentum and capitalize on emerging opportunities, while a premature or delayed pivot may hinder progress. Lastly, decisiveness is essential in deciding to pivot. Procrastination or indecision can lead to missed opportunities or prolonged periods of stagnation. Entrepreneurs must be willing to embrace change and act decisively to navigate their start-ups toward a new direction. Taking calculated risks and demonstrating leadership in decision-making sets the tone for a smooth pivot execution and instills confidence in the team and stakeholders.

Successful Pivot Strategies

Pivoting is a defining moment in the life of a start-up, and choosing the right strategy can be the difference between survival and failure.[6] Successful pivot strategies require a keen understanding of market dynamics, customer needs, and the start-up's unique strengths. This section delves into various approaches that have proven effective for start-ups seeking to pivot and achieve success. One powerful pivot strategy involves leveraging the start-up's existing core competencies and strengths to explore new market opportunities. By identifying areas where their expertise can be applied innovatively, entrepreneurs can broaden their product or service offerings and tap into previously untapped customer segments. This approach reduces the need for radical changes and allows the start-up to build upon its established brand reputation and customer base. A well-known example of this strategy is Instagram's pivot from a location-based social check-in app to a photo-sharing platform. Recognizing its core competence in photo sharing, Instagram evolved to meet the rising demand for visually appealing content, ultimately becoming a dominant player in the social media landscape. Customer feedback and insights are invaluable resources for successful pivots. Entrepreneurs should actively engage with their customers to understand pain points, preferences, and emerging trends. By listening to customer needs and being receptive to their suggestions, start-ups can uncover unmet demands and areas for improvement.

In rapidly evolving industries, embracing technological advancements and innovation can be a game-changer for successful pivots. Entrepreneurs should constantly monitor emerging technologies and trends that align with their start-up's mission. Incorporating cutting-edge technologies can enhance product offerings, streamline operations, and enable the start-up to remain competitive. A remarkable example of this strategy is Netflix's pivot from a DVD rental service to a streaming platform. Anticipating the shift towards online media consumption, Netflix harnessed the power of streaming technology to revolutionize the entertainment industry. This pivot allowed them to transcend geographic limitations and create a global streaming service that reshaped how people consume content. Start-ups can explore pivot opportunities by expanding their reach into new geographic markets or target demographics. By analyzing the potential of untapped markets and adapting their offerings to suit local preferences, start-ups can significantly scale their customer base. Successful market expansion pivots require thorough research, cultural understanding, and localized marketing strategies. A notable example is Airbnb's pivot towards international expansion. Initially, Airbnb focused on the American market but later recognized the opportunity to cater to travelers worldwide. They adapted their platform to appeal to different cultures and languages, facilitating global access to unique accommodations and travel experiences. I have elaborated on this section across three aspects. The first is adapting business models. The second is about expanding target markets. The third is embracing technological disruptions.

Adapting Business Models

Adapting the business model is a pivotal pivot strategy that involves reimagining how a start-up creates, delivers, and captures value in the market.[7] As market dynamics evolve and customer preferences change, start-ups must be agile in modifying their business models to remain competitive and relevant. This pivot approach requires a deep understanding of the start-up's target market and a willingness to explore alternative revenue streams and distribution channels. One effective way for start-ups to adapt their business models is by embracing subscription-based revenue streams. The subscription model offers a recurring revenue stream, providing start-ups with a more predictable income and fostering a loyal customer base. By offering customers the option to subscribe to their products or services regularly, start-ups can strengthen customer relationships and ensure consistent engagement. A notable example of this pivot strategy is Adobe's shift to a subscription-based model for its software suite. The company transitioned from traditional one-time purchases to a subscription-based service called Adobe Creative Cloud. This pivot provided a steady revenue stream for Adobe, allowing them to continuously deliver updates and improvements to their software. For start-ups in the technology sector, embracing a Platform-as-a-Service (PaaS) model can be a transformational pivot. A PaaS model allows start-ups to provide a platform that enables other developers or businesses to build and deploy applications. By transitioning from offering standalone products to becoming a platform provider, start-ups can attract a broader user base and create a network effect. This pivot strategy enables the start-up to benefit from the ecosystem's growth around its platform.

Start-ups can also pivot their business models by adopting an omnichannel approach, providing customers with a seamless experience across multiple channels. By integrating physical and digital touchpoints, start-ups can meet customers where they prefer to engage, enhancing their overall experience and increasing customer retention. An omnichannel pivot enables start-ups to cater to diverse customer preferences and capitalize on the benefits of both online and offline sales channels. A notable example of this strategy is Warby Parker, an eyewear company that began as an e-commerce retailer but later pivoted to establish brick-and-mortar stores. By blending the convenience of online shopping with the personalized in-store experience, Warby Parker successfully created a unified customer journey that drove customer loyalty and growth. Another successful pivot strategy is shifting from a product-based business model to a service-based model. Start-ups can pivot their offerings to focus on providing ongoing services and customer support. By offering value-added services, start-ups can build stronger customer relationships and differentiate themselves from competitors selling similar products. This pivot approach often involves bundling complementary services with the core product or transitioning to a subscription-based service model. An illustrative example of this strategy is the transformation of Xerox from a photocopier manufacturer to a leading provider of business process outsourcing and managed print services. By diversifying its offerings to include various document services, Xerox expanded its revenue streams and customer base.

Expanding Target Markets

Expanding target markets is a pivot strategy that involves broadening the reach of a start-up's products or services to new geographic locations or previously untapped customer segments.[8] This strategic pivot enables start-ups to capitalize on emerging market opportunities and diversify their customer base. By understanding the needs and preferences of different target markets, start-ups can tailor their offerings to resonate with diverse audiences, leading to increased growth and market penetration. Geographic expansion is a common pivot strategy where start-ups venture into new regions or countries to tap into additional customer segments. This approach allows start-ups to capitalize on the demand for their products or services in new markets and diversify their revenue streams. Successful geographic expansion requires in-depth research into the target market's cultural, economic, and regulatory nuances. Additionally, adapting marketing and distribution strategies to suit local preferences is essential for building a strong presence in new territories. A well-known example of this strategy is Airbnb's global expansion. Initially founded in the United States, Airbnb expanded its services to various countries worldwide, allowing travelers to find unique accommodations in diverse locations. Expanding target markets can also involve focusing on niche customer segments with specific needs and preferences. By tailoring products or services to cater to niche markets, start-ups can position themselves as experts in their respective domains and gain a competitive advantage.

Vertical expansion is a pivot strategy that involves diversifying product or service offerings to address the needs of related industries or customer segments. By expanding vertically within a specific market or industry, start-ups can deepen their market penetration and revenue potential. Vertical expansion requires a keen understanding of customer pain points and opportunities for cross-selling complementary products or services. This pivot strategy allows start-ups to establish themselves as comprehensive solution providers, enhancing customer loyalty and retention. A prominent example of vertical expansion is Apple's evolution from a computer manufacturer to a technology ecosystem provider, offering a range of interconnected products and services that cater to various consumer needs. Recognizing and adapting to demographic shifts is a strategic pivot that allows start-ups to align with changing consumer preferences and behaviors. As demographics evolve, start-ups must adjust their marketing, messaging, and product offerings to appeal to different generations or cultural groups. Understanding various demographic segments' distinct needs and aspirations enables start-ups to stay relevant and relatable in a constantly evolving market. A compelling example of this pivot strategy is the growth of plant-based food start-ups targeting the shifting preferences of environmentally-conscious consumers seeking sustainable and ethical food choices.

Embracing Technological Disruptions

Embracing technological disruptions is a pivot strategy that involves leveraging cutting-edge technologies to transform a start-up's business model, operations, or offerings.[9] In the ever-evolving digital age, technology can be a powerful enabler for start-ups seeking to innovate and stay ahead of the competition. This pivot approach requires a proactive mindset, a willingness to adopt new technologies, and a visionary approach to harnessing their potential for transformative impact. Digital transformation is a pivot strategy that involves integrating digital technologies across all aspects of a start-up's operations, from customer interactions to internal processes. By embracing digital tools and platforms, start-ups can enhance efficiency, customer experience, and data-driven decision-making. This pivot approach requires a cultural shift within the organization, encouraging a digital-first mindset and encouraging employees to adopt new technologies. Successful digital transformation can lead to streamlined processes, improved customer engagement, and a stronger competitive position. An exemplary case of this pivot strategy is the transformation of Netflix from a DVD rental company to a digital streaming platform, revolutionizing how people consume entertainment. Start-ups can pivot by integrating Artificial Intelligence (AI) technologies into their products or services, enabling more personalized and efficient customer experiences. AI can be utilized for tasks such as data analysis, recommendation engines, and natural language processing, unlocking new possibilities for start-ups to deliver value to their customers.

Blockchain technology presents numerous opportunities for start-ups to pivot and disrupt traditional business models. By leveraging blockchain's decentralized and secure nature, start-ups can transform industries such as finance, supply chain management, and intellectual property rights. Blockchain adoption can increase transparency, reduce transaction costs, and enhance data security. A noteworthy case of this pivot strategy is the emergence of Decentralized Finance (DeFi) platforms that leverage blockchain to provide financial services without intermediaries, offering users greater control over their assets and financial activities. Embracing the Internet of Things (IoT) is a pivot strategy that allows start-ups to create connected devices and systems that collect and exchange data. By integrating IoT capabilities into their products, start-ups can offer enhanced functionalities and deliver real time insights to customers. This pivot approach enables start-ups to enter the realm of smart products and capitalize on the growing demand for interconnected devices. An illustrative example of this pivot strategy is the development of smart home devices that enable homeowners to control appliances, security systems, and energy consumption through mobile applications.

Executing A Successful Pivot

Executing a successful pivot is a critical phase in the entrepreneurial journey, where visionary plans and strategies must be translated into tangible actions. This section delves into the key elements and best practices that underpin the execution of a pivot, empowering start-ups to navigate the complexities and challenges of the transformation process with confidence and precision. Clear communication is the foundation of a successful pivot execution. Entrepreneurs must effectively articulate the reasons for the pivot, the desired outcomes, and the steps involved in the process. Transparent communication fosters alignment within the team, ensuring everyone understands the pivot's purpose and is committed to its success. Regular communication channels, such as team meetings and updates, can facilitate a cohesive approach to execution and encourage open dialogue for sharing insights and addressing concerns. Flexibility and adaptability are essential qualities for executing a successful pivot. Start-ups must be prepared to adjust their plans as new information emerges or market dynamics change. An agile approach allows entrepreneurs to respond swiftly to unforeseen challenges and seize emerging opportunities. As the pivot unfolds, entrepreneurs should remain receptive to feedback, monitor market reactions, and be willing to make adjustments to ensure the pivot stays on track and aligned with the intended goals.

Start-ups must prioritize activities and initiatives that drive the pivot's success while optimizing available resources.[10] Resource constraints may necessitate making difficult decisions, and entrepreneurs must focus on activities that yield the most significant impact. Assessing resource needs, aligning them with key objectives, and continuously evaluating progress can ensure efficient resource allocation throughout the pivot process. Executing a successful pivot requires collaboration across various functions within the start-up. Marketing, product development, operations, and customer support teams must collaborate to effectively implement the pivot. Cross-functional collaboration enables a holistic understanding of the pivot's implications and ensures that all aspects of the start-up align with the new direction. Encouraging collaboration, breaking down silos, and fostering a collaborative culture empower start-ups to leverage the collective expertise of their teams for a seamless pivot execution. Throughout the pivot execution, a customer-centric approach remains paramount. Customer feedback and insights should continue to inform decision-making and guide the pivot's direction. Listening to customers, gathering data, and monitoring customer behavior allows entrepreneurs to validate assumptions, identify areas for improvement, and make customer-driven decisions. An unwavering commitment to meeting customer needs ensures that the pivot resonates with the target audience and increases the likelihood of successful customer adoption. You will have more clarity once you read the sections ahead. I have elaborated on the aspect of communicating the pivot. It is followed by resource allocation and execution. The third aspect I have written about is learning from failed pivots.

Communicating The Pivot

Communicating the pivot is a critical aspect of executing a successful transformation. Effective communication ensures that all internal and external stakeholders understand the reasons behind the pivot, the intended direction, and the potential implications. Transparent and compelling communication builds trust, alleviates uncertainties, and garners support for the pivot, ultimately positioning the start-up for a smoother and more successful transition. When communicating the pivot, entrepreneurs must craft a clear and compelling narrative that explains the reasons for the pivot and the desired outcomes. The narrative should convey the vision for the future and the benefits the pivot will bring to customers, employees, investors, and other stakeholders. Articulating the story behind the pivot concisely and compellingly can engage and inspire stakeholders, aligning them with the start-up's new direction. Internal communication is paramount during a pivot as it engages and motivates the team, which is instrumental in the successful execution. Entrepreneurs should be transparent with employees, sharing the context behind the pivot and the opportunities it presents. Engaging the team in the pivot process, encouraging open discussions, and addressing any concerns will foster a collaborative and committed approach to executing the pivot.

Communicating the pivot to external stakeholders, such as customers, investors, and partners, is equally crucial.[11] Start-ups must reassure customers that the pivot enhances their experience and meets their evolving needs. Conveying the value proposition of the new direction can reassure customers and retain their loyalty during the pivot process. Investors need to understand the strategic rationale behind the pivot and the expected return on investment. Transparent communication with investors can help manage expectations and secure continued support for the start-up's pivot journey. For partners, open communication ensures that existing relationships remain intact and enables the exploration of potential collaborations in line with the pivot strategy. Timeliness and consistency in communication are essential elements of a successful pivot. Start-ups should communicate the pivot early, allowing stakeholders sufficient time to digest the information and adapt to the changes. Consistent messaging across all communication channels ensures that stakeholders receive a coherent understanding of the pivot's goals and direction. Entrepreneurs must proactively address any concerns or misconceptions that may arise, reinforcing the clarity of the pivot message. During the pivot execution, it is crucial to manage stakeholders' expectations realistically. A pivot is a transformational process that may take time to achieve the desired results. Entrepreneurs should set achievable milestones and communicate progress transparently.

Resource Allocation And Execution

Resource allocation and execution are fundamental to the success of a pivot. Careful planning, efficient use of resources, and effective execution are key to ensuring that the pivot remains on track and delivers the desired outcomes. This sub-section explores the critical considerations and best practices for allocating resources and executing a successful pivot. Before starting a pivot, start-ups must thoroughly assess the resources required for the transformation. It includes financial resources, human capital, technology, infrastructure, and other essential assets. Entrepreneurs should consider the extent of the pivot's scope and the new initiatives it entails. Assessing resource needs enables start-ups to identify potential gaps and make informed decisions about resource allocation during the pivot execution. Resource allocation during a pivot necessitates careful prioritization of key initiatives. Not all aspects of the pivot may require equal attention or resources. Start-ups should identify and prioritize initiatives that align most closely with the pivot's strategic objectives and have the highest potential for impact. By focusing on critical initiatives, start-ups can ensure that resources are channeled efficiently toward activities that drive the pivot's success. The pivot journey is likely to involve uncertainty and evolving circumstances. As such, resource allocation must be agile and responsive to changing needs. Start-ups should be prepared to reallocate resources as new information emerges and pivot requirements evolve. An agile approach to resource allocation enables the start-up to adapt quickly to unforeseen challenges and seize emerging opportunities during the pivot execution.[12]

Resource allocation during a pivot often requires making trade-offs. Start-ups may need to reallocate resources from existing operations or initiatives to fuel the pivot's progress. Entrepreneurs should carefully evaluate these trade-offs, considering the short-term impact on existing operations and the long-term benefits of the pivot. Managing trade-offs requires clear decision-making and strategically optimizing resource utilization for the pivot's success. Effective resource allocation and execution in a pivot context demand cross-functional collaboration. Different teams within the start-up need to work together to ensure seamless execution of the pivot initiatives. Collaboration fosters a shared understanding of resource needs and priorities and enables teams to leverage their diverse expertise to drive the pivot's success. Encouraging cross-functional collaboration also fosters a sense of ownership and collective responsibility for the pivot's outcomes. Constant monitoring and evaluation of the pivot execution are vital for success. Start-ups should establish key performance indicators (KPIs) and progress milestones to assess the pivot's effectiveness. Regularly evaluating execution against these metrics enables entrepreneurs to identify areas for improvement, make data-driven decisions, and adjust resource allocation as needed.

Learning From Failed Pivots

Learning from failed pivots[13] is a crucial aspect of the entrepreneurial journey. Despite careful planning and execution, not all pivots yield the desired outcomes. Embracing failure as a learning opportunity allows entrepreneurs to gain valuable insights, refine their strategies, and enhance their decision-making for future endeavors. In this sub-section, we explore the importance of learning from failed pivots and the key lessons that can be gleaned from these experiences. Failed pivots often stem from flawed assumptions about the market, customer needs, or the start-up's capabilities. An honest evaluation of these assumptions is essential for understanding why the pivot did not succeed. Entrepreneurs should critically assess the data and insights that inform their pivot decisions. Recognizing and addressing faulty assumptions enables them to make more informed and evidence-based choices in future pivot endeavors. Execution gaps can undermine even the most well-conceived pivot strategies. Entrepreneurs should closely examine the execution process to identify any shortcomings or missteps. Evaluating resource allocation, cross-functional collaboration, and overall project management can shed light on areas that require improvement. Understanding execution gaps empowers entrepreneurs to strengthen their organizational capabilities and project management practices for future pivot attempts.

Market dynamics and timing play a significant role in the success of a pivot. A failed pivot may result from launching the transformation at an inopportune moment or overlooking crucial market trends. Entrepreneurs should closely monitor market changes, emerging technologies, and competitor actions to ensure their pivot aligns with market demands. Reflecting on market dynamics and timing enables entrepreneurs to make more astute judgments for future pivot opportunities. Failed pivots can be disheartening, but resilience and adaptability are essential attributes for entrepreneurs to embrace and learn from these experiences. Acknowledging failure, understanding its causes, and persevering in the face of setbacks is key to personal and professional growth. Resilient entrepreneurs tend to persist, innovate, and succeed in future pivot attempts. Learning from failed pivots is part of a broader commitment to continuous improvement. Entrepreneurs should foster a culture of learning and improvement within their start-ups.

Companies That Understood Pivoting Well

Companies that have successfully embraced the art of pivoting share an agile and iterative approach to their business.[14] They understand that the initial business idea is just a hypothesis and needs constant validation and refinement. Instead of rigidly sticking to their original plan, they remain open to change and feedback. This flexibility allows them to adapt quickly to market shifts and customer demands, avoiding the sunk cost fallacy that can trap other businesses. They can iterate and improve their products or services based on real-world data and customer insights by breaking down their vision into smaller, manageable steps. This approach reduces the risk of large-scale failures and empowers them to respond swiftly to emerging opportunities and challenges. A customer-centric mindset is another critical strategy employed by companies that excel in pivoting. These companies prioritize understanding their customers' needs and pain points, engaging with their target audience, and listening to feedback. Doing so gives them valuable insights into what is working and what isn't. Instead of being solely focused on executing their original vision, they adapt and evolve their products or services to better meet customer demands. This customer-centric approach builds a loyal user base and helps companies identify new avenues for growth. They recognize that successful businesses are not built solely on a great idea but on an unwavering commitment to serving their customers in the best possible way. By continuously fine-tuning their offerings based on customer feedback, these companies stay relevant and competitive in a rapidly changing market landscape.

Faire

Faire[15] is a wholesale marketplace connecting independent retailers with emerging and established brands. The company's success story revolves around its strategic pivot to focus on empowering small retailers in the highly competitive retail industry. Faire began as a traditional wholesale platform in its early days, catering to various retailers. However, they soon realized that many small retailers faced challenges accessing quality products and competing with larger, well-established retailers. This realization prompted a significant pivot in their business model. Faire shifted its focus from being a typical wholesale marketplace to becoming a tech-enabled platform that empowers local retailers with data-driven insights and personalized product recommendations. They leveraged artificial intelligence to match retailers with products that resonate well with their specific customer base, optimizing their inventory and sales. This pivot enhanced the shopping experience for retailers and attracted a wider array of independent brands to join the platform. The data-driven approach allowed smaller retailers to thrive, providing brands access to a network of retailers genuinely interested in their products. This win-win strategy boosted Faire's growth, becoming a game-changer in the wholesale industry, strengthening the position of independent retailers, and fostering a vibrant ecosystem of small businesses. Faire's successful pivot demonstrates the significance of staying attuned to market demands and customer needs. By understanding the challenges faced by their target audience and being willing to adapt their business model accordingly, Faire effectively established itself as a key player in the wholesale market, empowering countless independent retailers and contributing to the growth of small businesses across various sectors.

Company Name: Faire

Founded: 2016

Significant reason(s) for success: The company continuously paid attention to the changing industry dynamics and incorporated substantial integrations into its offerings.

Dialpad

Dialpad[16] is a cloud-based communication platform offering businesses voice, video, messaging, and contact center solutions. The success story of Dialpad revolves around its strategic pivot from being a traditional business phone service to becoming a modern cloud communication platform. Initially known as Switch.co, Dialpad started as a consumer-focused voice-over IP (VoIP) service. However, the company soon recognized the potential and demand for cloud-based communication solutions in the business world. They realized there was a significant opportunity to cater to the needs of modern businesses that required more than just a basic phone system. With this insight, Dialpad boldly transformed its business model and targeted the enterprise market. They rebranded from Switch.co to Dialpad to emphasize their broader vision of offering a comprehensive communication platform for businesses of all sizes. The new Dialpad platform incorporated voice, video, messaging, and contact center capabilities, providing a unified and scalable solution for modern teams. Furthermore, Dialpad leveraged artificial intelligence and machine learning to enhance its services, enabling real time transcription, sentiment analysis, and smart call routing features. This focus on innovative technology and seamless user experience set Dialpad apart from traditional communication providers. Dialpad successfully positioned itself as a disruptive player in the cloud communication industry through this well-timed pivot. Their modern and versatile platform attracted many customers, including start-ups, small businesses, and enterprise-level corporations. Dialpad's commitment to continuously improving its services through regular updates and feature additions further solidified its position as a leading cloud communication provider.

Company Name: Dialpad

Founded: 2011

Significant reason(s) for success: The company was able to recognize evolving market trends and adapt to meet customer demands.

VTS

VTS, short for View The Space, is a technology platform that has transformed the world of commercial real estate (CRE). The success story of VTS[17] revolves around its strategic pivot to address the unique challenges faced by the CRE industry and create a comprehensive solution that has disrupted traditional practices. Founded in 2012 by Nick Romito and Ryan Masiello, VTS initially started as a platform for providing virtual 3D tours of available office spaces. While this idea showcased potential, the founders quickly realized that there was a more significant opportunity to leverage technology in addressing the pain points of commercial real estate professionals. VTS's journey toward success began with recognizing critical market gaps in the CRE sector. Traditionally, CRE professionals relied on fragmented and outdated tools, such as spreadsheets and emails, to manage their leasing processes. This manual approach often led to inefficiencies, delayed decision-making, and missed opportunities. VTS saw the need for a centralized platform to streamline and optimize the leasing lifecycle. In response to the market demands, VTS made a strategic pivot and transformed from a virtual tour provider to a comprehensive leasing and asset management platform. They expanded their focus to include end-to-end solutions for landlords, brokers, and property managers. The platform enabled users to track lease data, manage tenant relationships, monitor key performance metrics, and gain valuable insights into market trends – all in one place. The shift towards becoming an integrated leasing and asset management platform was a game-changer for VTS. It allowed CRE professionals to work more efficiently and make data-driven decisions, enhancing their ability to attract and retain tenants, optimize space utilization, and maximize property value. One of the key elements that set VTS apart was its emphasis on data-driven insights. By collecting and analyzing vast leasing data, VTS provided valuable market intelligence to its users. Landlords and brokers gained access to real time data on tenant preferences, market trends, and competitive properties. This data-driven approach empowered CRE professionals to make more informed decisions and stay ahead of the competition.

Company Name: VTS

Founded: 2010

Significant reason(s) for success: The company revolutionized the commercial real estate industry through tech innovation, which is a testament to the power of recognizing market gaps and strategically pivoting to address them.

Flockjay

Flockjay[18] is a tech education company that aims to empower individuals from diverse backgrounds to pursue careers in tech sales. The success story of Flockjay revolves around its strategic pivoting to address the significant opportunity in the tech industry's talent gap and bridge the diversity divide. Initially, Flockjay started as a platform to help aspiring tech entrepreneurs. However, the founders quickly realized the immense potential in addressing the lack of diversity in tech sales roles. They observed that sales positions, particularly in the tech sector, were often dominated by a homogeneous group of individuals, and there was a lack of accessible resources and training for underrepresented groups seeking to enter this field. With a mission to democratize access to tech sales roles and create a more diverse and inclusive industry, Flockjay made a bold pivot. They shifted their focus from supporting tech entrepreneurs to providing comprehensive sales training and career support for aspiring tech sales professionals from non-traditional backgrounds. By partnering with tech companies, Flockjay developed an intensive sales training program that covers essential skills such as prospecting, sales techniques, and customer relationship management. Moreover, they provided mentorship, coaching, and networking opportunities to help their participants secure high-paying jobs in the tech sales sector. Flockjay effectively addressed the talent gap in tech sales through this strategic pivot while empowering individuals from diverse backgrounds to break into the industry. The company's emphasis on inclusivity and equal opportunity transformed countless graduates' lives and created a more diverse and representative tech workforce. Flockjay's pivot not only catered to an underserved market but also aligned with the growing demand for diverse talent in the tech industry.

Company Name: Flockjay

Founded: 2012

Significant reason(s) for success: The company acknowledged a pressing need in the market and adapted its business model to fill that gap.

ShipBob

ShipBob[19] is a technology-driven e-commerce fulfillment company that empowers businesses to streamline their order fulfillment processes and deliver a seamless customer experience. The success story of ShipBob revolves around its strategic pivot to disrupt the traditional e-commerce fulfillment industry and cater to the evolving needs of online merchants. Originally founded as a consumer-facing on-demand shipping service, ShipBob soon recognized the tremendous opportunity to provide a comprehensive fulfillment solution for e-commerce businesses. They observed that traditional fulfillment methods were often slow, expensive, and lacked the flexibility required to meet the demands of the booming e-commerce sector. In response to these insights, ShipBob made a significant pivot, shifting its focus from serving individual consumers to helping businesses optimize their order fulfillment operations. They invested heavily in developing a sophisticated technology platform that integrates with various e-commerce platforms, enabling seamless order and inventory management. Moreover, ShipBob established fulfillment centers in strategic locations across the United States, allowing businesses to store inventory closer to their customers reducing shipping times and costs. This strategic distribution network enabled them to offer two-day shipping options, competing with larger e-commerce giants and leveling the playing field for smaller online merchants. By providing efficient fulfillment services, real-time tracking, and data-driven insights, ShipBob revolutionized the e-commerce fulfillment industry and enabled countless businesses to scale rapidly and deliver an exceptional customer experience.

Company Name: ShipBob

Founded: 2014

Significant reason(s) for success: The company identified the pain points e-commerce businesses were facing and offered a comprehensive and tech-driven fulfillment solution.

Tessian

Tessian[20] is a cybersecurity company that has revolutionized email security using machine learning and artificial intelligence. The success story of Tessian revolves around its strategic pivot to address the growing challenges of email-based threats and the protection of sensitive data. Tessian was founded in 2013 by Tim Sadler, Tom Adams, and Ed Bishop. The company started with a different focus, aiming to provide a tool for individuals and organizations to verify email recipients and prevent misdirected emails. However, as they delved deeper into the email security landscape, the founders recognized a more significant problem

– the human element. Traditional email security solutions primarily focused on filtering spam and known malware, but they often failed to detect sophisticated social engineering attacks that relied on human error. Hackers increasingly used targeted phishing emails and other tactics to exploit human vulnerabilities, making people the weakest link in an organization's security defense. With this revelation, Tessian pivoted from merely verifying email recipients to creating a comprehensive platform that leveraged machine learning to prevent data breaches and email-based threats caused by human error. They rebranded from Check-Recipient to Tessian, reflecting their new vision of applying cutting-edge technology to protect organizations from advanced email threats. The core of Tessian's innovative approach lies in its machine-learning algorithms that analyze and understand human behavior patterns in email communication. By analyzing vast amounts of data, Tessian's platform can detect anomalies and unusual email behaviors that may indicate a security threat. These behaviors include misdirected emails, data exfiltration attempts, and spear-phishing attacks. One of Tessian's key solutions is Guardian, which prevents misdirected emails. Using machine learning, Guardian analyzes the content and context of outgoing emails in real time, flagging potential misdirections before sensitive data is sent to the wrong recipient.

Company Name: Tessian

Founded: 2013

Significant reason(s) for success: The company identified the human element as a critical gap in email security and harnessed the potential of machine learning to revolutionize email protection.

Conclusion

In a start-up's dynamic and competitive world, a company's ability to adapt and embrace change often determines success. The strategic shift in business direction has proven to be a crucial tool for start-ups to navigate uncertainties, capitalize on opportunities, and stay relevant in ever-evolving markets. The success stories of various companies discussed in this chapter illustrate the power of pivoting at the right time and highlight the key strategies that have contributed to their achievements. The common thread among these successful companies is their agile and iterative approach to business. They recognize that the initial vision or business model is merely a hypothesis, and they actively seek feedback and validate their assumptions. By staying open to change and being willing to pivot based on real-world data, customer insights, and market trends, these companies were able to transform challenges into opportunities and stay ahead of the curve. Customer-centricity emerges as another key theme in the success stories of these companies. They prioritize understanding their customers' needs and pain points, going beyond just delivering a product to building strong relationships and providing exceptional experiences.

Moreover, these successful companies have showcased a deep understanding of market trends and emerging technologies. They keep a close eye on industry developments and are unafraid to embrace cutting-edge innovations to improve their offerings. Adopting technologies like AI, machine learning, and cloud computing gives them a competitive edge and can deliver more efficient, sophisticated, and data-driven solutions. Furthermore, the ability to pivot effectively also requires a culture of adaptability and a willingness to take calculated risks. The success stories demonstrate that the fear of failure should not hinder a company from exploring new avenues and making strategic changes when needed. Embracing failure as a learning experience allows these companies to quickly adjust their strategies and make informed decisions for future success.

This chapter is summarized in the following points for your easy-reference. I hope your start-up journey will be fulfilled after completing this book.

1. Recognizing the need to pivot is the first step towards this transition that would prove fruitful for your start-up.
2. You must recognize the signs of a necessary pivot and take action as and when required.
3. Evaluating potential pivots is equally important as it will decide how you are driving your start-up ahead.

4. Deciding to pivot depends on all these factors, and you must make it right.
5. There are many successful pivot strategies, but each start-up goes through its journey, and hence strategies that would work for it will depend on various factors.
6. Adapting business models is essential. Rethinking your business model is as vital as enhancing it.
7. Expanding target markets is the key. With the world rapidly changing, thanks to technology, expanding target markets seems inevitable for start-up success.
8. Embracing technological disruptions will work in your favor. Do not say yes to everything but keep an eye on what's growing big in the world and see if you can integrate its relevancy into your start-up.
9. Executing a successful pivot is difficult but can be achieved with substantial planning and focus.
10. Communicating the pivot is necessary for every stakeholder to be on the same page and be aware of the changes.
11. Resource allocation and execution are keys to smooth pivoting. As a start-up founder, you must take note of this.
12. Learning from failed pivots is as important as celebrating the successful ones. After all, every business objective you do not achieve is a stepping stone to the ones ahead.

References

1. Forbes (2022). *Council post: How to pivot successfully in business.* Available at: https://www.forbes.com/sites/theyec/2020/07/03/how-to-pivot-successfully-in-business/?sh=4269af3f7316 [Accessed 29 Jul. 2023].
2. Y Combinator (2022). *All about pivoting: YC start-up library.* Available at: https://www.ycombinator.com/library/6p-all-about-pivoting [Accessed 29 Jul. 2023].
3. Forbes (2021). *Council post: 14 signs that tell owners it's time to pivot their business.* Available at: https://www.forbes.com/sites/forbescoachescouncil/2021/02/24/14-signs-that-tell-owners-its-time-to-pivot-their-business/?sh=423b6798264c [Accessed 29 Jul. 2023].

4. Glauser, M. (2016). *4 to pivot into new revenue streams and grow your business #mainstreetentrepreneur.* Available at: https://www.entrepreneur.com/growing-a-business/4-to-pivot-into-new-revenue-streams-and-grow-your-business/274210 [Accessed 29 Jul. 2023].
5. Forbes (2022). *Council post: How to pivot successfully in business.* Available at: https://www.forbes.com/sites/theyec/2020/07/03/how-to-pivot-successfully-in-business/?sh=ad8d2e7316b7 [Accessed 29 Jul. 2023].
6. Forbes (2023). *Council post: 16 tips for successfully pivoting your business.* Available at: https://www.forbes.com/sites/forbesbusinesscouncil/2022/12/22/16-tips-for-successfully-pivoting-your-business/?sh=737ea39d37f9 [Accessed 29 Jul. 2023].
7. Medium (2019). *7 business model pivots you can learn from.* Available at: https://medium.com/wdhb/7-business-model-pivots-you-can-learn-from-d721cbfbea36 [Accessed 29 Jul. 2023].
8. Forbes (2021). *Council post: 14 effective ways to identify an untapped market for your business.* Available at: https://www.forbes.com/sites/forbesbusinessdevelopmentcouncil/2020/11/24/14-effective-ways-to-identify-an-untapped-market-for-your-business/?sh=6df003357ce6 [Accessed 29 Jul. 2023].
9. Katarina (2023). *How businesses pivot and stay relevant in the face of Disruptive Technologies.* Available at: https://www.howwe.io/insights/how-businesses-pivot-and-stay-relevant-in-the-face-of-disruptive-technologies/ [Accessed 29 Jul. 2023].
10. Liu, H. (2020). *Executing a successful pivot.* Available at: https://medium.com/@hollyhliu/executing-a-successful-pivot-39f62d81c48e [Accessed 29 Jul. 2023].
11. Monae, A. (2023). *How to effectively communicate a pivot in your business.* Available at: https://www.entrepreneur.com/leadership/how-to-effectively-communicate-a-pivot-in-your-business/452447#:~:text=Communicating%20a%20pivot%20in%20business,to%20communicate%20the%20new%20vision. [Accessed 29 Jul. 2023].
12. Atsmon, Y. (2016). *How nimble resource allocation can double your company's value.* Available at: https://www.mckinsey.com/capabilities/strategy-and-corporate-finance/our-insights/how-nimble-resource-allocation-can-double-your-companys-value [Accessed 29 Jul. 2023].
13. Forbes (2020). *Council post: 11 valuable lessons business owners can learn from failure.* Available at: https://www.forbes.com/sites/forbesbusinesscouncil/2020/07/29/11-valuable-lessons-business-own-

ers-can-learn-from-failure/?sh=44a38c8f17e0 [Accessed 29 Jul. 2023].

14. Natsir, C. (2023). *7 types of pivot strategies for business that you need to know*. Available at: https://www.hashmicro.com/blog/7-types-of-pivot-strategies-for-business-that-you-need-to-know/ [Accessed 29 Jul. 2023].
15. Taussig, A. (2022). *The secret to Faire's success – think global; Shop Local.* Available at: https://medium.com/lightspeed-venture-partners/the-secret-to-faires-success-think-global-shop-local-c2f2ca8fe116 [Accessed 29 Jul. 2023].
16. Swinscoe, A. (2023). *Dialpad is betting that TrueCaaS is the future of customer service*. Available at: https://www.forbes.com/sites/adrianswinscoe/2023/01/31/dialpad-is-betting-that-truecaas-is-the-future-of-customer-service-they-might-be-right/?sh=2155d65d4f6b [Accessed 29 Jul. 2023].
17. Businesswire (2018). *9 billion square feet now managed on VTS following the most successful quarter in company history*. Available at: https://www.businesswire.com/news/home/20181106005800/en/9-Billion-Square-Feet-Now-Managed-on-VTS-Following-the-Most-Successful-Quarter-in-Company-History [Accessed 29 Jul. 2023].
18. Jacobs, S. (2023). *Flockjay has the Cheat Code for a successful team*. Available at: https://www.saleshacker.com/flockjay-cheat-code-for-successful-team-podcast/ [Accessed 29 Jul. 2023].
19. Wilkins, P. (2021). *Why Shipbob is quickly becoming the best e-commerce fulfilment service*. Available at: https://www.forbes.com/sites/peterandrewwilkins/2021/10/27/why-shipbob-is-quickly-becoming-the-best-e-commerce-fulfillment-service/?sh=75a7fffb2be0 [Accessed 29 Jul. 2023].
20. O'Hear, S. (2018). *Email security start-up Tessian raises $13m led by Balderton and Accel.* Available at: https://techcrunch.com/2018/06/18/tessian/ [Accessed 29 Jul. 2023].

www.ingramcontent.com/pod-product-compliance
Ingram Content Group UK Ltd.
Pitfield, Milton Keynes, MK11 3LW, UK
UKHW041858031026
15587UKWH00008B/1301/J

9 788198 456489